Unsettling Assumptions

Unsettling Assumptions

Tradition, Gender, Drag

Edited by
Pauline Greenhill
Diane Tye

UTAH STATE UNIVERSITY PRESS
Logan

© 2014 by the University Press of Colorado
Published by Utah State University Press
An imprint of University Press of Colorado
5589 Arapahoe Avenue, Suite 206C
Boulder, Colorado 80303

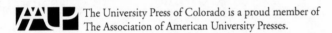 The University Press of Colorado is a proud member of
The Association of American University Presses.

The University Press of Colorado is a cooperative publishing enterprise supported, in part, by
Adams State College, Colorado State University, Fort Lewis College, Metropolitan State College
of Denver, Regis University, University of Colorado, University of Northern Colorado, Utah
State University, and Western State College of Colorado.

ISBN: 978-0-87421-897-8 (paper)
ISBN: 978-0-87421-898-5 (e-book)

Library of Congress Cataloging-in-Publication Data
Unsettling assumptions : tradition, gender, drag / edited by Pauline Greenhill, Diane Tye.
    pages cm
  ISBN 978-0-87421-897-8 (paperback) — ISBN 978-0-87421-898-5 (ebook)
1. Gender identity. 2. Sex role. 3. Gender expression. 4. Queer theory. 5. Manners and customs. 6. Folklore. I. Greenhill, Pauline, editor of compilation. II. Tye, Diane, 1957– editor of
compilation.
  HQ1075.U567 2014
  305.3—dc23
                                2014010139

Cover photograph: © Margarita Borodina / Shutterstock

Contents

Thematic Clusters

Autoethnography, ethnography, and ethnographers
Fehr and Greenhill, Ferrell, Magnus-Johnston,
Mullen, Pooley, Sawin, Tye

Custom and belief
Fehr and Greenhill, Ferrell, Mullen, Roth, Sawin,
Tye, Wallen

Ethnic drag
Fehr and Greenhill, Tye, Wallen

Film studies
Magnus-Johnston, Møllegaard, Roth

Material culture
Ferrell, Tye, Wallen

Men and masculinities
Fehr and Greenhill, Ferrell, Magnus-Johnston,
Mullen, Pooley, Roth, Tye

Narrative
Greenhill and Anderson-Grégoire, Magnus-Johnston,
Møllegaard, Pooley, Sawin, Vaughan, Xie

Postcolonial studies
Fehr and Greenhill, Møllegaard, Sawin, Wallen

Transbiology
Møllegaard, Roth, Xie

Transgender and Transsex
Fehr and Greenhill, Greenhill and
Anderson-Grégoire, Tye

Women and femininities
Møllegaard, Roth, Sawin, Vaughan, Xie

Acknowledgments

First and foremost we owe thanks to Michael Spooner, who has stuck with us through the thick and thin of this project!

Part of this work was funded by Pauline's Social Sciences and Humanities Research Council of Canada Standard Research Grant (SSHRC), 2008–2012, "Transgender Imagination and Enactment in Traditional and Popular Culture in Canada." Pauline also thanks the University of Winnipeg Research Office for funding support. We have tried to contact rights holders of copyrighted material for permission when applicable. Please contact us via the publisher if you have any questions or concerns. We thank *Marvels & Tales* for permission to use material from a longer and somewhat different version of Kendra Magnus-Johnston's chapter, there titled "'Reeling in' Grimm Masculinities: Hucksters, Cross-Dressers, and Ninnies" (2013, 27[1]). We thank *Ethnologies* for permission to use material from a longer and different version of Marcie Fehr and Pauline Greenhill's chapter, there titled "Our *Brommtopp* Is of Our Own Design: (De)Constructing Masculinities in Southern Manitoba Mennonite Mumming" (2011 [2013] 32[2]).

Feedback from reviewers for the press led to significant improvements to the collection; we thank these readers for their careful attention to each chapter and engagement with our aims. The responses from students in Pauline's Folklore and Gender course, winter 2012, were invaluable in helping us to understand how undergraduates would read each chapter. Liyana Fauzi was a fabulous research assistant. We thank John Alley, who first expressed interest in this work, and we thank the contributors for sticking with us through a long and sometimes quite arduous process.

Pauline thanks John Junson, the late Bobbie, and Neko for lightening the load. Diane thanks Peter, Callum, and R.D. for the same.

Thank you to Robin DuBlanc for copyediting. We also thank Linda Gregonis for indexing our work. Finally, Barbara Rieti named the book, coming up with a gloss on our work that would have been well beyond our creative powers!

Unsettling Assumptions

Introduction

Pauline Greenhill and Diane Tye

WHAT DO THANKSGIVING TURKEYS, ROCKABILLY AND BAR FIGHTS, and Chinese tales of female ghosts have in common? Each offers an example of how tradition and gender can intersect—sometimes with modes of drag— to unsettle assumptions about culture and its study. These topics, along with many others—a nineteenth-century French antiquarian, selkie stories, a fairy tale, films about the Grimm Brothers, Dutch-Danish ethnicity, a noisy Mennonite New Year's celebration, *The Distaff Gospels*, a kilt-wearing pipe band, Kentucky tobacco farmers, and international adoptions—are the subjects of this book. In the contributors' hands, these topics offer opportunities to trouble all three areas—tradition, gender, and drag—especially in terms of their intersections. Thus, each chapter not only questions taken-for-granted presumptions about them but also shows how traditional and popular culture can both (sometimes simultaneously) instantiate and resist hegemony. Whether coded or uncoded, folklore can demonstrate hetero-sexism, heteronormativity, and the complexities of patriarchy, but its many modes and forms also leave space for alternative understandings. And in traditional and popular culture, drag—the representation of oneself as another—can go beyond sex/gender into other aspects of identity.

Unsettling Assumptions began with the editors' desire to address the lacuna in teaching collections for courses on women/gender/sexuality and traditional and popular culture. (We do, however, hope this book will be of interest beyond those areas and disciplines, and so contributors foreground [inter]disciplinary preconceptions.) While students in our classes still found relevance in *Undisciplined Women: Tradition and Culture in Canada*, a volume of articles on interconnections of folklore/ethnology[1] and gender that we coedited in 1997, we thought it was time for something new. Since that date exciting research in gender and traditional/popular culture has resulted in numerous books,[2] but with the exception of Norma E. Cantú and Olga Nájera-Ramírez's *Chicana Traditions: Continuity and Change* (2002), focusing upon one specific group of women, there have been no essay collections

DOI: 10.7330/9780874218985.c000

in feminist folklore/ethnology studies sampling a broad range of current research linking gender studies with traditional and popular culture studies.[3]

When we first discussed the need for a new collection in 2009, we envisioned a broad-ranging and comprehensive group of papers that would address folklore's intersections with sex, gender, and sexuality. We hoped it would take a feminist look at cisgender[4] women and men as well as transpersons; hetero, homo, and bi sexualities; masculinities and femininities. We wanted to include examinations of archival and published collections of traditional and popular culture and ethnographic studies in various genres of tangible and intangible cultural heritage from different world regions and ethnocultural groups. And the chapters take theoretical and analytical perspectives not only from feminism but also from masculinity studies, queer theory, gender theory, transgender studies, and cultural studies.

UNSETTLING/RETHINKING TRADITION/TRADITIONS

Although this collection unsettles assumptions about folklore/ethnology and its study, *Unsettling Assumptions* is firmly situated within the discipline. Thus, the chapters draw on and develop the terms that comprise *Eight Words for the Study of Expressive Culture* (Feintuch 2003), a benchmark work that extends folklore/ethnology's relevance into cultural studies. Expanding and revising a special issue of the *Journal of American Folklore* published in 1995, Burt Feintuch's edited collection drew on Dell Hymes's understanding of expressive culture as "the capacity for aesthetic experience, for shaping of deeply felt values into meaningful, apposite form, . . . present in all communities" (Hymes 1975b, 346). Feintuch suggested that the symbolic and conceptual "common ground" (2003, 1) for talking about expressive culture in its social contexts lies in eight central ideas: group, art, text, genre, performance, context, tradition, and identity. "Together, they stand for expressive culture's social base, its aesthetic nature, its categories, and its relationship to time" (4). These core concepts remain at the heart of *Unsettling Assumptions*.

Feintuch indicated that the very idea of expressive culture "sweeps across scholarly disciplines and fields of criticism" (2003, 2). Thus, contributors to *Unsettling Assumptions* explore their territories from a variety of academic locations, including women's and gender studies, communications, cultural studies, film studies, literary studies, anthropology, and history. The perspectives are interdisciplinary, although contributors do not ignore established disciplines. But all chapters simultaneously link to folklore/ethnology, joining its pursuit of the local and vernacular, which has often challenged the canons of Western academic thought. "From long before it was fashionable, folklorists claimed that culture is plural . . . Our gaze tends to rest on cultural continuities, and it seems that we are advocates for creativity wherever it happens" (3). The chapters take up these preoccupations in new ways, unsettling established notions and asking readers to reconceptualize and reimagine the locations of, and possibilities inherent in, expressive culture.

Unsettling Assumptions spans what folklore/ethnology once considered the major genres: narrative, song, material culture, custom, and belief. But while the idea of genre remains in the language of folklore/ethnology, genre classification is no longer a primary analytical goal. "As a way of naming forms, genre is never finished; it is always changing, as ways of knowing shift" (Feintuch 2003, 5). Not only do many folkloric practices and texts bridge categories (Sims and Stephens 2005, 18), but the idea of genre is troubled by linguistic, cultural, and conceptual limitation. The history of the use of genre in folklore/ethnology studies is one in which initial efforts to stabilize the concept in the late nineteenth- and early twentieth-century beginnings of the discipline gave way in the mid-twentieth century to recognition that any system of classification is ever evolving, ever subject to new subgroups and new categories (Harris-Lopez 2003, 99–100).

The diversity of forms taken up in this collection—from music and ritual to food and narrative—reflects the eclecticism of contemporary expressive culture as well as the difficulty of assigning texts and ideas to simple, simplistic categories. The contents examine a broad generic and topical span: dress (Fehr and Greenhill, Tye), family folklore (Sawin), folktale (Greenhill and Anderson-Grégoire, Møllegaard, Magnus-Johnston, Xie), food (Roth), heritage (Wallin), humor/legend (Tye, Vaughan, Pooley), mumming/custom (Fehr and Greenhill), personal experience narrative (Ferrell, Sawin, Tye), music/song (Fehr and Greenhill, Mullen), and occupational folklife (Ferrell).

Most chapters defy efforts to classify their subjects within a single genre, speaking again to expressive culture's complexity. They reflect the degree of blurring (Geertz 1980) and overlap between genres that characterizes contemporary life. Concepts that speak to cultural interactions and interconnections, like intertextuality (see, e.g., Allen 2000)—the idea that texts influence and reflect one another—and paratextuality (see, e.g., Genette 1997)—the significance of material surrounding, explaining, and contextualizing any given text that influences its interpretation—have long permeated folklore/ethnology studies. From the 1960s, American folkloristics enjoined attention to folklore's textures—form and structure—and contexts—performative and sociocultural—as well as to texts (see, e.g., Ben-Amos 1971; Dundes 1964). Thus, for example, Magnus-Johnston argues that understandings of Grimms' fairy tales overlap with the cinematic treatments of the collectors themselves and vice versa; their filmed lives enmesh with the materials they collected.

Magnus-Johnston is only one contributor who explores the complexities of a variety of media that extend beyond face-to-face transmission. Roth considers the gendering and sexualization of the American Thanksgiving turkey through various sources—from prescriptive literature and Norman Rockwell paintings to contemporary films and videos. Tye's study of men wearing kilts draws on humor in personal experience narratives, legends, generalization narratives (Greenhill 1994), and sayings (L. D. Small 1975) shared among members of a pipe band. But all are prompted and supported by the online circulation of a larger body of narrative and visual humor.

Even historical texts' diffusion and communication become complicated. Xie examines folktales that have been reissued in many literary editions, while Vaughan explores how the fifteenth-century *Distaff Gospels* reveal a complex blending of the oral, literary, and vernacular that in turn draw on ecclesiastical traditions. She nevertheless discovers that by looking beyond contemporary literary conventions that caricature female narrators, the wisdom shared offers a more nuanced view of medieval women's lives. Greenhill and Anderson-Grégoire consider how one traditional folktale type explores issues of transgender and transsex, allowing for the imagination of gendered and sexual possibilities very much beyond the hegemonic and conventional. Similarly, in the cinematic and novelistic representations of selkie legends and folktales taken up by Møllegaard, traditional cultural forms act to check and balance mass-mediated ones; each is rarely untouched by the others. The chapters in *Unsettling Assumptions* suggest that the interconnections of traditional and popular culture have become even more intertwined and complicated since Peter Narváez and Martin Laba conceptualized the popular-traditional culture continuum in 1988. Indeed, the relationship might be better visualized as a series of intersections in three dimensions rather than as a two-dimensional line.

Given these complexities, the chapters unsettle what constitutes a traditional text. Building on Jeff Titon's notion that a text is any object of interpretation (Titon 2003), some writers focus on subjects that until recently would not have been considered folklore but classified instead as heritage (Wallen) or literature (Vaughan). Meanings take shape in context and in performance as the analyses beg the question: where is expressive culture based and to whom does it belong? In her entry on "group" for *Eight Words*, Dorothy Noyes wrote that folklore/ethnology's "influence as a discipline has often come from arguing for small groups against big groups" (Noyes

2003, 7). Some contributors indeed explore expressions of relatively small groups—a pipe band (Tye) or a rural community (Fehr and Greenhill). However, it is no longer possible to locate all expressive culture in intimate contexts. Tobacco farmers (Ferrell), Americans who celebrate Thanksgiving (Roth), and parents, agencies, and governments brought together by their stakes in transnational adoption (Sawin) also share (sometimes conflicting) traditions within their populous and geographically extensive communities.

Indeed, some chapters point to the many intersections of small and large groups. As Tye notes, wearing a kilt ties a man to other members of a particular pipe band at the same time as it creates commonality with men worldwide who seek a distinctive Scottish dress. Roth finds that American Thanksgiving celebrations create shared expression and opportunities for exchange and interpretation that extend from family to community to nation and beyond. Published versions of folktales (discussed by Vaughan and Xie) offer further examples of intersections between elite and folk traditions as well as between mass and personal communications. Together the chapters question the desirability and even the viability of such boundaries. Indeed, they suggest, with Noyes, that the idea of networks better suits the social grounding of expressive practices: "The community exists as the project of a network or of some of its members. Networks exist insofar as their ties are continually recreated and revitalized in interaction" (Noyes 2003, 33).

In their reexamination of expressive culture's social base, chapters in *Unsettling Assumptions* also question the location of the fieldworker/ethnologist. While Magnus-Johnston and Pooley do so through exploring others' techniques, practices, and modes, Fehr and Greenhill, Mullen, Sawin, and Tye cast the gaze toward their own cultures and experiences. Working within their own social networks and/or examining familiar places, they are linked with their subjects in time, space, and cultural location. Their analyses reflect a growing influence within folkloristic practice not just of reflexive ethnography but also of autoethnography (see Tye 2010). Dating from the 1970s, autoethnographic writing takes many forms, from fiction and poetry to photographic essays to fragmented and layered writing, as well as social scientific prose (C. Ellis 2004, 38). Such work intersects autobiography and ethnography, focusing at once on the self and on culture. Carolyn Ellis and Arthur Bochner describe how during the autoethnographic process, the researcher's gaze zooms backward and forward, inward and outward, so that distinctions between the personal and cultural become blurred, sometimes beyond recognition (Ellis and Bochner 2000, 739). Whether discussing Mennonite *Brommtopp* mumming, rockabilly, transnational adoption narratives, or kilt-related humor, writers here merge the ethnographic with the autoethnographic.

Unsettling Assumptions' contributors share a postcolonial commitment to grappling with the difficult questions of representation in reflexive field-work practice and autoethnographic writing. They reach beyond the goal of documenting historically othered cultural practices toward a respectful exploration of a multiplicity of voices that offers alternatives to dominant discourses, explored in particular by Møllegaard. But while contribu-tors strive neither to appropriate nor to speak for their subjects but rather empathically to acknowledge an absence and work it into presence, they recognize that even marginalized discourses can be problematic. As Fehr and Greenhill show, though the margin can be a site of resistance (see hooks 1990, 2000), oppression can also be reproduced there. And as Sawin argues, narratives can offer common ground for respectful dialogue between dispa-rate groups on difficult problems. *Unsettling Assumptions* challenges readers to imagine expressive culture in a broad range of locations and to reflect on how its basis in social acts leads to both continuity and change.

UNSETTLING SEX/GENDER (UN)CONVENTIONS

All chapters explore intersections of traditional expressive culture with sex/gender systems by challenging their conventional constructions and/or by using sex/gender as a lens to question, investigate, or trouble concepts such as family, ethics, and authenticity. Traditional and popular cultural expres-sions and performances can simultaneously communicate and counter established, hegemonic ideas of what makes women and men.[5] Often draw-ing on Judith Butler's famous concept of gender trouble (1999), contribu-tors further disturb modes for constituting sex/gender that move beyond inter/national, class, and sexuality divisions—and even the divide between life and death. The chapters also underscore expressive culture's central-ity to what Butler terms the performativity of gender (1990, 1993, 1999, 2004)—the idea that gender and indeed sex are created and re-created, not as overlay on a preexisting biological base but rather as an effect of continu-ous enacted reiteration. Thus Ferrell, considering Kentucky tobacco farm-ers, describes "traditionalized performances" of gender, noting that what constitutes (hegemonic) masculinity[6] not only changes through time but can be appropriated and then redefined by women as well as men.

The last few decades have seen an exciting upheaval of conventional ideas about sex, gender, and sexuality.[7] Fundamental concepts include the recognition not only of womanhood and femininity but also of manhood

and masculinity as socioculturally constructed, and the idea of intersectionality, which understands gender as multiply imbricated with race, nation,
ethnicity, ability, sexuality, and so on.[8] Arguably, folklore/ethnicity studies have been at the forefront of ethnographic research into masculinities.
For example, Stanley Brandes's landmark work *Metaphors of Masculinity:
Sex and Status in Andalusian Folklore* (1980) did not simply deal primarily with men, presuming them to instantiate humanness unmarked,[9] but
instead located and represented masculinity in its sociocultural manifestations. Works as disparate as Michael Robidoux's *Men at Play: A Working
Understanding of Professional Hockey* (2001) and Simon Bronner's edited
collection *Manly Traditions: The Folk Roots of American Masculinities* (2005)
explore how traditional and popular culture constitutes and enables the performance of Euro–North American[10] (and other) masculinities. These studies recognize that some forms of maleness become hegemonic—most often
those masculinities associated with young, heterosexual, White, middle and
upper class, able men. Such masculinities, then, become a standard against
which all men are measured, with nearly all found wanting. Because the
actual content of hegemonic masculinity shifts constantly, its measure can
never be truly and permanently reached by any individual.

Ferrell's and Mullen's chapters, in particular, explore questions associated with the multiple masculinities found in Euro North America, dealing
respectively with "tobacco men" and rockabilly music. Using queer theorist
Eve Kosofsky Sedgwick's terms, Mullen explores male homosocial desire[11]
by looking at social class, race, gender, and sexual representations in vernacular music lyrics. Often the homosocial is intersectionally inflected with
class and race. For example, clubs that allegedly admitted only White men
actually did so only in terms of their public performance or front stage (to
use Goffman's [1959] terminology). Such places usually employed men of
color and women workers backstage to cook, clean, and/or provide sexual
services. The invisibility of men of color—many of whom actually served
in the front stage in "all-White" clubs—and the fact that some women's
presence does not undermine the sex/gender prescription "all-male" in similar locations, underscores intersectionality's reach and power. For example,
politician Elsie Wayne, as mayor of Fredericton, New Brunswick, attended
several events at a men-only club—as a server, cross-dressed, and even
jumping out of a cake—underlining that the club did not actually exclude
women, it only excluded them as members and guests in positions of power
(discussed in Greenhill, Tye, and Cantú 2009, xxvii). Ferrell examines how
Kentucky tobacco farmers negotiate their growing economic marginality
and the perceived threat of feminization of their agriculture: from women

who participate in the business, from increased mechanization, and because the crop they grow has less and less sociopolitical and economic power.

Magnus-Johnston explores cinematic representations of the Brothers Grimm. She notes that folklorists' ideas of Wilhelm and Jacob Grimm as sober, politically astute scholars seeking to gather and promote German national language and traditions have been replaced in American film representations with very different figures. For example, strongly homosocially identified and queerly inflected, the Grimms of Terry Gilliam's (2005) *The Brothers Grimm*, the most recent and possibly most popular of the four she discusses, are bumbling con men concerned pretty exclusively with their own self-interest.

Pooley also considers how masculinity inflects the practice of folklore/ ethnology, considering the nineteenth-century French collector François Bladé's relationship with his primary male informant, Guillaume Cazaux. Sometimes reading between the lines in the materials Bladé collected, and sometimes invoking the ethnologist's own commentary about the folk with whom he worked, Pooley explores the adversarial connection between the two men. He argues that Bladé's concept of authenticity multiply implicates concepts of gender, including a class-inflected "combative masculinity." His touchstone is the complex legend text, "My Uncle from Condom," which Pooley understands as a gendered "conversation about place, time, and language."

Focus shifts to femininities with Vaughan's discussion of *The Distaff Gospels* as they decenter conventional male depictions of femininity and offer a female-centered view of medieval life. Her work shows that male-authored texts sometimes, perhaps unwittingly, give voice to women's traditions and perhaps even their opinions. That the women's views were intended to be taken as jokes by the original fifteenth-century male audience does not mean that audiences today should ignore them or doubt their significance. Even when traditional texts and practices appear conventional, they offer opportunities to glimpse other possibilities.

Sawin's postcolonial narrative analysis approaches international adoption through a lens that combines feminist and folkloristic paradigms. Rather than dealing with masculinity or femininity specifically, her work queries notions of parenthood and family as taken-for-granted, presumed universal concepts. In her chapter, personal experience and narratives about it connect with United Nations conventions and the often combative and unequivocal statements by adoptees and their receiving families. Rather than seeking compromise and unified narrative closure, Sawin looks for respectful dialogue between the parties.

While *Unsettling Assumptions* focuses around and about more or less conventional notions of masculinities and femininities, it frequently strays deliberately beyond those binaries into territories that question the sex/gender system so eloquently critiqued by Gayle Rubin (1984). Her description of the structures that make some forms of sex and sexuality socioculturally normative, and thus generally understood as both worthy and normal, while simultaneously making others evil and deviant is further elaborated and nuanced, rendered transparent in order to undermine its conventional taken-for-grantedness.

The Euro–North American conventions implicated in its sex/gender systems are undermined in Xie's chapter, which discusses Chinese folktales in which living men marry female ghosts. Sexual relations in these stories cross the boundaries between the living and the dead. Both tales she discusses specify the consummation of the marriages, and one ghost woman gives birth to a male heir. Such relations, economically valuable for the peasant men who marry dead noblewomen, offer kinship advantages for the female ghosts. Yet contrary to Vaughan's recuperation of *The Distaff Gospels*, Xie sees little room for women's perspectives. She argues that in these narratives, the sexual and economic benefits primarily direct toward male characters. Yet these stories undoubtedly divert from presumptions about marriage as a simple kinship exchange and about sex and sexuality as confined within the limits of mortality.

UNSETTLING/RETHINKING DRAG

Contributors address modes of representation of self as other that include men dressing as women and women as men, White Euro North Americans dressing as (often stereotypical) others (including blackface and whiteface), and humans dressing as animals (and vice versa) to explore the cultural transformations that result from such performances. The extension of the term *drag* to domains beyond sex and gender is deliberately provocative, but it productively assists contributors in bringing assumptions about cross-dressing to bear upon many aspects of identity. Roth's and Møllegaard's chapters open the question of transbiology as drag when it involves animals dressing as humans or humans as animals. Transbiology messes with sex/gender, using representations of animals or humans who masquerade or transform, particularly as another species, and/or who dislocate hard-and-fast distinctions between species, including between human and nonhuman.[12] The turkey sex/sexuality that Roth explores connects human-animal (highly proscribed), queer, and straight relationships. She contends that turkey sexuality implicates various forms of human sex, but also American culture's ethnoracial and social class inclusions and exclusions. This perspective becomes all the more convincing given its presence across a wide range of media and genres, including but not limited to blockbuster and independent films; advertisements; custom and ritual; and song parodies.

In transbiology, as contributors indicate, the concepts of biology and humanity both transform, and the allegedly rigid boundaries between species become permeable. Social anthropology has explored in depth how animal metaphors and taboos actually express notions about human culture (e.g., Douglas 1966; Leach 2000; Willis 1974). Disguise as an animal is not uncommon in traditional culture, but again, its transbiological implications have been underexplored (e.g., Greenhill 2008). As Halberstam argues, "Popular culture has already imagined multiple alternatives to male and female, masculine and feminine, family and individuality and . . . contemporary popular culture, specifically horror film and animation, can provide a rich archive for an alternative politics of embodiment, reproduction and non-reproduction. Such alternatives are important to visualize and recognize" (2008, 266). Notably, one of Roth's central examples comes from popular culture: the faux movie trailer from Robert Rodriguez and Quentin Tarantino's horror pastiche/parody *Grindhouse* (2007).

Also drawing on popular culture but in addition on traditional narratives about seals who transform into humans (and sometimes return to their nonhuman form), Møllegaard's work on selkie stories brings in Neil Jordan's *Ondine* (2009) and other films as well as Solveig Eggerz's novel *Seal Woman* (2008). Møllegaard's postcolonial analysis shows how the traditional transbiological narratives can be used in zones of contact between national groups. Biological difference can stand in the place of cultural difference. And again, a variety of genres—film, novel, and traditional narrative—speak to a common subject.

Along with transbiology, transgender—indicating a lack of correspondence between gender identity (social, cultural, psychological) and sex identity (biological, physiological)—also appears in *Unsettling Assumptions*. Susan Stryker argues the need to distinguish feminist, queer, and sexuality studies from transgender studies: "If queer theory was born of the union of sexuality studies and feminism, transgender studies can be considered queer theory's evil twin: it has the same parentage but willfully disrupts the privileged family narratives that favor sexual identity labels (like *gay, lesbian, bisexual,* and *heterosexual*) over the gender categories (like man and woman) that enable desire to take shape and find its aim" (2004, 212). She adds that "all too often *queer* remains a code word for 'gay' or 'lesbian,' and all too often transgender phenomena are misapprehended through a lens that privileges sexual orientation and sexual identity as the primary means of differing from heteronormativity" (214).

Transgender's place in folklore shows that imagining and enacting gender contestation has never been exclusively the province of the elite but has long been part of the heritage of the common and everyday. Much current literature on historic cross-dressing in European and Euro–North American cultures has focused on upper-class groups and individuals. Historic fictional and folkloric cross-dressing women have received considerable attention.[13] Male to female transgender, often considered in terms of contemporary drag and camp, has also been discussed historically.[14] Folklore/ethnology research again shows not only the historical depth and geographical breadth of cross-dressing, but also that it was by no means limited to a few class-privileged folks.

Thus *Unsettling Assumptions* ventures into the territory of queer and trans studies, explored by some folklorists/ethnologists (e.g., Greenhill 1995, 1997; see also Turner and Greenhill 2012) but by no means to the extent it has been analyzed by literary and historical scholars.[15] The concept of female masculinity (see, e.g., Halberstam 1998) is invoked in Greenhill and Anderson-Grégoire's work on a folktale about a girl who dresses and acts like a boy and eventually transforms physically into a man. In their work on "The Shift of Sex" tale type, the authors note that although the "girl's" magical transformation into a man is exactly what s/he wants, it comes as a result of the worst curse an evil character can conceive—that a man be turned into a woman or a woman into a man! In spite of the association of this "curse" with an evil character, it remains transgressively balanced. That is, despite the cross-cultural privilege associated with men (see Ortner 1974), such that a man being turned into a woman might arguably be more of a hardship than vice versa (discussed in Mills 1985), the curse evenly and fairly offers the transformation to both sex/genders.

Transgender enters Tye's work when she addresses how members of a Scottish pipe band negotiate masculinity in the context of wearing kilts—too easily coded as skirts and thus as female dress forms. Simultaneously, she explores the cultural obsession with the presumptive male genitalia under the kilt, marked by the traditional abjuration against wearing underwear when kilted. Fehr and Greenhill look at yet another primarily homosocial male practice, that of Manitoba Mennonite *Brommtopp* performers. Their rowdy behavior, by including female dress and sometimes even feminized roles, underscores gender by countering the traditional circumspection expected of males in that cultural and religious tradition.

Tye's and Fehr and Greenhill's work negotiates transgender via dress. Male Scottish pipers and male *Brommtopp* performers alike work to undermine any possibility that, despite apparently being dressed in women's clothing, they want to be understood as female. Cross-dressing, or drag, is most often understood in terms of gender: that is, involving a man dressing as a woman or a woman as a man. Yet the concept of intersectionality—the complex construction of identity in multiple and interlocking modes—raises the possibility that aspects other than sex/gender could be sociocultural constructions multiply inflected with other facets of identity (see, e.g., Somerville 2000). For example, the concept of race was long misconceived—and indeed culturally enjoined—as biological.[16] However, current scholarship not only recognizes race as a cultural construction but also attends to the cultural constructedness of Whiteness as an unmarked social location (see, e.g., Frankenberg 1993; Greenhill 1994, 2002). Concomitantly, then, masquerade and drag involve more than just sex/gender.

Because folklore/ethnology analysis sensitively attends to issues of reversal and inversion, contributors to *Unsettling Assumptions* explore not only constructions of gender and sexuality but also their construction and deconstruction in ethnic and gender drag. Katrin Sieg's notion of ethnic drag, which "includes not only cross-racial casting on the stage, but, more generally, the performance of 'race' as a masquerade" (2002, 2), addresses this issue. Examining, for example, theatrical representations in Germany, wherein White actors play the roles of people of color, Sieg outlines the alibis for this action, including a scarcity of actors of color, the alleged universality of White actors' representations, and pervading values of artistic autonomy and excellence above all other considerations. She argues that although such a practice may be orientalist, exclusionist, and xenophobic, it can also be politically progressive:

> After the Holocaust, the very word race was excised from public language and political analysis. Ethnic drag reveals what this linguistic break conceals, namely the continuities, permutations, and contradictions of racial feelings in West German culture. As a figure of substitution, ethnic drag both exposes and disavows traumatic holes in the social fabric, and facilitates both historical denial and collective mourning. As a crossing of racial lines in performance, ethnic drag simultaneously erases and redraws boundaries posturing ancient and immutable. As a pedagogy, it promises to reveal the dark inside of "Germanness" by taking up an outsider's perspective. As a technique of estrangement, drag denounces that which dominant ideology presents as natural, normal, and inescapable, without always offering another truth. As a ritual inversion, it purports to master grave social

contradictions, yet defers resolution through compulsive repetitions. As a symbolic contact zone between German bodies and other cultures, ethnic drag facilitates the exercise and exchange of power. And as a simulacrum of "race," it challenges the perceptions and privileges of those who would mistake appearances for essence. (2–3; see also Sieg 1998)

Fehr and Greenhill's chapter concerns how the discomforts with *Brommtopp*'s representation don't easily map onto the ethnic associations of the ethnographers. Fehr is Mennonite (as are the *Brommtopp* players); Greenhill is not. Some participants in the revival want to exclude potentially problematic references to race/ethnicity. Some do not. And ultimately, a univocal meaning cannot accurately be attached to such representations in any case. But it is telling that despite the numerous photographs clearly showing gender cross-dressing and ethnic drag by the performers, some interviewees refused to talk about this aspect of the costuming, denied it ever took place, and/or insisted that their comments be removed from the final version of the chapter.

Crucially, ethnic drag cannot be confined to situations of ethnoracial difference. Ethnolinguistic self-representations implicate postmodern sociocultural relations in Wallen's work on "Dutch drag" in Denmark. Though the folks who live on the island of Amager trace their heritage to Dutch settlers, the ties are in fact quite tenuous. Wallen helpfully contextualizes how Dutch ethnicity is celebrated by juxtaposing it with more problematized European responses to immigration by Muslims and other non-White-associated groups. She notes that while Dutch ethnicity can be voluntarily invoked, other ethnoracial groups may be unwilling or unable to try to pass within the mainstream.

UNSETTLING IMPLICATIONS/CONCLUSIONS

Some readers may find the most unsettling aspect of this collection the fact that the editors have declined to organize the book into thematic sections. Given their myriad overlaps and multiple inflections of our three subtopics in the chapters, our decision was simply to present each work in alphabetical order by the author's surname, and then to develop clusters of concepts/ideas and subjects/genres. One reader/reviewer suggested that "this flexible approach to organizing the materials . . . opens up space for teachers and students, and most importantly it valorizes the essays not as individually definitive pieces but as starting points for conversations about our attitudes and practices—the positions we take, consciously or not, within and counter to hegemonic culture and its hierarchies."

We concur!

Unsettling Assumptions calls for reexamination of disciplinary genre classification, expressive culture's relationship to popular culture and its social base, and issues of contemporary fieldwork praxis and representation characterized by a decreasing distance separating fieldwork and subject. It further draws attention to the ways in which the crossing of sociocultural boundaries has become not only a central part of everyday life for most citizens of the globe but also a central mode for exploring difference via various forms of drag—animal, cultural, and sex/gendered. Emphasizing the importance of context and performance to expressive culture's meanings, the chapters also highlight the significance of the everyday, not just in particular cultural nexuses but in larger discourses of authenticity, tradition, and identity.

Folklorists/ethnologists have long recognized expressive culture as international, shared, collective. Such relations are the subjects of international tale-type, ballad, and motif indices, for example. Yet the (inter)discipline's contribution to wider ideas around global flows, as a window on economies and international relations, has been less obvious. In *Unsettling Assumptions* these relations become more explicit. Expressive culture emerges as fundamental to folks' sense of belonging to a family, an occupation or friendship group and, most notably, to identity performativity. Within larger contexts, these works offer a better understanding of cultural attitudes like misogyny, homophobia, and racism as well as the construction and negotiation of power. They often raise more questions than they answer. This problem reflects the difficulty of the issues and the fact that they require continuing attention and vigilance, a task the contributors to *Unsettling Assumptions* take up with scholarly rigor and enthusiasm. But the collection also offers a balanced recognition that its chapters will never be the only answer, let alone the final one.

NOTES

1. Because our French colleagues find the English term *folklore* problematic, and to recognize the different trajectories of European-based ethnology studies and American-based folklore studies, we use the term *ethnology* in addition to *folklore* (see Greenhill and Narváez 2002a, 2002b) when we refer to the area of study and research.

2. They include Bourke (1999); Burke (2004); Gaunt (2006); Greenhill (2010); Lawless (2001); Magliocco (2004); Rieti (2008); Sawin (2004); Thomas (2003); Turner (1999); Tye (2010); Ware (2007); and Whatley and Henken (2000).

3. Arguably, the *Encyclopedia of Women's Folklore and Folklife* (Locke, Vaughan, and Greenhill 2009) could be included, but encyclopedias don't make good teaching texts and are generally more retrospective than programmatic.

4. *Cisgender* refers to those whose gender identity matches the behavior or role conventionally considered appropriate for their sex.

5. For further information on women's folklore, see Greenhill, Tye, and Cantú (2009); on folklore about women, see Greenhill (2009); and on women folklorists/ethnologists, see Cantú, Greenhill, and Saltzman (2009).

6. Hegemonic masculinities are those recognized as privileged, normative, and prescriptive within a group (see Kimmel and Messner 2012).

7. In addition to Butler's aforementioned work, see Stone's "The 'Empire' Strikes Back: A Posttranssexual Manifesto" (1991), which rethinks transgender and transsex, and the works of Connell (e.g., 2005), Kimmel (e.g., 2000), and Messner (e.g., 1995) on masculinities.

8. See, for example, Crenshaw (1991) and Collins (2000).

9. Markedness, an idea from linguistics, offers a useful distinction for sorting out particular kinds of relations between concepts. The unmarked element is generally taken for granted as the norm, and the marked element is usually seen as a development or a change from the unmarked norm. Marking is invariably physical, in that the marked term is longer and incorporates the unmarked. For example, *man* can often be used as a generic to talk about people or humans in general; whereas *woman*—a specific kind of man—rarely is so used. *Man* is unmarked, and *woman* is marked. One of the first feminist criticisms of academic research and scholarship pointed out that not only were women excluded from research as subjects and objects alike, but also that male subjects and objects were presumed sufficient to account for all of humanity (see, e.g., Eichler and Lapointe 1985). The fiction that *man* stands for all human beings is countered by the unlikeliness of the following description: "Man is a mammal, which means that he breastfeeds his young."

10. We use this term to underline significant differences between the cultural presumptions of North Americans of European extraction and those of African, Asian, Indigenous, and other backgrounds.

11. The term *homosocial* came into common use in gender studies beginning with Sedgwick's *Between Men: English Literature and Male Homosocial Desire*, which examines "social bonds between persons of the same sex" expressed in fiction (1985, 1). Now applied to same-sex relationships of all kinds—not always sexual ones—it has become useful in exploring dynamics within apparently all-male and all-female groups.

12. Scholars like Franklin (2006), Giffney and Hird (2008), Halberstam (2008), and Hird (2004, 2006) have begun to map the territory.

13. Consider, for example, Cromwell (1999); Dekker and van de Pol (1997); Dugaw (1989); Greenhill (1995, 1997); Hotchkiss (1996); and Wheelwright (1989).

14. See Ekins and King (1996); Farrer (1996a, 1996b); Newton (1972); and Woodhouse (1989).

15. For example, Epstein and Straub (1991); Herzog (2009); Macías-González (2007); and Rachamimov (2006).

16. Artifacts of the racist idea that races are biological entities result in, among others, social and legal prescriptions against miscegenation—sexual relations, particularly reproductive ones,between members of different races (see, e.g., Lemire 2002); Nazism; ethnic cleansing; and apartheid. Substituting the more culturally inflected term *ethnicity* can elaborate, or alternatively obscure, the biologicalized concept of race.

1

Three Dark-Brown Maidens and the *Brommtopp*

(De)Constructing Masculinities in Southern Manitoba Mennonite Mumming

Marcie Fehr and Pauline Greenhill

FOR MOST ADULT EURO NORTH AMERICANS, THE SEASON from Christmas to New Year's has some (often vestigial) religious significance but remains characterized primarily by formal ritual obligations of feasting, gift giving and receiving, and visiting (see, e.g., Bella 1992; Caplow 1982, 1984; Cheal 1988). Periodic moments of play and socializing (sometimes involving alcohol!) may break up the structure, but for the most part drinking (sometimes to excess) offers the only relief from the often socially and financially expensive obligations. Yet in the past and to some extent the present, various Euro–North American and other cultural groups marked the period from Christmas Eve on December 24 to Twelfth Night on January 6 with rowdy, disguised playful/ludic (see Huizinga 1950) or carnivalesque (see Bakhtin 1968) behavior that mainstream Euro North Americans associate more with Halloween than with this holiday season (see Santino 1994).

Many such customs, termed the "informal house visit" (see Halpert and Story 1969; Lovelace 1980; and Pettitt 1995), involve a group (usually composed of young men) perambulating from one location to another within a community, to the households of socially and culturally proximate families and individuals. The visits include performative aspects—often dancing and singing—as well as the expectation of a reward—usually food and/or drink—and some sociability with the visited household. The cultural and social surround of one such form, Newfoundland Christmas mumming, has been well documented. Also called mummering or janneying, it has been

  DOI: 10.7330/9780874218985.c001

Figure 1.1. Brommtopp players, Sommerfeld, 1914 (Toews and Klippenstein 1974, 304) photograph by Peter G. Hamm (1883-1965) (Photo Courtesy Mennonite Heritage Centre, Winnipeg [Peter G. Hamm Coll. 526.27.5])

variously explained as a ritualization of social relations and solidarity, an expression of otherwise repressed hostilities, an indication of fear of strangers, and a dramatization of socioeconomic relations or sex/gender roles.[1] We find aspects of all these motivations in the *Brommtopp*.[2]

A seasonal informal house visit custom performed well into the twentieth century by young men, almost always on New Year's Eve, in rural Manitoba Mennonite villages where the church tolerated it, *Brommtopp* is named after the musical instrument, a friction drum, used during the performance (see figure 1.1). The *Brommtopp*, constructed from calfskin, a barrel, and horsetail, sounds when its player pulls and rubs rhythmically on the horsetail, producing a difficult to describe thrumming sound: "The player, by situating the drum against a wall, could cause sympathetic vibrations which sometimes shook the china from the shelves. The singers had to shout their song in order to be heard over the racket of the brummtupp" (Petkau and Petkau 1981, 92). Writing in a local history, Jake Bergen remembered, "If everything was made real well this strange instrument would make the dishes in the kitchen cupboard rattle" (2005, 189). Traditionally, a group of some dozen teenage boys and young married men would drive (originally in a horse-drawn sleigh or buggy; later by car) and/or walk from house to house within their own village and sometimes beyond. At each residence, the group would sing the traditional song, which could vary from one location to another but generally asked for money in return for good wishes (Toews 1977, 303–304).

As social historian Ervin Beck comments, the "'Brummtopp Song' must have many variant stanzas, since the young people who sing it while performing the New Year's mummers' play typically compose or alter stanzas to make the song fit the household in which they are performing" (1989, 774–775).[3] As the lyrics imply, players could receive money, liquor and/ or food, often the traditional *Portzeltje* (New Year's fritters) (see, e.g., Beck 1989; Epp-Tiessen 1982) in exchange for their performance.[4] Their rowdy behavior contrasted with the usual expectations of decorum for house visits, as we'll detail below.

Costume varied from place to place. As local historians describe, Blumenfeld performers had elaborately specified roles:

(a) Policeman: His role was to keep order in the group that tended to become unruly in their merrymaking. He would knock on the door to say that a group of people wanted to present a New Year's Wish. If the group was welcomed, he ushered in his troupe. He was the steward of the evening's collection. The policeman was uniformed and wore a red stripe on his trousers.
(b) Clown: The clown's attempts to add humour to the performance were hilarious and ridiculous. But everyone loves a clown! His costume can be imagined.
(c) The Couple: The man and woman tried to pose as a hen-pecked husband and a nagging wife.[5] They were dressed in styles typical of that year.
(d) The Singers: The group of approximately 15 young men sang the song of New Year's wishes. They were dressed in white costumes sewn from flour sacks. They had black stripes on their trouser legs and wore white flathats. All were masked.
(e) The Brummtupp Player: He was dressed like the singers. Upon entering the house, he would find a place in the room that was close to an inside wall or near a china cupboard. (Petkau and Petkau 1981, 91; see also Bergen 2005)

At other locations, costumes seem more improvised, using blackface and whiteface instead of masks (see also V. C. Friesen 1988; Schroeder 1999; Toews 1977) (see figure 1.2). Photographs of *Brommtopp* players indicate that many employed both gender drag—some men dressing as women—and ethnic drag (Sieg 2002)—representation as othered ethnoracial groups like Jewish, Chinese, and First Nations peoples (see figure 1.1).

Figure 1.2. Brommtopp players from near Plum Coulee, December 31, 1930. (Photo Courtesy Tammy Sutherland and David Dyck)

The performance, singing and sometimes dancing followed by socializing, rarely lasted longer than ten to fifteen minutes before the group moved on to the next household.

Most participants assume the tradition has roots in Prussia, predating Mennonite immigration to Russia in the 1780s and then to Manitoba in the 1870s (Petkau and Petkau 1981, 82–92).[6] Interviewees told us that active local performances stopped in some locations as early as before the end of the Second World War, and in others as late as the 1950s or early 1960s (see also Epp-Tiessen 1982; Petkau and Petkau 1981). As writer Armin Wiebe told us:

> Something happened in the era that I was growing up, in the '50s . . . and probably happened well before that. But there seemed to be an attempt to distance the church from . . . the folk traditions . . . And even in my experience, I remember one church that I spent my teenage years in, it seemed like the church went from having guitars used to accompany singing to singing cantatas. And the guitars—more sort of country gospel kinds of singing—got pushed out. A real shift occurred in the late '50s and '60s when the Low German language became less used. In my own experience as a teenager, my generation still spoke Low German socially, but my oldest sibling, six years younger, never became quite fluent. They could speak it to some extent and understand it but weren't fluent. And I think that's also around the time when television became [*laughs*] accessible with the arrival of KCND, and the transmitter was there and the signal was strong enough. And the school system had been really working hard to improve English skills, and churches started switching from German to English. All those kinds of things happened around that time. And along with that, a lot of other traditions became not cool [*laughs*]. (KM2008-1, 2)[7]

Folkloric revival (see Rosenberg 1993) of the practice may have begun at the Sunflower Festival in 1977 in Altona, when a group of then middle-aged men did a *Brommtopp* performance.[8] But from the first decade of the twenty-first century, a group has regularly performed on the afternoon of New Years' Eve at seniors' homes like Eastview Place in Altona. These performers have also appeared at events in Neubergthal village, a designated Manitoba Historic Site reflecting the early years of Mennonite settlement. Organizers incorporated *Brommtopp* performances into a series of concerts sponsored by the Mennonite Heritage Village in Steinbach in 2010 (see figure 1.3). All these events included performers dressed in gender drag but not ethnic drag. The presentation incorporates mimicking actions from the song. Thus, for example, when the lyrics refer to fried fish, one man places plastic fish on all four corners of a table on the stage. At the verse about silver coins, another rattles a Folger's coffee can containing money at the audience. All perform the final stanza together, using their arms to describe a golden band and jumping as the "dark brown maidens" rush out of the house.

Several research consultants, including one who withdrew his name and information, vehemently deny that cross-dressing and ethnic drag were ever part of the *Brommtopp*. Many of those who acknowledge the presence of such practices disagree with our interpretation, arguing that *Brommtopp* is an entertainment only, and can have no other meaning. While we respect their right to hold such opinions, we do not share them. We deconstruct masculinities and their relation to the cross-ethnic, cross-racial, and cross-gender costuming in the traditional and revival manifestations of *Brommtopp*. In working through this material, we experienced the anxiety of trying to balance a fair account of the practice with our recognition that, historically and currently, it risks invoking profoundly sexist and racist stereotypes. Our exploration of the tradition seeks to address such anxieties and discomforts head-on. By employing feminist, queer, trans, and postcolonial lenses and theories, our analysis of the *Brommtopp* explores how the opportunities it once gave young men—and now gives older men—for transgender, transethnic, and/or transracial identity exploration offer insight into the fragmentation of hegemonic masculinity in Mennonite societies.[9] This research is primarily based on seventeen interviews by Pauline Greenhill, six by Marcie Fehr, and one by Kendra Magnus-Johnston conducted between spring 2009 and winter 2010, with folks who participated in or otherwise experienced the practice in the south-central Manitoba communities of Altona, Blumenfeld, Hochfeld, Neubergthal, Plum Coulee, and others on the so-called West Reserve of Manitoba Mennonite settlement (see figure 1.4).

Figure 1.3. Poster from a series of concerts organised by the
Steinbach Mennonite Historic Village in 2010

MENNONITES AND LOW GERMAN IN MANITOBA

Until as recently as the last thirty to forty years, Mennonites in rural
Manitoba communities were somewhat culturally detached from the Euro–
North American mainstream. Villages offered socioreligious islands in a sea
of greater diversity. As Armin Wiebe noted:

> Long after I had left home it dawned on me one day that where I had lived
> was in reasonable biking distance from a French community but there
> was never really any interaction with them . . . I think I was in grade four
> when we had moved to town and the teacher asked, "What do you call
> people who live in Manitoba?" and I was going to shoot up my hand and
> say, "Mennonites!" and luckily something stopped me [*laughs*]. Because

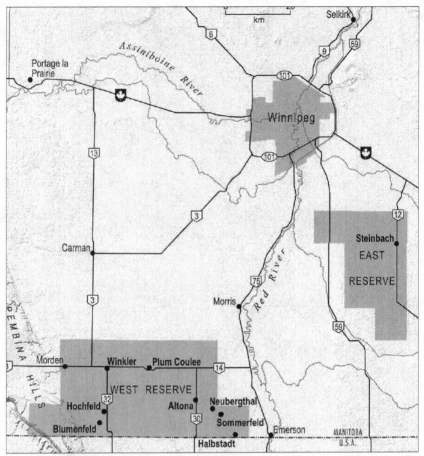

Figure 1.4. Map of portion of Manitoba showing East and West Reserves of Mennonite settlement

up until that time I was under the impression that that was what it meant, you know: that Mennonites were people who lived in Manitoba [*laughs*]. (KM2009-1, 2)

Southern Manitoba Mennonite communities and cultural expressions weave elements of displacement, dissent, pacifism, and conscientious objection with self-sufficiency informed by religion. Mennonites trace their history to the sixteenth century and the Reformation era in Switzerland and the Netherlands, and then to migrant communities in Prussia (Poland) and Russia. During the eighteenth and nineteenth centuries, Prussia dictated that Mennonite churches be plain, with no bell, towers, or pointed windows. Such concepts of "modesty"[10] permeated forms of (in)visibility including gendered

Figure 1.5 Marcie's paternal Grandmother, Mary Fehr, in traditional Old Colony Mennonite dress in front of the Fehr family home in Winnipeg, June, 1970. Mary's youngest son—Marcie's Uncle Gary—is standing on the steps. (Photo Courtesy Mary Fehr)

Figure 1.6 (from left to right) Great-grandfather Fehr, Isaac Fehr (Marcie's paternal Grandfather), Great Aunt Nettie, and Great-grandmother Fehr in Hochfeld, Manitoba, 1931. (Photo Courtesy Mary Fehr)

and uniform dress codes, nonmaterialism, and Luddite ideals (J. Friesen 2001, 4–6) (see figures 1.5, 1.6, and 1.7). In Russia, by 1870, the government introduced a universal military service policy but granted Mennonites the so-called *Forsteidiensts*, alternative service in forestry. The government also pressed them to teach Russian in their schools alongside High German, but left them free to speak Low German (a North German dialect with some Dutch influence) in everyday communication (Staliûnas 2007; Thiessen 2003, x–xiii). Some 17,000 conservative Mennonites migrated in the 1870s to North America (J. Friesen 2001, 6–8), seeking more extensive rights and privileges.

Most Mennonites who came then to Manitoba settled southeast and southwest of the city of Winnipeg, in rural areas known as the East and West Reserves.[11] The first immigrants arrived in 1874 from the Bergthal and Borosenko colonies in South Russia and laid out their farm villages on the eight-township East Reserve (Reimer 1983). Those who came in 1875, finding the East Reserve unsuitable for farming, occupied land further west, between the Red River and the Pembina Hills (Francis 1955; Reimer 1983; Warkentin 2000). Relatively quickly, Mennonites lost the autonomy to establish their own social and economic systems, including for land tenure and education. The Manitoba School Attendance Act (1916) enforced "attendance in public schools where English was the primary language of

Figure 1.7 Girls who attended Hochfeld School, in Hochfeld, Manitoba, 1936. Back row center: the only teacher, who did not speak Low German. (Photo Courtesy Lena Rempel)

instruction mandatory for all children between the ages of seven and four-teen" (Sawatzky 1971, 13). This policy established a hierarchical system of linguistic spaces, specifically: English for school; High German for church; and Low German for home and everyday life. Recalling his personal experi-ence as a first generation Mennonite-Canadian, Jac Schroeder notes: "All the children spoke 'Low German' . . . at home. The Provincial Government gave to the School Board the privilege of also teaching German as a second language. But this had to be done outside of the regular school hours of 9:00 A.M. to 4:00 P.M. when only the English language could be spoken. The School Board decided to add half an hour from 8:30 A.M. to 9:00 A.M. for instruction" (1999, 153).

The government-sanctioned compartmentalization of High German in institutionalized education both supported the class superiority that came from its association with Church activities and limited its use to those two locations. Without an established writing system,[12] Low German lacked the central tool to facilitate skills on the North American wage market (Francis 1955; Loewen 1983, 1999; Warkentin 2000). Some resisting Mennonites guarded their traditions in the private sphere. But many folk practices dis-appeared as the language central to them became obsolete, ousted by the capitalist system that flooded Mennonite subjectivity and culture. As socio-linguist Suzanne Romaine indicates, "Schooling and literacy create a divi-sion between those whose credentials give them access to town as opposed to those who have no negotiable skills on the wage market. English is a kind of cultural capital with a value in the linguistic market place" (1994, 93).

MENNONITE MASCULINITIES

Brommtopp does not mesh well with outsiders' views of historical or current Mennonite culture and tradition. The hegemonic, historical, exoteric image for rural Mennonite men presents stoic and *sober* (both literally and figuratively) business owners and farmers. However, as historian Royden Loewen (2006) suggests, Mennonite masculinity changed drastically after the Second World War in response to economic crisis. Mennonites began to commercialize their farms, specializing in wheat, poultry, and beef. Men's move to commercial poultry farming in particular represented gender transgression. Collecting eggs and slaughtering chickens, with their everyday physical and social relationship to cooking and kitchen work, were traditionally women's work. Thus men who commercialized poultry doubly transgressed gender roles, first by linking their identities to a feminine domain, and second by masculinizing traditionally female work for the sake of capitalism. The pressure to adapt and re-form commercial farming led to a masculinity crisis. Indeed, traditional gender roles and expectations for both women and men shifted to sustain economic security in a time of cultural strife.

Further, as larger commercial enterprises replaced small farms, Mennonite men and women increasingly sought employment outside their villages. Smaller families increased the need for farmhands from the community and beyond. Shifting roles meant that men were no longer the sole laborers outside the home, nor the breadwinners at the homestead farm (see figures 1.8 and 1.9). Well before the Second World War, many women found paid labor in urbanized areas, especially Winnipeg, as seamstresses, housekeepers, and cleaners (Epp 2008, 176). The trend to find off-farm labor increased after 1945. The original communities became less localized, their populations decreased, and extended families fell out of touch. With fewer local connections, smaller families, and a decrease in communal farming practices, the resultant destabilization of hegemonic masculinity left little room for what were once performative boyhood practices like the *Brommtopp*. When the maintenance of a local cultural economy made the performance of the most mainstream, conservative Mennonite identities and their strict gender scripts themselves deviant and resistant with respect to the mainstream (urban Euro North Americans), *Brommtopp* performances and other Low German traditions became culturally anomalous.

Figure 1.8 Great Aunt Lena Rempel plowing grass on Rempel family farm, (circa 1940). (Photo Courtesy Lena Rempel)

BROMMTOPP

Most traditional participants and audiences experienced no sense of *Brommtopp* as an inappropriate or disjunctive social practice. Many research consultants, recalling their childhood and youth in the 1920s to 1950s, described a much-anticipated fun and wholesome atmosphere when the *Brommtopp* players would arrive and perform. Jake Schroeder recalls: "We lived half a mile from Grandma and Grandpa's and when we knew that they were going to come over there, and they might miss our house, we would all go over to Grandma and Grandpa's. It was a whole bunch of people in the house waiting for the *Brommtopp*, 'cause this was exciting! This was something that we looked forward to! It was good entertainment!" (PG2009-24, 25).

Neighbors in Mennonite communities recognized one another; families attended church together, worked communally on each other's farms and village projects, and followed *faspa*, a weekly family house-visiting tradition, usually after Sunday church services.[13] Loewen claims that "it was only an odd farmer [who] would not be glad to stop his work for a while when a guest appeared on the yard. Village culture encouraged visiting" (1983, 167). Calls on Sunday after church brought large families un/expectedly to each other's doors for food, refreshments, and conversation. Kin and friends gathered to discuss sermons, farming, relatives, and sometimes world events that someone had read about in a newspaper from Winnipeg

Figure 1.9 From left: Great Aunt Tina, Great Aunt Lena, and Great Aunt Nettie Rempel picking corn on Rempel family farm (circa 1940). (Photo Courtesy Lena Rempel)

or gathered from local village papers such as the *Mennonitische Rundshau* or the *Nordwesten* (168).

Doors were never locked, and folks rarely arranged meetings ahead of time. The idea of the feared stranger was only a distant possibility, as "not only was one fulfilling a scriptural injunction by having an open home; it was also a sign of prestige if one had many guests" (Loewen 1983, 168). However, many respectful social codes were transgressed in the *Brommtopp* tradition. When entering the host house, performers never removed their boots and overshoes and therefore trod the dirty, melting snow onto the kitchen or parlor floor. Also, the musician in charge of the *Brommtopp* drum poured water over the horsetail for lubrication and optimum sound, leaving behind a pool of dirty water that needed to be mopped up. The aftermath of a performance often mixed excitement with resentment, as the women of the house were, by gendered default, left to clean up after the messy gang of costumed singers. Indeed, some consultants suggest that the end of the *Brommtopp* tradition could be attributed to the replacement of easily cleaned linoleum tile and wood floors with carpeting and broadloom. However, interviewee Bruno Hamm linked the tradition's demise to other gendered concerns: "Because some of them had their floors all waxed and polished for New Year's and then on New Year's Eve and someone comes and messes it all up? Takes a pretty good mother to accept it" (PG2009-12). Ideally, women shouldn't care about having extra messes to clean up, or indeed wish to put their own interests above those of their family and community. Thus, this pollution explanation of why the *Brommtopp* tradition ended is strongly gendered. When outsiders' values—like the idea that women should be attentive to their own individualistic concerns—enter the traditional Mennonite home, they also endanger the social climate in which *Brommtopp* originally flourished. But these same values also foster the revival of *Brommtopp* by older men as an expression of another time and place, remembered with nostalgia. For, as we argue, this rowdy tradition was not only about its young male performers' sex/gender others but also about their ethno/racial/religious others. This concern for expressing self and difference remains salient for the revival performers as well.

Some consultants depicted the *Brommtopp* performance as far more obnoxious and vulgar than others remember—or are willing to disclose. David Schroeder recalls: "They would simply yell the minute they were on the yard and we all had dogs [that] warned us that somebody's on the yard, so it was often pretty rowdy until they got into the house. They would be dressed differently sometimes and . . . would be very boisterous, purposefully boisterous. So they made a lot of racket outside" (PG2009-15, 16). But Alvina Giesbrecht, a young girl at the time the *Brommtopp* would visit her family home, remembers, "There'd be . . . a lot of jokes and maybe even some off-color ones. . . . Filthy ones" (PG2009-01). Di Brandt, Mennonite writer, scholar, and artist, describes her family's historical experience of the *Brommtopp*: "It was definitely a disruption. You didn't expect it. No one would have announced it or anything. It wasn't like they would have said, 'Let's wait up for the *Brommtopp* people to come!' No, certainly not. As for the noise, that was exactly the thing, making a lot of noise, being rude and . . . irreverent. Everyone would be, sort of, 'Oh, good,' you know, embarrassed. People would think, 'Oh, ergh, here they are again!'" (PG2009-08).

Consultants agree that not every community member enjoyed or welcomed the *Brommtopp*. The tradition incorporated more than merely a song and dance in exchange for baked goods and well wishes—or even alcohol. Indeed, even when it flourished, its aesthetic and behavioral ideals diverged incongruently with everyday social norms for Mennonites such as the aforementioned modesty, uniform dress, strict heteronormative gender scripts, and sobriety. Further, traditional Mennonite Christian interpretations order that depicting oneself as anything other than one's birth body and face blasphemes against humans' creation in God's image. Thus, while actual dress and occupational opportunities have evolved with urbanization and modernization, nevertheless the *Brommtopp* costuming, then as now, jars with stereotypes of Mennonites.

TRANSGENDER MENNONITE MEN

As would be expected of a liminal, seasonal, disruptive tradition, the costumed alternative identity of *Brommtopp* allowed young men to engage in behavior that would otherwise be codified as socially inappropriate. Typical *Brommtopp* performers in the practice's heyday would be young, Mennonite men, embodying hegemonic masculine identities, from the same town or village. Now, those in *Brommtopp* revival performances are elderly patriarchs. For both groups, everyday behavioral license would be greater than for any other man or boy, or for any woman or girl. Indeed, the alibi of a pious, hardworking male serves as license for a performer to substitute cultural and gender subalterns for his hegemonic identity, providing the fluidity and privilege to perform a *Brommtopp* persona. Thus, social conventions of gender scripts could be explored under the guise of an accepted male ritual.

Still, possibly in an effort to suspend or displace anxieties about cross gender dress, the transperformers' feminine beauty (or lack thereof) could be scrutinized. Writer Eleanor Chornoboy in *Faspa with Jast* calls the mummers "far too noisy men singing out of tune and looking like ugly women or goofy men" (2007, 61). Neither the historic nor the revival performances demonstrate any effort by the cross-dressed men to represent a conventionally attractive woman. In the revival performances, the transgendered costumed men mark their performative nonperformance of womanhood by wearing their jeans or dress pants under their skirts and aprons as well as by leaving on their everyday men's shoes. This careful attention to detail in order *not* to pass as a woman shows concern that their gender/sex and—for the traditional performers, sometimes sexually transgressive—behavior could too uncomfortably resonate with everyday life.[14] Thus, judgments on the beauty of male-to-female *Brommtopp* costumers, as well as their disinterest in passing,[15] can serve to control and repress trans expressions and identities as well as to fortify internalized homophobia.

Armin Wiebe's prize-winning novel *The Salvation of Yasch Siemens* (1984) tellingly suggests that cross-dressed performers may have stirred anxiety for traditional *Brommtopp* players and their audiences. His hero reflects: "Those other badels [scoundrels] wouldn't have the nerves to put on a dress . . . his grandfather said a woman couldn't play the brummtupp. It just wouldn't be right . . . I don't know what do to because nobody told me that if I had a dress on I would have to do stuff like a woman, too" (1984, 16, 22). The connection a man might feel to transgressing his gender script in *Brommtopp* would nevertheless remind him that he should not wish to pass as a woman in real life. Bruno Hamm, when asked if men had cross-dressed as women in the *Brommtopp* group he performed in, said. "You know, I don't really remember that. I don't think so, because in those days it was [either] women [or] . . . men, nothing like, mixed" (PG2009-12). So taboo was this subject that one consultant denied that *Brommtopp* players ever cross-dressed during an interview conducted in a hall decorated with a famous picture of a local *Brommtopp* group clearly depicting gender (and ethnic) drag. We note that this individual also participated in the revival performances we saw, though he was not one of those dressed as a woman.

In traditional *Brommtopp* visits, even when a player's primary identity would be obscured with masks or makeup, the community usually knew who he was. Interviewee Alvina Giesbrecht commented, "You'd see something like that even though. . . . cross-dressing, as far as a man was concerned, you would still recognize him" (PG2009-01). Yet periodically, planned trickery could lead to private guessing games between audience members, or could be deliberately calculated to fool and embarrass women. One interviewee and past *Brommtopp* performer, who asked not to be identified, described how some men would switch costumes with fellow players to trick their wives when arriving to perform at their family homes. The trickster friend, now doubly disguised, would cuddle up to the woman—playfully, physically, and sometimes intimately interacting with her—and then remove his mask to reveal he was not her husband. The woman would sometimes leave the room or hide her own face. Though she was supposed to feel ashamed for not recognizing her husband—she would know his costume, having typically been the person who pieced it together—and thus for interacting inappropriately with another man, we imagine that in some circumstances the situation also offered play opportunities for women.

Heterosexuality, fidelity, and honoring one's spouse are highly valued identities for Mennonite men and women. Thus, the social contract between the two men who are doubly disguising their identities creates a space of permissible male sexual openness and play while shaming the wife's sexual agency. This act of double disguise and the permissive space of comedy allow men to explore intimate possibility, disturbing the hegemonic ideals of heterosexual coupling, especially when the man happens to be cast as a female character. In these instances of switching costumes, and indeed in other instances of disguise in *Brommtopp*, just as in Cajun country Mardi Gras, "real life social relationships were negotiated under the surface of a cultural game" (Ancelet 2001, 152; see also Sawin 2001). Unfortunately (and we certainly don't mean to downplay this consequence), from the men's perspective this happens at the expense of the confidence and sexuality of women.

THE SPACE BETWEEN BOY AND MAN

Another transgressive aspect of *Brommtopp* was its frequent association with drinking. Alcohol use, typically discouraged among Mennonites, varies in social acceptability from village to village. As described in the *Brommtopp* song itself:

> We wish the master . . .
> > a jug of wine
> > To induce the Master to jollity. (Toews 1977, 304)

Thus, not only drinking but indeed intoxication ("jollity") becomes a central aim in the song's world. Some interviewees denied offering or using alcohol, yet others indicated that audiences gave it to performers as a (sometimes more than) token exchange. In some cases, a drunken (or suspected drunken) *Brommtopp* performer could suffer drastically negative social consequences. Alternatively, as one interviewee who asked not to be identified claimed, the overindulging man or boy could simply be left behind to sleep it off. Some research participants also described judgment on a performance as too energetic, too jovial or obnoxious, resulting in suspicion that the player was drunk or even alcoholic! As Menno Kehler explains, in one case, "Everybody thought, 'Well, that guy's just a terrible drunk.' He just got so wound up because it brought back memories, eh? Man, could he sing . . . Even his church elders talked to him about it and heard that he'd been very drunk . . . He was so hurt. He never sang . . . again. He disappeared. But he would never! But that's what people saw, eh?" (PG2009-13, 14).

Clearly the rambunctious, energetic behavior a *Brommtopp* performer embodied was not codified as socially appropriate for a Mennonite adult man. Boyhood and youthful narrative embodiment of play, dress-up, and foolery transgressed the presumed manhood of a *Brommtopp* performer. Consultants confirmed that traditional players were usually young men, commonly unmarried and thus, like their cognate Nova Scotia belsnickles, "occupied a distinctly transitional position, being no longer children, but just on the verge of assuming their full roles and responsibilities, having to give up the carelessness of boyhood and the peer group and face up to the stronger social demands and constraints of adulthood" (Bauman

1972, 238). As the markers of perceived succession into manhood are not only culturally relative but also subjective, it is possible that the young men and boys of historical *Brommtopp* groups were negotiating their transitional stage from boy to man through disguise, ritual, altered consciousness from alcohol, and socially inappropriate behavior. Barry Jean Ancelet's description of traditional Cajun Mardi Gras practice argues that "as young boys become young men and young girls become young women, they shed their adolescence by stepping outside themselves and imitating their elders in public, yet in secret" (1989, 2). Alvina Giesbrecht, asked why the young men in the photographs of *Brommtopp* groups shown to her would have chosen to disguise themselves, said, "These young people, these young men would not have wanted to let their parents know what they were doing, that would be one thing. Now, the parents might . . . they might have known, but they just let them go ahead and do it. But they were not supposed to be doing it, really, it was actually a no-no" (PG2009, 1). Such passive sanctioning meant that while they were in public settings such as neighbors' homes, for the *Brommtopp* players as for Mardi Gras participants, "the ritual consumption of alcohol serve[d] to loosen inhibitions, while the mask serve[d] as a sort of cocoon, providing a cover for the changes occurring in the real self underneath" (Ancelet 1989, 2).

The potentially deviant queering of hegemonic manhood, paired with the manifest anxiety of the transitional masculinity embodied by the *Brommtopp* players, often scared young children. Consultants who remembered the tradition from their childhood often said they feared the *Brommtopp*'s strange sound and the weirdly costumed people, even when they recognized their parents' friends and neighbors. As they became older, however, fear could be replaced by excitement. One minister's daughter, who asked to remain anonymous, a teenager at the time, followed the players through her community. She commented: "I remember that my dad wasn't home. My dad wouldn't have allowed us to go with [them]. My sister and I went with them from house to house . . . I'm sure that if he had been home, we wouldn't have been able to." Interviewee Eleanor Chornoboy talked about "us kids sitting on the staircase and looking at these guys in awe because they didn't act as adults at all" (PG2009-21, 22). In *Faspa with Jast,* she notes: "The noise and odd looking adult men scared . . . youngest daughter Anna. But not wanting to miss a thing, she hid behind the door and peered through a small crack to see big men acting as silly as her toddling brothers" (2007, 61). Clearly, men's roles were sufficiently restricted that children recognized that the *Brommtopp* players were not fulfilling the scripts their communities normally dictated to them.

Indicating a poignant overlap of traditional meaning and purpose, folk-lorist Richard Bauman's discussion of masculinity in the Nova Scotia bel-snickling argues that "in frightening and intimidating the youngsters of the household, [performers] were gaining release from the time, just recently left behind, when they themselves were fearful children, terrified of the strange and the supernatural and subject to external mechanisms of moral control" (1972, 240). We also note that at the revival performance in summer 2010 in Steinbach, when the *Brommtopp* began to sound, a four-year-old girl climbed onto her father's lap, hid her face in his chest, and only peeked at the stage for the rest of the presentation.[16]

ETHNIC DRAG AND PRIVILEGE

The many intersections of identity play integral to the *Brommtopp* performance associate each song verse with a different archetype from a historical heteronormative extended family and household group. While the *Brommtopp* song has many melodic permutations, and like other traditional songs its texts vary, it follows a common overall structure. The general archetypes represented in all versions brought to our attention have been, in order of their usual appearance: a patriarch known as master of the house; an elderly matriarch; a young daughter; an elderly female housekeeper; a young son with a sword and pistol set; a boy who keeps the horses; a pig herder/shepherd, usually wielding a whip or stick; and, in the last verse, three young girls of color who come running out of a house. Historical photographs show that performers sometimes dressed in costumes not explicit in the song, such as clowns, animals, and First Nations, South or East Asian, and Jewish stereotypes, as well as wearing masks and/or using blackface or whiteface (see figure 1.10). The song itself does not clearly call for gender cross-dressing. Indeed, we first recognized the link between costumes and song verses when we saw a revival performance in the seniors' home, Eastview Place in Altona, on December 31, 2009. And only the last verse implies any kind of cross-ethnic or cross-racial dress:

> We draw a golden band over the house
> and three dark brown maidens rushed out. (Toews 1977, 304)

We have few details about how the historic performances actually incor-porated—if at all—the costumes and disguise evident in the astonishing number of posed pictures of *Brommtopp* groups, dating from the second to the middle decades of the twentieth century. No photographs of actual performances have come to our attention. Further, we have encountered

Figure 1.10 Brommtopp group, photograph courtesy Marge Friesen, Altona, Manitoba.

considerable difficulty in persuading most interviewees to give many details about gender or ethnic drag. Clearly, recent revival performances have raised anxieties regarding the inclusion of the last verse with the "three dark brown maidens." Some seek to explain it away as only tradition and entertainment.[17] Yet the program published for the Singing in Time: Mennonites and Music concert, which we attended, avoided the issue, rather than accurately translating into English the final verse, as the group sang it in German. Clearly, the greatest concern was that the "English" (non-Mennonite) attendees would (mis)interpret the verse and its representation as racist. So in the English translation, instead of "three dark brown maidens," "three pretty maidens" jump from the house. Avoiding the possibility that the song and practice could actually be racist, the decision to include while excluding the "three dark brown maidens" reinforces racism as a trivial and historically bound variable for which blame can be displaced for the sake of traditional continuity. The artifice implies that whatever such words and representations might have meant then, now they reference the past only, and specifically the *Brommtopp* performance, not any contemporaneous or current attitudes and practices. But we find it somewhat bizarre that, despite the obvious ethnic stereotypes, arguably much more offensive than any linguistic reference to skin color, organizers deemed the photograph in figure 1.10 perfectly acceptable for the cover of the same concert program. Representations cannot be divorced from what they (potentially) depict; in this case, the images in the photograph invoke the actual marginalization of ethnoracial minorities in historic and present-day Manitoba.

However, racial and ethnic anxieties indeed manifested through imitation in historical *Brommtopp* performances. In the late nineteenth and early twentieth centuries, when the tradition flourished in Manitoba, most Mennonites were—as discussed above—new immigrants, members of an ethnoreligious minority invoking a narrative of persecution in early modern Europe. The implications of identity crisis in the cross-ethnic dress and imitation found in *Brommtopp* renders visible the construction of immigrant identity, which "emerges out of the fragmentation of colonization, transportation, and migration of peoples, and cultural diaspora" (Clary Lemon 2010, 8). It complicates the construction of identity in the simplistic discourse of posturing the self as known in relation to the mysterious, even incomprehensible, other. In a tremendous irony, the *Brommtopp* song itself is preserved in otherwise English-language community histories and in books and articles on Mennonite folklore in High German. Indeed, some controversy remains as to whether or not the song was originally performed in Low German—the informal community language—or in High German—the formal institutional language.[18]

The identity crises of Mennonite communities cannot be detached from the *Brommtopp*'s presentation of what cultural theorist Katrin Sieg calls "ethnic drag," which "includes not only cross-racial casting on the stage, but, more generally, the performance of 'race' as a masquerade" (2002, 2). A lumpen functionalism argument would make Brommtopp ethnic drag "a way of expressing and releasing tensions within a rapidly emerging culture" (Ackroyd 1979, 112). Though one group, First Nations peoples, apparently sparked fear and the other reflected the more comfortable, ubiquitous rural Manitoba towns' Chinese restaurants (see Marshall 2011), both quintessentially represented what Mennonites were *not*. On one level, this racial masquerade offers a flattering view of a strong impression of exotic difference; on another it reflects appropriation and privilege. By "perform[ing] an ethnic identity in order to negotiate the rigid stereotypes of self and other" (Benbow 2007, 517), the White males in *Brommtopp* groups, then and now, may work through their cultural anxieties of the gendered and/or ethnoracial other. Yet clearly, in *Brommtopp*, "the impersonation of ethnic others by a subject that stages and conceals its dominance . . . in the form of a series of displacements" (Sieg 1998, 297) takes place at the expense of marginalized races and ethnicities.

Nevertheless, we argue that the essentialization of race and ethnicity is not simply rehearsed but instead problematized in the practice of *Brommtopp*. As Sieg says, in ethnic drag, "ethnicity [is] underscored as a drag performance in the sense that actors displayed its signs at a distance, rather than in the mimetic mode of merging actor and role. Its signs were shown to be attributed to bodies, rather than originating in them" (2004, 126). The performers' White, male privilege to perform race as masquerade to construct, as well as preserve, their religious, ethnic, and gender identities in crisis is indeed problematic. Yet *Brommtopp* also fractures the understanding of "the palpable, physical effects of ethnicity on bodies that are forced to identify" through race (315). *Brommtopp* performances challenge the deterministic convergence and construction of race and ethnicity as well as of gender. Through the understanding of ethnicity and gender as socially constructed, and embodied through performance, events like *Brommtopp* foreground the construction of—and consumption of—race, ethnicity, and gender. Events that include performances crossing socially vested lines need to be placed in the hierarchically structured systems of class, gender, and ethnicity, and to account for radically unequal positions of access to representation and cultural exchange. But at the same time, a deeper understanding of the *Brommtopp*'s gender and ethnic drag implicates taken-for-granted notions of assimilation into Canadian ethnicity, adulthood, and hegemonic gender scripts, illuminating while disturbing more conventional identities.

NOTES

Funding from the Social Sciences and Humanities Research Council of Canada, Standard Research Grant "Transgender Imagination and Enactment in Traditional and Popular Culture in Canada" (Pauline Greenhill, principal investigator, 2008–2012), made this research possible. Emilie Anderson-Grégoire, Kendra Magnus-Johnston, and Merrick Pilling gathered and prepared materials. Roland Sawatzky offered invaluable background from the Mennonite Heritage Village in Steinbach. Thanks to interviewees Di Brandt, Eleanor Chornoboy, Mary Fehr, Alvina Giesbrecht, Bruno Hamm, Menno Kehler, David Schroeder, Jake Schroeder, Erika Thiessen, and Armin Wiebe for their invaluable insights. The positions we take in this chapter are not necessarily ones all of these individuals would share, agree with, or even approve of. Carol Toews and Jonathan Sawatsky at Eastview Place, Altona, gave help and cooperation. Margruite Krahn helped us make connections with the community. For permission to use photographs, we thank David Dyck and Tammy Sutherland, Marge Friesen, The Mennonite Heritage Centre (Peter G. Hamm Coll.) 526.27.5, and Marcie's great-aunt Lena Rempel and grandmother Mary Fehr. Weldon Hiebert drew the map. We also appreciate Diane Tye's careful reading and many suggestions and Royden Loewen's keen eye for nuances and historical references.

1. Halpert and Story (1969), including Chiaramonte (1969); Faris (1969); Firestone (1969); Szwed (1969); and Clyde E. Williams (1969); as well as Firestone (1978); Handelman (1984); Robertson (1982, 1984); Sider (1976), and others have extensively detailed the practice's forms; we do not reprise them here.

2. Orthographic variations abound. Using *Brommtopp*, we follow Jack Thiessen's *Mennonite Low German Dictionary* (2003). Other possibilities in newspaper articles, local histories, autobiographies, and so on, include *brummtupp, brumtup, brummtopp, brumtop,* and *bromtop.*

3. Beck talks about the tradition across Anabaptist culture; we are unaware of any *Brommtopp* mummers' play being performed in Manitoba.

4. Thiessen's dictionary offers two alternatives: *Portzeltje* and *Porzeltje*. He also calls these fritters *Niejoahschküake* (2003, 188). Epp-Tiessen (1982) uses *porzeltje*; Toews (1977) uses *portzelky*.

5. The "woman" would be a cross-dressed man.

6. Erika Thiessen, who emigrated from Russia to Paraguay in 1947 and came to Manitoba in 1956, remembers the *Brommtopp* from her girlhood in Russia (PG2009-07). See also Voth (1994).

7. This citation system gives the initials of the interviewer—Pauline Greenhill or Kendra Magnus-Johnston—the year of the interview, and the interview reference number(s).

8. *Revival,* as folklorists use the term, refers to a return to a cultural tradition, often after a period in which it was inactive. Revivals of tradition sometimes include members of groups other than those who originally participated in it. Thus, for example, the 1950s and 1960s folk music revival in Europe and North American included many participants and performers who were not directly linked to source traditions in that they did not come from families and/or communities in which folksongs were commonly performed, and/or many who performed songs from ethnolinguistic groups other than their own.

9. Though multiple forms of masculinity exist within any society, some are recognized as privileged, normative, and prescriptive, and are thus termed hegemonic (see Kimmel and Messner 2012).

10. *Modesty* refers to religious and social dictates that people dress plainly—for important occasions, preferably in black—be well covered, and subsist with minimal material goods.

11. This terminology describes the plots of land the Manitoba government set aside for Mennonites (see, e.g., Reimer 1983).

12. High German was the written language in Mennonite communities, and newspapers like Steinbach's *Die Mennonitische Post* continue. Some churches still sing in German. Recent work toward establishing Low German as a written language includes Thiessen (2003).

13. For *faspa,* the woman of the house needed to be prepared with baked goods and fresh coffee or face humiliation: "No woman wanted to run out of food on Sunday Faspa, regardless of how many guests arrived. She wanted to be seen as prepared, hospitable, and well-organized. To run out of food would suggest otherwise" (Chornoboy 2007, 57).

14. In a different Canadian prairie context, mock-wedding cross-dressing raised similar concerns around critique of gender roles rather than attempts to pass as female (see Taft 1997).

15. Elaine Ginsberg argues that "'passing' has been applied discursively to disguises of other elements of an individual's presumed 'natural' or 'essential' identity, including class, ethnicity, and sexuality, as well as gender, the latter usually effected by deliberate alterations of physical appearance and behaviour, including cross-dressing . . . and forces reconsideration of the cultural logic that the physical body is the site of identic intelligibility" (1996, 4; see also Schlossberg 2001).

16. See also Patricia Sawin's (2001) discussion of children's fear in contemporary Louisiana Mardi Gras.

17. Greenhill (2002) discusses various alibis for racism in Morris, an "English men's dance tradition."

18. When we asked ethnomusicologist Doreen Klassen why the *Brommtopp* song was not included in her *Singing Mennonite* (1989), she answered that it was in High German, and the book included only Low German songs.

2

Cutting a Thousand Sticks of Tobacco Makes a Boy a Man
Traditionalized Performances of Masculinity in Occupational Contexts

Ann K. Ferrell

In November 2000, at the second annual Kentucky Women in Agriculture conference in Louisville, I had a brief conversation with an attendee whose husband raised tobacco. She told me their future seemed increasingly uncertain; their growing quotas were being cut, and her husband now worked a full-time job off the farm while continuing to raise a small amount of tobacco. For him, she told me, it was not just a crop or a source of income; it was a way of life, and she was afraid of what it would mean to him if a time came when he could no longer grow tobacco. Although conversations about tobacco farming—both its culture and its politics—were relatively common in Kentucky at the time, and although I never saw this woman again, this particular discussion became the seed that grew into my research about Kentucky tobacco.

Her story held power for me as a gendered narrative, central to the decline of tobacco production, that was relatively absent from public discourses. Raising tobacco, a multigenerational tradition for this woman's husband, was worth fighting to hold onto. Working off the farm in part supported his ability to continue raising tobacco and to maintain the family farm that had passed to him from his father, suggesting symbolic as well as economic reasons for raising tobacco. Meanwhile, his wife and the other women attending this conference were exploring new farming opportunities through the exchange of information about agricultural diversification and sustainability, not exclusive to but in a context of the decline of tobacco production. This chapter examines the performance of tobacco work as commensurate with

DOI: 10.7330/9780874218985.c002

the performance of a particular locally valued masculine identity, providing a gendered case study of an occupational context in the midst of change.

My ethnographic fieldwork with Kentucky burley tobacco growers began in 2005, with intensive fieldwork during the 2007 crop year (January 2007 through February 2008). I began this work after observing that tobacco was increasingly understood as on its way out due to changing societal acceptance of its products, rising overseas production, and the legislated end to the federal tobacco program—a system in which, since the 1930s, growers agreed to production allotments in return for minimum poundage prices.[1] I quickly learned that while those who continue to raise this crop do not all agree that it is on its way out, many of their discussions are structured around change, serving to continually compare the past and present. The end of the federal program has been widely heralded as the most dramatic change; many growers stopped growing tobacco when the program ended, and those who continue now contract directly with tobacco companies with no guaranteed market.[2] They also face changing farm technologies and labor circumstances as well as a stigmatization of not just the crop but also those who grow it.[3] One of the questions that they frequently hear (and I heard during and after my fieldwork) is "Why don't you just grow something else?" Gender is central to the complex and layered answers to this question. Tobacco work is certainly not unique in this regard; the relationships between gender, occupational identity, and economic crises—local and global—demand further investigation.

For instance, while the gendered stories of the current period of transition in tobacco regions remain largely absent from media reports, gender is central to other recent public discourses about economic change. The "Great Recession" that began in 2008 was initially described by policy makers, pundits, and media outlets as gendered. The term *mancession,* coined by a professor of economics and visiting scholar at the conservative American Enterprise Institute (see Perry 2010), spread like wildfire through analyses of the downturn and its repercussions. The mancession, according to many media accounts, resulted in a "gender role reversal" (D. Harris 2010). Stories in both national and local news provided example after example of stay-at-home dads and working moms. Characterized as the most recent battle in the war of the sexes (Baxter 2009), the mancession, proponents argued, made women the "victors." Major mainstream publications proclaimed, "Women will rule the world" (Bennett and Ellison 2010) because America had reached the "end of men" (Rosin 2010).

Men's overrepresentation in fields hit particularly hard by the recession, such as construction and manufacturing, is generally understood to have resulted in a larger number of job losses for men than for women at the start of the recession.[4] Women, who have tended to be employed in the education and service sectors, initially saw fewer job losses. However, despite predictions that "women are taking control of everything" (Rosin 2010), the economic picture began to change in 2009. A report released in May 2010 found that "as job losses slowed in the final months of 2009, women continued to lose jobs as men found employment" (U.S. Congress Joint Economic Committee 2010, 3). Other economic reports demonstrated not only that initial gendered trends changed course but also that throughout the recession, women of color and young women and single women of all races were among those with the highest rates of unemployment. Yet, mancession pronouncements continued (see McKelway 2010). As one commentary, reporting that March 2011 Bureau of Labor statistics "showed that of the 1.3 million jobs created in the preceding 12 months, some 90 percent went to men," asked, "By now the burning question is what explains the media's fixation on the idea that men's job-loss woes exceed those of women?" (Rivers and Barnett 2011, 1).

Access to jobs—like access to education, according to a long-standing discourse that girls and women are taking over schools—is presented as a zero-sum game; men suffer when women make gains. "Women are taking control—of everything" (Rosin 2010). Such "crisis" rhetorics provide provocative headlines but are problematically based on cultural conceptions of gender as a neat and tidy binary. It is precisely because economists across the political spectrum identify gender as a central factor in employment (even when they differ in their final analyses of who "loses" or "wins") that occupational traditions offer a crucial context for deconstructing gender as a binary.

In this chapter, I argue that feminist folkloristics has a place in dismantling these discourses, and folklore offers both theory and method applicable to a study of gender that moves beyond the provocative to a more complex and nuanced understanding of its multiple performance contexts. Ethnographic research offers opportunities for looking closely at gendered ideals as they are deployed in specific communities and in particular circumstances. Folklorists have much to offer to this task but also much more work to do. Occupational folklore scholarship has tended to focus almost entirely on men, with little attention to their construction as gendered subjects. Such studies have also privileged the creative over the economic, often "demonstrat[ing] the existence of the aesthetic impulse in the workplace" (M. O. Jones 1984, 176), as though the impulse to create art can be distinguished from the very real need to make a living. In contrast, I argue that there are connections between the expressive and the instrumental, and between economic need and aesthetic impulse, and that these connections are gendered. I suggest an understanding of multiple masculinities as traditionalized performances of gender.

MULTIPLE MASCULINITIES

In recent years, feminist research and action has extended from a near-exclusive attention on women to work on men. Such moves, however, have been tempered with caution. In the introduction to the second edition of the classic work *Masculinities*, R. W. Connell describes a reluctance to write the original book "because there was already a genre of 'books about men' that had become hugely popular. This was a mixture of pop psychology, amateur history and ill-tempered mythmaking, and I hated it. Backward-looking, self-centered stereotypes of masculinity were the last thing we needed" (2005, xii). Women writing about men risk, as Judith Newton and Judith Stacey put it, "recentering the very male authority we seek to challenge and revise" (1995, 297). However, as anthropologist Ruth Behar argues, "Feminist revision is always about a new way of looking at all categories, not just at 'woman'" (1995, 6). Newton and Stacey ask "whether a postmodern feminism can afford, any more than modernist feminism, to be a project for women only" (1995, 289). Rather than focus exclusively on women, feminist research has increasingly extended to the study of gender more widely conceived. Further, according to gender theorist Judith Butler, "In this effort to combat the invisibility of women as a category feminists run the risk of rendering visible a category which may or may not be representative of the concrete lives of women. As feminists, we have been less eager, I think, to consider the status of the category itself and, indeed, to discern the conditions of oppression which issue from an unexamined reproduction of gender identities which sustain discrete and binary categories of man and woman" (1988, 523). Like Butler, I question naturalized gender categories as a binary opposition. The argument that centering one gender results in the *de*centering of *the other* gender only serves to reinforce the dominant binary view of sex/gender systems.

Scholars who argue that there is no homogenous "masculinity"— rather, there are *masculinities*—challenge binary gendered constructions: "In research on men and masculinity the concept of 'multiple masculinities' has been developed to convey how specific and various forms of masculine subjectivity are constructed in relation to multiple social sites where people are engaged" (Brandth and Haugen 2005, 15). In *Men's Lives*, editors

Michael S. Kimmel and Michael A. Messner and their contributors demonstrate how masculine ideals differ dramatically, for example, across race, class, sexual orientation, gender identity, and age (2012). Connell maintains that beyond recognizing multiple masculinities, "we must also recognize the *relations* between different kinds of masculinities: relations of alliance, dominance, and subordination" (2005, 37). Particular forms of masculinity become "culturally exalted" over others and thus hegemonic: "the configuration of gender practice which embodies the currently accepted answer to the problem of the legitimacy of patriarchy" (77). Connell is particularly interested in the instability of hegemonic masculinities in changing circumstances, both within and seemingly outside of gender relations.[5]

Using the work of Connell and others, Nicole Power has examined the crisis plaguing fishermen of Newfoundland in recent decades as a crisis of masculinity.[6] Her reading of the discourses surrounding the effects of the restructuring of the fisheries also suggests a critique of the zero-sum game model in which men are assumed to be suffering if women make gains. She argues that "men's economic position has declined due to restructuring, rather than competition from women" (2005, 19). Power also distinguishes between fishermen and working-class men studied by others, between fishermen with different-sized operations, and between fishermen and men who work in local fish factories. Distinct masculine ideals apply to each category. The differing circumstances faced by men in Newfoundland and by Kentucky burley tobacco farmers points to the imperative to recognize multiple masculinities based on occupation as well as history and region.

Folklore scholarship on men and masculinity has too often echoed the media discourses cited above, implicitly arguing that men are losing and therefore women must be winning. For instance, Simon Bronner argues, "For all the reminders that men are different from women in ways other than anatomy, the distinctive cultural traditions that contribute to a conveyable sense of masculinity still need definition, especially in an era when manliness, if given consideration, is often criticized and suppressed" (2005, xii). Such an approach not only reinforces gender as a binary opposition, it simplifies the experiences of men by suggesting that all masculinities are the same. Yet, a central concept of folkloristics—tradition—offers an alternative frame for examining masculinities when combined with Butler's concept of gender as performance. In order to understand the gendered transitions taking place in Kentucky tobacco communities and beyond, I propose a new approach. In the remainder of this chapter I offer an understanding of gender as *traditionalized performance*, and I then apply this approach to fieldwork data. In large part because of tobacco's economic importance in the regions in which it has historically been grown, particular masculinities tied to its production once "occupie[d] the hegemonic position in a given pattern of gender relations," to borrow from Connell (2005, 76). A speech given to the Burley Auction Warehouse Association in 1990 by John M. Berry Jr. (former Kentucky state legislator and brother of poet and essayist Wendell Berry) reflected on what it meant to him to come from a family of five generations of tobacco farmers. He notes that when he was growing up, "people distinguished themselves and gained stature in the community, based on how many sticks they could cut or strip in a day, or how neatly they could tie a hand [of tobacco], or if their crops consistently topped the market" (Burley Tobacco Growers Co-operative Association 1991, 129–130). As the economic and therefore political importance of tobacco has waned, so too has the hegemonic position of tobacco-based masculinities.

GENDER AS TRADITIONALIZED PERFORMANCE

In the 1970s and 1980s, folklorists updated our understanding of tradition. Dell Hymes asserted that tradition should be understood as rooted not in time but in social life, as process: "to traditionalize" (1975b, 353). His challenge to the notion of tradition as *the way things always were* is echoed in the work of Richard Handler and Jocelyn Linnekin, who argued against the assumption, in both scholarly and commonsense definitions, that tradition is bounded and natural. Practices and ideologies alike are performed in "an ongoing reconstruction of tradition . . . which is not natural but symbolically constituted" (1984, 276). These scholars' concepts of tradition share affinity with Judith Butler's gender theory; each argues constitution through *doing*. Butler describes the embodied performance of gender as a "style of being" and goes on to say that "this style is never fully self-styled, for living styles have a history, and that history conditions and limits possibilities" (1988, 521). She understands gender as constituted in performative acts rather than simply existing in intrinsic and stable identities. According to Butler, "In this sense, gender is always a doing, though not a doing by a subject who might be said to preexist the deed" (1999, 33).

　　Linking and developing these ideas, I understand gender as *traditionalized performance*. In doing so, I depart from the usage of "performance" as folklorists have defined it since the 1970s, as framed moments in which something identified as "folklore" can be observed, documented, and interpreted in an appropriate context, and which is most valued for its aesthetic qualities. Thus, most folklorists have used *performance* to mean "not merely behavior" (Hymes 1975a, 13) but "a unifying thread tying together the

marked, segregated esthetic genres and other spheres of verbal behavior"
(Bauman 1975, 291). While folklorists note particular moments when an
individual might "breakthrough into performance" (Hymes 1975a), performance in Butler's sense and as I use it here is ongoing and inevitable. She sees
it as comprising behaviors that can be understood as series of discontinuous
acts that appear continuous and therefore "natural," but also as "the styliza-
tion of the body and, hence, . . . the mundane way in which bodily gestures,
movements, and enactments of various kinds constitute the illusion of an
abiding gendered self" (1988, 519). Understanding gendered performances
as traditionalized helps to illuminate the active process involved in enactments of gender based on what Handler and Linnekin call "model[s] of the
past" (1984, 276). While tradition, as Hymes argued, need not be rooted
in time, in both lay and scholarly usage the idea carries an authority based
on a linkage of the present with the past. Tradition is therefore particularly
useful for understanding gendered performances in periods of transition, as
people grapple with change.

TOBACCO PRODUCTION AS TRADITIONALIZED
MASCULINE PERFORMANCE

Burley tobacco, a type that is blended into cigarettes, has historically been
raised primarily in Kentucky and parts of Tennessee, and Kentucky remains
the largest burley-producing state. Although I have not conducted the comparative fieldwork to be sure, my work with burley growers (who are clear
that they raise *burley* tobacco) suggests the possibility of different masculinities in different tobacco regions. This assertion is in part based in the
specialized knowledge necessary for raising different types of tobacco as well
as the degrees of mechanization of the production process. For instance,
flue-cured tobacco production (dominant in North Carolina, which leads
the nation in total production) has largely been mechanized. In contrast, a
burley tobacco masculinity continues to rest in part on physical labor that
has not—*cannot,* according to many growers—be mechanized.

Tobacco is culturally understood in Kentucky as a men's crop. Caroline
Sachs (1983) notes that the designation of particular crops as "men's" or
"women's" recurs across agricultural systems; women are more likely to
have responsibility for subsistence crops and men for cash crops.[7] Such
designations are "associated with the gender that controls the management
and disposition of the crop" (6) and result from traditionalization. With
respect to burley tobacco, men traditionally directed the labor of women,
children, and other men hired at critical points in the production season.

Traditionally, women played essential roles in tobacco production at all stages, but these have diminished in most farm families as many women moved to off-farm jobs and as larger tobacco acreages led to increased dependence on hired labor. Yet, tasks alone do not make tobacco a men's crop; indeed, the performance of work and the performance of masculinity have become commensurate.

Power has identified a similar situation for Newfoundland fishermen. According to her, particular "activities also present men with opportunities to demonstrate masculinity. In other words, the culturally valued abilities and skills required to perform many of these services are distinctly masculine" (2005, 74). The specific and particularized activities that are commensurate with masculinity are different for fisherman and for tobacco farmers, demonstrating that rather than homogenous, ideals of masculinity are multiple and localized. This suggests the need to understand what specific activities are commensurate with a particular masculinity. A complete description of the complex gendering of the processes of growing, harvesting, curing, and marketing tobacco is beyond the scope of this chapter. I will focus instead on cutting tobacco and preparing it for market as representative examples because these aspects of tobacco work are particularly understood as male activities and because they are undergoing significant changes.

"Tobacco man" as a descriptor sums up the traits of a localized, idealized masculinity in the burley tobacco region in which I conducted fieldwork. Wendell Berry writes: "As a boy and a young man, I worked with men who were as fiercely insistent on the ways and standards of their discipline as artists—which is what they were. In those days, to be recognized as a 'tobacco man' was to be accorded an honor such as other cultures bestowed on the finest hunters or warriors or poets. The accolade 'He's a *tobacco* man!' would be accompanied by a shake of the head to indicate that such surpassing excellence was, finally, a mystery; there was more to it than met the eye" (1991, 54).[8] The category has been around for decades, as evidenced by Virgil Steed's narrative of life and work on a Kentucky tobacco farm, in which he notes: "Local farm tenants call themselves 'tobaccomen'" (1947, 43).

What makes a tobacco man is the competent performance of activities and practices that have, through a process of traditionalization, come to define the category (see Sacks 1995). Seemingly circular, category-bound activities recall Butler's performativity, as the category is constituted and maintained through the doing of activities. Such performance differs from that of other occupational categories, such as soybean or corn farmers, and from categories of men in nonfarming occupations. While the term might resemble others that appear to exclude women, such as "postman," it denotes not merely an occupational category used by insiders and outsiders alike but also (and more significantly) an excellence in the simultaneous performance of both work and gender that only an insider recognizes.[9]

Tobacco is a labor-intensive crop, often called a "thirteen-month crop" because the ground is frequently being prepared for the coming year's crop even as the previous year's crop is being marketed. I focus first on cutting tobacco, described in overt terms of masculine performance. Although mechanical harvesters have been designed and tested since the late 1950s, with the exception of fewer than a handful of large farmers, burley tobacco continues to be cut entirely by hand.[10] Cutting usually takes place in August, and it is hot, back-breaking work. The cutter picks up a *tobacco stick*—a wooden stick, about four and a half feet long and three-quarter by one inch in diameter—thrusts it into the ground at an angle, and puts his metal spear on the upward end. He then grabs a plant with one hand and, with a tobacco knife in the other, cuts the plant off at ground level. With the tobacco knife still in one hand, he seizes the stalk with both hands and spears it onto the tobacco stick. He does this six times per stick. Standing between two rows, he alternates cutting a plant from each, cutting a *stick row*. A very good cutter cuts 1,200 to 1,500 sticks, with six tobacco plants per stick, in a day—about an acre. Stories are told of men who can cut up to 2,000, or who could do so in their prime. When the process is done well, the cutter never stops, never stands upright, and never puts down his tobacco knife; the sticks do not fall over, and the stalks do not split out. Good cutters are *lean, agile, fast* but *steady, men* with *stamina*. Such descriptions serve as markers of a number of other distinctions including age, gender, and race.

One farmer told me that being able to cut 1,000 sticks used to make a boy into a man. A tobacco crop serves as a rite of passage in other senses as well. The vast majority of the tobacco growers I interviewed described being given their first patch of tobacco when they reached a particular age, ranging from nine to teenaged. This first patch symbolized moving out of boyhood and into manhood, as the young man was now responsible for his own crop. Greater responsibility and increased competence in tobacco differentiated not just boys from men but also men from women. Women sometimes cut tobacco, but they are noted as exceptions:

> Noel: Yes, yes, that is the problem with tobacco . . . it's not for every-
>   one because of the hard work at harvest time.
> Ann: So is that the hardest work?
> Noel: Yes, yes.
> Ann: What makes it the hardest work?

Noel: Without a healthy body, without a lot of stamina, you cannot compete in the tobacco field. It separates the boys from the girls.

Noel explicitly genders cutting tobacco with the statement that it "separates the boys from the girls." "Girls" can refer not only to females but also to males who are perceived as inadequately performing masculinity, in the widespread tradition of using feminine labels for derogatory purposes.

Men often reminisce about cutting tobacco when they were young, racing brothers or friends down the rows. Informal competition led to formalized cutting contests in which performance became the primary rather than secondary function. The audience, no longer limited to other cutters, could include hundreds of spectators. In our discussion of the Garrard County Tobacco Cutting Contest, county extension agent Mike Carter told me, "We've had very few people enter that are not good cutters. Because most of them are aware of the level of competition and they don't want to embarrass themselves." Such contests formalized accepted understandings of what it meant to be the best tobacco cutter, and therefore to demonstrate one's masculinity for others in a meta-performance. Organizers developed detailed scoring systems that take not only speed but also accuracy and neatness into account.

According to Mike, prior to the establishment of cutting contests, conversations about who was the best cutter took place at "the little country stores and poolrooms and, you know, Farm Bureau meetings." The Garrard County contest began in the late 1970s, a period of both heightened consciousness about tobacco farming as "heritage" and of a labor shortage that, by the 1990s, had led to the current dependence on Latino men to do the majority of the cutting.[11] Because the future of tobacco was uncertain, the cutter's skills were in danger of becoming obsolete, leading to the celebration of both the activity and the men. The contest continues today, and it may take on new meanings as tobacco farmers themselves do less cutting. More and more Latino men enter the contest each year, and they are not universally welcomed. I wonder if the day that Latino cutters outnumber Whites will mean the contest's end because it would mean "we" are no longer performing *for each other* the skills that made "us" men for generations. Indeed, for Whites, "tobacco man" is a White and hegemonic category, despite past and present tobacco work carried out by African American and Latino men.

Many tobacco growers now cut very rarely or never. Instead of working one row over from a buddy, many spend a large portion of their day driving alone in their pickups and tractors, overseeing the work of other men whom they perceive as different from themselves based on language, culture, and connections to the crop and the land. This change symbolizes an intricately linked set of altered work responsibilities, relationships with the crop, and meanings of the tobacco man masculinity, noted through comparisons of the present with the past.

A GOLDEN AGE OF MASCULINITY

Timothy Lloyd and Patrick Mullen identify a "golden age" of commercial fishing in the personal experience narratives of retired Lake Erie fishermen. For these men, the past was a better time characterized by "more primitive technology, harder work, clearer water, more abundant fish, and less governmental restriction" (1990, 80). Similarly, Amy Shuman describes a "golden age" for a community of artisans in Pietrasanta, Italy, in which "stories serve as nostalgic reminiscences that glorify a lost past and lament the present state of events" (2005, 62). Their narratives, according to Shuman, offer allegories of the past that comment on the present. Throughout my interviews and conversations with tobacco growers, nostalgic stories and expressions of change arose, comparable to Lloyd and Mullen's and Shuman's examples. The referenced time periods were not necessarily consistent, but were most often that of the speaker's father or grandfather, in contrast to the Italian stone carvers' golden age, a quite specific "period of the early 1900s, when artisans worked in large studios employing hundreds of workers" (62). The golden age of tobacco production, then, fluidly addresses cultural practices that reinscribe a performed identity.

Wendell Berry's description of the tobacco man, quoted above, firmly places the ideal in the past: "In those days, to be recognized as a 'tobacco man' was to be accorded an honor such as other cultures bestowed on the finest hunters or warriors or poets" (1991, 54). County extension agent Dan Grigson described the lessons he learned from his father about doing a job the right way, particularly after he had been given two-tenths of an acre of his own tobacco to raise. I asked if he would describe the farmers with whom he now works in the same terms that he depicted his father, and he replied:

> Sure, there are a lot of good tobacco farmers. There are folks who grow tobacco. There are folks who I call "pretty good tobacco farmers." And then there's that upper level who just—they're "tobacco men." They're— tobacco women or tobacco men.[12] But they do the extra, they always seem to have a good crop, even in a dry year or, you know, too wet of a year,

they'll still come out with a very good crop of tobacco. Detail people. People, again, who are good managers and make things work. They take care of getting the soil samples and making sure the fertility's right. Selecting the best varieties, making sure pests are under control. Topping at the right time, cutting at the right time, and watching those doors and curing that crop down. And then, take a lot of pride in making sure that when they prepare it for market it's prepared well. Not just all thrown together and grades are not mixed up, no weed trash or anything like that in there. They truly have pride in doing a good job.

Through his articulation of a difference between *tobacco men*, "pretty good tobacco farmers," and those who simply continue to raise the crop, Dan describes levels of competency in the work performance. At the "upper level," the tobacco man knows the proper cultural practices required to raise and market a good crop and performs them consistently because he has "pride," frequently used as a descriptor that moves the activities from practice to performance.

Like tobacco cutting, preparing the crop for market and handling the final sale have traditionally been controlled by men through traditionalized performances—even though women were historically heavily involved in the work process.[13] Cured tobacco was tied into a *hand*, formed as the leaves are stripped from the stalk in a particular grade. The stems are held tightly in one hand, leaves pointed toward the floor. When a handful has been stripped, a *tie leaf* of the same grade is wrapped around the stems and then woven through the leaves, holding the hand together. Simple as this may sound, tying a "pretty" hand of tobacco is far from easy; it is a performance requiring technical as well as artistic skill in which farmers took great pride. Once he brought the hands to the warehouse for auction, a tobacco man made sure that employees arranged them carefully when unloading. A man sometimes waited long periods for the preferred warehouse employee who had the ability to make the tobacco look its best. While debates continue about how much the tobacco's appearance affects price, growers uniformly described its symbolic importance. One retired farmer told me that appearance "didn't help your price but it, but a lot of people just, you know, didn't like sloppy tobacco." The iconic tobacco warehouse, then, offered a homosocial space in which tobacco men performed for one another.

In the late 1970s and early 1980s, burley tobacco began to be pressed into bales instead of tied in hands. Although some decried the move to the new packaging method as removing the pride from tobacco, a new but similar aesthetic moved with it. In many stripping rooms tobacco is placed in the bale box neatly, in alternating layers, the stems butted up against the sides to form a bale that is uniform in texture and color with no leaves hanging out. Tobacco grower Martin Henson and I discussed changing farm technologies:

Martin: Things have come a long way, come a long way. I've often wondered what my daddy would say if he'd seen me baling tobacco. [*laughing*]

Ann: What would he say?

Martin: I don't know. [*laughing*] He's probably turned over, several times, and you know, just—

Ann: Why?

Martin: Well, I know, for years he raised tobacco, he raised tobacco until he was eighty-four, when he passed away. He raised tobacco for probably seventy-some years, seventy-five years, hand tied it, everything was neat, just prim and proper. Now you just throw it in there and tramp her down and go on. [*laughing*]

While Martin described his father turning over in his grave at the idea of baled tobacco, a farmer a generation younger narrated with awe the neatness of his own father's bales. Clarence Gallagher described a particularly messy load of tobacco that he had seen, and I asked him what his deceased father—about whom he'd talked throughout the interview—would have said about it. He responded, "Oh my goodness. Dad's—I wished I had took some pictures of tobacco that he had fooled with. And just actually showed you what older people did. I mean his, his bale just looked like . . . you know, you could just shoot a rifle right down the side end of them, you know what I mean, just never—everything was just—just neat."

Taken alone, Martin's rumination on his father's possible opinion might be read merely as a negative judgment on the baling of the precious leaves. However, placing it next to Clarence's description of his father's bales highlights the men as well as the tobacco. Their comments demonstrate how tobacco growers describe change through comparisons with "my father's day." Fathers—particularly those who are deceased—model the ideal performance and serve as implicit judges of today's production and therefore of today's tobacco men. In such comparisons, tobacco growers now always come up short; they are not the hardworking men their fathers were. Clarence told me, "We're lazier. I raise more tobacco than my dad did, but the man worked harder. He worked harder. He worked harder than I ever worked, as far as raising tobacco."

But other standards also apply. Mike Carter told me: "I wouldn't say [my father was the] most progressive farmer, but if you showed him, if he saw others doing something and it proved to be—I never thought that he put much stock in it being easier, more easily accomplished, but it—if it was [*laughing*] something that was maybe quicker, or accomplished the same purpose with maybe less expense, he was willing to adapt." Mike distinguishes between something "easier" versus quicker or less expensive; a previous generation "worked harder." Yet, whether their sons describe them as early or late adopters of technology, these tobacco men adapted; indeed, part of the tobacco man's performance is adaptability, though it is limited to particular kinds of change.

Today's growers see their jobs as easier than their fathers' in part because they are increasingly removed from physical labor. But more and more, they also lack physical contact with the tobacco plant. Just as many growers no longer cut their own tobacco, many also no longer strip and bale it themselves, instead paying others to do so. Marketing circumstances have also changed. Now that growers contract directly with tobacco companies, instead of taking their tobacco to the warehouse where they performed for other tobacco men, the sale is now accomplished by appointment at a "receiving station." The audience is now primarily tobacco company buyers rather than other growers. Moreover, instead of tobacco men spending hours or even days at the warehouse with other farmers, now for the most part they merely pull up, drop off their load, get their check, drive away, and resume work.[14] Growers often say there was more pride in tobacco in their fathers' days. The crop itself, each leaf, was once respected; tobacco men didn't treat it poorly, step on it, or throw it in the baling box. Ultimately this care had economic motivations; the individual leaves paid for the farm, bought the children's shoes, and so on. But through traditionalized ideals of masculinity, respect for the crop led to respect for the man who produced it. As the circumstances of tobacco production have changed, so too has the status of tobacco man masculinity.

BEYOND "CRISIS"

The current period provides serious challenges for tobacco growers' economic futures as well as their masculine identities. Beyond particular performative acts such as cutting or stripping tobacco and preparing it for sale is the decision of what to farm. The changing buying habits of tobacco companies as well as the growing awareness of tobacco's harmful effects and the steady drop in use that has followed have resulted in increasing encouragement for tobacco men to diversify their farms to other crops. Elsewhere, I argue that diversification requires that farmers make major shifts (Ferrell 2012a).

Raising green peppers or tomatoes is neither economically nor symbolically commensurate with raising tobacco. Though as I have noted, part of the performance of *tobacco man* is the ability to adapt, moving to other crops is a different kind of change. According to Henry Glassie, "Change and tradition are commonly coupled, in chat and chapter titles, as antonyms. But tradition is the opposite of only one kind of change: that in which disruption is so complete that the new cannot be read as an innovative adaptation of the old" (1995, 395). For tobacco men, diversifying to other crops represents a complete symbolic and economic disruption of tradition that is as much about gender as it is about tobacco.

Many successful diversification efforts are taking place on Kentucky farms, and women play active—often leading—roles in these efforts. Organizations such as Kentucky Women in Agriculture work at the grassroots level to empower female farmers. Although my research focus has been tobacco growers, I frequently saw and heard about women's expansion of traditional farming activities such as gardening to more public arenas. Mike Carter and I discussed women's general lack of involvement in tobacco production—although there are exceptions—and he then told me:

> Mike: Now, when they switch to vegetables, more typically you would see both spouses involved in it. Sometimes with the lady taking a lead.
> Ann: Why do you think that is?
> Mike: Not sure that a female farmer's not more prone or more apt to try different enterprises than her male counterpart.
> Ann: More willing to try something new?
> Mike: Yeah. You know, I mean, they are farmers. The male gender, it seems to me, gets more comfortable in what he's used to than, what, a female farmer or maybe the female gender as a rule, would. [She] wouldn't be in that same comfort level, she would be more interested in trying something different.

Alice Baesler[15] responded similarly when I asked her whether she thought that women bring a particular perspective to farming. "I think so—I think sometimes you might get hung up on the big picture of what you're trying to do. And sometimes women can come up with, with a[n] idea that just might work, that's just a little different." Women also commented to me about their tobacco-farming husbands that tobacco is "all they know," suggesting a belief that these farmers would not be willing to learn new crops. I often encountered such ready articulations of the idea that women are more willing than men to change. The gendering of tradition is in need of further study, as it too is not a simple binary in which men are aligned with tradition and women with progress.[16] In this case, the expectation of male farmers as stubborn is an aspect of the traditionalized performance itself. Women have always been involved in tobacco production, but men controlled it. Statements that women are more willing to change suggest an articulation that as women increasingly step forward as leaders, they bring fresh perspectives because they are new to such positions. Nationally, the number of women farmers is growing while that of men is dropping, not unlike the increasing move by women into male-dominated fields and particular types of higher education. But does this suggest an end of men, that women are taking over agriculture? By no means. For the time being, even though more women are successfully farming, agriculture remains male dominated.

Whether they continue to raise tobacco or try to grow something else, fewer and fewer tobacco growers can perform the traditionalized tobacco man masculinity. Simply lamenting a crisis of masculinity neither leads to a deeper understanding of gendered relationships nor helps either women or men as they struggle with cultural and economic changes that have very real consequences not only in theory but also in daily life—in factories, construction sites, fisheries, Kentucky farms, and other workplaces. Connell notes that the concept of crisis "presupposes a coherent system of some kind, which is destroyed or restored by the outcome of the crisis." Masculinity, Connell argues, cannot be in crisis because it is not a coherent system but "rather, a configuration of practice *within* a system of gender relations" (2005, 84). The changing economic and cultural landscape demands analyses of systems of social relations and the deconstruction of gender as a binary opposition. Such work must continue to problematize monolithic conceptions of masculinity in favor of more nuanced understandings of gendered performances that have become traditionalized in particular localized contexts. Men facing the restructuring of the fisheries of Newfoundland have very different challenges than those facing the possible end to tobacco production—not only because of the nature of their work, but because it has become commensurate with their understandings of themselves as men.

NOTES

1. In 2004 the U.S. federal tobacco allotment program ended. During its seventy-plus years, growing and selling tobacco was limited to those with an allotment, and thus tied directly to land. The program kept tobacco production rooted in specific regions (see Stull 2009).

2. Kentucky tobacco production dropped over 30 percent in 2005, the year following the end of the program (United States Department of Agriculture 2008).

3. I trace this stigmatization of tobacco and its growers elsewhere (Ferrell 2012b).

4. Susan Faludi describes this phenomenon's manifestations in the 1990s. The head-lines she cites as examples of a "masculinity crisis" (1999, 6) strikingly resemble those I cite above. She notes, "It's often been observed that the economic transition from industry to service, or from production to consumption, is symbolically a move from the traditional masculine to the traditional feminine. But in gender terms, the transition is far more than a simple sex change and, so, more traumatic for men than we realize" (38). Much as I argue here, Faludi demonstrates that viewing such transitions in binary terms is far too simplistic.

5. See also Connell (2005) for a helpful overview of approaches to masculinity/masculinities.

6. Power is careful to distinguish her use of "crisis" from "its use in 'masculinity crisis' literature" and "the anti-feminist factions of the men's movement" (2005, 21).

7. Crop gendering has long been acknowledged in the literature on gender and devel-opment and has served as a basis for agricultural policy recommendations in regions that receive development aid from Western countries. Often, an understanding of local concep-tions of "women's crops" and "men's crops" has been used to address women's vulnerabilities in such contexts. See Doss (2002) and Carr (2008) for critiques of the practical application, despite acknowledged cultural constructions, of "men's crops" and "women's crops."

8. The aesthetic dimensions of the tobacco man performance alluded to by Berry are generally accepted in tobacco communities—production is often described as "an art"—demonstrating how they implicate both folklore performance theory—a material "aesthetic genre" (Bauman 1975)—and Butler's ideas of performativity.

9. Similarly, Power argues that "to be a 'fisherman' a man does more than simply fish" (2005, 70). See also Mary Hufford's discussion of "foxman" among foxhunters in the New Jersey Pine Barrens (1992, 94), Roger Abrahams's "man-of-words" (1983), and Jeannie Thomas's description of the "cowboy continuum" upon which members of western livestock culture place themselves based on performed masculine identities, with cowboys at one end and farmers at the other (1995, 215).

10. Flue-cured growers mechanized their cutting practices in the late 1970s, a decade after they adopted mechanical technologies that dramatically decreased labor at other stages of the growing season, cutting their labor costs from 370 to 58 person-hours per acre (Daniel 1980, 264).

11. Latino workers, primarily from Mexico and primarily male, now do the vast major-ity of cutting on Kentucky farms, just as they now do much of the harvest work on farms across the country; they currently account for at least 75 percent of total labor hours (Snell and Halich 2007).

12. Dan's statement that "They're—tobacco women or tobacco men" demonstrates a recovery pattern that I witnessed in a number of interviews. Consistently, an acknowledg-ment that some women do raise tobacco often followed instances in which the speaker had referred to farmers specifically as male and then corrected himself. After the recovery, speak-ers eventually returned to male nouns and pronouns for the remainder of the interview. I believe that my presence as a woman interviewing primarily men about a male-dominated arena made them hyperaware of gender and their use of gender-specific language.

13. After burley tobacco is cut, it is hung in a tobacco barn—still on the stick, and also by hand—to air cure for six to eight weeks, depending on the weather and farm size. Once cured, the leaves are stripped from the stalk—usually by hand, but in some cases this process has been mechanized—and separated into distinct grades, each of which has a different pric-ing structure. Currently, most growers strip their tobacco into three grades, though they told

me of periods in which there were seven or more grades as well as brief periods in which they stripped it only into one or two grades. Although men traditionally controlled the work, families once spent weeks or months together stripping the crop.

14. See Benson's analysis of the climate of tobacco sales in North Carolina (2008).

15. Alice defies the categories I've described above. She raises 300 acres of tobacco and is also a founding member of Kentucky Women in Agriculture and Partners for Family Farms, organizations with memberships almost exclusively comprised of diversified farmers.

16. Bauman and Briggs (2003) suggest that the gendering of tradition has historically fluctuated: in periods in which tradition has been valued, it has been understood as patriarchal, passing through the father's line. In periods in which modernity and progress have been valued over tradition, it has been understood as passing through the mother's line from mother to daughter.

3

"If Thou Be Woman, Be Now Man!"
"The Shift of Sex" as Transsexual Imagination

Pauline Greenhill and Emilie Anderson-Grégoire

> "Fairy tales. . . concern themselves with sexual distinctions, and with sexual transgression, with defining differences according to morals and mores. This interest forms part of the genre's larger engagement with the marvelous . . . The realms of wonder and impossibility converge, and fairy tales function to conjure the first in order to delineate the second: magic paradoxically defines normality. Hence the recurrence, in such stories, of metamorphoses, disguises and . . . impossible tasks" (Warner 1994, 133).

A TRANSGENDER IMAGINATION—THINKING ABOUT OR EXPRESSING THE idea that a person, self or other, is or could be a different sex/gender than it appears—works in several traditional genres. Here, "transgender" and "trans" disconnect conventional gender identity (social, cultural, psychological) from canonical sex identity (biological, physiological). We use *transgender* and *trans* as encompassing terms to include transsexuals,[1] who identify as another sex than that of their birth, who may or may not want, or enact, hormonal or surgical interventions to match their sex identity to their gender identity; intersexuals (previously "hermaphrodites"), whose biological identity includes both male and female markers; cross-dressers or transvestites, who dress as another sex; and genderqueers or genderfuckers,[2] who feel their sex/gender identity to be between, beyond, or in addition to the binaries of male and female. We recognize that these are not the only or even the least contested uses and that they can combine in various ways (see, e.g., Stryker and Whittle 2006).

Elsewhere, Pauline Greenhill argued that in the traditional ballad genre in English, the trans imagination seems limited to two possibilities. First,

    DOI: 10.7330/9780874218985.c003

these song texts may circle around a male character *forced* by circumstances to dress in women's clothes, or female characters *choosing* to cross-dress and take traditionally male work roles as soldiers, sailors, pirates, or highway robbers. Second, ballads may portray a male character expressing desire for transsexual transformation. He may either wish that he himself were female and thus a potential lover to a male character, or that another apparent male (in fact a cross-dressed woman) were female, again to enhance sexual possibilities. With only changes of clothing and occupation, or declarations of wishes, then, ballad transgender remains quite restricted (see Greenhill 2013, 2014).

However, for a specifically transsexual imagination—the textual representation of a bodily change of sex/gender—the traditional folktale, particularly the fairy tale, seems the place to go, though examples are few.[3] Volume 1 of Hans-Jörg Uther's (2004) revision of Antti Aarne and Stith Thompson's tale-type indices, which includes the classic wonder tales, offers only two unequivocal examples: ATU 363 ("The Corpse Eater") and ATU 514. We deal with the latter here.[4] In "The Corpse Eater," transformation is limited, entirely temporary, and contingent. In "The Shift of Sex," however, the female-born protagonist usually begins by cross-dressing to access male play and work. S/he rescues and then marries a princess who proves less than pleased to discover her bridegroom's female sex. Ultimately, after s/he accomplishes impossible tasks, generally with the help of a marvelous horse, a supernatural curse transforms her/his biological sex to male.[5] The princess is satisfied with her mate, and the expected "happy ever after" concludes the tale. In this chapter, we investigate versions of "The Shift of Sex" to demonstrate how they imagine transgender and specifically transsex.

Feminist transphobe Janice Raymond (1979) might read this text as the reinstallation of a heteronormative imperative, requiring heterosexual marriage and partnering, because it precludes a lesbian relationship between protagonist and princess. Nevertheless, the tale can instead be interpreted—as can trans itself—as a subtle exploration and undermining of sex and gender. Particularly because transformation results from a curse, "The Shift of Sex" also presents a telling ambivalence about gender, sex, and sexuality that characterizes genderqueer. While the curser considers as negative her (more rarely his) action, it comes as a blessing to the recipient, and the tale's audience is invited to join his relief at manifesting the desired sex as well as gender. That becoming a man is a curse also inverts the patriarchal assumption invariably making male the preferable sex/gender.

NOT SHIFTING SEXES—MADAME D'AULNOY'S "BELLE BELLE OR THE KNIGHT FORTUNÉ"

Before we turn to ATU 514, we look at the related tale type ATU 514**, "A Young Woman Disguised as a Man Is Wooed by the Queen," because it demonstrates how the narrative can be rendered more sex normative (though it remains gender nonconforming).[6] Those few other folklorists who have included ATU 514 in their studies tended to show discomfort about the tale and/or its relation to tradition, and presume its links to ATU 514**. Stith Thompson called "The Shift of Sex" "a story which was developed by literary writers of the seventeenth and eighteenth centuries, and which has been collected in a few countries from oral raconteurs" (1946, 55).[7] In fact, accounts of cross-dressing adventurous warring women (who sometimes magically or miraculously change sex) appear in various forms of French popular literature dating from at least the twelfth century. They include the *Roman de Silence* (twelfth century), in which the heroine is raised as a boy; *Ide et Olive* (fourteenth century), an epic in which a woman cross-dresses to escape incest with her father; and from the same century, *Osre*, a play in which the heroine cross-dresses to escape her murderous husband; and *Miracle de la fille d'un roy*, about a princess who dresses as a man to escape her father's incestuous intentions (Carol Harvey, personal communication).

However, Elisée Legros suggests that "The Shift of Sex" is a "quite altered" version of Marie-Catherine d'Aulnoy's "Belle Belle or the Knight Fortuné" (1962, 99), the "only one of Mme. Aulnoy's tales . . . constructed around a disguise" (Mitchell 1978, 72).[8] This narrative begins, as do some versions of ATU 514, with a noble but poor father sending his daughter, Belle Belle, off to war in his place.[9] She receives a magical horse from a fairy in disguise whom she helps. Dressed as a man, Belle Belle becomes Fortuné (Lucky) upon reaching an inn in the city (and is then referred to using male pronouns): "She arrived in a beautiful populous city. She attracted all eyes, and people followed and surrounded her, and everyone said: 'Has anyone ever seen a more handsome, better made, and more richly dressed knight; how graceful he is in handling this superb horse.' The people welcomed him with great ceremony, and he reciprocated in a polite and civil manner. When he wanted to enter the inn, the governor, who had admired him while walking by, sent a gentleman who begged him to come to his castle" (d'Aulnoy 1998, 223–224).

Fortuné acquires seven human magical helpers, Strong-Back, Fleet-Foot, Good-Shot, Quick-Ear, Impetuous, Drinker, and Glutton, on their way to join the king's army. The queen (the king's sister) falls in love with the disguised knight, while Belle Belle is attracted to the king:[10] "Fortuné could not help gazing from time to time at the king. He was the best-looking prince in the world, in all ways considerate, and Belle Belle, who had by no means renounced her sex by taking a dress that hid it, felt a genuine affection for him" (d'Aulnoy 1998, 233). When the queen finds that her feelings are unrequited, she tricks the king into sending Fortuné off to do impossible tasks, which he completes thanks to his magical helpers. Eventually he vanquishes the king's enemy, again assisted by his helpers. The queen becomes so angry over Fortuné's lack of interest in her that she tells the king that he has attacked her, and he is sentenced to death. Her servant, also in love with Fortuné, gives the queen a slow poison. Fortuné is tied to the stake but when his coat and vest are removed so he can be stabbed, his biological sex is revealed. The queen dies and the king marries Belle Belle (see Barchilon 1975; Carver Carpasso 1987; Paton 1907; Ritchie 2003).[11]

Clearly, this narrative renders both sex/gender identity and sexual orientation extremely complex. Belle Belle knows she is not Fortuné, and she struggles with her unrequited love for the king and lack of interest in the queen and her servants: "I love a king without any hope that he loves me, nor that he knows how much I suffer" (d'Aulnoy 1998, 234).[12] Pronoun use in the tale demonstrates sex/gender as a potentially queer performative (see Butler 1999). Crucially constructed in social discourse rather than in costume alone, Belle Belle is not referred to as male when she changes clothes, nor even when the fairy gives her a man's name; "she" becomes "he" only once s/he arrives in a town where other people admire the handsome, rich knight. Her explicit performativity (see Schneider 1997) becomes particularly striking when d'Aulnoy juxtaposes the dual identities of Belle Belle and Fortuné, as in the would-be execution scene that reveals Belle Belle's womanly attributes: "what was the astonishment of the assembly when they discovered the alabaster bosom of Belle Belle! All present understood that this was a girl unjustly accused. . . . the people, who loved Fortuné, freed *him*" (d'Aulnoy 1998, 267; our emphasis). Within a few sentences of her revelation of Belle Belle's sex to the other characters, d'Aulnoy reverts to the male "Fortuné," naked female breasts notwithstanding!

This tale has been analyzed primarily from psychological and historical/political economic perspectives.[13] The latter tend to highlight the tale's "significant statements, challenges, and—most crucially—questions about the nature of the social order," according to Lisa Brocklebank. She sees "the cross-dressed figure as a touchstone to contest official order and socially constructed representations of power . . . a potent critique of the status quo that begins with an examination of gender norms . . . By highlighting the performativity of gender and gender relations, ["Belle Belle"] also call[s] into question the production of other modes of power that claim a 'natural' status to sanctify their existence and dominance" (2000, 127). "Belle Belle" simultaneously critiques masculinity and sociopolitical hierarchy, "emasculating the male king and empowering the female peasant" (135).

Anne E. Duggan suggests that "writers such as Charles Perrault identified salon women, or 'independent' women, as a threat both to the rule of men and to the monarchy" and that d'Aulnoy countered this view by creating "idealized feudal and matriarchal worlds, based on reciprocal relations between all nobles, regardless of their gender" (1998, 199–200). In "Belle Belle," d'Aulnoy "proposes . . . the re-establishment of the former alliance between the feudal nobility and the monarchy, along with the participation of noble women in political affairs" (203). Belle Belle resembles actual cross-dressing and troop-leading salon women, and her story "creates utopic spaces based on notions of civility in order to provide a 'place' . . . for . . . disenfranchised nobles" (199).

Others have seen "Belle Belle" as a reflection on and critique of contemporary notions of masculinity, rather than a comment on femininity and women's roles.[14] For example, Adrienne E. Zuerner notes that "although cross-dressing violated biblical and social codes, the text reiterates that Belle-Belle [*sic*] disguises only to serve the crown and thereby recuperates transvestism for an indisputably worthy cause . . . [The] transvestite heroine . . . [balances] 'feminine' and 'masculine' traits (kindness *and* military acumen, artful discourse *and* physical and moral courage, filial loyalty *and* skillful diplomacy)" (1997, 196–197).[15] The king's love for Fortuné is a "challenge [to] seventeenth-century norms of masculinity. Male homoeroticism . . . necessarily denaturalize[s] masculinity since man is seen to abandon his 'naturally' superior position" (203).[16]

Similarly, Francis Assaf discusses "Belle Belle"'s relation to social roles. He specifically addresses its implicit criticisms of the laws of succession preventing female heirs from inheriting the crown and male domination in general by "showing how a supposed inferior becomes indispensable to the restoration of monarchical power, power which, unfortunately, she seems to suggest, remains ultimately in the hands of weak and incompetent men, unable to manage their kingdom or to carry out even a defensive war" (2003, 273). The specifics of Assaf's description, perhaps even more than the narrative itself, suggest an analogy to Joan of Arc, as Belle Belle would have to d'Aulnoy's contemporaries.[17]

The psychological analysis by Amy Vanderlyn DeGraff, in contrast, sees the tale as indicative of what she calls "the voyage of self-development" (1984, 61). Belle Belle "must outgrow the phase" of being in disguise in order "to move on to heterosexuality." Fortuné's reaction to the queen's "passion" for him is "problematic," because "instead of revealing her female identity, a revelation that clearly would have ended her problems with the queen, she chooses to remain silent." Instead, "Fortuné is not quite ready to give up her disguise because emotionally she is not quite ready to move on from this stage of indeterminate sexuality to a mature stage of heterosexuality" (66). In conclusion, "Although Belle-Belle's masculine disguise kept her desexualized thereby enabling her to explore and discover aspects of herself, nevertheless the time had come to accept her sexuality and a mature heterosexual relationship. Not doing so was potentially destructive to Belle-Belle. Doing so would mean the attainment of happiness and many of the riches life has to offer. The story ends with the wedding of Belle-Belle and the king" (67).

In addition to the heterosexism, homophobia, and transphobia of the foregoing, DeGraff fails to understand Belle Belle/Fortuné's transgender position. Indeed, the character's reluctance to reveal biological sex is a rational choice. The text itself suggests that the tale's perspective on the concluding marriage may not be as univocally positive as DeGraff suggests. Fortuné relinquishes his identity only when the marriage date is decided, when Belle Belle takes up women's dress; "Belle Belle returned to her woman's clothing and appeared a thousand times more wonderful in them than she did in those of a knight" (d'Aulnoy 1998, 268). Further, the tale's final section deals almost entirely with Belle Belle's concern for her horse, who disappears. She searches for him for four days. When he magically reappears with her family and guardian fairy, her love for them all receives the most narrative attention, not her relationship with her future husband. The ending is evidently happy for Belle Belle, but in general, DeGraff fails to take notice of the ambivalence in this fairy-tale plot, and of the genre as a whole (see also Howells 1997).

Anne Defrance, in the penultimate chapter of her work on d'Aulnoy, similarly sees "Belle Belle" as pertaining to homosexuality, but notes the different approaches it takes to same-sex attraction among women and among men. Belle Belle's cross-dressing mends the original castration.[18] Yet the men in the tale, who should be powerful (in a patriarchal political economy), are controlled by women—the father by his daughters, and the king by his sister. Even Fortuné is subject to the queen's machinations. The helpers, the horse, and the fairy's magic wand remain true possessors of the phallus, which is thus underlined as imaginary, as symbol (1998, 309–320). The queen's attraction, unlike the king's, is manifestly heterosexual; she wants the love of someone who presents as a man. In fact, then, the undisciplined heterosexual attraction of a woman (the queen) is punished, whereas the same-sex attraction of a man (the king) is rewarded with heterosexual marriage.[19]

Christine Jones's sophisticated analysis, simultaneously attentive to the text, tradition, and the actual representation of transgender, points out that the queen's death at the end is not *"necessary . . .* because she is no longer a threat to the courtly couple once Belle-Belle's identity is made public. Her elimination is desirable, however, since she comes to embody sexual monstrosity in the narrative. The queen serves, then, as a symbol of sexual misconduct and its consequences. Significantly, fear of such misconduct is traditionally associated with the transvestite, but is here entirely displaced onto the Queen and the transvestite incurs no blame for having inspired sexual desire in women. The Queen becomes the narrative scapegoat for the condemnation of homoerotic desire." Tellingly, however, the queen's role is pivotal and eventually positive in the narrative: "The Queen's attempts to kill Fortuné ultimately facilitate the restoration of the King's fortune" (2003, 394). The double role of this condemnation of the queen's desire—it transfers "this vice" from Belle Belle/Fortuné to the queen—"dissociates sexual and political order." In the end, the principal named character becomes "a valiant and powerful *woman* in power without the perfunctory masculine persona" (395).

The tale offers considerable opportunity to explore both lesbian and gay possibility. While Belle Belle herself remains consistently attracted to a man, refusing the queen and her servant, the latter two characters can be understood in recognizable lesbian terms. That is, their desire for Fortuné may involve a conscious attention to her/his butch presentation (see Case 1988/1989; Quimby 1995). They seem uninterested in anyone else. Belle Belle's change of clothes changes neither her felt gender identity nor her sexual orientation. Others define Fortuné as male—to Belle Belle's consternation in the case of both the king, who fails to recognize her as female, and of the queen, who fails to deduce that she is not male. But the Belle Belle inside Fortuné's male clothes, as it were, remains female and heterosexual. Her maleness is enacted exclusively at the level of a performance that does not render its subject fundamentally male. Her case may remind some of the tragic twentieth-century John/Joan case, in which an identical male twin whose genitalia had been damaged in a botched circumcision became a test subject for psychiatrist John Money's conviction that sex/gender identity was a matter of nurture, not nature. Despite surgical, hormonal, and behavioral interventions attempting to render "John" female, his resistance and fundamental rejection of these endeavors ultimately supported the idea that sex/gender identity (at least in his case) was resistant to such intrusions.[20]

Lacking an actual sex change, "Belle Belle" is clearly ATU 514** (see also Tubach 1969, 134) rather than ATU 514.[21] Yet in his work on "the great fairy tale tradition," Jack Zipes includes "Belle Belle" with Giovan Francesco Straparola's "Constanza/Constanzo," Giambattista Basile's "The Three Crowns," and Henriette Julie de Murat's "The Savage" (more or less related tales involving similar gender disguise, magical helpers, and eventual marriage to the king) under the rubric of "Disguised Heroes." Describing the central protagonists as male—heroes, not heroines—despite their biological sex shows Zipes's recognition of their fundamentally male roles (2001, 159–219). Assaf comments: "We see in this tale a synthesis of reality and the marvellous which makes the story possible and even plausible" (2003, 271).[22] It is, then, perhaps more realistic than ATU 514's instantaneous magical sex change. We appropriate his insight to our own—that d'Aulnoy's narrative, and even more its traditional counterpart in ATU 514, expresses transgender imagination and transgender possibility quite explicitly throughout.

"THE SHIFT OF SEX"

Renowned folktale scholar Bengt Holbek considered "The Shift of Sex" anomalous.[23] His problems with ATU 514 resulted from his classificatory imposition of a heterosexual pair in the division of tale modes. The protagonist's sex change precluded the tale fitting into his structural division of masculine and feminine. He argued that "in a masculine tale, the two main characters are the low-born young male . . . and the high-born young female . . . Conversely, the two main characters of the feminine tale are the low-born young female . . . and the high-born young male" (1987, 417). "The Shift of Sex" initially involves a lowborn young female and a highborn young female—not a possibility in Holbek's scheme—but resolves into a lowborn female-to-male transsexual—thus, male—and a highborn female: his masculine tale. Yet that designation fails to reflect the tale's hyperfeminized narrative conflict between the girl and the princess.

ATU 514 is not the only tale to raise problems with Holbek's gendered schema, as Risto Järv's work helpfully explores. First, Holbek's actual attribution of some types is questionable. For example, he calls ATU 312 ("Maiden-Killer [Bluebeard]") a masculine tale (1987, 167), though the protagonists are a lowborn female and a highborn male, which qualifies it as a feminine tale in his classification.[24] Second, though a change of the protagonist's sex within a particular tale is uncommon, the interchangeability of protagonists' sex from one version to another is not. In ATU 720 ("The

Juniper Tree"), while the character "persecuted by the step-mother and devoured by the family" (Järv 2005, 53) is a boy in the Grimms' version, in many others it is a girl.[25] Such variability calls into question Holbek's presumption that protagonists' sex can define the narrative's gendered focus. It raises further problems with his association of masculine tales with male tellers and feminine tales with female tellers; "we may expect to find a definite correspondence between the sex of the narrator and the 'gender' of the tale" (1987, 167). Following Holbek's logic, "The Shift of Sex" and "The Corpse Eater" would have tellers and audience confined only to transfolk.

Finally, naming tales "masculine" or "feminine" also presumes the primary protagonist's gendered actions. Many of Holbek's masculine tales open with the (male) hero seeking his fortune, and his feminine tales with the heroine on the threshold of marriage. ATU 514 again raises a problem, because it begins with a girl who seeks her fortune and ends with a marriage that raises her/his social status, as is usual for a male character. However, tales like "Peg Bearskin" (ATU 711) (see Greenhill, Best, and Anderson-Grégoire 2012) also have plucky female heroes whose actions, until the very end of the story, are more like those of the male fortune seeker than of the female bride-in-waiting.

Different versions of "The Shift of Sex" published in English and French, as well as English or French précis of versions or tale types collected in other languages, offer an opportunity to explore this narrative across time and space as an expression of trans imagination, and specifically as a discursive manifestation of transsexuality. Some forms, for example, in Greek tradition, as discussed by Mariléna Papachristophorou, do not include transgendering moves. She suggests: "The ecotypal forms deal with the same radical change of nature as AT 514, even with an upheaval of the natural order; it could take the form of an overt transsexualism, an unexpected rejuvenation, a humanization, a transformation of death to birth, or an inversion of source/origin. In spite of local differences, the problematic remains the same: it is always about a desire to transgress natural laws, to change the human condition; it is about a woman who, having become other, begins a new life cycle" (2002, 202). We concur that there are similarities in those tales that deal with other forms of transformation. However, concerned as we are with transgender and transsex specifically, we do not deal with them here.[26]

An Armenian version of ATU 514 begins with an old woman who "dressed her daughter in boys' clothes, so that she could play with the neighbours' children." S/he finds the king's daughter, who is lost, and on returning her, gets instruction from the horse Luzilar: "When the king asks you to make a wish, tell him you desire to possess me, and nothing else." When s/he does so, the king replies: "Luzilar is worth my entire kingdom . . . If I give her to you, I might as well give you my daughter too!" After the wedding feast, "the princess realized that her husband was a woman like herself" (Downing 1972, 83). The princess and queen conspire to make the king send "the girl" on a series of three impossible tasks. Following Luzilar's advice, s/he succeeds. When s/he completes the final one, the victim, a mother devil, curses her: "If thou be man, be now woman! If thou be woman, be now man!"[27] On the husband's return, the wife tells her father, "I find that my husband is a man after all . . . I would not change him for any other" (86).

A Greek version more closely resembles "Belle Belle," with a father (not mother) with three daughters (not one), summoned to the army. Each daughter offers to go in his place. The elder two fail tests of bravery, "but the youngest showed herself capable of playing the warrior and dressed as a youth she went off to war, helped always by her faithful horse who possessed . . . the gift of speech." Sometimes the protagonist's apparent gender finds ambivalent acknowledgment, such as that s/he "acquitted *her*self *manfully*" (our emphases), and as a result the king and queen choose her/him as husband for the princess. Just like in Belle Belle, once s/he is recognized as male, the description generally changes to male pronouns: "The supposed bridegroom set a sword between himself and his bride," and when the princess is dissatisfied, the monarchs conspire "to get rid of him." The "impossible and fatal" quests are successful. The sex change involves giants who "cursed her 'If you are a boy you shall be turned into a girl; if you are a girl you shall be turned into a boy.'" And yet ambivalence remains; "the heroine became a *boy* and *her* marriage was happily concluded" (Dawkins 1953, 298; our emphases).[28]

The narrative itself offers no indication that the princess or her parents have any suspicion about why the husband puts a sword between her/himself and her/his wife. But it is clear that the character's sex/gender raises a problem. We draw attention to the pronoun switches in Dawkins's précis because they indicate where a fairy-tale collector (or teller, we do not know which) locates the change of sex/gender identity. In this version, the only time the protagonist becomes "him" is in the context of the sexual relationship (or lack thereof) between her/him and the princess, before her/his corporeal alteration. Yet the "he" of this section reverts to "she," even though his body has become male.[29] Thus, the tale's denouement queers the narrative: "Then the girl—but now she was a boy—went to the house and told them to get water ready for a bath. She went into the bathhouse and had a good bath and then went to her wife. She let down her hair and said to her wife: 'A long time since I had my hair combed; come and comb it.' When the wife saw the hair she thought it must be a girl. But when they went to lie down the sword at once disappeared from between them. Next day she went full of joy and told her mother" (Dawkins 1953, 311).

Another Greek version has the protagonist initially male and becoming female because of a fairy's curse. Then, after going to war, and following the same sequence, s/he is cursed by a "gigantic negro": "If you are a man be a woman, if a woman, then become a man" (Dawkins 1953, 300; see also Chauvin 1904, 43). Dawkins's collection notes an Albanian version in which the transformation results because a king wants a son and has a daughter instead. "To save the girl's life the angry and disappointed king was induced to believe she was really a boy." Her/his horse helper assists her/him in getting cursed (as above) by the jinn, and "*she* became a *boy* and so saved *her* life" (Dawkins 1953, 301; our emphases).

Another Albanian version (translated into French), closer to Dawkins's Greek version, has a father who must go off to war or send a son, but has only daughters. The first two propose that their father should provide them with husbands.[30] "Marry me [to someone], she said. And the second said the same as the elder. But the youngest in turn said, Father, reassure yourself, because I will go to war" (Dozon 1881, 107–108). Further, the narrative switches between male and female referents and pronouns, but tellingly, the magical and knowing horse always refers to the main character as "my master," not "my mistress." Queerly, having accomplished her/his first heroic deed, the hero is referred to as male, and usage reverts to female pronouns only to illustrate the transformation s/he undergoes: "The girl felt that she had changed into a boy, and said to her horse, 'Gallop on, my horse, I was a girl and I have become a boy, I was a mare and I have become a stallion'" (120). Equally queerly, the French uses the female/feminine form of the verb "to become," even when s/he has transformed to boy and stallion.[31]

A version from the Cape Verde Islands also queers the narrative extensively. A prince (apparently uncomplicatedly male) named Bonito dreams of the beautiful Aldraga Jiliana (implicitly female), "enchanted at the bottom of the sea, seven towers of Babel, who lives on the Gold Mountain, where no male fly ever goes, much less a split of a human." He is so upset by his dream that "when in the morning the servant brought him coffee, he did not take it" (Parsons 1923, 281). Helped by his magic horse, Bonito kidnaps her. However, she will not speak, and the king announces that he will marry her to anybody who can make her do so.

"Then came Marco, he had an enchanted mule" (Parsons 1923, 283). Though Marco is identified with male pronouns throughout, the queen asserts that Marco "is not a man." He cries in despair, but the magical mule (always "she") assists him with a supernatural test, advising him to not "take the fruit of women, take only that of men" (284) when he goes to a farm with Bonito. The mule kills Bonito's magic horse to distract him so that he and Marco do not bathe together, though they "undressed to their drawers." Having passed these tests, Marco and Aldraga are married. The queen sends her servant to spy on their wedding night, and she hears Aldraga calling to Marco, "Come, let us lie down, because I come from a country where woman marries woman" (285). The monarchs plan to murder Marco. He hears a voice calling "Marta, Marta!"—his godfather San Pedro, who informs him that he has come to save him: "'I came to put on you, all finished, what a man has.' Then he became a man withal." When the queen arrives to murder him, "Marco took his male organ, he gave it to the queen in the mouth, he broke all the teeth in her mouth" (286).

The brutal rape that provides the denouement may seem rather unexpected, but it underlines a transformation in Marco/Marta from someone who cries at the prospect of a problem (culturally feminized), to a physical male—and a hyperviolent one at that. Nevertheless, this tale suggests lesbianism in Aldraga's lack of consternation that Marco is apparently female. Since she does not reappear in the story, the audience does not know how she feels about Marco's transformation.

SEX CHANGE IN FOLKTALES

Given its anomalous qualities, it is not surprising that considerations of ATU 514 are few. W. Norman Brown explores the discursive deployment of the motif of sex change in Hindu narrative. "The notion that a human being may suffer a change of sex is familiar to the West" (1927, 3). But when "the purposes for which the motif is employed" are "to make good the pretence that a girl is a boy" (6), such narratives offer a good gloss for the action in "The Shift of Sex."[32] Remarkably for Brown's time, in tracing "the origin of the idea," he notes that "there is, first, the frequent desire of members of one sex to belong to another." (Note that he does not limit that desire to women who wish to be men, and thus avoids patriarchal presumptions of the primacy of maleness.) Though he comments that these stories could be "mere wish fulfilment," his evaluation of transgendering desires as "frequent" was by no means a majority view among academics of his time—nor, indeed, of the early twenty-first century. Likewise, though he also notes that "there are definite types of sexual perversion that might supply a starting point for the notion" (22), his confusion and conflation of sexuality with transgender is not uncommon even in some recent thinking (as described in Stryker and Whittle 2006). Further, his recognition of what would now be termed inter-sex is remarkable: "There are physiological phenomena that might be mentioned in this connection, especially hermaphrodism" (Brown 1927, 24).

Brown's work looks progressive in contrast with that of Jessica Hooker, who gives passing attention to ATU 514 among other stories in which women dress as men. Asking "what happens to fairy-tale women who deviate so far from traditional female roles as to clothe themselves as knights and take up arms[?]" she responds, "A major message . . . appears to be that women may not pass entirely into the male sphere of action with impunity." Her argument echoes Raymond's, though Hooker does not cite it. Disappointed that sword-bearing women either don't retain their weapons permanently or they relinquish their original sex, Hooker comments, "Women who take up the sword have two options: to be re-domesticated by a husband, or to sacrifice their femininity and become actual men, for in wielding this power symbol of masculinity they represent an intolerable threat to male physical dominance" (1990, 178). Drawing on folktale representations of military women, she argues that "on the one hand, the heroines are vindicators of adventurous womanhood; they are models of valour and confidence and far outshine the male characters in the stories, seemingly proving that anything a man can do a woman can do better. However, in each case the girl loses her femininity completely by the end of the tale. Also, none of these heroines is fully accepted or appreciated until after her transformation" (181). Yet in "The Shift of Sex," the protagonist welcomes her imposed transformation—that is, s/he desires transsexual embodiment. Further, the princess/wife's acceptance of her husband's change is unmitigated by concerns about inauthenticity that female-to-male transsexuals (FTMs) face in contemporary North American cultures—that is, the idea that they are not "real" men. The princess simply expresses herself satisfied with her husband and asks that he no longer be assigned dangerous tasks.

Donna Lanclos directly considers the role of ATU 514 in Hispanic societies as expressing the psychological transformation required of biological boys, following feminist Nancy Chodorow's (1978) theories of human development. Though culturally focused, Lanclos's reading, like Hooker's, is less sophisticated and paradoxically less current than Brown's. For example, she contends that this story couldn't be about "hermaphrodism" because it "occurs in fairly low percentages in all populations" and yet "the tale has a meaning which resonates with a much greater percentage of the population" (1996, 73). We agree that ATU 514 tales speak to nontranssexuals, including the present writers, but Lanclos's presumption seems a too-close reproduction of Holbek's proposition that if men tell and appreciate masculine tales and women, feminine tales, then only transpersons could tell and appreciate transgender tales. Research with actual tale audiences indicates that appreciation of and identification with a story do not depend upon a gender match with the main protagonist (e.g., Stone 1997; see also Werhun and Greenhill, forthcoming).

Lanclos presumes that "The Shift of Sex" is a men's tale about men's experience, and is thus of interest primarily to men. She repeats the transphobic errors of Raymond and Hooker, apparently unable to conceive of the protagonist's transsexual transformation as anything but a loss of womanhood: "Had a woman told the tale, the protagonist might have exercised her will within feminine roles. Perhaps a tale like AT 514 should not be interpreted as an instance of 'wishful thinking' in tale-telling by women, but rather as a tale told by men, *about* men. I suggest that AT 514 *is* a boy's tale . . . symbolic accounts of the journey a boy raised in a traditional Hispanic family must take on his way to manhood" (1996, 74). Lanclos compounds her error by presuming uniformity between female and feminist views, suggesting that any female teller would create/reproduce only bold and forceful women. Yet even Bruno Bettelheim recognizes that "whatever the sex of the hero," a story can be relevant to any teller or listener. Arguing the relation of fairy-tale characters to children's development, he suggests that "the male and female heroes are . . . projections onto two different figures of two (artificially) separated aspects of one and the same process which *everybody* has to undergo" (1976, 226). In his discussion of audiences, if not in other details of his analysis, Bettelheim is absolutely correct.[33]

Both "Belle Belle" and versions of "The Shift of Sex" offer arguments addressing what Judith Halberstam and others call "female masculinity." They "pry apart" masculinity's relation to maleness (Halberstam 1998, 2), making one or both available to (hitherto) female-identified persons. For the main character in ATU 514, the resolution of acquiring a male body and using it for sexualized purposes—in at least one case, that of rape— allows not only phallic power but also phallic expression. S/he—starting off female, ending up male—instantiates what appears to be a classic transsexual narrative, beginning by dressing as male and doing male work, and finally being transformed through others' interventions into a biological male. Belle Belle readily accepts the circumstances that place her in male clothing and roles, but does not apparently desire a male sexual identity.

Nevertheless, s/he by no means unequivocally embraces the return to female gender, diverting herself before her marriage with a search for her beloved horse! Arguably these two characters situate themselves at different locations on what Halberstam calls a "masculine continuum" (1998, 141–173).[34]

MAGIC PARADOXICALLY DEFINES NORMALITY

> The escapism or retreat from reality prevalent in supernatural tales blatantly contravenes the dominant literary esthetic of realism . . . Fairy tales specify with extraordinary precision and economy a culture's prototypical quest for identity; they are *par excellence* narratives of initiation, becoming, and maturity; they are themselves susceptible to becoming (and have become) powerful instruments of socialization and acculturation . . . In spite of their lesser prestige compared to "high" literature, fairy tales are a particularly apt means of studying the construction of sexuality and gender differences . . . They present many of our most central myths about what divides the sexes and what constitutes desire. By that same token, they reveal more explicitly than other texts the conflicts, contradictions, and tensions on which those myths are founded. (Seifert 1996, 1–3)

Lewis C. Seifert's comments about fairy-tale unreality as a privileged mode through which to explore cultural paradoxes resonate well with our understanding of "The Shift of Sex." In its many variants and near relatives, this tale works to produce ways for individuals to express feelings about their sex/ gender identity that contradict conventional interpretations. That the story further achieves this process by complicating the relation between sex/gender identity and sexual attraction allows it to work magic to reconcile reality. As Marina Warner suggests, "Fairy tales . . . often seek to define, within a romantic contest, appropriate male and female conduct, to endorse the correct version and—usually—reward it . . . [Some] stories dramatize trials of identity in which the heroine . . . is concealed . . . and her sex is put to the proof" (1994, 135). The notion that the sex of a heroine—or for that matter a hero—must be tested and proved through narrative opens the possibility that humans, apparently male or female, may not be what they seem (and indeed, it echoes notions of sex/gender as performative). Within the versions of ATU 514, the cross-dressing, genderfucking, and possible lesbianism/ bisexuality of the protagonists never attract a narrator's negative commentary within the tale. Instead, the situations in which the protagonists find themselves become complicated by the reactions of others. The intolerance of forces beyond the main character him/herself drive the problems s/he encounters, the obstacles s/he faces, and ultimately, her/his sex change.

But Warner further notes "a strongly marked shift toward fantasy as a mode of understanding, as an ingredient in survival, as a lever against the worst aspects of the status quo and the direction it is taking" (1994, 415). She approaches Kenneth Burke's (1973) famous notion of literature as "equipment for living." Particularly for those whose living is arduous because they don't fit their society's notions of appropriate behavior, appearance, gender, financial solidity, and so on, the presence of even fantastical literary representations of alternatives that they may live on a daily basis can be profoundly meaningful. In later work, Cherie Werhun and Greenhill (forthcoming) follow up on this idea, asking individuals to identify particularly important works of fiction in their lives, and how those works relate to their experience and understanding. As such, as Catherine Velay-Vallantin comments, "In fact these narratives are stories of power" (1992, 10). "Our stories are nothing other than a symbolic questioning, in a representative mode" (12). The metamorphoses, disguises, and impossible tasks that serve as narrative devices in fairy tales may be closer to everyday experience than the most conventional among readers and hearers might guess. That these stories represent these transformations allows an opening of worlds—both for those who fit in, and for those who do not.

NOTES

Funds from a Social Sciences and Humanities Research Council of Canada Research Development Initiatives Grant, "Transgressive Tales: Reading Queer and Trans in Traditional Fairytales," supported this work. Anne E. Duggan helped to make our translations more graceful and accurate.

1. We use the spelling preferred in Stryker and Whittle (2006).

2. Jacquelyn N. Zita calls "genderfuck" "tampering with the codes of sex identity by mixing male and female, masculine and feminine, man and woman signifiers on one body" (1994, 125).

3. Cross-dressing sometimes occurs, though the most common transformations—both of dress/role and body—are between human and animal forms.

4. Bengt Holbek suggests, "The characters of fairy tales do not change sex (except in the curious case of AT 514 where a girl assumes the hero's role)" (1987, 423).

5. Here, "getting the curse" makes one male, not female.

6. All translations are our own.

7. It is unclear whether he intended to suggest that its origins were literary—"developed" is ambiguous—or simply that writers had worked with the idea; no source information illuminates his contention.

8. For biographical information about d'Aulnoy, see Brocklebank (2000, 129); DeGraff (1984, 2–3); and Mitchell (1978, 126–127).

9. Anne Defrance notes that the mother's absence remains unexplored and unexplained (1998, 199). The circumstances recall "Beauty and the Beast" (ATU 425C; *beauty* is "belle"

in French), not only because of the father's recent poverty but also because the two elder sisters fail through their love of wealth and lack of kindness.

10. The situation of a woman falling in love with a woman in male disguise appears in many ballads (see, e.g., Greenhill 1995). In "Belle Belle," two characters use "inclination" when thinking about their feelings for Fortuné. The queen's servant, herself in love with Fortuné, believes that if *she* were queen she would be so great that the knight would have no choice but to love her out of gratitude "even if he didn't love me out of inclination." But the king also muses on his knight, "of whom he was inclined to be particularly fond" (d'Aulnoy 1998, 235). In current English, *inclination* can connote sexual orientation, and the same potential double entendre existed in seventeenth-century French (the language of d'Aulnoy's time) (Norton 2002).

11. D'Aulnoy has at least one other "Belle" who cross-dresses, Belle-Etoile (see Hannon 1993).

12. D'Aulnoy further queers the hero/ine's angst about the king, initially using "Belle Belle" and reverting momentarily to female pronouns, yet twice later in the story showing Fortuné thinking about his love for the king with not a female pronoun in sight.

13. More exclusively literary analytical perspectives include Birberick (2005) and C. Jones (2003).

14. See also James Taggart's reading of Spanish and Mexican tales in terms of their expression of masculinity (1997).

15. Caroline T. Trost similarly finds Belle-Belle/Fortuné "androgynous not only with respect to her changing of name, clothing, and role, but at a more profound level as well. Her personality amalgamates qualities considered typically masculine or feminine" (1991, 60).

16. In this specific case, Fortuné is socially elevated, and the king arguably debased by his love for a class inferior. However, homoeroticism does not necessarily create equality among participants.

17. On Joan of Arc, see Thurston (1910). We thank Carol Harvey (personal communication) for reminding us that crucially, though Joan wore men's clothing, her followers and detractors alike always knew her as female. However, cross-dressing was one of Joan's cited crimes, and she repeatedly refused female clothing in prison though her captors offered her holy Communion, which she greatly desired, if she would dress as a woman.

18. She refers to Freud's notion that women, lacking the penis, are sociopsychologically constructed as castrated beings. By claiming male status, Belle Belle symbolically regains the allegedly lost phallus.

19. Maya Slater, also compelled by Belle Belle's disguise, finds its success "implausible" and cannot figure out "why . . . the queen fail[s] to realize Fortuné's true sex" nor why he does not "confess the truth to the queen" (1982, 73). She also misrecognizes the tale as one for children.

20. The subject of these experiments, David Reimer, committed suicide at the age of thirty-eight (http://articles.latimes.com/2004/may/13/local/me-reimer13); see also Colapinto 2000). Judith Butler movingly and respectfully discusses Reimer's resistance to Money's interference and refusals to reduce himself as a person to his anatomy (2001). We also note that trans can be used as an alibi to refuse and erase lesbianism (see, e.g., A. M. Smith 1995).

21. A traditional version was collected in the Cape Verde Islands by Elsie Clews Parsons (1923, 286–287).

22. Assaf does not deny the homoerotic possibilities of the tale but sees it instead as expressing the vocabulary of the period, "in many ways less tainted with intentions and implications more or less Freudian than ours" (2003, 272).

23. Only three other types join it: "Some tales must be disregarded . . . The records of these tale types have not been included in our statistical break-down" (Holbek 1987, 618).

24. For a discussion focusing on this and similar tales, see Greenhill (2008).

25. For a discussion of filmed and other versions of this tale, see Greenhill and Brydon (2010). See also Torborg Lundell's (1983) criticism of the different attitudes to male and female protagonists betrayed by the Aarne-Thompson tale-type index. Note that these problems have been significantly addressed in the latest version of the tale-type index (Uther 2004).

26. The tale can be resolved without resorting to a sex transformation. In one Latvian version, the girl "sends her brother in her place . . . and he marries the princess" (Arājs and Medne 1977, 435). In a Mexican version, the "brave widow," who has succeeded at impossible tasks, gives a princess she is offered to her son (Philip 2003, 54–58).

27. In a Georgian version, the sex change is to the persecuting witch, and the cross-dressed female protagonist marries the prince (Kurdovanidze 2000, 51).

28. Précis of apparently similar tales are found in Cardigos (2006, 129) and Hodne (1984).

29. It is possible, of course, that this directly translates a shift in how the teller identifies the girl/boy, but in transliterated texts, in the absence of access to the original version, we cannot know.

30. The collector/translator says the reasoning is that a son-in-law could replace the father.

31. The switch could result from the writer's concern for French grammar, being unwilling/unable to change any subject's gender halfway through a sentence. From this point on, the now physically male hero is referred to with male pronouns.

32. Uther notes Indian versions of the tale (2004, 302).

33. Greenhill (2008) offers a brief consideration of childhood identification with cross-gender and cross-species characters.

34. Halberstam criticizes the presumption in such a continuum that would make transgender and transsex some kind of ultimate representation of female masculinity. We suggest no hierarchical distinction between Belle Belle and the protagonist of "The Shift of Sex."

4

From Peeping Swans to Little Cinderellas
The Queer Tradition of the Brothers Grimm in American Cinema

Kendra Magnus-Johnston

" [THE] GOD-AWFUL, KITSCHY FILMS ABOUT THE BROTHERS GRIMMS' lives
and how they came to write fairy tales . . . 'frame' the Grimms in such a way
that the background to their lives and the purpose of their collecting tales
are totally distorted to create lively entertainment . . . The Grimms come
off more as lovable fops than serious scholars, and history itself is mocked.
Entertainment is always more important than truth. We live in realms of fiction . . . So, perhaps the only way we can glean some truth about the Brothers
Grimm will be through fiction and popular culture" (Zipes 2002, x).

The brothers Wilhelm (1786–1859) and Jacob Grimm (1785–1863),
apart from their fame as the collectors, editors, and publishers of traditional
European folktales, were also accomplished librarians, scholars, teachers,
legal historians, philologists, translators, academic human rights activists,
and the founders of Germanic studies. While it is true that they are probably
the most internationally renowned duo of story collectors in the world—
their *Children's and Household Tales*[1] helped establish the transnational
appeal of literary folktales and fairy tales—the diversity and volume of their
work is substantial. Despite their work's range and substance, however, the
Grimm Brothers rarely escape the sentimental distortions that circulate in
popular media.

Misconceptions about the brothers abound. They are credited with
"defining folklore romantically and scientifically, internationally and
nationally, historically and contemporaneously . . . for alternately espous-
ing fragmentation and unity, international diffusion and romantic nationalism, historical reconstruction and cultural fieldwork, blatant literary
license and fidelity to tradition" (Bronner 1998, 184). In many cases, the

DOI: 10.7330/9780874218985.c004

brothers are embedded in their association with folktales and fairy tales. They are mythologized as culturally transcendent persons with a universal spirit. Such cultural transcendence leaves them susceptible to appropriation or, as some have argued, "Americanization" (e.g., Bronner 1998). Donald Haase attributes the universalization of the Grimms in the American literary tradition as deriving from "the Anglo-American attitude toward the German as the other—an other who must be *dominated, tamed, and civilized*" (2003, 64). In the midst of this contradictory legacy, the Grimms' cultural representation exists somewhere between manipulated facts and creative fiction.

Their mediated representations in popular American film act to define, contain, and fix the Grimm Brothers' identities, conflated with specific aspects of their research. Those films and television shows produced thus far tend to feature their folktale work, focus on perpetuating misconceptions associated with their process of collection, and ignore almost entirely or explicitly downplay the rest of their scholarship. North American assumptions about folktales and fairy tales as children's literature seep into each film; and thematic elements of the tales imbue the brothers with particular characteristics. The plots invariably parley the tension between feminized oral traditions and a masculinized literary heritage. The films also express uneasiness about, and often explicitly parody, the queerness of two brothers whose fraternal love overshadows any other heterosexual and/or nonincestuous romantic possibility.

This chapter will explain how American biographical films (biopics) featuring the brothers negotiate their failed masculinity.[2] In the films, they are derogated through their limited agency in their gender and sexual performance. Usually against their will, they variously cross-dress; undergo coercion by patriarchal and/or matriarchal authorities; fall victim to transbiology (human-animal transformation); and experience crippling self-doubt and/or personal illness. Moreover, their seminal contribution to folklore studies is invariably depicted as "children's literature," a genre incongruous with hegemonic masculine preoccupations.[3]

The films invoke foundational concepts of gender and sexuality as produced through actions; indeed, the inflated comedic sexualities of the brothers appear socially constructed and highly performative. As Alexander Doty points out, film "comedy is fundamentally queer since it encourages rule-breaking, risk-taking, inversions, and perversions in the face of straight patriarchal norms." Curiously, the restoration of the status quo is not "contained or recuperated by traditional narrative closure" in any of the Grimm films (2000, 81). That such recuperation could be unnecessary might speak more to a generic convention of fairy-tale film and children's texts generally than to socially progressive representations.

As depicted in *The Wonderful World of the Brothers Grimm* (directed by Henry Levin and George Pal, 1962), *Once upon a Brothers Grimm* (directed by Norman Campbell, 1977), *The Brothers Grimm* (directed by Terry Gilliam, 2005), and even in their cameo appearance in *Ever After* (directed by Andy Tennant, 1998), the brothers' communicable story appears as little more than a device, or a framework, from which to exploit their stories, rather than an opportunity to explore who the brothers were as historical figures. As they are title characters in their own biopics, one might expect some degree of fidelity; however, in each film there is "no attempt to be totally faithful to their documented biographies" (Staples 2008, 142).[4] Rather than artistically re-creating the lives of Wilhelm and Jacob, American cinematic representations concurrently celebrate and interrogate the cultural value of the folktales the pair collected and published. Assumptions about gender and the tradition of storytelling are enmeshed and negotiated in these representations.

Disentangling the fictions from the truths about the Grimm Brothers is a valuable pursuit, but it is not the topic of this chapter. I nevertheless take a moment to clarify a few biographical details. The brothers were born in Germany and lived together for the majority of their adult lives, publishing multiple scholarly books. Their focus was not on children's literature per se but on folklore, philology, and linguistics, which stemmed from their shared "sense of imaginative nation-building." In other words, the brothers were German nationalists who "sensed that they were doing monumental research about tales, legends, customs, proverbs, and expressions stemming from the people." Biographer Jack Zipes writes that while "Jacob was more introverted, serious, and robust; Wilhelm was outgoing, gregarious, and asthmatic—they were inseparable and totally devoted to one another" (Zipes 2002, 28). Wilhelm married, but Jacob remained a reclusive bachelor his entire lifetime (2003, xxvi). Zipes attributes their scholarship to their "great moral integrity," which they apparently inherited from their father (xxiv). The brothers were renowned for their industriousness and attention to detail as well as for their commitment to each other: "The Grimms insisted on a quiet atmosphere and a rigid schedule at home so that they could conduct their research and write without interruptions. Although Wilhelm continued to enjoy company and founded a family—he had three children with Dortchen—he was just as much married to his work as Jacob, and nothing could ever come between Jacob and him" (18). The American cinematic portrayals that comprise this sampling therefore negotiate the controversial history of German nationalist zeal on the one hand, and the incestuous implications of brotherly love on the other. As a result, the films capitalize on the comical potential of two brothers with personality conflicts while emphasizing the financial benefits of publication.

Moving chronologically through the films, representation becomes progressively more critically self-reflexive and metanarrativistic. Other characters' awareness of the Grimms' abilities to affect the stories by virtue of their authorial presence, their power invariably to "give it a happy ending" or "finish the story," offers a critical position on the brothers' influence as the contaminators of cultural texts and the patriarchal appropriators and silencers of female storytelling. What is particularly fascinating is which fictions are recuperated and consistently repeated. While borrowing some of the brothers' cultural capital or notoriety, the films themselves tend to subject the Grimms to degrading, often emasculating, experiences.

The films feature the brothers as either incidental characters—a backdrop—to the anthology of segmented stories that are the central focus or as authors inserted into the narratives they have imagined. Parallels among the three films in terms of characterization of the Grimms include both the intermittent feminization and masculinization of one or both and their mutual failure to perform hegemonic masculinity. An overview of the films also reveals excessive heterosexualization of one brother, especially when seen in contrast to the other. Wilhelm is portrayed as heterosexual and sociable (in the later two films he pursues women sexually ad nauseam). Although in the first, Wilhelm is happily married, he perpetually forgets that he has any family-oriented responsibilities. Jacob receives one romantic liaison per film; despite historical accounts that he was a lifelong bachelor married to his work, the filmmakers literally invent a love interest for him, presumably to offset the manifest sexual tension between the two male leads. All three biopics demonstrate that the brothers do not meet American cinema's normative standards for heterosexual masculine performance.

THE WONDERFUL WORLD OF THE BROTHERS GRIMM

The Wonderful World of the Brothers Grimm (henceforth *Wonderful*), which had its theatrical release in 1962, was planned to coincide with the 150th anniversary of the earliest edition of the Grimm tales. Much of the hype surrounding the film related to the novelty of the medium, three-strip Cinerama, which projected the film in a widescreen format on a massive curved screen measuring 105 feet by 35 feet. The technological impressiveness of the film's presentation arguably overshadowed the work itself; as

Terry Staples surmises, "*The Wonderful World of the Brothers Grimm* . . . is about Cinerama" (2008, 142). Critics largely dismissed the film's representation of the brothers and focused instead on the creative narrative sequences dispersed throughout the film. The *New York Post* observed that "in some curious ways these episodes water down the story of the Brothers Grimm" (quoted in Lochner 2010, 4). Indeed, the interruption of the Grimms' narrative by three live-action fairy-tale sequences results in a juxtaposition between the fantastic quality of the stories and the blandness of the biographical elements of the Grimms' lives.[5]

Wonderful describes two brothers contracted to trace the family history of a duke. While Jacob (played by Karl Boehm) is dedicated to the task at hand and aware that income is needed to support Wilhelm's family, Wilhelm himself (played by Laurence Harvey) is preoccupied with collecting local folktales, which he calls a "priceless literary heritage." Wilhelm warns (on numerous occasions) that unless the stories are "written down and published, they'll soon be forgotten." The film is interspersed with three narrative sequences, which Wilhelm purchases, overhears, or himself recounts to children. He buys a rose to trade for a story from a female flower vendor; he eavesdrops on an old woman who "has the power to bewitch and beguile and create a world of beauty . . . she tells the most wonderful fairy tales ever heard . . . [and] only children are invited." Away from these storytellers and his notes, Wilhelm often struggles to remember the stories. In one scene he observes, "Funny, I just can't seem to remember any, they come and go, slip away, it's a pity there isn't someone to write them down." Obviously, remarks such as these serve blatantly to promote the necessity of the Grimms' future achievements.

Notably, *Wonderful* sets up a conflict between the brothers that reappears in the other two films, figuring one as the hapless dreamer and the other as the stern, fiscally oriented realist. In one scene, two old women remark that Wilhelm, a "poor moonstruck ninny," is "off in the clouds again"; when "the whole world [is] on fire . . . he can't even smell the smoke." When Wilhelm overhears, he responds, "True, the whole world is at war, blood is flowing everywhere, real blood, not dragon's blood . . . nor witch's brew, which can turn an old hag into a beautiful young princess. That is my world, dear ladies. If you prefer yours, I beg you keep it with my fond blessings and a cordial good day." If the film's diegetical real world is coded as a masculine realm, an explicitly public sphere, the location Wilhelm describes, populated by hags, princesses, and witches, is feminine, where delusions that empower the oppressed can reign, albeit within the confines of one's personal imagination. The pleasure Wilhelm derives from this feminine, unproductive realm is therefore coded as queer in the film, a preoccupation for ninnies, not real men.

In another scene, Wilhelm pleads with Jacob after destroying the duke's entire family history for the sake of eavesdropping on an elderly story-teller: "These are pure gold. You can't realize how valuable they are!" Jacob responds coldly, "You ruin everything you touch . . . I'm sorry for you. But much more sorry for your family with nothing to live on but dreams." It is Wilhelm's fragile health that reunites the brothers. In his feverish delir-ium, Wilhelm hallucinates numerous fairy-tale characters (including Tom Thumb, Cinderella, Little Red Riding Hood, Rumpelstiltskin, Hansel and Gretel), who disclose that their "lives depend on you—if you die, then we'll never be born!"[6] Symbolically, the scene suggests that the oral tradition is outmoded and precarious; until committed to the supposed permanency of print, apparently, these characters risk extinction. Elsewhere, Wilhelm sug-gests that oral tradition is also less democratic (despite the aristocratic elit-ism of literacy!). He directly chastises an old female storyteller, credited with "the power to bewitch and beguile," declaring to her, "Those stories don't just belong to a few children, they belong to children all over the world now and forever after." Wilhelm, therefore, is presented as the man who saved a "priceless literary heritage" that, unless "written down and published," would soon have been forgotten.

Apart from the gendered hierarchy wherein the aristocracy's masculin-ized "literary heritage" is privileged over the folk's feminized oral traditions, in *Wonderful*, folktales are further trivialized as primarily for children. The film concludes after Wilhelm resolves to transcribe the stories while working with his brother on more scholarly pursuits. The book titles that fly across the screen range from *Tom Thumb* and *Rumpelstiltskin* to *German Grammar* and *Legal History.* In the final scenes, when the brothers are honored for their "literary and scholarly excellence," Wilhelm is disillusioned when the praise excludes "frog and dogs and hags and dragons." In spite of his admis-sion that Jacob was "right about the fairy tales . . . quick reading, quickly forgotten," children greeting their train begin chanting, "We want a story!" whereupon Wilhelm begins: "Once upon a time there were two brothers."

These concluding words frame the film as a fairy tale retold and adapted from an oral tale (like the Grimms' own *Kinder- und Hausmärchen*). The narrative infidelity in *Wonderful*, coyly framed within the conven-tions of the fairy-tale genre, is reminiscent of the Brothers Grimm who appear peripherally in *Ever After*. Although women are featured as the primary storytellers in both films—in *Wonderful* as the flower vendor and the bewitching old woman, and in *Ever After* as Danielle's or the "real"

Cinderella's great-great-granddaughter—it is men, the Brothers Grimm in *Ever After* and the filmmakers in *Wonderful* (Henry Levin and George Pal), who have the authority to appropriate the story as they see fit for popular consumption. In both films, feminine oral storytelling is undermined by the determination of printed text; in *Wonderful,* this takes place during Wilhelm's dream sequence when he learns he needs to give birth to the characters. Fittingly (though ultimately ironically), the film presents with supreme confidence the literary record—in contrast with oral tradition—as the prime technological apparatus. Yet the success of any medium can be somewhat precarious. *Wonderful* was made in Cinerama, itself predicted to trump all other media. However, given that so few films were ever made in Cinerama, one can reasonably conclude that it proved less profitable than print.

ONCE UPON A BROTHERS GRIMM

Similar to the conventional framing of *Wonderful, Once upon a Brothers Grimm* (henceforth *Once*) is framed by a large, gilded storybook, opened by a distinctively masculine hand. The live-action, made-for-television musical features Jacob (Dean Jones) and Wilhelm Grimm (Paul Sand) getting lost in an enchanted forest on their way to accept an award from the king. The film begins with the brothers gaily riding in a carriage singing of their work:

> Who collected stories by the pound? Put them all together leather bound?
> Who worked hard with pen and ink when it was sink or swim?
> Him and me! Me and him! The Brothers Grimm!"

Of their popularity:

> People all would say, "Who are they?" But today they will say:
> "Look who's here! Give a cheer!"

And finally of their future fame:

> Who will be so famous they may need a pseudonym? . . . The Brothers
>   Grimm . . .
> This makes all our wildest dreams seem pale. This is almost like a fairy tale:
> Fame beyond all measure from a treasury of whim.

The song is particularly emphatic about the Grimms' need for compensation ("sink or swim"), not for their romanticized folklore scholarship but for something that is measured "by the pound," for tangible rewards like fame (enough to "need a pseudonym") and fortune ("treasury"). Reminiscent of Wilhelm's entrepreneurial spirit in *Wonderful*, the brothers in *Once* recognize that folktales are "pure gold."

The carriage driver refuses to chauffeur the brothers into the forest after sunset because a family legend tells of a supernatural phenomenon that punishes anyone entering the forest after dark. Jacob declares that "fairy tales are just stories. They're not to be taken seriously!" He repeats several variations of his incredulity throughout the narrative; however, his declarations are undermined and indeed punished because the forest really *is* an enchanted and dangerous place. Jacob's position, as in *Wonderful*, contrasts sharply with that of Wilhelm, who is an ardent believer. Jacob supposes that Wilhelm has let "the folklore [he's] been collecting take possession of [him]"; Jacob even serenades his brother on the subject in the song "Life Is Not a Fairy Tale":

I find it inconceivable that you find things believable
That I find are naive-able at best . . .
Life is not some childish plot, but what you see and feel.

It is not until after their extensive experiences in the enchanted forest, in which Jacob is humbled in many ways (most memorably as a cross-dressed grandmother to Little Red Riding Hood, but otherwise as a man-turned-swan) that he is able to conclude the film with the song "Life Can Be a Fairy Tale," where "magic carpets can sail to enchanted lands" and "things that I thought inconceivable all at once are quite believable." The songs echo the narrative arc of *Wonderful*. Wilhelm believes in the timeless significance of fairy tales as a matter of "imagination," "the dreamer's way," where "once upon a time is that happy rainbow only those who dream pursue," and "you can be a child at eighty or be fully grown at ten." Wilhelm's position, in both *Wonderful* and *Once*, results in his characterization as naive, fanciful, and almost entirely reliant on his brother's ability to problem-solve (or rather, to resolve the problems Wilhelm creates).[7]

Once effaces the intimacy and vulnerability associated with homosexuality and provides heterosexual alibis for both male leads. In both *Once* and *Wonderful*, Jacob's stern attitude and reluctance to pursue women is excused by his devotion to his scholarship; in *Once*, for example, when Jacob meets a "sweet lady" (an ambiguously available single mother), he refuses her advances:

Jacob: – Sweet lady, I must return to reality.
Queen: – There could be a sweet reality here.
Jacob: – Not for a man who doesn't believe in fairy tales.

In another scene, Wilhelm wins the hand of one of the Twelve Dancing Princesses. However, when propositioned by one, he responds, "From my point of view the situation is impossible. I mean, how could I pick one of you when I love all of you?" As in *Wonderful*, it appears that neither brother can successfully maintain a healthy heterosexual relationship. Potentially, these failures can be attributed to their other primary affections: scholarship and each other.

Other campy[8] moments oscillate between overt presentations of mutual affection and subversive dialogue between the brothers and within their respective musical performances. In one scene, for example, Jacob as half swan, half man, spies on his brother, only to refer to himself as a "peeping swan." In another scene, when Jacob disbelieves that Wilhelm had been turned into a frog, the human Wilhelm inquires (with raised eyebrows), "Wanna see my wart?" The prospects of these respective transgressions are both comical and sexually loaded. That Jacob would experience sexual gratification from watching *his brother's* exploits with the Twelve Dancing Princesses as a Peeping Tom or that Jacob might want to see Wilhelm's genital warts (presumably transmitted during his time in the frog princess's chamber) are doubly titillating as threefold taboos (homosexual, incestuous, and voyeuristic).

Many scenes between the brothers are perceptibly coded as romantic. When they are reunited after Wilhelm's failure to measure up to the Frog Princess's desire for a "green Apollo," Wilhelm calls out to Jacob, "I've never been so happy to see anyone in my whole life!" He subsequently runs and jumps into Jacob's arms, and Jacob twirls him around and around. In disbelief, Jacob asks, "How did you get away from me without me seeing you go?" The brothers' obvious delight in reuniting might have appeared less queer if it had not been sequenced directly following Jacob's failed heterosexual escapade as a frog. Rather than a "Mama's boy," Wilhelm figures as Jacob's boy, requiring gay consolation from his eternal heterosexual rejection.

In *Once*, the characters are fully aware and self-conscious of their scripts in the stories and complain about the limitations of their existence. Little Red Riding Hood, for example, tells Jacob—then cross-dressed as her grandmother and resisting his role in the fairy tale—how the story is supposed to go: "A handsome prince disguised as a hunter is going to rescue Grandmother and me and take me out of this dreary hut." In disgust/astonishment, the wolf decries, "A hunter? You're throwing me over for a hunter?" She responds blankly, in a mechanically even, high-pitched voice, "I don't want a wolf. I want a prince." His response: "But I'm a prince of a fellow." Despondent, Red responds, "But you don't believe in marriage . . . A girl wants stability, a castle of her own, a prince by the fire." The Frog Princess, like Little Red, anticipates the Grimm script.[9] Playing croquet, she sings that her "heart is beating so wildly" because the frog she "will revere" is on his way; she describes him as her "green Apollo" and asks, "Who needs a man again?" because her frog "is equal to any ten" and "tall and strong [who] fills my heart with song." She then deliberately knocks her golden ball into the water and is greeted by a temporarily froglike Wilhelm. She throws herself at him, cheering, "Oh, goody!" as he hops into her bed; sitting beside him she asks, "Oh, froggie, would you mind very much if I kissed you?" She is disappointed, to say the least, when she discovers her frog prince is none other than the lowly scholar Wilhelm Grimm.

Ironically, each story Wilhelm witnesses in the film leaves him unsatisfied and alone. He apologizes to the frog-loving princess for his inadequacy, for as "a humble scholar," he is unworthy of the princess he allegedly invented in his own folktale and fairy-tale collection. He complains, "It's *my* fantasy, so I should have gotten the princess!" The film exposes an ironic tendency of the stories themselves; they often supported the aristocratic ideals that so frustrated the Grimms in their real lives.

Instead of controlling the fairy-tale creatures, as foreshadowed in *Wonderful* (through birth), the Grimms fail to exert *any* control over the scripts and find themselves trapped within them (hence Jacob's role as the grandmother opposite Little Red and the wolf). Instead of the Grimms and their authorial powers, it is the "hags of the dark forest" who control this realm; and it is solely by virtue of Cinderella's fairy godmother's goodwill that the brothers escape. Because Jacob fails to perform any of the lead roles, he is ultimately forced into supplementary positions as the grandmother in "Little Red," one of the six swans, and as a helper in "Hansel and Gretel" and "Rumpelstiltskin." Wilhelm, in contrast, appears as the frog in "The Frog Prince," the suitor in "The Twelve Dancing Princesses," and the "Dummling" in "The Golden Goose."[10] That each brother is unable to successfully integrate himself into the tales, despite his best efforts (Wilhelm, for one, works relentlessly), reveals the brothers' failings as heteronormative masculine men.

The playfulness with which both Wilhelm and Jacob are treated in *Once* renders their folktales escapist entertainment as opposed to communicating their significance as cultural and historical documents. The king's conclusion that it is "good to dream and to use your imagination, but even in dreaming good must conquer evil. Little children must be pure of heart and noble of spirit and purpose and . . . survive the peril to discover the value of truth and to live happily with love ever after" glosses over the culturally situated representations of good versus evil binaries. As with the oral folk traditions controlled by the storytellers in *Wonderful*, the enchantments in *Once* also take place in a matriarchal universe, wherein women appear as the authoritative agents. In both films, however, the brothers' income is afforded by patriarchs (in *Wonderful* it is a duke, and in *Once*, a king). Although at the end of the film, the king emphasizes the tales' importance to folkloric tradition, as "the ancient tales of Germany will now live forever," the lack of Germanness among *any* of the characters underscores instead the American appropriation of German folktales and of the Grimms in the film.

THE BROTHERS GRIMM

Terry Gilliam's idiosyncratic representation in his 2005 film *The Brothers Grimm* (henceforth *Brothers*) offers a prequel to the Grimms' public lives. Set in 1811, one year prior to the publication of volume 1 of *Kinder- und Hausmärchen*, the film reinvents its subjects as two conmen who travel the German countryside pretending to vanquish evil spirits. "Will" (Matt Damon) and "Jake" (Heath Ledger) are rejuvenated as wayward, morally questionable grifters. The pair's infamy is one of the primary gags running through the film. In presenting the Grimms as con artists proficient in "subterfuge, theft, and buggery," Gilliam creates an authorial team that cannot be trusted. Despite their convincing sales pitch, to "save your land from evil enchantments," audience members know that the brothers are little more than traveling grifters, a dubious pair of nineteenth-century ghostbusters (lorebusters?). Their costumed armor, which they introduce early in the film as "enchanted," is revealed as simply "shiny"; their oversized technological equipment is faulty; and their "expertise" in lore is revealed as inert as Will scans the forest in search of "trees on tracks," "the forest on wheels," or an elaborate "pulley system," only to conclude that the perpetrators are "better funded than we are."

Soon after the audience has ascertained the dubiousness of the brothers' enterprise, Will and Jake are apprehended by the French general Delatombe (Jonathan Pryce) and dispatched to the village of Marbaden under the supervision of Delatombe's Italian henchman and torture expert, Cavaldi (Peter Stormare). The primary narrative leads the brothers to resolve why countless young girls from the small village have mysteriously disappeared. They eventually discover that the supernatural force responsible is the Thurungian Queen (Monica Bellucci), a centuries-old witch who is attempting to restore her youth by killing the girls.

In the film, the Thurungian Queen is a powerful matriarchal figure, albeit a villainous one. She, like the "hags of the dark forest" in *Once* and the bewitching storytellers in *Wonderful*, has mystical powers bound up with fairy tales.[11] The enchantments in *Once* also exist in a matriarchal universe, whereby women appear as the authoritative agents, constricted to the scripted possibilities of their respective tales. In *Brothers*, the presence of powerful female characters emasculates the Grimms' authority as fairy tale "experts." When not attempting to flee or shrieking in fright, Will recoils in disgust or exhibits a pathetically weak stomach. He actually falls over at one point after witnessing a momentary frog kiss and gags into his handkerchief when the village's female trapper callously skins a rabbit. The presence of the trapper, Angelica (Lena Headey), and the ways in which she interrogates the authority of the Grimms is strongly gendered. Edina Fecskó's psychoanalytic reading of *Brothers* highlights Angelica's "hermaphrodite nature" as she "bears both masculine (hunter) and feminine (she is capable of the rescuing kiss)" attributes (2008, 308). Following my analysis of the brothers' nonnormative sexual performance, it is appropriate that s/he serves as a love interest to *both*. In a scene following Will's admission that his enchanted armor is bogus ("I made that armor; it's not magic, it's just shiny!"), Angelica coyly emphasizes the absurdity of his costume. She asks, "So tell me, famous Brother Grimm, how exactly do *you* intend to save us?" as she licks her finger to shine his false armor (it squeaks loudly). Other feminized moments include the two separate occasions when Will dons women's clothing; in one of the two he is referred to as a "little Cinderella."

Despite his performance as the overbearing, protective older brother, Will falls short of the romantic hero archetype. On several occasions he simply tries to flee the scene, at one point abandoning his brother altogether, yelling, "Never fear, Jake, I will return for you!" Unlike the Jacob who literally carries and figuratively suckles Wilhelm in *Once*, or the Jacob who reminds Wilhelm to responsibly carry out duties related to his employment and personal relationships in *Wonderful*, Jake, like Will, is neither heroic nor particularly dependable in *Brothers*. In terms of masculinity and sexuality, however, the Grimms in *Brothers* are aligned with the oscillating representation in the other films.

Wilhelm Grimm is depicted as a socialite who, as Jake phrases it in the film, has "enough bullshit to fill the palace of Versailles." Will uses his skills to defraud, pacify, flatter, and entice for self-interested, financial, and sexual gratification. At one point Marcusio Cavaldi urges the brothers to "go and sell your oil of snake, Grimmy." Similarly, when the brothers visit the village of Marbaden, they are approached by a villager who immediately inquires about what the men are selling: "What's your business?" Will, as though adopting the rhetorical strategies of a used-car salesperson, says,

"Grimm's the name. Two 'm's." Later, he self-promotes by illustrating his latest endeavors to impress the film's love interest: "the men who vanquished the mill witch of Karlstadt, the frog boy of Glutenhof, and the cannibal chef of the Schwarzwald in the gingerbread house of terror." The audience, of course, knows that Will's "a little chit, a little chat" is little more than, as Jake describes, "a little huff, a little puff." Jake fares little better; even when he stands up to Will, he shrinks in pain from the force of his blow to his brother's face. Although Jake is presented as primarily interested in "mythical damsels and princesses" in contrast to his philandering brother, his gift for scholarship and keen interest in popular lore lend credibility to the Grimm enterprise. Like Will, Jake is a skilled raconteur; in a drunken stupor, he proclaims, "I've got a story! I've got a story!" only to recount an obviously made-up adventure in which he and his brother journeyed "to hell and back." The tall tales cited by the brothers each enlist adventures of grandeur that are little other than methods of overcompensation.

Audience members' willingness to imagine the Grimms as romantic heroes on horseback venturing from village to village, either to gather stories from an authentic folk collective or to "save [the] land from evil enchantments," is perhaps reinforced by the scarcity of English biographical works that set the record straight.[12] The representation of the brothers in the film could prompt readers to visit the Grimm texts for the first time or to revisit them with an eye toward the editorial interventions of the collectors and the rhetorical construction of the fairy tales. By extension, a reader might also interrogate the motivations and rhetoric of the director and screenwriter of *Brothers*. An audience might assume that the film is a prequel to the Grimms' scholarly future, as is the case with other fictional biographical films.[13] Similar to the foreshadowing that occurs in *Wonderful*, at several points in *Brothers*, Jake urgently declares that he needs to "write down" the events that occur in the film. Nevertheless, an accurate description of the Grimms is perhaps unnecessary for readers to appreciate their works. Furthermore, directors such as Gilliam characteristically dispense with historical accuracy in favor of pastiche. Rather than mock the conventions of film, in *Brothers*, Gilliam mocks the esteem of canonical authors. His film is ironic to the extent that its subjects are agents in their own story; Gilliam does not seek to revise or subvert the Grimms' work or the conventions of such a fantastic retelling.

In the closing of *Brothers*, Will and Jake discuss their future prospects as a "turning point." The brothers say they are "on the verge of an alternative career path, one that uses all our new expertise." Their know-how early on, of course, is revealed as "lucrative"; as Jake explains, "There's money to be made in witches." Of the two, Jake is far less interested in money, but when offered his "half," he resolves that he would prefer to "take the beans, thanks." It is unclear, however, whether the "beans" refer to the magical, apparently noble pursuit of fairy-tale scholarship that the brothers presumably pursue *after* the adventure featured in the film, or the "beans" generated from the book trade. The ethical dilemma centered on popularizing and profiting from folktales—that is to say, appropriating the texts of others into a bound collection—is treated as commonsensical in each film. "Beans," rather, are used to contrast the two brothers' conflicting worldviews:

Jake: This is not your world, Will . . . The story—it's happening to us now. We're living it. It's alive, it's real, it's breathing, and we can give it a happy ending . . . we'll bring [the missing girls] back.

Will: Bring them back with what? Magic beans?

Jake: Why do you say that?

Will: Because magic beans don't work! They don't bring people back to life. They did not then and they will not now!

By the end of the film, however, the "magic" required for happy endings is replaced with brotherly love and good old-fashioned violence; beyond the final sword fight and shattering defeat of the queen, "believing" in one another is what enables the Grimms to walk out of the final frame of the German countryside in a brotherly embrace, "without a bean" to their name. The "beans" not only symbolize hope and the futility of "happily ever afters," they also invoke financial security at the end of the film and signal a resolution between enlightenment and romanticism through contemporary capitalism.

In the closing of the film, Jake responds to Will's suggested "career path" by reaffirming that "this is the real world . . . We are men without country, enemies of the state, and worst of all we haven't a single bean to our name." Will responds, "It's a good name, though, isn't it?" and Jake confirms that it's "a damn good name." The closing lines of the film do not interrogate the tenuousness of the Grimms' future as storytellers or the controversies surrounding their transcriptions of oral folktales, but instead simplistically reduce the film to a namesake. Thus, the closing scene of the film reminds viewers that the only certitude offered here is a disembodied name with distinctly commerical properties.

And yet, the authorial seal with which canonical texts are stamped is temporarily broken as audiences are shown the constructedness of authorship. As a construction of the past, *Brothers* can be conceptualized as pastiche, a form that Nicolas Haydock (2002) suggests is a practice of both assemblage and forgery. Because there is no real version of history that the film's viewers have themselves witnessed, audiences judge the authenticity of cinematic representations in terms of *other* artificial, fictitious film depictions. As they are biopics, one might measure the accuracy of the films' portrayals of the Grimms based on *other* Grimm films. Indeed, when the characterization of the respective brothers is consistent across films—or at the very least familiar—audience members may be more apt to trust the film's accuracy. Blatant inconsistencies, such as the reversal of the brothers' characterization, are what encourage an audience to remain skeptical of the Grimms' authorial neutrality. Gilliam's characterization of the Grimms as both real and constructed demonstrates the postmodern propensity for questioning truth.

The countless visual references to Grimm fairy tales are presented transiently in *Brothers*; that is to say, the Grimm fairy-tale characters do not serve any purpose in the film beyond a visual cameo. Similar to *Wonderful*'s use of the stories as temporary digressions that interrupt the primary narrative, *Brothers* offers tropes for readers familiar with the resonance of a red cape, a glass slipper, and long billowing hair from a tower window. By framing the film with fairy-tale conventions that begin with "Once upon a time" and end with "And they lived happily ever after," Gilliam does not interrogate the conventions of the genre or ironize the stories themselves. Of the three films, only in *Once* do self-reflexive fairy-tale characters explicitly interrogate the narrative conventions of fairy tales, and in particular how those conventions constrain their gender performance. All three films subtly interrogate gender conventions by underscoring the brothers' inability to meet the standards of ideal masculinity as outlined in their own opus. In other words, either fairy-tale characters overtly question the gender scripts of the Grimms' fairy tales or the Grimms' performance does. In all three instances, the fictionalization of the Grimms dismantles the gender scripts of canonized fairy tales.

While audience members may recognize the fairy-tale tropes, the film does not demonstrate the liberating possibilities of the stories *for* the people. Literary scholar Susan Cahill, in one of the few articles that investigates *Brothers* at length, writes that by staging illusionary folk legends only to appear to defeat the chimeras, "the Grimms' use and abuse of the spectacle, by staging the public's fears and simultaneously constructing themselves as heroes within this fantasy, can be read as analogous to certain uses of the cinema" (2010, 63). *Brothers*' story *as* fairy tale is hardly liberating in its interpretive possibilities—at least if one reads the overarching "Snow White" story affected by the mirror queen as central. On the other hand, if readers consider the focal narrative as the Brothers Grimm rather than their literary works, the *process* of fabricating stories becomes the crux of the film's critical potential. The Grimm brothers as scam artists may not challenge readers with *new* adaptations of folktales, but the story does hold out for the deconstruction of authorship and its supposedly neutral, yet somehow sacred, authority.

THE GRIMMS READ THROUGH THEIR CULTURAL PRODUCTIONS

The auteurial freedom exacted by Gilliam, Levin and Pal, and Campbell is not entirely unlike the editorial vigor with which the Grimms' revised, edited, added to, and basically rewrote many of the classic tales to reflect what Haase terms their "own aesthetic and moral values" (1999, 360). The films, like the Grimms' collection of "authentic" folktales,[14] are subject to creative contamination. For Zipes, "To contaminate an oral folk tale or a literary fairy tale is thus to enrich it by artfully introducing extraordinary motifs, words, expressions, proverbs, metaphors, and characters into its corporate body so that it will be transformed and form a new essence" (2001, 103). Rather than simply preserving an oral tradition, Zipes posits, the brothers were "the greatest contaminators of fairy tales in the nineteenth century" (101). Rather than further pollute the fairy tales offered in the Grimms' collection (which many *other* filmic adaptations have pursued),[15] these filmmakers project their own aesthetic and moral values onto the scholars. What the films reveal is that the Grimms are subject to the same interventions as their folktales; paradoxically, they have become just as malleable as the stories they themselves collected and edited.

These representations of the Grimms provoke audiences to consider both the history of each figure's public persona and how each is constructed in the popular contemporary imagination. Of the three films, *Brothers* is perhaps most creative in its reinvention of the Grimm Brothers as deintellectualized, depoliticized, and dehistoricized romantic antiheroes. In a featurette released with the film on DVD, "Bringing the Fairytale to Life," Gilliam clarifies a crucial detail about the film: "Let me just say from the start that this has got nothing to do with the real Brothers Grimm, other than the fact that they were collectors of German folktales and we owe them a lot of thanks." Rather than thank them, however, Gilliam clarifies that in his film, "we're using them." The brothers are reduced to their names, for as Gilliam suggests, the Grimms represent little more than an idea or "name" for contemporary readers.

The fantastic nature of the two later films, in contrast to the dramatization of the Grimms in Levin and Pal's work, infuses the brothers' biographical details with supernatural fairy-tale adventures. This infusion results in a postmodern interrogation of what is "real" and teases out the cultural constructedness (and instability) of the Grimms' authority as canonical authors and "contaminators" of oral folk traditions. Although *Wonderful* certainly fictionalizes the Grimms, the genre within which it frames them offers the most serious treatment of the brothers as historical figures. The individual and oppositional traits given to them are arguably flexible and perhaps dependent upon the actor cast in the role.

Each film, by emasculating and bowdlerizing the Grimms, suspends the idolization of the scholars as authoritative historical personae and underscores the performativity inherent in their existence as public figures. By representing the Grimms with disreputable qualities, primarily as shady operators, Gilliam liberates the stories from their authorial reputation. At the very least, both of the most recent films sully the popular interpretation that valorizes the Grimms' creative genius by playfully derogating them to a logical extreme. And by framing the brothers within the conventions of their work, each film interrogates the editorial efforts imposed by the Grimms as well as the cultural understandings of folktales. Thus, these cultural productions discourage a reading of the Grimms' stories that is bent on the esteem of the brothers' characters or in fixing the narratives to a particular category (children's literature, for example). Audiences are encouraged to read with one eyebrow raised, mindfully considering the fabricated and forever-evolving nature of cultural production, apparently regardless of the medium.

NOTES

Jack Zipes's feedback was instrumental to the final editing stages of the work; I owe him, Pauline Greenhill, and Diane Tye much gratitude for their insightful suggestions.

    1. Jacob and Wilhelm Grimm's *Kinder- und Hausmärchen* was published in seven editions during the Grimms' lifetime as the Large Edition (Grosse Ausgabe). The Grimms also published a Small Edition (Kleine Ausgabe) with fifty tales from 1826 to 1858. There were ten different editions.

    2. *Masculinity*, as used here, does not refer to an inherent male nature but to a "dominant fiction authorizing the continued representation of certain types of gender performances (like the breadwinner), marginalizing others (like the mama's boy), and forbidding still others (like the homosexual)" (Cohan 1995, 57).

    3. Perry Nodelman argues that children's literature is culturally coded as "women's writing," and that the stories' configuration as "tales of repression" or "wish-fulfillment

fantasies of escapes from repression" echoes the experiences of women and disempowered individuals generally (1988, 33).

4. Terry Staples's (2008) "Brothers Grimm in Biopics" is the sole publication I could find that examines all four films.

5. Although it would be valuable to review the textual elements of the three sequences in the film—"The Worn Out Dancing Shoes" ("Die zertanzten Schuhe"), "The Gifts of the Little Folk" ("Geschenke des kleinen Volkes"), and "The Singing Bone" ("Der singende Knochen"), I focus on their framing rather than their textual content.

6. The line itself implies that Wilhelm needs to give birth to these fictional characters, taking an oral, feminized tradition and masculinizing it into print. As a duo, the two brothers—homosexually, incestuously, symbolically—parent the multitude of fairy-tale characters who encircle Wilhelm's bed. All the while, Jacob waits at Wilhelm's bedside.

7. Whenever Wilhelm is in trouble, he desperately and pathetically calls out for his brother: "Jacob! I'm in trouble!" In one instance, Wilhelm flees from a king and royal guards who wish to reprimand him for maneuvering his way into the princess's chamber under "false pretenses." When Jacob is visibly shocked and declares, "That's no Wilhelm I know!" it is unclear what Jacob finds out of character for Wilhelm: his deceptiveness or his heterosexuality?

8. Alexander Doty outlines camp's primary interests as "taste/style/aesthetics, sexuality, and gender—or, rather, sexuality as related to gender-role-playing." He further clarifies, "Camp's mode is excess and exaggeration. Camp's tone is a mixture of irony, affection, seriousness, playfulness, and angry laughter . . . There is nothing straight about camp" (2000, 82).

9. In another scene, after Jacob saves two children from a hungry witch, Gretel declares, "I was supposed to burn up the witch! What are you doing in this story, anyhow?" Jacob's failure to properly navigate or follow the script is aligned with his inability to acknowledge the pleasurable possibilities of the fairy-tale realm, which would permit/encourage any nonnormative expression of sexuality that Jacob desires.

10. "Dummling" is the name of the youngest son, and hero, of "The Golden Goose" ("Die goldene Gans"). Bruno Bettelheim sees the Dummling as "the fairy tale's rendering of the original debilitated state of the ego as it begins its struggle to cope with the inner world of drives and with the difficult problems which the outer world presents" (1976, 75). Wilhelm's positioning as Dummling is telling in light of his dependency on his brother and his insufficiency as an appropriate heterosexual partner for any of the women he pursues in the film.

11. Susan Cahill's (2010) article on feminine representation in *Brothers* offers an insightful critical gender analysis by exploring the representation of the queen. In particular, Cahill argues that the film is a site in which cultural anxieties about femininity as spectacle and an object/agent of the gaze are staged.

12. With the exception of Zipes's *The Brothers Grimm: From Enchanted Forests to the Modern World*, "we still do not have a 'definitive' biography of the Grimms in English," and as a result fiction has arisen "out of the shortcomings of history" (2002, x).

13. In the closing of *A Knight's Tale* (directed by Brian Helgeland, 2001), Chaucer proclaims that he might "write some of this story down," suggesting that the film narrative could be the textual origin of *The Canterbury Tales* rather than the other way around. Such a statement is inherently postmodern as it seems to interrogate what is real and prompts readers to question their assumptions about historical truth. A similar framing technique is taken up in *Ever After*.

14.   The concept of authenticity in the adaptation of oral folktales to the literary canon lacks stability, as the Grimms editorially intervened in each folktale they published. As Zipes has argued, the Grimms were not simply "collectors of 'pure' folk tales, they were creative 'contaminators' and artists." As Zipes has it, the Grimms' major accomplishment "was to *create* an ideal type for the *literary* fairy tale" (2002, 31).

15.   As discussed in Greenhill and Matrix (2010); and Zipes (2011).

5

Global Flows in Coastal Contact Zones
Selkie Lore in Neil Jordan's Ondine *and Solveig Eggerz's* Seal Woman

Kirsten Møllegaard

Kann ikki ráða sær heldur enn kópur, tá ið hann sær húðina (To have as little self control as a seal that sees its coat).

Faroese proverb (Petersen 2006)

Once a selkie finds her sealskin again, neither chains of steel nor chains of love can keep her from the sea.

Tadgh in *The Secret of Roan Inish* (1994)

SELKIE LORE

THE ANIMAL SPOUSE IS AN ENDURING MOTIF, not only in traditional folktales but also in contemporary film and literature. Folklorists generally agree that, traditionally, tales of animal bridegrooms have been told primarily among women (Warner 1994, 276; Tatar 1999, 27), while animal bride tales mainly have circulated among men (Sax 1998, 21; Leavy 1994, 118). Since storytellers past and present "have always told tales relevant to their lives" (Zipes 2012, 95), story worlds function metaphorically as mirrors that reflect the social and cultural registers of the tellers' lived experience, geographical location, and historical time, thus refracting gendered points of view through the prism of the story's plot. From the latter perspective, animal bride tales interrogate woman's cultural role as other in relation to man, her body as locus of sexual desire and wellspring of children, and her ambiguity as bearer of culture. In animal bride lore, woman's otherness is symbolized by her transbiological transformation from animal to woman,

DOI: 10.7330/9780874218985.c005

93

and by the assumed subservience of both woman and animal to man. Exotic, strange, and tragic, the animal bride crystallizes conflicts and tensions arising from men's hegemonic power over women and the way marriage, as a patriarchal institution, enforces men's right to control women's sexuality.

At the same time, animal bride tales destabilize the validity of male hegemony by emphasizing through various plots involving trickery, violence, forced marriage, domestic drudgery, escape, and orphaned children that male control over women ultimately is doomed to fail. Like "Bluebeard" (ATU 312), one of the few classic fairy tales directly dealing with the prohibitions and transgressions within marriage, folktales about seal wives unsettle notions of a happy-ever-after. When the seal wife finds her skin, she follows her heart and returns to the sea, thus demonstrating women's capability of taking agency and breaking free of the chains that patriarchal society has imposed upon them. In Lacanian terms, by finding her husband's key to the chest, the seal wife swiftly appropriates the phallus as the means to access knowledge and possession of her own identity (symbolized by the sealskin), leaving behind an empty chest (home) and a key (phallus) that has lost its significance as a symbol of control. Shuli Barzilai notes, "It is indeed issues of power and control that generate the successive stories of texts designed to represent the humiliation of women and vindicate the hegemony of men. The affirmation of male dominion is dialectically dependent on female fallibility. In terms borrowed from Jacques Lacan, the husband is constantly compelled to seek reassurance about the whereabouts of the phallus" (quoted in Zipes 2012, 54). As in the story "Bluebeard," which Barzilai refers to, the phallus in selkie lore is represented by the husband's control of the key to the chest that hides the selkie's coat, and more abstractly by his knowledge and possession of the magic sealskin, her only means of escape from his house.

"The Sealskin," a folktale from southern Iceland, provides an example. A man from Myrdal steals the skin of a seal woman while she dances on the beach and locks it in a chest so that she cannot return to the sea. Unmoved by her tears, he takes her home. They marry and have children. One day he forgets to take along the key to the chest while he is away. The woman immediately gets hold of the sealskin and heads for the sea. Her final words to the children are:

> This I want, and yet I want it not,
> Seven children have I at the bottom of the sea,
> Seven children have I as well here above. (Ashliman 2000)[1]

Regional legends about seal folk (called selkies, selchies, or silkies in the British Isles), who temporarily shed their skin to dance or linger upon the shore, are known throughout the North Atlantic region. Alan Bruford reports of the migratory legend of a man stealing a selkie's hide that "there are hundreds recorded all along the Atlantic coasts from Ireland to Iceland" (quoted in J. M. Harris 2009, 9). Selkie narratives belong to a large cluster of legends, folktales, and fairy tales about animal brides who transform from beast into human form, and sometimes back to animal form again. In contrast to many beast bridegroom tales, for example, "East of the Sun and West of the Moon" (ATU 425A), "Beauty and the Beast" (ATU 425C), or "The Frog King" (ATU 440), whose male protagonists are cursed with animal form and attain happiness only when transformed into wholesome human form through the mediating effect of a good woman, the human form is usually a curse for the animal bride because her human incarnation separates her from her animal kin and entraps her in a patriarchal human social order where women function "as domestics and breeders, born to serve the interests of men" (Zipes 2012, 80). The impermanence of both her animal and human form suggests transbiological fluidity and unsettles the boundaries within which the human condition is perceived as distinct from the animal world. Selkie narratives depict this fluidity as a parallel, otherworldly social order by positing the seal woman as bound by social and emotional obligations to others in the ocean-dwelling community of seals (Leavy 1994, 200). Unlike the animal bridegroom, who often is represented as a cursed princeling wielding social rights in the human world, which he, despite his beastly form, is part of, the seal woman is a stranger, an exotic other, in the human world. She has a past history of family and kin in the ocean, which precedes the obligations imposed upon her as wife and mother on land. In this regard, seal wife tales bear witness to women's resistance to traditional gender roles as mothers and wives as well as to men's fear of the runaway wife.

My purpose here is twofold: in order to examine how folkloric texts inform contemporary cinematic and literary depictions of women, immigration, and otherness, I first contextualize Irish filmmaker Neil Jordan's film *Ondine* (2009) and Icelandic-born American writer Solveig Eggerz's novel *Seal Woman* (2008) with folktales from Iceland, the Faroe Islands, Ireland, Scotland, and the Scottish Isles that involve a union between a man and a seal woman.[2] Taking into account how gender conflicts and the ambiguity about transbiological transformation in folktales speak of complex social realities, my next step is to consider *Ondine* and *Seal Woman* in relation to postmodern intertextuality and generic flexibility by exploring

Trudier Harris's point that any text "can have a variety of relationships to comparable texts and categories of genre that have preceded it" (1995, 523). *Ondine* is set in present-day Ireland and *Seal Woman* in Iceland in the late 1940s; in both, historical realism about the social facts facing solitary women immigrants mingles with legends about supernatural seal women who get caught along the shoreline and eventually marry landsmen, though never losing their longing for the sea. As postmodern texts, *Ondine* and *Seal Woman* demonstrate how expansive selkie lore has become, and how their representation of gender ties in with generic choices (Bacchilega and Rieder 2010, 32).

Unlike the enchanted long-long-ago, far-far-away settings of animal bride fairy tales grouped under "The Man on a Quest for His Lost Wife," (ATU 400) or "The Animal Bride" (ATU 402), selkie narratives have typically been told as legends relating to specific places and common people within the living memory of the local community. Seal wife tales often have some traditional fairy-tale motifs, most notably the use of magic numbers (three and seven), helpers (a child accidentally finding its mother's seal-skin), and the transformative power of the selkie's magic coat.[3] But they also include many real-life, strikingly modern themes relating specifically to ideas about gender, power, and otherness as well as the social and economic pressure to marry and rear children in the rural subsistence economies along the North Atlantic shores.

David Thomson's collection *The People of the Sea: A Journey in Search of the Seal Legend* illustrates these concerns. He wrote down the stories he heard while traveling from the Shetland Islands to County Kerry, Ireland, in the late 1940s. A Kerry man, Sean Sweeney, told him about the MacNamaras, whose "first father found their mother on the strand, and he hid her cloak away in the thatch and married her." The woman apparently never spoke. She laughed only three times: once when a stranger refused a meal she offered, a second time when a girl slipped on a flagstone that hid a treasure of gold, and the third time when her cloak fell to the floor from where her husband had hidden it in the rafters (1980, 171).[4]

Like many other collectors of folklore, Thomson sensed that cultural change was imminent: "I came to the seal places during the years of transition and knew even then that contact with industrialized society had begun to make some storytellers shy of expressing themselves to their own children" (1980, xxii). The foreboding sense of social change, in particular depopulation of small coastal communities, gives Thomson's collection a sheen of nostalgia and a sense of urgency to capture the associations and connectedness between people, places, and stories in folktales and local legends. Thomson and Traveler storyteller Duncan Williamson, who started collecting stories on the west coast of Scotland in the early 1940s, both mention the sacredness of the stories, the need to protect family secrets, and the humility required to live in close proximity to the sea. Williamson explains, "Stories from tradition are magic—because they are given to you as a present—you are let into the personal lives of your friends" (2005, 3). In the preface to his recollection of growing up on the Outer Hebrides in the 1940s, John M. MacAulay writes, "One learned to respect, not only the sea, but also what lived and moved upon and within it" (1998, xvii).

Emerging from the intimate setting and haunting narratives about magical seal folk recorded by Thomson, Williamson, and MacAulay is a double vision, similar to that of fairy tales, "on the one hand charting perennial drives and terrors, both conscious and unconscious, and on the other mapping actual volatile experience, [which] gives the genre its fascination and power to satisfy" (Warner 1994, xxi). This observation connects to postmodern retellings because stories "enable us to live through the present's uncertainties . . . [thus tying] story to history (knowledge), values (ideas), and figuration (vision) . . . [and signaling] that mastery of such narrative ingredients produces power, as both privilege *and* empowerment" (Bacchilega 1997, 24). As the following discussion will show, these narrative ingredients also allow double vision to function as a gendered perspective in storytelling both in film and fiction.

Double vision is a central dimension of both Neil Jordan's and Solveig Eggerz's adaptation of traditional selkie lore. Three questions guide my discussion of their works: first, what makes selkie stories meaningful in the intertextual and ontologically ambivalent, gendered discourses in which they emerge? Second, how does selkie lore narrate geographical place in relation to shifting historical currents in settlement and migration? And third, as metaphor, how are selkie legends incorporated into cultural discourses that (re)produce images of the other?

ONDINE

Ondine was conceptualized during the 2007–2008 Writers Guild of America strike. Unable to work on his American studio production, director Neil Jordan took the opportunity to return to his native Ireland and make a low-budget fantasy movie on location in the small seaside town where he owns a house. Jordan, who has written and directed films on both sides of the Atlantic, has often depicted Ireland as a place of brutal conflict and intolerance. His Irish films include the critically acclaimed *The Crying*

Game (1992), the historical drama *Michael Collins* (1996), and the uncanny portrayals of disturbed youth in adaptations of novels by Patrick McCabe, *The Butcher Boy* (1997) and *Breakfast on Pluto* (2005). In one interview, Jordan states, "I've done so many things in Ireland about brutality and violence—punishing, unforgiving things. I suppose I wanted to do something just gentle, like those early fairy tales of Yeats and Lady Gregory, which are terribly childish, terribly romantic, quite beautiful" (Rafferty 2010). In another, Jordan adds that *Ondine* "is my version of 'The Little Mermaid,' I suppose" (Faust 2010).

Ondine, a complex family melodrama, engages in the nostalgia for the west of Ireland, which since the days of W. B. Yeats and the Celtic Revival has been claimed by various nationalist movements both as a repository for authentic Irish culture and identity and as a place of mythic meaning (Ó Giolláin 2000, 3–29). *Ondine* was filmed with support from the Irish Film Board in Castletownbere, a West Cork fishing village on the Beara Peninsula (Faust 2010). Cinematographer Christopher Doyle turns the dull, overcast, damp Irish summer landscapes and seascapes into an otherworldly place, strangely liquid and fluid with promise of enchantment. An *Irish Times* reviewer calls this place "a lovely Nowhere" and an "unreal dreamland," further questioning the film's supposed regional authenticity by noting that actor Colin Farrell's "Cork accent comes and goes" (Clarke 2010). American reviewers more readily accept the premodernity of "one of those wee Irish fishing villages that belongs to another time" (Rea 2010), describing the film as "blarney carried to rhapsodic heights" (Rainer 2010).

Inevitably, reviewers also note *Ondine's* thematic affinity with American director John Sayles's Irish fantasy film *The Secret of Roan Inish* (1994), adapted from the Scottish novella *Secret of the Ron Mor Skerry* by Rosalie K. Fry (1959). *Ondine*, however, incorporates a broader array of European folktales and fairy tales, including "the German folktale from which the film derives its title, the Scottish Selkie tradition, and Hans Christian Andersen's 'The Little Mermaid'" (McGuirk 2010, 243). It makes overt references to the Grimm version of "Snow White" (ATU 709) and to *Alice in Wonderland*. *The Secret of Roan Inish*, securely focused on selkie lore, allows no major global flows in popular culture or politics to dilute the magic or disrupt the fetishization of the west of Ireland as the land of Celtic myth and folklore. Sayles's exclusion of other folk traditions allows Emily Selby and Deborah Dixon to situate *The Secret of Roan Inish's* selkie lore specifically in relation to the Celtic "Otherworld," which they argue is a female space "dominated by powerful female Celtic deities and other supernatural entities" (1998, 20). *Ondine*, less concerned with origins of tradition, refers vaguely to selkie lore as a "Scottish thing" and mingles it with broad references to European folklore, including undines (water nymphs), mermaids, and the haunting singing of sirens. Both films associate femininity with water, the supernatural, and the exotic, but only *Ondine* is concerned to show the vulnerability of the female other in a predatory masculine social order.

Further, *The Secret of Roan Inish* has characters with Irish names (e.g., Fiona, her cousin Tadgh, and the selkie Nuala) and uses the Gaelic language to express resistance to English colonialism.[5] *Ondine* has much broader geographical scope. Its cast speaks English with various regional dialects and foreign accents, and names like Syracuse and Ondine refer to places and myths from beyond Ireland. *The Secret of Roan Inish* concerns healing and reestablishing a family broken apart by death, migration, and loss of home by way of one brave girl's determination to find her little brother, reared by seals. *Ondine* deals with moving on after loss and trauma, and trusting a foreigner, who may or may not be a magical creature, enough to form a new family with her. Several reviewers express disappointment with *Ondine*'s lack of fixed genre. Donald Clarke describes the central story as "slippery" and "insecure" (2010), while other critics note the perpetual and essentially unresolved questions the film raises: "Is Ondine a selkie (seal woman) or is she simply a girl on the run seeking asylum?" (Rainer 2010).

Syracuse (Colin Farrell), a scruffy fisherman down on his luck, struggles to stay sober for the sake of his wheelchair-bound daughter Annie (Alison Barry), seriously ill from kidney disease. Stuck with the nickname Circus for his erstwhile drunken antics, Syracuse has a recalcitrant relationship to Maura (Dervla Kirwan), his alcoholic ex-wife. Annie, a precocious child who compensates for her lack of physical mobility with wise observations about the blundering adults around her, lives with Maura and her hard-drinking Scottish boyfriend, Alex (Tony Curran), who—seal husband style—has abandoned his wife and three children in Scotland.

One day, Syracuse finds a barely breathing young woman (Alicja Bachleda-Curus) in his trawl net. Fearful of the authorities, she refuses to be taken to the hospital. He wonders if she is an asylum seeker, and if she has swum "all the way from Arabia." She claims to have no memory of who she is or where she is from. She calls herself Ondine, has long mermaid tresses, and wears a netlike, knitted dress.

Syracuse takes her to his mother's abandoned cabin, nestled picturesquely among the rolling green hills overlooking a secluded cove. Under his breath, Syracuse muses, "If it depends on me, you can stay forever, happily ever after, once upon a time." Like Disney's Snow White, another vagrant persecuted heroine, Ondine starts cleaning house and tidying up—performances communicating her "natural" inclination toward homemaking and hence her inherent female goodness. She also helps herself to some of Syracuse's mother's old clothes and sleeps in her bed with the innocent trust of a fairy-tale orphan.

Ondine changes Syracuse's luck for the better. She sings fish into his nets and lobsters into his pots in montages that meld her singing with the soundtrack's ambient, dreamy serenades by Icelandic band Sigur Rós. To Syracuse, Ondine and her ways are very "strange and wonderful," an expression that he often uses when he asks Annie about her day. While Annie is in dialysis, he tells her a story about a fisherman who pulled in his nets and found a woman. The girl wants to know how the story ends, but Syracuse has no answer. "That's a real shitty story," Annie remarks. She suspects there may be more to her father's half-finished fairy tale. She drives her electric wheelchair to her grandmother's cabin and finds Ondine swimming in the cove. Annie decides that Ondine must be a seal woman.

While Annie desperately wants to believe that Ondine has come directly out of an enchanted world, Syracuse is too wrapped up in his own post-alcoholic euphoria to question her identity. Maura soon becomes jealous. The uglier and more evil-stepmother-like Maura, the biological mother, becomes in her possessive, aggressive behavior toward Syracuse, the more angelic Ondine, the beautiful stranger, seems. Paul McGuirk notes, "There is never any real conflict between Syracuse's position and Ondine's" (2010, 245). The real conflicts are between Ondine and Maura for Syracuse's love and attention, and between Ondine and the drug smuggler Vladic (Emil Hostina), who comes to claim her back. Maura and Ondine are responsible for the film's two deaths: Maura kills Alex in a car accident, and Ondine, who knows that Vladic can't swim, pushes him into the harbor. Both deaths inaugurate new beginnings. Annie receives a kidney transplant from Alex. Syracuse decides to marry Ondine, whose real name is Johanna, to prevent her from being deported. The wedding brings closure to *Ondine* as a contemporary fairy tale, but it also illustrates the social fact that marriage to a national citizen is one of the few ways solitary immigrants without independent means can settle legally in another country. The wedding, presented with deportation as its only alternative, makes the romance between Syracuse and Ondine more pragmatic than a Disneyfied fairy-tale ending. Although the characters seem to genuinely care for one another, the complexity of Ondine's immigration status suggests that her behavior toward Syracuse and Annie may, at least at some level, have been calculated with marriage in mind.

Yet, fairy-tale style, Ondine must prove her worth in crucial tests: she saves Annie from drowning and she kills the beast, Vladic, whom she describes to Syracuse as "a monster from a fairy tale." The fact that Ondine takes action where Syracuse hesitates exposes her bravery vis-à-vis foes stronger than she, and it reverses her role from victim to saving angel. By marrying Syracuse, she saves both him and Annie from Maura's alcoholic clutches. As McGuirk observes, "Syracuse, like many of Jordan's male protagonists, operates with extremely fuzzy and blurred boundaries. Syracuse is a rather well-intentioned, if somewhat hapless character" (2010, 245). Syracuse's passivity and selfishness, his inability to break with poisonous Maura and fully commit to Ondine, the fact that he falls off the wagon, and his many other displays of weakness of character aid in strengthening Ondine's position as the film's most caring, self-sacrificing character and stereotype her as an ideal woman.

The colonial fantasy about the sexualized, exotic woman who willingly betrays her own kind (Vladic) out of love for a White man (Syracuse) is perhaps *Ondine*'s lasting point. McGuirk explains that, like the "grumly guest" in the old Scottish ballad of the seal man of Sule Skerry who returns to claim the child he fathered with a human woman,[6] Vladic is demonized as the dark, evil foreigner

> who insinuates himself into the host community for his own advantage,
> and when he has achieved what he set out to achieve, takes away what he
> considers his right without any consideration for those whom he leaves
> behind because his allegiances lie elsewhere. Jordan's Ondine, on the other
> hand, is fully assimilated. She kills her seal-husband and thus cuts her
> ties with her other world, her home country. This is the perennial wish or
> fantasy of the host community: that, if, in what it sees as its generosity, it
> accepts "outsiders," they should assimilate and unequivocally cut their ties
> with their own culture—and by extension, remove any threat that that cul-
> ture might pose. (2010, 245)

Indeed, when Vladic accuses Ondine/Johanna of betraying him, he snarls, "You speak their language now." She counters, "You don't belong here." Her wish to belong, speak the language, and shed her old identity is valorized discursively within the film by showing how this abused, exploited Romanian woman, who is goodness incarnate, desires the flawed but essentially wholesome West, (im)personated in Syracuse's character. Eggerz takes a different perspective on this colonial fantasy in *Seal Woman*. Comparing *Ondine* to *Seal Woman* expands on the generic choices and values embedded in both works, and the ways in which folklore can serve multiple intertextual functions in postmodern texts.

SEAL WOMAN

Seal Woman incorporates the violent themes of Faroese and Icelandic selkie narratives, in which men's cruelty toward captured selkies leads to bloodshed and murder, to enable the protagonist Charlotte to process the violent events she witnessed in Berlin during World War II. Max, her Jewish husband, was humiliated, harassed, and eventually died in a concentration camp, her child disappeared, and she ended up having to prostitute herself when the Red Army entered Berlin and soldiers bought sex with food. Eggerz turns to folklore and a sense of place in order to explore the powerful motif of the dislocated, traumatized war bride in this narrative based on historical events. During the late 1940s, 314 German agricultural workers arrived in Iceland on one-year contracts. The vast majority stayed on and eventually married Icelanders (Eggerz 2008).

After the chaos of World War II, Charlotte, still reeling with pain from having lost her beloved husband and been separated from her only child, travels to Iceland to work as a contracted farm laborer. Dazed by trauma and numbed by violence, Charlotte immerses herself in the near-medieval working conditions on an isolated coastal farm in Iceland. The farmer, Ragnar, a quiet man, has lost his first wife to tuberculosis. He lives with his widowed mother, a healer fluent in the myths and lore of the land. Charlotte and the old woman form a bond of mutual respect and solidarity, but the younger woman lacks Ondine/Johanna's strong desire to assimilate culturally and linguistically. Charlotte's mind is constantly haunted by the memories of the war and her losses. Resigned to accept her new life, she eventually marries Ragnar and bears him two sons.

The novel contrasts two very different worlds: the old-fashioned, otherworldly farm in Iceland with its drudgery of physical labor and minimal comforts, and vibrant, decadent, cosmopolitan Berlin where Charlotte lived a privileged life as an artist with a caring husband. In Iceland, overcome by longing for her old life, she desires to die. She finds comfort for her distress in the legend of the seal woman, who has, in Charlotte's retelling, "two children on the land and two in the sea" (Eggerz 2008, 221). Similar to Ondine/Johanna's double identity, Charlotte identifies with the seal woman's divided self because she cannot reconcile her past with her present. In Charlotte's version, a landsman steals the seal woman's hood while she dances naked on the beach; he promises to return it if only she'll marry him. She complies, but he rescinds his promise, saying he will give the hood to her "later, after we've been married for a while" (219). She becomes a mother, and he forgets his promise. However, the sight of three dead seals on the beach, killed by hunters, awakens the seal wife's longing for the ocean. As her husband helps skin the seals, she falls ill. As soon as she is well enough, she rummages through her husband's chest until she finds her hood. Then, like Henrik Ibsen's Nora, "she walked out the door," returning to the sea (221).

Charlotte tries to drown herself twice. Eggerz frames her protagonist's unsuccessful suicide attempts and her odd memories of them with the folktale. In contrast, the descriptions of her relationship with Ragnar and the hard work on the farm are solidly grounded in historical realism. But the beach and the tug of the ocean's rolling currents draw her into a strange nowhere, a blank space harboring her repressed memories, a dark abyss aching with tumultuous pain threatening to well up and drown her. If the ocean symbolizes the destructive forces of historical change, it is significant that Ondine needs to be rescued from it, while Charlotte willingly throws herself into it.

Charlotte reaches a consciousness of being a link in a long chain of women whose entire existence has been defined by their gender roles in traditional Icelandic fishing and farming communities. "Standing high on the hill, overlooking the ocean, Charlotte felt her place in time, right behind the medieval women who had stood here, breathing in the muttony steam, seeking the longship that carried their men on the ocean" (Eggerz 2008, 164). Yet, even though the "tug of the ocean" and its "barking sound" echo her past and intrude into her present to cause chaos, they also produce in her a sense of freedom from the bonds that bind her to Ragnar and the land they work together (216–221).

Charlotte throws herself into the sea when she thinks she hears her lost child calling her. She recognizes, upon being pulled ashore, that she likes her Icelandic children's fear of losing her. In the absence of a truly caring husband, their fear makes her feel wanted: "It matched her own fear for the safety of these pups born to her in middle age" (Eggerz 2008, 18). The vocabulary of the folktale—"pups"—helps her identify her loyalties. She also finds some happiness with the clumsy Ragnar, but to her chagrin she must compete with the farm animals for his love: "She knew he'd never look at her the way he looked at a cow that gave rich milk, or at [a] horse that could carry him to the interior without a slip. But she sensed that he considered her an asset to the farm" (244). The breaking point comes the day Ragnar asks her to paint their sons and the child she lost. Art becomes an outlet that allows Charlotte to reconnect with the individualistic, creative part of herself that she has repressed in her life on the farm.

Eggerz's incorporation of the traditional selkie story projects complex images of gender roles into what appears to be a monolithic cultural landscape. Charlotte's transformation speaks of how women often learn to compromise and adapt by entering into preexisting gender roles that await them as constituent parts of any patriarchal structure. Like the selkie whose coat is taken away, Charlotte must learn to adapt to life without a magic portal back to happy prewar Berlin. In comparison, Ondine/Johanna hides her coat (a backpack full of drugs) so that she can stay in Ireland.

Ragnar's needs seem almost primitive in comparison to Charlotte's, but his life, too, is complex and hinges on forces beyond his own control. He wants a wife who can work with him on the farm. He wants children to carry on the work when he is old. Ragnar is tied to the land and his role as farmer and husband; it is the only life he knows. He does not care to know anything about Charlotte's previous life. What he wants is someone who will stay in his life, on his farm, in his country. As soon as Charlotte acquires the rudimentary vocabulary for working on the farm, he stops teaching her new words. Her inability to master Icelandic becomes a social muteness that disempowers her as woman and makes her other, stranger. It prevents her from belonging, speaking (out), or forging a sense of self strong enough to cope with the intrusion of the past into the present. Eggerz's representation of Charlotte's self-destructive inclinations thus offers a stark contrast to the way in which Jordan represents Ondine/Johanna as deftly slipping into the social position awaiting her as Syracuse's bride and Annie's stepmother. Eventually Ragnar is forced to accept as part of his responsibility that he must help Charlotte cope with her past. Unlike Syracuse, who remains the same immature boy-man throughout *Ondine*, Ragnar grows and becomes a better man.

Like the man from Myrdal who steals the selkie's coat in the folktale, Ragnar does not court Charlotte. He just says, "'Is it alright then?' His look said he meant her—and him. 'Yes,' she said for the second time in her life" (Eggerz 2008, 39). On their wedding night, she had "vowed to make love to him all night long. But suddenly he opened her legs and thrust himself inside her. It was over too quickly" (48). The next morning she wonders, "How many aprons would she wear out with no reward but this man's hands on her at night?" Amorous rewards belong to her happy days in Berlin with a sophisticated lover for a husband. The wearing out of aprons, a symbol of female domesticity, counts the days of her present reality in Iceland. For Ragnar, a wife is a first and foremost a work partner. Romance is far from his way of thinking. Grounded in the settler culture of the North Atlantic, he knows that successful farms depend on the ability of married couples to work together to ensure the survival of crops and livestock. Charlotte's romantic notions of spending the mornings making love are rudely inter-rupted by a neighing horse—Ragnar whispers, "He's happy for us"—and "the sound of chickens fussing in the henhouse" (49). There is no happy-ever-after for Charlotte, except for the possibility that she may in the end be reunited with her lost daughter. Even so, the novel hints at the complexity of such a reunion and the pain it may entail.

Eggerz's depiction of Charlotte's destiny offers a historical perspective on labor-seeking migration and settlement in northern Europe. But in spite of the novel's narrow historical focus, its attention to the individual destiny of one woman does not detract from its deeper perspective on what Gayatri C. Spivak (1988, 271–313) refers to as the silencing of the subaltern woman—economically, politically, and culturally—and the need for the subaltern to speak for herself. Charlotte's ability to "speak" through her paintings underscores Spivak's point that patriarchal Western societies' logocentrism imposes the illusion of cultural homogeneity in heterogeneous populations. The story of the seal woman allows Charlotte to understand her own transformations in nationality, location, and identity while at the same time giving narrative frame to the historical memory of migration and settlement in the coastal regions of the North Atlantic.

A POSTMODERN PERSPECTIVE ON SELKIE LORE
AND THE COASTAL CONTACT ZONE

In the broadest sense, selkie lore is about humans' relationship with nature and about the precarious boundaries that culture maintains to define humanness. At the same time, selkie tales express desires, longings, and social tensions that arise from cultural norms and gender roles in specific cultural and geographical settings. *Ondine*'s and *Seal Woman*'s generic complexity reflects and refracts the gender and identity politics performed in coastal contact zones. As contemporary retellings, *Ondine* and *Seal Woman* are situated in "a web whose hypertextual links do not refer back to one authority or central tradition" (Bacchilega and Rieder 2010, 25) but reflect the expansive "crystallization," or "interplay of multiple structures" (Walter Burkert, quoted in Zipes 2012, 9), of postmodern fairy tales.

Since the turbulent aftermath of World War II and the fall of the Iron Curtain, new patterns of cultural and national identity have emerged in Europe. In *Ondine*, the Romanian drug mule slips into the fairy-tale identity of the selkie because Syracuse and his daughter want to believe in her reality. As Ondine/Johanna says, being a selkie "is one truth." Other "truths" become meaningful in other contexts because identity is performed and negotiated situationally. Like Charlotte in Eggerz's novel, Ondine/Johanna seeks to mend a fissured identity in a tight-knit fishing community that defines itself by its homogeneity and is suspicious of strangers. Where Charlotte eventually learns to live with her scars visible and some wounds still bleeding, Jordan aims for smooth suture and a happy-ever-after in *Ondine*.

Both works support John Frow's claim that "texts—even the simplest and most formulaic—do not 'belong' to genres but are, rather, uses of them; they refer not to 'a' genre but to a field or economy of genres, and their complexity derives from the complexity of that relation" (2006, 2). Frow's understanding of texts as responding to, and organized by, "the social setting in which they occur (a setting which is a recurrent type rather than a particular time and place), and . . . the genre mobilized by the setting and by contextual cues" (16) complements Cristina Bacchilega and John Rieder's discussion of hybridization and generic complexity in contemporary fairy-tale films (2010, 26–27). They agree with Frow that "genres create effects of reality and truth" and work semiotically (2006, 19), stating, "To say that generic strategies involve an economy of genres means, first, that generic choices have values attached to them, and, second, that making those choices involves taking a position on other choices and values" (Bacchilega and Rieder 2010, 32).

In *Ondine* and *Seal Woman*, the range of values embedded in choice of genre reflects two competing but mutually informing positions. On the one hand, they demonstrate an undercurrent of nostalgia for traditional gender roles, place (Ireland and Iceland, respectively), and a mythic past (Celtic and Norse) seen as made stable by patriarchy, monocultural sovereignty, and pastoralism. On the other hand, they challenge such idyllic perceptions of the mythic past with the intrusion into the local environment of global flows stemming from wartime displacement, survivor's trauma, illegal immigration, and drug trafficking. Both texts incorporate pastoral representations of a simple life in tucked-away rural communities at the edge of the sea, but neither sentimentalizes the drudgery of work, the poverty, the sexual predation, or the xenophobia that rural isolation harbors. Rather, film and novel alike incorporate the shoreline to signify a site of cultural transmission, with female strangers coming from unknown lands—with histories muted by violence and trauma—and their attempts to settle and create families with the local men who find them.

Two main themes emerge in *Ondine, Seal Woman*, and the folklore on which they draw. First, the narratives occur in coastal contact zones, which mark a geographical frontier as well as a metaphorical border between land and sea, civilization and wilderness, the known and the unknown. The shoreline is, metaphorically speaking, a threshold with a liminal tidal zone where cultural beliefs transacted between natives and strangers, humans and animals, the natural and the supernatural collide and "compete along that border for interpretative dominance" (J. M. Harris 2009, 6). Shorelines and borders, and the cultural values and choices they represent in relation to gender and identity, offer compelling metaphors in the postmodern reworking of selkie lore in these two texts. But border sites are also heavily invested with territorial markings and performances where meaning about the female stranger, doubling as foreigner and other, is continuously produced and interpreted in terms of territorial dominance and national identity. The selkie's shedding of her skin and transformation into a woman happens precisely where ocean and land meet, and where she, being literally out of her own element, is most vulnerably exposed to a social environment alien to her own. Here, also, the landsman immediately recognizes her as a valuable prize—a bride without (apparent) kin of her own, which removes any obligation on his part to honor social duties to in-laws.[7]

Furthermore, the border locates power imbalances between naturalized citizens and illegal immigrants, which are translated into the legal language of social rights and entitlements. Jason Marc Harris points out, "Globally, borders are historically fraught with anxiety" (2009, 6), not only because invaders cross borders but because frontiers as semiotic frames establish ontological domains and thus participate in narrating human existence in relation to geographical place. In this situation, Mary Louise Pratt's definition of contact zones as "social spaces where disparate cultures meet, clash, and grapple with each other, often in highly asymmetrical relations of domination and subordination" (1992, 4) may extend to reflect the fundamental struggles between disparate, gendered, ontological domains embedded in selkie lore that involve a man who sees a seal woman shed her skin, steals it, conceals it, and forces the selkie to become his wife.

Second, as suggested by Bacchilega and Rieder (2010), one set of values and choices entails others. Said differently, culturally constructed borders participate in, interact with, and reflect upon other aspects of social organization. In my intertextual positioning of these texts, selkie lore participates on various narrative and semiotic levels in articulating desires and anxieties in human relationships with others, notably those involving specific gender roles (husband and wife) and assumptions and fears about others (illegal immigrants, strangers, animals). Animal bride tales may indeed, as Barbara Leavy argues, express universal, slanted views of women as being closer to nature than men. She states, "A basic assumption about woman is that her beast form defines her essential being" (1994, 222). But in light of *Ondine's* and *Seal Woman's* incorporation of global flows in immigration and their two female protagonists' social positioning as defined in relation to the complexity of such flows, historical time and geographical place also play a role in the representation of gender and social conflicts.

Animal bride tales may, as Leavy points out, communicate universal themes about "culture's triumph over nature" (1994, 40). However, selkie lore also thematically concerns the culture clashes Pratt (1992) refers to as taking place in the contact zone between creatures of different social domains and with disparate understandings of the world. Perceptions of seals as a different "people" with their own moral codes and cultural organization are apparent in Williamson's collection of seal legends. In one instance, three young men meet seal people "dressed in furry kind of suits. And talking among themselves, some talking in half Gaelic, half broken English and Gaelic" (2005, 131). Such descriptions suggest a perception of human-seal relations as similar to intercultural human relations and the unease and difficulties that arise in such encounters. At the same time, the reference in several of the legends collected by Williamson to seals speaking Gaelic evokes mythology about cultural and linguistic affinity between seals and humans. The seal may function as symbolic exponent of the ancient Celtic culture that historically has been oppressed linguistically, politically, and economically by the English.

The prominence of history and geographical place also means that *Ondine* and *Seal Woman* invariably evoke the *social* aspect of folktales and contemporary folktale retellings, by which I mean these two texts' commitment to think critically about historical and current issues—the aftermath of World War II for German civilians and the effects of the collapse of the Soviet Union for people in Eastern Europe; the breakdown of traditional family structure and the current downturn in the economy; and the legal and illegal international trafficking of women as brides and/or workers. The 2008–2012 financial crises that plunged Iceland and Ireland, after years of unprecedented prosperity, into severe economic hardship also invite a consideration of how *Ondine* and *Seal Woman* as cultural texts pass on allusions to the vulnerability of small national economies in late capitalism, in particular fringe economies depending directly or indirectly on larger structures like the European Union. Generic choices and values thus interact with other sets of choices and values, in which coastal contact zones function as social spaces of multivarious cultural interaction awash in "the fundamental struggle to define identity and power amid a chaotic world whose borders ebb and flow with countless perils" (J. M. Harris 2009, 6).

Postmodern trends in generic complexity and mixing do not seek to exclude the existence of meaningful generic structure. The point to recognize is that "genre is quintessentially intertextual" (Briggs and Bauman 1992, 147). The blurred boundaries between a novel or film's realism and legend or fairy tale do not dissolve ontological differences between the fictive and the factual. Rather, Linda Hutcheon observes, "The boundaries may frequently be transgressed in postmodern fiction, but there is never any resolution of the ensuing contradictions. In other words, the boundaries remain, even if they are challenged" (2002, 69). *Ondine* and *Seal Woman*, set in the "real" world at specific historical times and geographical locations, both weave strands of legend and fairy tale into the narration to destabilize or decode the way the protagonists experience the "real." The "real" is, of course, a generic strategy. As Hutcheon warns, "Our common-sense presuppositions about the 'real' depend upon how that 'real' is described, how it is put into discourse and interpreted. There is nothing natural about the 'real' and there never was—even before the existence of mass media" (31). Similarly, there is nothing "natural" about gender because it is a social construct. Jordan's invocation of the domestically inclined, persecuted fairy-tale heroine naturalizes a patriarchally endorsed female gender role as a result of his choice of genre (fairy-tale/fantasy film), while Eggerz's contrastive narrative flow between historical realism and folktale allows gender roles to remain dialogic rather than fixed.

Indeed, as Cathy Lynn Preston argues, "The blurring of the boundaries between fairy tale and legend, like the blurring of the boundaries between fiction and nonfiction, creates a site of cultural production in which social transformation has both imaginative and material possibility" (2004, 209). Noting the fragmented, piecemeal nature of fairy-tale retellings in electronic media texts and television that communicate information about gender and identity by intertextual references, Preston concludes that "contemporary texts have cumulatively achieved a competitive authority [vis-à-vis older fairy tales], one that is fragmented, multivocal, fraught with contestation, and continually emergent" (212). *Ondine* and *Seal Woman* try to make sense of human lives that have been fractured and violated by historical events. Old stories cannot save people cut adrift from their homelands and traditional way of life; rather, in both texts, new circumstances force the protagonists to generate new identities based on meaningful fragments of old stories that are repositioned and retold in relation to changes in space and time.

The colonial fantasy of "white men saving brown women from brown men" (Spivak 1988, 296) that emerges in contemporary selkie lore shows the importance of situating contact zones in the context of gender, migration, and cultural difference. In *Ondine*, Ondine/Johanna is pursued by a swarthy "seal husband." He wears black clothes, drives a black car, and eats fish out of the can using a pocketknife. He lurks, scowls, and uses violence to gain what he wants. Knowing his secrets and alien (seal) nature, Ondine/Johanna kills him. Slaying the villain/drug smuggler, though, does not make her a heroine. Her goodness and selfless willingness to assimilate into Western culture certainly ennoble her, but the position of true hero goes to a male protagonist. Syracuse becomes Ondine/Johanna's Western prince because only he can save her from deportation back to Romania (understood as a fate worse than death) by offering her marriage. In this manner, the underlying perception of Eastern Europe as violent, primitive, and dangerous is confirmed in a representation of the West as the subject of desire and the geographical site of Ondine/Johanna's happy-ever-after.

As a result of migration—be it under the banner of slavery, conquest, migration, or human trafficking—cross-cultural exchanges have generated "new and complex identities" (Loomba 1998, 175). The cultural transmutations resulting from these historical movements implicate folklore studies because, as Donald Haase argues, "creolization, multivocality, and hypertextuality" are constituent parts of the way folklore is transmitted and (re)incorporated in specific historical contexts and locales (2010, 31). Intertextuality follows global flows. *Ondine* and *Seal Woman* are only two examples of the rich body of folklore-inspired narratives in various media that demonstrate the intertextual complexity and generic flexibility of postmodern texts.

NOTES

1.   I am drawing on a version of "The Sealskin," which was first translated from Icelandic into German, "Das Seehundfell," by Åge Avenstrup and Elisabeth Treitel. It was later translated from German into English by D. L. Ashliman (2000).

2.   A large body of regional legends deals with romance between a woman and a seal man, adoptions or abductions of children by seals, humans adopting seal pups, hunters punished for killing seals, seals rewarding humans for help, seals saving humans from drowning, conflicts between seals and humans competing for ocean resources, or a combination of such themes.

3.   In addition to pelts or coats, selkie lore features belts, caps, pouches, and other objects made of sealskin as possible objects of transformation.

4.   B. S. Benedikz relates a similar narrative from Iceland, but with a seal man as the protagonist who laughs three times (1973, 4).

5.   *The Secret of Roan Inish*'s story within the story, told by Fiona's grandfather, involves an English schoolmaster who puts a collar of shame around the neck of Sean Michael, who refuses to speak English. Sean Michael eventually joins the resistance movement, traffics guns for the *fianna*, and dies in an English jail.

6.   For more details on the Orkney ballad "The Silkie of Sule Skerry," see Thomson (1980) and Williamson (2005).

7.   The gruesome conclusion to the Faroese legend from Mikladadur on Kalsoy, "The Seal Woman," shows the consequences of a miscalculation on the man's part: after returning to the sea, the seal woman visits her human husband in a dream, begging him not to kill her seal husband and pups. He ignores her plea, kills her mate and the pups, and cooks them for supper for the children he fathered with the seal woman. The seal woman comes back to curse not only him but all men of Kalsoy, saying that her revenge is not complete until so many men have drowned or fallen off the cliffs that they can reach all around Kalsoy arm in arm (Andreasen 2010).

6

"Let's All Get Dixie Fried"
Rockabilly, Masculinity, and Homosociality

Patrick B. Mullen

Rockabilly music originated as a blending of African American rhythm and blues and Anglo-American country music in the early to mid-1950s and was a significant factor in the development of rock 'n' roll. A major starting point for rockabilly was Sun Records in Memphis, Tennessee, where producer Sam Phillips made the original records by Elvis Presley, Jerry Lee Lewis, Carl Perkins, and others that helped define the sound and style of rockabilly and emerging rock 'n' roll. Some of these records became regional hits and later spread to other parts of the United States and Canada, and eventually to the rest of the world. An early Carl Perkins's song contains a phrase that expresses some of the essential traits of the rockabilly ethos. The setting is a southern honky-tonk bar where a group of men are urged by their hero Dan to join him in getting violently drunk. He does this by yelling out in their in-group language, "Let's all get Dixie fried." This song and other seminal rockabilly songs about drinking and fighting describe communal behavior that reflects and helps maintain a masculine regional culture.

Eve Kosofsky Sedgwick's concept of homosocial desire as defined in her 1985 book *Between Men: English Literature and Male Homosocial Desire* is relevant to understanding these rockabilly lyrics. This might seem like a huge stretch from Sedgwick's focus on eighteenth- and nineteenth-century British literature, but I think there is a basic similarity in the representations of masculine behavior in literary works and vernacular lyrics. There are also significant differences, and I tried to keep Sedgwick's warning in mind: "Any attempt to treat [her formulations] as cross-cultural or . . . as universal ought to involve the most searching and particular analysis" (19). A lot of

DOI: 10.7330/9780874218985.c006

what Sedgwick has to say does not fit rockabilly masculinity, and I have expanded and altered her theory to some degree, but many of her primary theoretical points do fit when they are adapted to the specific context of mid-twentieth-century American vernacular and popular culture.

She starts with the fundamental social science definition of homosocial as "social bonds between persons of the same sex . . . obviously meant to be distinguished from 'homosexual' " (1985, 1). She calls this bond "homoso-cial desire," which means not just sexual attraction or love but more broadly the "social force, the glue . . . that shapes an important relationship . . . even when its manifestation is hostility or hatred" (2). This applies equally to women's relationships with other women and those of men with other men. Relevant examples would include a women's book club or softball team, and a men's bible study group or touch football game. The easiest way to express the concept for men in everyday terms is *male bonding,* but Sedgwick's analysis is much more complex and multilayered than that term expresses. Her theory is based on a social structure that she describes as a "continuum between homosocial and homosexual—a continuum whose visibility, for men, in our society is radically disrupted" and marked by what she calls an "invisible line" (1–2).

Men in Euro-North American society tend to deny the existence of this continuum because they make a sharp distinction, represented by the invisible line, between their all-male social relationships in politics, sports, and business, and male homosexual relationships, a stance that is rooted in homophobia and based on what Sedgwick calls "obligatory heterosexuality" (1985, 2–3) and earlier what Adrienne Rich called "compulsory heterosexu-ality" (1980). It's important to keep in mind that the invisible line between all-male social relations and homosexual relations is a social construct, an imagined distinction, albeit one with very real consequences.

Some masculine homosocial behaviors can be perceived as homosex-ual; a football team holding hands in the huddle or patting each other on the behind is part of a broad cultural pattern that crosses race, class, and regional lines. Male displays of camaraderie and physical affection take place not only at football games but also at fraternity parties, bachelor par-ties (C. N. Williams 1994), bars and honky-tonks, and in buddy movies and on television. Folklorist Alan Dundes, in his 1978 article "Into the Endzone for a Touchdown: A Psychoanalytic Consideration of American Football," explained such behaviors in football as repressed homosexual-ity, but Sedgwick's theory of a homosocial continuum provides a more intricate and sophisticated explanation of the relationship of hetero- and homosexual. She implies that Freudian explanations such as Dundes's are oversimplified when she says, "The fact that [these cultural enactments] can look, with only a slight shift of optic, quite startlingly 'homosexual,' is not most importantly an expression of the psychic origin of these institutions in a repressed or sublimated homosexual genitality. Instead it is the coming to visibility of the normally implicit terms of a coercive double bind . . . For a man to be a man's man is separated only by an invisible, carefully blurred, always-already-crossed line from being 'interested in men' [in a sexual way]" (1985, 89). Masculine homosocial behavior reflects this "coercive double bind" or "obligatory heterosexuality"—terms that suggest the cultural force behind homophobia.

Masculinity scholar Trent Watts, though he does not refer to the invisible line, does offer further evidence of the cultural determination to maintain the distinction between hetero- and homosexual behavior: "[There is] an argument about sexuality that most southern white men have traditionally understood: that some instances of same-sex contact—depending upon one's role in the encounter—do not compromise one's manhood. Showering together in gym, and patting butts and holding hands on the football field, for instance, are viewed as wholesome rites of passage, and anyone noting the homosocial elements of these encounters invites condemnation as a troublemaker" (2008, 12–13). The label of "troublemaker" would probably include the authors of scholarly articles who examine homosocial behavior. Dundes did not use the term *homosocial*, but the fact that his article about latent homosexuality was met with indignant outrage by football players and fans could itself be seen as evidence of the invisible line, a public denial of the homosocial/homosexual continuum.

Sedgwick's study of homosociality emphasizes the intrinsic roles of homophobia and misogyny, especially the idea that "homophobia directed by men against men is misogynistic, and perhaps transhistorically so." She adds, "(By 'misogynistic' I mean not only that it is oppressive of the so-called feminine in men, but that it is oppressive of women)" (1985, 20). Sedgwick uses the homosocial/homosexual continuum as a means of exploring "historical power relationships," especially the domination of men over women in patriarchal societies (2). This is a concept that gender scholars term "hegemonic masculinity," "the maintenance of practices that institutionalize men's dominance over women" (Connell 1987, 185); and, an even more relevant point for my study, "homosocial interaction, among heterosexual men, contributes to the maintenance of hegemonic masculinity" (Bird 1996, 121).

Michael A. Robidoux's research on a specific homosocial group provides ethnographic evidence: "The shared male experience of professional hockey not only promotes segregation between men and women, it also segregates and devalues other men that do not fit within this hegemonic structure" (2001, 142). But Sedgwick's writing established these principles even earlier, and my study, like hers, is based on a "structural paradigm" of "the isolation" and "subordination . . . of women." This underlying structure "is a distortion that necessarily fails to do justice to women's own powers, bonds, and struggles" (1985, 18).

Homosocial desire can be seen in the rhythm and blues, country, and rockabilly lyrics under consideration here, especially in the drinking and fighting that is described in two songs. This behavior can be seen as a performance of masculinity, a social display that has an audience. Actual masculine social behavior at honky-tonks and bars provides contextual evidence to reinforce this setting as conducive to getting drunk and fighting; as country music historian Bill Malone says, "The honky-tonk was essentially a masculine retreat . . . a place to aggressively assert one's manhood" (1998, 246). Fighting among drunken men also fits Sedgwick's point about homosocial desire sometimes being expressed through "hostility" and "hatred." But what are they fighting about? Sedgwick cites an intriguing theory that helps explain masculine aggression as homosocial desire. She borrows a concept from René Girard (1965), *Deceit, Desire, and the Novel: Self and Other in Literary Structure*, to provide a more specific relational structure within the homosocial context, an idea she refers to as "the folk wisdom of erotic triangles": "Girard traced a calculus of power that was structured by the relation of rivalry between the two active members of an erotic triangle. What is most interesting for our purposes in his study is its insistence that, in any erotic rivalry, the bond that links the two rivals is as intense and potent as the bond that links either of the rivals to the beloved: that the bonds of 'rivalry' and 'love,' differently as they are experienced, are equally powerful and in many senses equivalent" (1985, 21).

I see evidence of Sedgwick's homosocial structure and Girard's erotic triangle in the descriptions of fighting in several rockabilly songs. The rivalry between men is clear in the songs' focus on their drunken fighting, but the lyrics of these particular songs leave out any references to women. How can there be a triangle? Women are not explicitly mentioned, but the circumstances of the behavior and the context in which the songs are performed imply the presence of women and an erotic triangle between a woman and two men. The rivalry between the two men is apparent, but the erotic connections between the men and the woman are hidden because, as Sedgwick would suggest, they exist on a subconscious level.

Contextual and textual evidence for the erotic triangle can be found in actual behaviors at honky-tonks and in cheating songs of this period, but pre-rockabilly country songs configure the triangle in several different ways and usually lack physical altercations between men. Country music scholar Dorothy Horstman says that cheating songs at the time omitted "any admission of damaged manhood" (1986, 199), which explains the lack of references to rivalry between a husband and his wife's lover in the songs. This could also be the explanation of why rockabilly songs about fighting don't give the reason for fighting; to do so might reveal at least one man's "damaged manhood" and undermine the very masculinity he is trying to project by fighting.

Cheating songs often concentrate on the hurt felt by the one who is being cheated on or the regrets of the cheater. For example, Floyd Tillman's "Slipping Around" (1949) is from the perspective of a married man and addressed to the woman he is having an affair with; the only reference to the other man in the song is when the married man says to his lover, "You're tied up with someone else." He is also "tied up with someone else," so there is an implied square instead of a triangle. Hank Williams's "Your Cheatin' Heart" (1952) admonishes the woman who is cheating on him without ever referring to the man (or men) she is cheating with (for other examples of cheating songs, see Horstman 1986, 197–210, 217–218, 224, 228–229).

Like "Slipping Around" and "Your Cheatin' Heart," rockabilly fighting songs and numerous other cheating songs express the erotic triangle incompletely, not laying it out explicitly but implicitly suggesting it. Some cheating songs concentrate on the emotions of the husband or wife whose spouse is cheating, and some on the man or woman who is cheating. It's as if you have to look at the corpus of country cheating and rockabilly fighting songs to discern all the complex variations of the erotic triangle or square. There are, of course, other reasons besides the erotic triangle that men fight at bars, such as any perceived insult or slight, but even here there may be a woman as intended audience for the homosocial performance of masculinity.

Scholars in masculinity studies have considered male bonding at least since Lionel Tiger's 1969 book, *Men in Groups*. He sees male bonding as biologically based behaviors that can be expressed through aggression and at times escalate to violence (158). He does not use the term *homosocial,* but later studies of male bonding use it extensively. Tiger's emphasis on male aggression and violence relates to the centrality of fighting in country and rockabilly lyrics and also fits certain categories of American masculinity identified by later gender scholars.

E. Anthony Rotundo calls one category "passionate manhood" (1993, 2–6), "the essence of which," according to Craig Thompson Friend, "was celebration of male emotions through acts of competition, aggression, force, sexuality, [and] self-fulfillment" (2009; ix, also see Bederman 1995, 22–23). These broad categories have been applied more specifically to southern manhood; for instance, Trent Watts establishes the persistence of the image of "hell-raising young men" in White southern masculinity. He speaks of a "period of wandering, especially among women, beer, and cars," as part of "the transition from boyhood to manhood" in southern culture (2008, 2). This could also describe the masculine behavior in country and rockabilly lyrics in the 1940s and 1950s.

Feminist approaches to masculinity such as Sedgwick's have been a significant part of the scholarship since the 1960s and 1970s; however, some recent scholarship downplays the power dynamic of feminist theories and focuses more on male fears and anxieties about their masculine identities. For instance, Michael Kimmel in *Manhood in America: A Cultural History* says, "Manhood is less about the drive for domination and more about the fear of others dominating us, having power or control over us. Throughout American history American men have been afraid that others will see us as less manly, as weak, timid, frightened" (2006, 4). Simon Bronner also emphasizes this masculine perspective and attaches less importance to feminist approaches in his introduction and opening essay in *Manly Traditions: The Folk Roots of American Masculinities* (2005). I think both feminist and masculinist interpretations are relevant, but my own focus will be on the gender power differential in homosociality.

In addition to the homosocial continuum, the theoretical frame for this essay draws upon my background as a folklorist who uses reflexive ethnography and autoethnography, especially their concern with the influence of subjective position on field research. Since my knowledge of rockabilly, rhythm and blues, and country music includes, in addition to research in published scholarship, personal experience as a youthful fan from the late 1940s to the early 1960s, I will incorporate into the analysis my subjective position in relation to American vernacular music during this period. Subjectivity in this case includes aesthetic judgments about music based on personal opinions that combine what I remember feeling then with what I've learned since. Specifically, my experiences include homosocial behavior as a teenager in junior high and high school and as a young adult in southern bars and dance halls similar to those described in the songs that are the subject of this chapter.

The song lyrics and my experiences can both be considered cultural representations, one composed and performed by singer/songwriters based on their experiences at the time and the other orally told or written by me based on memories of events that happened contemporaneous with theirs fifty to sixty years ago. My recollections can be classified as the traditional genre of personal experience narrative or life story which, as Jeff Todd Titon points out, are subject to the process of "fictionalizing," that is, artistically enhanced in order to engage a listener (1980). Interpreting homosociality involves the interaction between these performed cultural representations and the social behavior they are based on.

The homosocial power dynamic can be identified on several levels, including in rockabilly song lyrics, in behaviors at the bars and honky-tonks where the music was played, and in the music industry itself. As pop music scholar Sheila Whiteley points out, "The bonds which produce particular [musical] cultures (whether rock or rockabilly) are primarily homosocial, and that knowledge is highly male-centered and serves to reinforce gender boundaries" (1997, xxv). As a result, talented women rockabilly singers such as Wanda Jackson, Janis Martin, and Barbara Pittman did not receive the attention that male rockabilly performers did. They were relegated to a secondary position in rockabilly and several had to develop alternate careers in country music or gospel. Consequently, the scholarship on rockabilly has not dealt with women singers as extensively as it has with men. According to popular-music writer David Sanjek, "The milieu the predominantly Caucasian male [rockabilly] performers inhabited routinely rejected the presence of women other than as the objects of sexual appetite" (1997, 139). Even though women were left out of some song lyrics and, to a certain extent, the rockabilly music business, gender difference is essential to analyzing both.

Another essential element in understanding masculinity in vernacular music is the socioeconomic class context in which the music was played. Bill Malone refers to honky-tonk music of this period as evoking "the ambience and flavor of the working-class beer and dancing clubs where the style was born" (1998, 245). The violence that took place among men at these bars and dance halls has long been associated with their lower socioeconomic status. All of the singers and songwriters cited here (with one exception, Red Foley), both White and Black, came from hardscrabble rural working-class backgrounds and played in bars with audiences from the same class culture. I don't have enough space to go into much depth on class dimensions of the homosocial/homosexual continuum but will consider one issue—the perception of social class difference by young men within a homosocial southern dance hall context in the early 1960s.

Finally, masculinity in American vernacular music cannot be analyzed without considering the emulation by White singers, musicians, and song writers of Black masculine performance style, a historical process that can be traced back to nineteenth-century blackface minstrelsy and continues to the present (Gubar 1997; Lott 1993; Roediger 1991). As Eric Lott points out in his book *Love and Theft: Blackface Minstrelsy and the American Working Class*: "What appears in fact to have been appropriated were certain kinds of masculinity. To put on the cultural forms of 'blackness' was to engage in a complex affair of manly mimicry . . . to wear or even enjoy blackface was literally, for a time, to become black, to inherit the cool, virility, humility, abandon, or *gaité de Coeur* that were the prime components of black manhood" (1993, 52). He is describing nineteenth-century behavior, but this also is true of White male singers' emulation of Black performers in the twentieth century, especially during the period we are considering here. Examples of White male mimicry in the twentieth century would include country singer Jimmie Rodgers's emulation of African American blues singers in the 1920s and 1930s, Elvis Presley's blending of rhythm and blues and country in the 1950s, Mick Jagger's mimicry of blues and soul music in the 1960s, and White rapper Eminem taking on the cultural and musical style of Black rappers starting in the late 1990s. In all these cases and with the rockabilly singers we are focusing on, this is more than imitating a musical style; it is also assuming a Black masculine persona that White men imagined as both cool and more primitively sexual.

Like rockabilly singers, the White teenage boys who were an important fan base for rockabilly and emerging rock 'n' roll were also attracted to African American rhythm and blues. In the early 1950s, when I was thirteen, I was listening to R & B on Black radio stations in Baton Rouge, Louisiana, and Baytown, Texas, before I had even heard of Bill Haley, Elvis Presley, or any of the other White inventors of rock 'n' roll. I was aware of racial difference in the music and preferred Ray Charles, Big Joe Turner, the Penguins, Lavern Baker, and Johnny Ace to the White pop music on the radio at the time or the imitative covers of Black recordings by the Crew Cuts, Pat Boone, and Georgia Gibbs that soon followed. As a White boy who grew up in the segregated South, I associated R & B music with Black sexuality and on some level I understood that the "dirty bop," the most popular dance at Horace Mann Junior High School in Baytown, was outlawed because it was clearly based on African American dance styles. Rock 'n' roll was condemned by White southern adults as "nigger music" which, of course, made it more appealing to our rebellious instincts.

At twelve and thirteen, boys' social behavior was also rigidly homosocial; I didn't drive and was too shy to ask a girl for a date anyway, so that meant going to movies and dances with male friends. We bonded with other boys around our favorite R & B, rockabilly, and rock 'n' roll music:

we collected records, got together to listen to music, and talked about new music we heard on the radio the night before. At the time, I wasn't aware of girls bonding over their interest in popular music, but later in high school and college, I knew girls who were huge fans and socially bonded with other girls over music. In the early 1950s, an audience of White teenagers hearing R & B on Black radio was already primed for rockabilly, at that point in time the latest in a long line of musical borrowings from African Americans by European Americans.

Following in this at least century-old American cross-racial tradition, in the early to mid-1950s record producer Sam Phillips and singers Elvis Presley, Jerry Lee Lewis, Carl Perkins, and other White inventors of rockabilly and rock 'n' roll based their hybrid music on White country music, especially Hank Williams and other honky-tonk singers, and direct borrowings of Black R & B hit records of the late 1940s and early 1950s (Escott and Hawkins 1980; Morrison 1996; Mullen 1984). There were White country songs from the 1930s and 1940s that were about drinking and fighting that established this as a traditional theme for rockabilly songs.

A good example is "Tennessee Saturday Night" by Red Foley, which was a big hit in 1948. It describes a small rural town in Tennessee where people drink moonshine whiskey, or as the song puts it, "Get their kicks from an old fruit jar," and then "Somebody takes his brogan knocks out the light," and finally, "They all know the other fellow packs a gun / Ev'rybody does his best to act just right / 'Cause there's gonna be funeral if you start a fight." The repeated refrain is "Civilized people live there alright / But they all go native on Saturday night" with the word *native* suggesting primitivism and stereotypes of African Americans. There were similarly themed songs from the African American R & B tradition of the same period. "Drinkin' Wine Spo-dee-o-dee" is about wild drinking and fighting, and it was originally an R & B hit in 1949 that became a rockabilly hit in the 1950s.

I am using just two major examples of rockabilly songs in this essay, but there are others that reflect the same kind of wild behavior associated with excessive drinking including "Ubangi Stomp" and "Jungle Rock" (with the suggestion of primitivism again), "Whole Lotta Shakin' Goin' On," "Let's Get Wild," "Have Myself a Ball," "We Wanna Boogie," and "Tear It Up." Not all these songs are in homosocial settings, but many at least suggest the importance of masculine social relationships, and "Drinkin' Wine Spo-dee-o-dee" emphasizes an all-male social environment. Jerry Lee Lewis first heard Stick McGhee's R & B version of the song in 1949 when he was fourteen, and he played it at his first public performance that same year. He later recorded it and continued to play it throughout his career (Tosches

1982, 64–65). The song was widely popular among early rockabilly bands; besides Lewis it was recorded by the Rock n Roll Trio, Malcolm Yelvington, and Sid King and the Five Strings. The title refers to an African American drinking custom of the 1940s that involved taking a shot of port wine, followed by a shot of whiskey, then another shot of port. "Nice sweet jacket for all that bad whiskey," as one Black character in Jack Kerouac's *On the Road* says (1957, 68).

Stick McGhee's version of the song reveals some of its appeal for rockabilly performers and their fans. It opens:

> Down in New Orleans, where ev'rything is fine
> All them cats is drinkin that wine. (Quoted in Mullen 1984, 85)[1]

The version continues by indicating the cats' "delight / When they gets drunk, start singing all night," but they soon get to "fighting all night / Knocking down windows and tearin' out doors." McGhee enumerates their wine choices, including elderberry, port, sherry, blackberry, half 'n' half, as well as the prodigious amounts: pints, fifths, quarts, and even half a gallon. Further, the song enjoins a communal ethic:

> If you wanna get along, in New Orleans town
> Buy some wine and pass it all around.

Rockabilly versions of the song changed the lyrics slightly and in the case of Sid King and the Five Strings radically enough that it sounds like a different song. Jerry Lee Lewis's version (released in 1959) is close to the original but makes one significant change. McGhee says, "singing all night" in the first stanza, but in the second he sings, "fighting all night" and adds "Knocking down windows and tearin' out doors," emphasizing the violence. Jerry Lee drops all mentions of fighting, using "singing all night" instead, and he omits "Knocking down windows and tearin' out doors" entirely. This seems out of character for Jerry Lee Lewis, given his reputation as a wild man onstage and in his personal life. I suspect producers made the change since Lewis loved Stick McGhee's recording and had been singing the song since he was fourteen.

Two previously released recordings, Malcolm Yelvington's in 1954 and Johnny Burnette's Rock n Roll Trio in 1957, keep McGhee's reference to "fighting." Johnny Burnette sings, "They start fightin' all night," and Yelvington's goes a step beyond Stick McGhee's original with "Then they start fuckin' and fightin' all night." I think these uncleaned-up recordings capture rockabilly's masculine cultural attitude in a way that Lewis's doesn't, as rockin' as his music and vocals are. The rockabilly fighting lyrics had been around for five years before Lewis's version of the song was released, influencing and reflecting southern country masculinity.

African American dance music with lyrics that described wild drinking and partying appealed to rockabilly musicians and their audience, and reinforced their stereotyped images of Blacks as primitive, more natural and uninhibited than Whites (for more on race in vernacular music, see Mullen 1984, 2008, 117–130). The lyrics of the versions by Stick McGhee and the White rockabilly singers are similar, but the meanings could be very different with the shift from an African American to an Anglo-American context. My emphasis is on White perceptions of Black masculinity, not masculinity as Black men would define it but as White men emulated what they imagined it to be.

Both the R & B and rockabilly versions of "Drinkin' Wine Spo-dee-o-dee" are celebrations of homosocial male bonding through getting drunk and fighting. This hell-raising behavior is described as exclusively masculine. Jerry Lee addresses his "honey" once, but women aren't mentioned at all on Stick McGhee's, Malcolm Yelvington's, and Johnny Burnette's recordings. This might suggest that for men to really let loose, women as a civilizing influence must not be present. The drunken fighting is represented as pleasurable, even referred to as "their delight." This kind of masculine behavior as related to men's oppositional construction of the feminine is cited often in gender studies. For example, Elizabeth Lunbeck in *The Psychiatric Persuasion: Knowledge, Gender and Power in Modern America* says that drinking asserts "a glorious manhood unfettered by the nagging demands of women who would, had they their way, ensconce men at home, squander their wages, forbid them to drink—in short emasculate them" (1994, 245). Men are celebrating their freedom from women's control and at the same time expressing their masculinity within a homosocial setting.

There were, of course, women in the actual world of bars and honky-tonks, and there must have been fighting over women, but these rockabilly and R & B lyrics imagine a world that leaves women out, suggesting the men are completely self-sustaining—to have a good time all you need are your buddies and plenty of wine. The absence of women in the lyrics expresses a manifestation of power over them by exclusion from the social scene in which they are present in reality. As I said earlier in the chapter, women aren't referred to explicitly, but their presence is implied in the songs. As Sedgwick informs us, "The status of women, and the whole question of arrangements between genders, is deeply and inescapably inscribed in the structure even of relationships that seem to exclude women—even in male homosocial/homosexual relationships" (1985, 25).

Even though the songs seem to be all about men, women are there on a subconscious level that is necessary for maintaining misogynistic attitudes. Leaving women out of the song on an explicit level also means one corner of the erotic triangle is missing; this in itself indicates an exercise of power, removing the woman as necessary to the triangle, putting all the emphasis on the relationship between men, perhaps in some cases consciously or subconsciously moving from homosocial to homoerotic. The actual honky-tonks and bars represented in these song lyrics were, I'm sure, not limited to homosocial behavior. In spite of the invisible line, homosexual interactions must have taken place, with the participants risking homophobic violence and death.

Rockabilly covers of African American rhythm and blues songs like "Drinkin' Wine Spo-dee-o-dee," Elvis's version of Roy Brown's and Wynonie Harris's "Good Rockin' Tonight," and Billy Lee Riley's take on Billy "The Kid" Emerson's "Red Hot" were the standard at first, but it was inevitable that White rockabilly performers would write their own versions of uninhibited drinking songs. Carl Perkins was one of the first rockabilly performers to write songs that were influenced by African American music and reflected a White perception of wild Black Saturday nights in a homosocial setting. His most famous song was "Blue Suede Shoes," but he wrote another hit, "Dixie Fried," that captured the essence of the crazy drunken hillbilly rocker. It begins:

Well, on the outskirts of town, there's a little night spot.
Dan dropped in about five o'clock. (quoted in Mullen 1984, 79)[2]

Dan "flash[es] a quart" and "hollers . . . 'Rave on cats . . . It's almost dawn and the cops are gone. / And let's all get Dixie fried.'" Again, fighting starts; Dan pulls a razor, "but he wasn't shaving." The cops return and lead him away, but "Dan was the bravest man that we ever saw. / He let us all know he wasn't scared of the law." He leaves a note for his "hon" saying, "'It ain't my fault . . . that I'm in here.'"

As with the other song we looked at, this one, imaginary as it is, is still grounded in a real time and a place. In an interview Carl Perkins described the violent behavior he had observed in southern honky-tonks: "I'm talking about rough places, where half the people went there to fight . . . And a lot of these places had chicken wire around the juke box and us to keep the bottles from hitting" (quoted in Weiser 1978, 6). The interviewer asked him, "Are these the kind of clubs that inspired you to write your kind of songs?" Perkins replied, "Yep, there's no doubt about it. Yes sir." He must have had "Dixie Fried" in mind.

Like Jerry Lee Lewis's "Drinkin Wine Spo-dee-o-dee," Carl Perkins's sound is as raucous as the activities being described. To me his voice sounds especially rough and dirty when he switches from his narrator role to play Dan in the first person and his singing suggests that his raving is truly crazed. Also similar to "Drinkin Wine Spo-dee-o-dee" is the way "Dixie Fried" puts the emphasis on drinking and fighting as homosocial behavior. Women aren't mentioned in the song except for the "hon" whom Dan tosses a note to through the jailhouse bars. She isn't placed at the honky-tonk but only in the outside world where women and police could be co-conspirators to keep men under control. The lack of women and dancing in the song again places the emphasis on male bonding. There are no direct sexual references in "Dixie Fried," but plenty of alcohol and violence, perhaps indicating displaced sexuality. And again, the erotic triangle is never explicit but implied by the drinking and fighting of the male rivals.

The singer/narrator in this song is someone who was there to observe Dan's actions firsthand; he admires Dan and seems to express the group's attitude toward him: "Now, Dan was the bravest man that we ever saw / He let us all know he wasn't scared of the law." The attitude of the singer and group makes Dan a rockabilly hero whose drunken behavior, including the flashing of a razor, is to be emulated. He pays for his transgressions by being arrested and thrown in jail, but in the end he is still unrepentant, hollering from his cell, "Rave on cats . . . I've been Dixie fried."

The outsider, on-the-edge masculine hero is at least partially created out of unspoken references to race, such as the use of a widespread stereotype of Black criminal behavior at the time, the razor as weapon. Given traditional performances of "Dixie" in blackface minstrel shows and all the White southern unrepentant Confederate associations of the song, its use in this context could signify southern masculine Whiteness with an implied attempt to make their drunken behavior distinct from that of racial constructions of primitivism, to have it both ways: to behave like the imagined uninhibited Black man but to hold onto their own White identity. The song and especially the word *Dixie* took on different meanings within shifting historical contexts from the nineteenth to the twentieth century. This racial construction was so prevalent in the 1950s that it became an essential part of the invention of rock 'n' roll. As rock critic Greil Marcus says, "Rockabilly fixed the crucial image of rock 'n' roll: the sexy, half-crazed fool standing on stage singing his guts out . . . Rockabilly was the only style of early rock 'n' roll that proved white boys could do it all—that they could be as strange, as exciting, as scary, and as free as the black men who were suddenly walking America's airwaves as if they owned them" (1982, 169). I don't think Marcus meant to describe a homosocial environment, but the elements are certainly here: "white boys could do it all," they didn't need women to have a wild, uninhibited good time. There is a kind of narcissism here, with the intended audience of women rendered invisible.

The outsider rockabilly hero can be seen as dependent on the homosocial setting, away from the societal control of women in a free-for-all atmosphere of drinking and fighting. Like all heroes, Dan is to be emulated by those who consider him a hero, reinforcing culturally learned masculine behavior. Other men are attracted to him similar to the way men at a gay bar might be attracted to someone who has attributes they admire and desire except without any acknowledged sexual dimension. This attraction is another indication of the continuum between homosexual and homosocial and of the permeable nature of the invisible line, which as a social construct depends on subjectivity—certain behavior perceived in different ways by gay men and straight men (Thomas Cameron, personal correspondence, 2010).

Both "Dixie Fried" and "Drinkin' Wine Spo-dee-o-dee" are good examples of upbeat rockabilly dance music, and one of the ironies here is that the songs don't mention dancing at all. It's as if fighting has replaced dancing, and this seems appropriate given the implied homosocial meaning of the songs and the social environment in which they are set. Even though it's usually alright for women to dance with women, men can't dance with other men because that would be perceived as homosexual; fighting then becomes a violent replacement for dancing. Think of all the movies in which fighting is accompanied by rock music and the connection becomes more apparent. Also, many men who go to honky-tonks without women *almost* dance with other men while standing around the dance floor watching the dancers. Moving in time with the music with another man is okay as long as you don't touch him, face him, or dance behind him, but keep your gaze on the dance floor. Homophobia demarcates the invisible line even as men dance inches apart and sometimes accidentally touch. If the touch is perceived as not accidental, that is enough to start a fight.

The homosocial/homosexual continuum can be found across socioeconomic class boundaries, from men's book discussion groups to pickup basketball games, from college fraternity parties to labor union meetings. But are there different perceptions of homosocial behavior in different social classes? For instance, how is fighting and drinking perceived differently by class? The middle and upper-middle class often perceive lower socioeconomic working-class men as being more violent. Since country and rockabilly music originally came from southern rural working-class people and continue to be associated with them, the drinking and fighting depicted in lyrics still conjure up class images.

To cite a personal example, when I was in college in southeast Texas in the early 1960s, my friends and I would go to a rock 'n' roll bar in Louisiana on Saturday nights where we could buy liquor at eighteen. It was similar to southern honky-tonks of the 1940s and 1950s in terms of loud dance music played by local bands, excessive drinking, and frequent fighting. Most of the young men there, from whatever class background, came with other men, not with dates; there were some couples but women also came mainly with other women. Some men asked women to dance and on some occasions a woman asked a man to dance, but much of the social interaction was within two groups, one made up of women and the other of men, definitely what we would now call a homosocial gathering.

There was a perceived class difference between the college boys and the local guys our age. We were in college, and they were already working at local refineries and chemical plants. We saw them as tough and pugnacious, ready to brawl at the slightest provocation. I don't know how they saw us—perhaps as "wimps"—with good reason, since we fit the stereotype. Fights broke out among the locals every time we went to the Big Oak, but our college group assiduously avoided them. Bouncers threw brawlers out, so most of the altercations took place in the parking lot, and when we college boys went back to our car we carefully walked as far away from the fights as we could. This was so in spite of the fact that most of us came from working-class backgrounds and were the first generation from our families to go to college. Upward mobility and going to college were enough to make us and our working-class age cohorts aware of class difference even though we both behaved in similar ways, getting drunk and running in packs. Both socioeconomic groups were engaged in homosocial behavior, but the working-class guys seemed more likely to fight, at least as we perceived them. Neither group was conscious of any of this as homosocial or homosexual in any way. We both maintained the invisible line; we both were homophobic and misogynistic in our unspoken assumptions. I don't want to generalize too broadly from this personal subjective example, but I suspect the pattern might be borne out more widely in American social class behavior. More research is needed.

We had fun, we got drunk, we danced on the sidelines, and all with little interaction with women. Not that we didn't want to be with women, to dance with them or take a woman out to the car to "make out." Whenever

I tell personal stories about going to the Big Oak I mention wanting desperately to dance with one girl from my college who was "cute" and a great dancer—so good that one of the bands named a song after her, "Band Doll," obviously a sexist term, but that word wasn't in our vocabulary or our consciousness at the time. I worked up the nerve to ask her to dance only once, and dancing with her was the high point of my Big Oak experiences. Our focus on her presence suggests an underlying erotic triangle, but for college boys one that lacked fighting with another guy over a woman. From my observation, the locals behaved in similar ways—they drank, they hung out together, and periodically they would ask a girl to dance. The big difference was they fought and we didn't. The masculine behavior of both male groups offers evidence to support Sedgwick's theory of a homosocial-homosexual continuum with misogynistic and homophobic implications, but this was also, in some ways, an expression of our social isolation from women.

There was a power dynamic in pretending we didn't need women, but there was also an implicit desire for women we were denying. We were bonding with each other in ways that suggested homosocial desire in Sedgwick's sense of "the social force, the glue . . . that shapes an important relationship," and at the same time coping with the lack of women in our lives. Our male bonding sent out a message that we didn't need women, but of course we did. Viewing women as unnecessary and even antithetical to the masculine urge to get drunk was a means of expressing dominance over them, but the concept of homosocial desire also suggests a need for women that fulfills the man-to-woman connection in the erotic triangle. This would also be true in honky-tonk and rockabilly lyrics that leave women out—implying the ironic nature of homosocial desire, the denial of needing women as an underlying expression of the need for women. Sedgwick's concept of homosocial desire is a structural pattern, a deeper level of meaning that performers in the social drama are not always conscious of. Performing masculinity often obscures the meaning of the performance from the audience and the performer.

One of the conclusions I can draw from my examination of social class, race, gender, and sexual representations in vernacular music lyrics and male behavior of this period is that all of them exist in continua that are disrupted by artificial constructs that have negative social and cultural consequences. Within the vernacular songs we've considered there is homosocial behavior that is part of a continuum that must be denied by heterosexual men because of their homophobia and their need to prove their masculinity. There may be a biological difference between heterosexuals and homosexuals, but that is not what the homosocial/homosexual invisible line is about.

It's about perceptions of difference grounded in homophobia and misogyny maintained culturally over a long historical period. Obviously, imagined differences are also basic to the maintaining of class, gender, and racial divisions. For instance, as Henry Louis Gates Jr. pointed out over twenty-five years ago, "Race, as a meaningful criterion within the biological sciences, has long been recognized to be a fiction" (1985, 4), and class, gender, and sexual orientation also depend on imagined social constructs for their divisiveness and manifestations of power.

Finally, though, and ironically, American vernacular music itself undermines all the divisions that have been socially constructed to keep us apart because the music ignores the boundaries between class, race, gender, and sexual orientation and produces instead a wonderful mixture of ethnic, regional, class, gender, and racial elements in rock 'n' roll, country, R & B, jazz, hip-hop, Cajun, zydeco, conjunto, salsa, Latina, and on and on (Spitzer 2003). James Baldwin expressed this idea more eloquently than I ever could: "Each of us, helplessly and forever, contains the other—male in female, female in male, white in black and black in white. We are a part of each other" (1985, 690).

NOTES

1. For the full text of this song, please see http://www.lyricsfreak.com/s/stick+mcghee /drinkin+wine+spo+dee+o+dee_20188840.html.

2. For the full text of this song, please see http://www.lyricsfreak.com/c/carl+perkins /dixie+fried_20780589.html.

7

Man to Man
Placing Masculinity in a Legend Performed for Jean-François Bladé

William G. Pooley

A FOLKLORIST AND A LEGEND-TELLER

In the writings of nineteenth-century European folklorists, gender's influence is sometimes obvious but often obscure. In a period when male domination of the public sphere and literary writing went largely unchallenged, collectors offered far fewer gendered assessments of their male informants than of the women whose traditions they gathered. Nor did they reflect upon the fact that, with only a few exceptions, folklorists and collectors of the time were men. If it is important to think about how their own masculine identities shaped folklorists' misogyny and myopia toward female informants (Kodish 1987), a related and more covert challenge is to discover how ideas about gender operated in relationships where they went unremarked or unmarked: those between men. In this chapter, I take up these issues in the work of Gascon fieldworker Jean-François Bladé (1827–1900). In his collections' introductions, Bladé wrote about female informants in very gendered ways, describing their innocence and purity or reminiscing about the songs and stories of the female servants of his youth (1881). In contrast, there is a telling silence when it comes to characterizing the men he collected from. Here I explore Bladé's construction of masculinity and consider its impact not only on his collecting but also on his understanding of folkloristic concepts, most notably that of authenticity.

Jean-François Bladé was born into a bourgeois family in the town of Lectoure in southwestern France in 1827 (see Alleman 1930; Courtès and Bordes 1985; Lavergne 1904). Over his lifetime, he worked as a notary and judge and wrote works of fiction and history (see the bibliography compiled

DOI: 10.7330/9780874218985.c007

by Pic 1985), but today he is best remembered for his monumental collections of songs, stories, and proverbs, which earned him the posthumous title of the "Grimm of Gascony" (Lafont and Anatole 1970, 685). While the Brothers Grimm have been the subject of much academic research, beyond biographies little has been written about Bladé since his death in 1900. Critical analysis of his work consists largely of a colloquium held in his native town of Lectoure in the 1980s and several articles by Patricia Heiniger-Casteret (Arrouye 1985b; Heiniger-Casteret 2004, 2009).

In this chapter I look at Bladé's relationship with the one informant to whom his name is linked for posterity, the mysterious Guillaume Cazaux. According to the register of births, marriages, and deaths in the Archives départementales du Gers, Cazaux was a former *domestique*, born in 1782 in St. Mezard. He died in 1868 in Lectoure, just a year after Bladé left the town for good. One of Bladé's biographers devoted a whole chapter of her work to this octogenarian storyteller (Alleman 1930, 168–211), and the narratives Cazaux told Bladé have even appeared as a separate edition (Lafforgue 1995). The figure of this informant, whom Bladé called his most "defiant" (Bladé 1885, 32) dogs the memory of the folklorist like his shadow.[1]

At first glance, the men could not be more different. Bladé attended the seminary in Auch and then law school in Toulouse and Bordeaux before going on to Paris (Alleman 1930, 101–135), where he moved in bohemian circles and became a confessed disciple and friend of the poet Charles Baudelaire (Lavergne 1904, 8). Cazaux, by contrast, was completely illiterate. Bladé left an enormous quantity of written work that mixed autobiography with other genres. Cazaux left no such traces for later researchers and only some sparse archival references document his life. Today we know Cazaux through what Bladé wrote about his "suspicious," and apparently secretive, narrator, and through the texts of the stories Cazaux told the collector.

AUTHENTICITY, GENDER, AND THE HISTORY
OF FOLKLORE COLLECTING

The legacy of nineteenth-century European folklorists is overshadowed by suspicions of forgery and fraudulence. In France, one of the most popular and influential works of the first half of the century, Théodore Hersart de la Villemarqué's collection of songs entitled *Barzaz Breiz* or "The Bard of Brittany," published in 1839, was outed as a "fake" by François-Marie Luzel almost thirty years later, in 1868 (Postic 1997). Despite the best efforts of the generation of determined fieldworkers and theorists between the 1870s and the start of the twentieth century, this taint has never fully been dissipated

(Laurent 1989). For writers such as Michel de Certeau, Dominique Julia, and Jacques Revel (1986), James Lehning (1995), and Marie-Noelle Bourguet (1976), the rather odd bunch of men who called themselves *traditionnistes*— there are no well-known French female fieldworkers from this period—were part of a growing romantic obsession with popular culture, an obsession that hinged on the "beauty of death." Popular culture was first repressed, and then mourned by the very agents who repressed it (de Certeau, Julia, and Revel 1986). Bourguet, along with de Certeau, Julia, and Revel, suggests that in seeking out the purest and most pristine expressions of a disappearing bucolic world, or campaigning to eradicate the dangerous popular "superstitions" that still "survived," folklorists essentialized the rural populations they studied (Bourguet 1976; de Certeau, Julia, and Revel 1986). If the most obvious essentialization involved class, associating folklore exclusively with agricultural laborers, a similarly essentializing attitude to gender predominated. According to Jennifer Fox, the influence of Johann Gottfried von Herder encouraged male folklorists to see traditions and tradition bearers in dualistic terms based on gender (1987).

This selectivity renders collections of songs, stories, and proverbs like Bladé's problematic, but should it make them unusable? I want to suggest that this outcome is not only unsatisfying, it also sidesteps the interest and importance of even the most suspect folklore collections. If all literature is written by authors in conversation with other writers and acquaintances, folklore collections offer an extreme case, not simply composed by the person whose name appears on the cover but by other storytellers, singers, and informants. Criticisms about the authenticity of folklore collections are built on an understanding of authorship that gives all agency and all responsibility for their contents to the men who published them. No leeway remains for the ways that the results refract conversations between the folklorists and the folk.

Giuseppe Cocchiara's *The History of Folklore in Europe* remains a standard account, examining how early modern period ideas about "primitives," "savages," the "Orient," the New World, and national identity coalesced into an interest in the traditions of "the people" (1981). Originally published in Italian in 1952, Cocchiara's book deals with ideas and theorists, and takes little interest in the practices of folklore collecting. His list of "folklorists" includes a number of thinkers who never undertook fieldwork, many of whom did not call themselves folklorists, not least because the term *folklore* did not appear until 1846. Such an intellectualized focus on the history of the discipline ignores two important issues. The first is the possibility, central to the study of popular history, that the folk themselves and their traditions were constantly changing, rather than a timeless culture to be discovered outside of elite culture. The second is the insight that contact between fieldworkers and performers was not a fixed situation but an evolving conversation.

Three strands of the history of folklore—the history of ideas, the history of popular culture, and the social history of collecting folklore—cannot be dissociated. On its own, the history of ideas loses its grounding in the ways that informants, folklorists, publishers, and readers behaved. The history of popular culture also suffers from this severance; no "popular" culture can be independent of its "invention" by elites (see P. Burke 1978, especially 65–87; S. Kaplan 1984). Between these two diverging research threads stands the story of how collectors and informants oriented themselves to one another, and how such relationships changed. The fact that the fieldworkers were men stands at the center of this knot, silently coloring their attitudes to authenticity and authority. Rather than portraying fieldworkers as what Diane Tye has called an "invisible force," objectively recording authentic traditions (1993, 115), this chapter focuses on how masculinities operated in the interactions between men like Bladé and Cazaux.

THE "CAUSE OF FOLKLORE": AUTHENTICITY AND BLADÉ'S COMBATIVE MASCULINITY

Bladé's biography points to a man who embodied culturally specific ideals of masculinity. As a notary and part-time judge, Bladé belonged to a provincial elite of *notables*, the French term for the well-to-do (see Singer 1983). He mixed with the bourgeoisie and aristocracy at a local salon (Larrieu-Duler 1981, 100). His professional status conferred legal authority on him, and he bolstered this with a series of publications on history and folklore, which established him as the point of reference for subsequent Gascon folklorists (Lafont and Anatole 1970, 685). He married, and his son Étienne went on to a successful career in the bureaucracy. In the different spheres of law, family, and local and national erudition, Bladé possessed an easy authority. And yet, it is striking how insecure this authority appears in his writings. Regina Bendix has written that "invocations of authenticity are admissions of vulnerability, filtering the self's longings into the shaping of the subject" (1997, 17). Bladé described a reassuringly authentic and stable concept of popular traditions, a concept intertwined with ideas about gender. But his writings appear to be a constant battle against male adversaries, as if the power he wielded as a wealthy and successful man was not secure but had to be constantly defended.

Bladé was forthright about his attitudes to popular traditions, referring to "our peasants" as the bearers of the traditions he sought out (1885, 35). In his thinking, this stability was associated with a sense of place, class, and education. The best informants were peasants from the countryside, illiterate men and women with stable memories, rather than those who changed their materials from performance to performance:

> It is principally among those who cannot read that one must seek the real informants [*témoins*]; because those who cannot read do not rely on what Montaigne called "the memory of paper."
> At the beginning of my research, like many of my colleagues, I fell upon a certain type of narrator, undoubtedly the most common, but who only merit limited trust. For them, the integrity of the story is not guaranteed by any hallowed form. Little concerned with style, and preoccupied above all with ideas and facts, they are always verbose, diffuse, and completely unable to restart their narration in the same terms. These are very dangerous guides, whose only use is to put one onto the trail of more exact and sober narrations. Those who possess such narrations get to the point by the quickest means. If one asks them to restart, each one constantly does so in the same terms. When one makes them treat the same theme separately, one finds but a small number of variants in the facts, and one notices numerous similarities in the style. (Ibid., 29–30)

A critic of the reliability of his predecessors, Bladé also struggled with his own conception of where authenticity resided. Composed in the period after Villemarqué's ballad collection had been denounced by Luzel, Bladé's writings on history and folklore refer to fakes and frauds and the "reprehensible practices" of the *Barzaz Breiz* (1885, 22). Bladé's first academic writings were denunciations of falsified historical documents, and he continued to publish vitriolic articles on medieval manuscripts and the origins of the Basques (1861, 1862, 1869).

Perhaps this vehemence stems partly from projected guilt (see especially Salles-Loustau 1985; Traimond 1985). In a poem reproduced after his death, Bladé referred to one of his enemies as "haunted by the demon of literature" (quoted in Lavergne 1904, 14). He castigated rival folklore collections for "smel[ling] of provincial romanticism from a mile away" (Bladé 1885, 25). Similar accusations were later applied to Bladé himself (see for example, Arrouye 1985a, 8; Lafont and Anatole 1970, 365). By locating the authenticity of the stories he collected in the anonymity of "our peasants" and yet simultaneously preferring certain skilled narrators, many of whom were dead by the time his collections were published, Bladé founded his publications' credibility on his own romantic sensibility. He wrote of his deep, affective link to his native Gascony in terms that stressed his nostalgia and pain as well as a world in the process of disappearing: "For more than a quarter of a century I have traveled through the pale world of memories, haunted by visions of the ancestors. Many times dreams of the past consoled me for the sorrows of the present. The select few [can author] individual works of genius. As for me, I am a good witness. I listen and retell the old songs and legends of times gone by. It is enough to gild my declining life, and to raise a poor researcher to the powerful and calm joys of the great poets" (1885, 42).

Subsequent researchers have pointed out that this self-image licensed Bladé to modify and touch up the narratives he collected (Lafforgue 1995; Salles-Loustau 1985; Traimond 1985). But the question of recasting or rewriting is complicated. Bladé was caught between his role as a special witness to the dying traditions and his belief in an intangible, ephemeral, and disappearing rural memory. This dilemma led him to a strangely self-defeating conclusion; Bladé wrote that the "veritable traditions" had in fact been destroyed by his own work. He suggested the scenario of "a critic . . . [coming] to investigate my aptitude and sincerity as a collector." This critic would discover all of the tales and legends Bladé collected, but only because his published works were so successful that they had been read to all of the "little peasants" of the region. Authenticity resided in the anonymous oral tradition uncontaminated by literacy, but Bladé imagined that his own fieldwork would destroy this aural purity. The critic who heard the stories "would have taken simple echoes for the sounds of the first origin" (1885, 29). His ideas on these issues were clearly confused, as if Bladé still clung to an "outdated" romanticism (Anatole 1985, 14) at the same time as he wanted to be a part of the new, more rigorous group of collectors, such as Luzel and Félix Arnaudin. Bladé spoke of his "brutal fidelity" (1885, 32) to the words of his informants and his role as a "good witness" (42).

If his folklore collections' introstuctions are structured around fond childhood memories and romantic descriptions of Gascony, the footnotes in his more academic *Études sur l'origine des Basques* [Studies on the Origins of the Basques] are characterized by aggression. He refers to his two greatest scholarly rivals, Augustin Chaho and Justin Cénac-Moncaut, as variously "old," "mad," "infectious," "liars," "worthless," and "beneath criticism" (1869, 61, 62, 70–71, 215, 229, 265, 286). He labels their work "mirages," "trickery," and "etymological fantasies" (339). At one point, he refers to Cénac-Moncaut's "innate penchant for falsehood" (465). These accusations are tempered by sudden outbreaks of heroic generosity on Bladé's behalf, mitigated with snobbery: "M. Cénac-Moncaut is no doubt an excellent man; but it is a complete waste of time trying to discuss any point of political or literary history with him" (449).

These polemics over documentary authenticity have less to do with the "analytical method" that Bladé laid claim to in the introduction (1869, i) than a form of competitive masculinity in which he professed his own sincerity and honor while pouring insults on his literary enemies. Robert Nye has suggested that nineteenth-century French bourgeois masculinity owed more to an aristocratic, even ancien régime model of honor than to the contemporary ethic of hard work (1993).[2] Bladé's comments about toil and determination in his historical works seem to fit this model, emphasizing heroic efforts rather than simple laboriousness. He describes his "ardor," the "size of the obstacles" to be overcome, "attacking the difficulties" and the "difficult and perilous" nature of this work (1869, i, 364). Behind these comments, it is always possible to identify a model of Bladé the academic warrior, engaged in combat for the "cause of folklore" (1881, 2:x).

A VISION OF CAZAUX

Bladé perceived the man he considered his most important informant through his own combative vision of masculinity. Most readers first meet Guillaume Cazaux not through the words of his stories but in the visual and personal description Bladé wrote in the introduction to the collection:

> Cazaux caused me much more difficulty [than the other informants]. He was an old man, quite plump, with a muddy complexion, seamed with a thousand wrinkles, with small, lackluster, and misty eyes, dressed, according to the season in either a gray frock or a coarse, blue woolen outfit, but whatever the weather he wore his otter skin cap. From working with his hands for more than sixty years, this illiterate octogenarian had saved up enough to buy a little garden, so he could live soberly in his small house in Lectoure in one of the little streets next to the place d'Armes. After the death of my poor father, I voluntarily managed Cazaux's interests, and he never failed to come the day after each payment was due to claim the small amount of income that I collected for him. During one of these visits, I discovered by chance that I was in the presence of a totally outstanding narrator, acquainted with [a large amount of material], superstitious in completely good faith, but more defiant on his own than all my previous informants [*témoins*]. In order to tame him, I made all sorts of submissions and used the treasures of a diplomacy conquered by ten years of practice. But Cazaux never talked except when he wanted to.
>
> During the warm weather, we would meet, every evening, on the corner of the road that comes off the end of the Esplanade, which dominates the

vast countryside, closed off in the distance by the vague blue line of the Pyrenees. Once he was certain that the two of us were alone, Cazaux grew thirty years younger. His gaze lit up. In his slow, serious voice, he dictated, with ample and serious gestures, sometimes silencing himself in order to gather his thoughts, or cast a suspicious look around us. I wrote rapidly, and later corrected the texts under the sometimes tyrannical control of my narrator. I know for certain that Cazaux held back from telling me things and that he died thinking me unworthy of noting half of what he knew. (1885, 31–32)

Aside from the importance this description ascribes to the markers of class, such as rustic clothing and a body molded by the vicissitudes of labor, the clearest message that emerges is Bladé's concern with domination and resistance, suspicion, honor, and worthiness.

This element of competition and struggle is less evident, if not completely absent, in Bladé's descriptions of his female informants. Unlike in his treatment of Cazaux, Bladé emphasized the purity and innocence of the women who sang for him and told him stories, regretfully writing that he knew Catherine Sustrac when she was "young, simple, naive," but that the forty-year-old had lost her "most precious gifts" and "virginal clarity" from her exposure to the world (1885, 31). The importance of feminine innocence to his idea of authenticity finds its most extreme representation in the figure of Sereine, the possibly fabricated young girl whom Bladé described in the introduction to his collection of folksongs. "All of the poetry of my *pays* [region], Gascony, came to life, fresh and rejuvenated, in the soul of this child" (1881, 1:xxviii). One evening, when they were alone, Sereine told the young Bladé that she would be dead by the next day. Under the influence of his grandmother, Bladé resolved to collect the poetry of his *pays* as a tribute to the now-dead girl (xxix–xxx). This apparently autobiographical episode has aroused the suspicions of Jean Salles-Loustau, who points out that it bears a striking resemblance to a short story by Gérard de Nerval published many years before (Salles-Loustau 1985, 198).

COLLECTING PRACTICES: FROM BLADÉ'S VISION TO CAZAUX'S SPEECH

Bladé's statements about the authenticity of his collections and his attitudes to gender are troubling, but there are clear dissonances between Bladé's statements about his collecting and the materials actually found in *Contes populaires de Gascogne* [Folktales of Gascony]. An obvious one concerns class. Bladé's informants were nowhere near as socially homogenous or as illiterate as his reference to "our peasants" suggests. In fact, he collected stories from his uncle, who was a relatively well-off local priest as well as from his aristocratic grandmother, the local judge with whom he worked in his professional capacity as a notary, and even his own son, Étienne, who went on to a career in the Parisian administration.

Even more crucially, comparing Bladé's statements about his informants to the materials he published reveals that Cazaux plays a disproportionate role in Bladé's self-representation as a folklorist. Cazaux, who earns a longer description than the rest of Bladé's informants put together, is an important male storyteller but, contrary to what subsequent writers have assumed (Lafforgue 1995), he was by no means Bladé's most prolific narrator. Cazaux told Bladé nineteen stories, while Pauline Lacaze told twenty-seven. Bladé's judgments about the importance of his narrators were not a reflection of how many stories or songs they gave him. In the case of Cazaux, they seem paradoxically opposite; he was an important storyteller because of what he refused to say (see Pooley 2012).

Evidence of Bladé's fieldwork methods is based largely on Patricia Heiniger-Casteret's 2009 discovery of some of his fieldnotes, all of which were thought to have been destroyed. Heiniger-Casteret suggests that Bladé recorded some materials verbatim while he sketched only outlines of others. In order to supplement this understanding of Bladé's practices and how they interacted with the world of his informants, I turn to the example of a legend that Bladé recorded from Cazaux. Instead of starting from a default position that questions whether the text is absolutely faithful to the words of the informant—surely a chimeric ideal in any case—I want to ask what kinds of conversation are enacted by the words of the story and the scholarly apparatus that Bladé builds around them. If the visual description of the preface speaks in Bladé's voice about the "defiance" of Cazaux, what message do the words Bladé printed in the name of Cazaux convey?

The following is my own translation from Bladé's French text, supposedly itself a translation from the "birth dialect" of Cazaux, Gascon. Bladé placed a series of factual notes and corrections throughout the text that merit attention for the ways in which they interact with Cazaux's story.

The Legend Text: "My Uncle from Condom"

> I had an uncle (God bless him!) who died at an old age in Condom, a long time ago now. He lived out of town on the road to Nérac. My uncle was a very smart man. But he had such a simple air, so simple that no one suspected a thing. By doing more than one type of work he had enough to live

off his profits. In his youth, before the great Revolution, my uncle was first a valet for a horse dealer and for a long time went round the fairs of the Grandes Landes and those of the Pyrenees, from Bayonne to Perpignan. Later he worked for himself and became a smuggler.

My uncle learned a lot from this life, which helped him later on. He understood and spoke the languages of the countries he had traveled through. He knew all the paths to follow to avoid the police. He knew which farms you could find some dinner and somewhere to sleep if you paid well enough, without the fear they would sell you out. My uncle often gave gifts to women whose husbands were in power, golden jewelry, silk fabric. More than once he even lent them money, which he never saw the color of again. That's how my uncle came to have more than sixty thousand francs, without ever having been tortured nor put in prison.

When the great Revolution drove out the priests and the nobles, the good, brave man changed his line of work. He earned as much as a thief by secretly taking people into Spain, people who were being hunted down to be guillotined. I bet that in that period alone he would have built up almost forty thousand francs, if he hadn't been forced to leave three-quarters of it to those thieves in positions of power who were protecting him.

My uncle, and he was no liar, he told me lots of things that happened to him. Here are two that are worth retelling.

As a child, you must have seen the abbé de Ferrabouc, who died the parish priest of Saint-Mézard.[3] During the Revolution, this abbé fled into Spain, and it was my uncle who took him to the frontier. They wanted to go by Saint-Bertrand-de-Comminges[4] to reach the valley of Aran.[5] But they were warned that the routes were guarded throughout the Pyrenees all the way to Foix.[6] My uncle and the abbé de Ferrabouc were therefore forced to make a large detour through Languedoc in order to get, via Limoux and Aleth, to a wild and wooded part of the country called Capcir.[7] This region borders on the Spanish Pyrenees; they speak Catalan there. But it belongs to France. The people of Capcir are not bad people, except there is a race of men there who kill Christians when they can, and eat them raw, or cooked in the oven.

My uncle had heard about that, but he wasn't sure it was true. He spoke and understood Catalan as well as anybody, but he pretended not to know a word. As for the abbé de Ferrabouc, he didn't understand one bit.

So my uncle and the abbé de Ferrabouc found themselves one evening at seven in the region of Capcir, two leagues from the Spanish frontier. They were famished and didn't have the strength to put one foot in front of the other.

"Monsieur l'Abbé," said my uncle, "here is a charcoal burners' hut. Let's go in to eat something and sleep. Tomorrow, we will set off before daybreak and we will be in Spain before sunrise."

"As you wish, my friend."

The two of them went into the hut, where they found seven people eating their supper, three men, a woman, and three children, the eldest of whom was not yet twelve. The two travelers were not badly welcomed. They were given something to eat and drink. The eldest charcoal maker knew a little of the Gascon *patois* [dialect], but my uncle pretended not to understand Catalan.

At nine, the old charcoal maker said to his three children in their language: "It's late. Go to bed."

"No," said the eldest. "I want to eat one of the priest's legs."[8]

So the old charcoal maker took a stick and drove out the children. My uncle was still pretending not to understand.

"Ha, ha, ha! Monsieur l'Abbé," he said, laughing, "pretend to laugh like me. If you don't, we are lost. Ho, ho, ho! These charcoal makers belong to a race of men who kill Christians when they can, and eat them raw, or cooked in the oven. Hee, hee, hee!"

"Ha, ha, ha!" said the abbé de Ferrabouc. "We both have our knives and our steel-tipped canes. Ho, ho, ho! Let's try and get out of here without injury. Hee, hee, hee!"

"My friend," said my uncle, "we would like to go to sleep."

The old charcoal maker led them to a little room full of straw. "Sleep there, and don't worry or fear. Tomorrow morning we will give you some breakfast before you leave. Good night."

The charcoal maker left, and my uncle heard him say to his wife: "In an hour, those two men will be sleeping like logs. Get my knife ready. We have enough to eat well for two weeks."

But my uncle had already softly, softly opened the little window of the room. One minute later, he and the abbé de Ferrabouc were outside and fleeing toward the Spanish frontier.

That's what happened to my uncle in the region of Capcir. Now I'll tell you what he saw and heard in the Grandes Landes.

My uncle had taken a noble to Spain, I can't remember his name. The journey went well, and the noble left France through the mountains at Saint-Jean-Pied-de-Port, in the Basque country. My uncle was returning alone across the Grandes Landes through the pine forests with fifty well-earned gold *louis* that he was carrying hidden under his clothes in a leather belt. It was the night of Saint-Jean.[9] It could have been around eight.

All of a sudden, my uncle heard metal clashing behind him and horses at full gallop.

"The police!"

Immediately, he jumped off the road into the pine trees and hid in a thicket. The police went by, still at full gallop, and went off, I have no idea where to. So my uncle thought to himself: "Those people certainly weren't after me. But it would be best not to find myself in their way. It's a nice night. I will sleep outside, under a pine tree."

So my uncle pressed deeper into the woods and lay down on the sand at the bottom of a pine tree as tall as a bell tower, careful to keep his dagger and his steel-tipped cane within hand reach. He quickly fell asleep. He was woken by the sound of little voices shouting just as the stars signaled midnight.

"Hee! Hee!" came the voices from the top of the pine tree as tall as a bell tower.

"Hee! Hee!" came the reply from the tops of the other trees.

"Hee! Hee!"

At the same time, all sorts of different spirits fell onto the sand like rain, in the form of flies, glowworms, dragonflies, crickets, cicadas, butterflies, stag beetles, horseflies, wasps, but not a single bee. From underground other spirits swarmed out in the form of lizards, toads, frogs, salamanders, and men and women the size of a thumb, dressed in red and with golden tridents.

Immediately, all of these people began to romp around and dance in a circle on the sand, on the tips of the stalks of grass, the heath and the gorse bushes. The spirits sang as they danced:

> "Hee! Hee!
> All the little plants
> In the fields
> Flower and seed
> On Saint-Jean's day.
> Hee! Hee!"

Half dead with fright, my uncle made the sign of the cross. But the spirits kept on singing as they danced:

> "Hee! Hee!
> All the little plants
> In the fields
> Flower and seed
> On Saint-Jean's day.
> Hee! Hee!"

So my uncle was no longer scared, and thought to himself: "These spirits are nothing to do with the Devil and his nasty lot. They mean no harm to Christians."

All of a sudden, the dancing and singing stopped. The spirits had seen my uncle.

"Man, my friend, don't be afraid. Come, come and dance and sing with us."

"Spirits, thank you. I have traveled a long way and I am too tired to do as you do."

So the spirits began to sing and dance.

"Hee! Hee!
All the little plants
In the fields
Flower and seed
On Saint-Jean's day.
Hee! Hee!"

The ball lasted until daybreak. Immediately, the flying spirits went back up into the sky, the others went back underground, and my uncle found himself alone, lying on the sand at the bottom of a pine tree as tall as a bell tower.

[Bladé notes:] *Told by the late Cazaux, of Lectoure. Belief in both cannibal mountain dwellers in the Pyrenees and in benevolent spirit gatherings during the night of Saint-Jean is still widespread in Gascony. But the details concerning the uncle from Condom and the abbé de Ferrabouc belong to Cazaux alone. I have classed this mixed* superstition *with the Malevolent Beings because of the charcoal makers of Capcir.*

DIFFERENTIAL NOSTALGIA

The problem in studying "My Uncle from Condom" is the deceptive mono-vocality of the text. It appears as an uninterrupted and coherent flow of stories in Cazaux's voice, when in reality this polished piece of writing is a result of the processes of entextualization and translation by Bladé, in which the illiterate Cazaux would have been unable to fully participate. Folklorists who study legend materials today, such as Linda Dégh, have criticized such texts: "The [historical] collector's interest was usually focused on publishing a smooth story, rather than one that was whimsically interrupted by comments and set in a situational context. But it is precisely these circumstances that bring legends to life, and the omission of them in legend transcripts unfortunately renders legend texts almost unrecognizable and fit only for variant documentation" (2001, 53).

For many contemporary folklorists, the essence of the legend is debate (Bennett 1999, 32–36; Dégh 2001, especially 2–3; Dégh and Vázsonyi 1971; Goldstein 2004, 8; Tangherlini 1994, 7). Dégh writes that "legends appear as products of conflicting opinions, expressed in conversation . . . Disputability is not only a feature of the legend, it is its very essence, its raison d'être, its goal" (2001, 2–3). Timothy Tangherlini differentiates legends from tales by suggesting that while tales are more often narrated by one person, legends are a "negotiated process" (1994, 7).

How smooth is Cazaux's text really, and how much conversation with his audience might he include in his narration? This is, after all, a highly personal string of related narratives, whose protagonist is the teller's own uncle. The events are set in nearby, named places that both Cazaux and Bladé knew. They concern a period of history, the years of the Revolution, which posed significant problems of commemoration to the nineteenth-century population, who had lived under emperors, kings, and democratic republics. A narrative that raises all of these questions, not to mention ones about the existence of fairies and whether cannibals really live in the mountains, demands an answer from its original audience, Bladé. Perhaps it is even a challenge to his credulity, a typically Gascon tall tale to test how much he can be trusted, or how much he can be fooled, or whether he will get the joke (see Mark 1991).

The recurring footnotes that Bladé inserts into the text are one way to answer; they enact a conversation that focuses on shared acquaintances, language, and place. Cazaux, like modern legend narrators, bolsters the reliability of his account by referring to as many details as possible that corroborate what he is saying (Goldstein 2007). Bladé cannot resist destroying these claims in his footnotes. The language of the men of Capcir, Bladé tells us, is clearly wrong. The abbé de Ferrabouc or Herrebouc gave no indication to Bladé that the adventure Cazaux relates ever happened to him. Bladé calls into question the vision of history that Cazaux presents in his fantastical legend. If the message of Cazaux's story is about how disrupted and dangerous the revolutionary period was, Bladé refuses to engage on paper in the discussion.

Bladé's footnotes concerning places in the other legends Cazaux told are also revealing. Whenever Cazaux mentions a village, stream, or valley, Bladé provides the reader with geographical and historical details to locate these places in a world of scholarly knowledge. Cazaux's attitude to these places is of a much more intimate kind. In a memorate he told about his own childhood, called "L'homme vert" ("The Green Man"), for instance, the young Cazaux falls asleep on the rocks by the hospital in Lectoure (Bladé 1885, 344). In "Les sirènes" ("The Sirens"), the river Gers is not just a geographical landmark, it is a workplace for the boatmen and a fishing opportunity for the hero of the legend (369–371). In "Les sept belles demoiselles" ("The Seven Beautiful Fairies"), a stream named the Esquère is a path to be followed by the Deserter, anxious to avoid meeting the police (341). Cazaux knew landmarks and regions, such as the forest at Ramier or the rocks at the hospital, from long-term intimacy. He walked these places for eighty years, and they belonged to his acquaintances and family, themselves anchored to specific locations, like the uncle who lived "out of town on the road to Nérac."

Like modern ghosts (Thomas 2007, 32), Cazaux's spirits have a fondness for liminal places around the house, but it is also important to notice that their peregrinations match the seasonal movements of male agricultural workers. These spirits spend the summer in the fields and meadows, and the winter locked up in "the loft, in the oven and in the holes in the wall," just the same as the men who would have done most, if not all, of the work further from the home (Segalen 1983, 86–114, especially 99).

If Bladé has little interest in this intimate and gendered sense of place, he pays similarly little attention to the sense of time that Cazaux seems to invite him to share through his legends. For Cazaux, the time of the legends is personal and cyclical: personal in that it refers back to his childhood, as in the case of "The Green Man," or recent family history, as in "My Uncle from Condom," and cyclical in that fairies in both "My Uncle from Condom" and "The Seven Beautiful Fairies" always appear at the same time of year, perhaps reassuring storytellers and audiences about the possibility of stability during the upheavals of the Revolution and Napoleonic period. If the political and social changes of the time were radical and irreversible, the language of the supernatural grounds them in a sense of continuity with the traditions of the past. This sense of time is silently homosocial: Cazaux's stories evoke the memories and traditions of his uncle, father, and other men, but at no point does he tell a legend from a woman's point of view.

This cyclical men's time goes unmentioned by Bladé, whose efforts within the text and the introductions to his collections were focused on a different view of time, one emphasizing a faded, revolved world, which associates childhood with regional traditions and innocence. In this context, it is worth thinking about Ray Cashman's (2006) idea that not all nostalgias are the same. If Cazaux's nostalgia is for his own childhood and the men of his family and social life, Bladé's nostalgia is a more generalized longing for the innocence of a rural world threatened by modernization. When Cazaux mentions landmarks such as the rocks at the hospital, Bladé points out: "These rocks were north of Lectoure near to the old fountain of Saint-Esprit. The new road [*chemin de ronde*] built there destroyed all of it" (1885, 343). This intrusion of "modernization" into the countryside, which has been an important narrative for historians at least since the work of Eugen Weber (1976), is not something that Cazaux raises; Bladé interjects it into the text.

Cazaux does reminisce about times gone by, even suggesting that some of the supernatural beings in his legends have now disappeared, but the emphasis is on seasonal cycles. Although Gargantua and the Horned

Men have left the region, Cazaux never claimed they have ceased to exist. Gargantua is probably in Spain, and the king of the Horned Men is trapped underground (Bladé 1885, 347, 359). Cazaux admits that even when he was "little, people already said that the Green Man didn't show himself as often as in the past," but this does not mean that he no longer exists. Cazaux himself saw him twice and, as he points out, "In Lectoure, there has always been and there always will be a Green Man" (343).

Richard Bauman urged folklorists to turn their attention away from a conception of folklore as belonging to homogeneous groups. He wrote that "folklore performance does not require that the lore be a collective representation of the participants, pertaining and belonging equally to all of them. It may be so, but it may also be differentially distributed, differentially performed, differentially perceived, and differentially understood" (1971, 38). In the case of Cazaux's performance to Bladé, it seems that the two men had different concerns and different ways to understand places and time, both of which could be called nostalgic, but in diverging ways: personal and homosocial in the case of Cazaux, and historical and combative in the case of Bladé. These differential nostalgias clash at times, but the overwhelming impression reading the text is of interplay, misappropriation, and translation, not least since both men presented a world where men were the most important agents, performers, and audiences.

WHOSE MASCULINITY?

When dealing with a text like "My Uncle from Condom," whose relationship to the original oral performance of Cazaux is impossible to prove, I am drawn time and time again to write in terms of Bladé's concerns. But the conversation or dissonance about senses of place and time between the words of the legend and the footnotes points to a more important disjuncture. Where, in all that Cazaux said, is the "defiance" that Bladé visualized as such an important part of his character? Is Cazaux, like his uncle, "so simple no one suspected a thing?" Coded threats (Radner and Lanser 1993) did make up a part of Cazaux's attitude to Bladé (Pooley 2012), but in the case of "My Uncle from Condom," the message of an invitation to share in a homosocial form of local memory seems clearer, even if Bladé's notes suggest that he misinterpreted or ignored these implications. Cazaux's invitation offers what he knows to Bladé. It makes him a participant in the same intimate relationship to the landscape and local men that Cazaux speaks from, and invites the folklorist to reflect on the existence and significance of strange, supernatural beings in the recent past.

Cazaux did not exist simply as a product of Bladé's writings. In the archives of the Gers department, his birth and death were recorded by the French state, and his will was preserved by the notary who succeeded Bladé in Lectoure. These archival documents confirm that Cazaux was a bachelor, but they also reveal that he was hardly poor; he owned 132 acres of land. This does not necessarily conflict with Blade's image of the former *domestique*, although it seems Bladé deliberately underplayed Cazaux's wealth. The term *domestique* could have referred to anything from a day laborer to a man responsible for managing a large farm for an absent owner, and his wealth when he died suggests that Cazaux was much closer to the latter than the former.

Cazaux's legend about his uncle presents a vision of masculinity that is particularly well suited to the life of a bachelor who worked for others. The story is about male solidarity, at the complete exclusion of women, just as Cazaux's life depended on work solidarities and involved no marriage. It is also about independence, a hero who looks out for his client and friend, the abbé, but is just as happy wandering the Landes on his own. This ability to be independent and this invitation to solidarity fit well with the biographical picture of Cazaux the man, but it is also noticeable that what Cazaux actually says in his legends fits poorly with what Bladé says about Cazaux's narrative repertoire. These are not the heroic stories that Bladé described as possessing such a "proud shape" in the introduction to the collection (1885, 30). Cazaux's legend protagonists display a noticeable lack of courage, running away from monsters and surviving by their wits. Stories like "My Uncle from Condom" deal in uncertainty and fear, male bodies under threat of cannibalism or, in other narratives, witchcraft (Pooley 2012). And perhaps it cannot be emphasized enough that all of these tales of surprise and fear are stories about men. Cazaux told Bladé just one legend, "Les treize mouches" ("The Thirteen Flies") that featured a female character who took any proactive role.[10]

CONCLUSION: MASCULINITY AND AUTHENTICITY

How can Cazaux's distinctly unheroic legends be reconciled with the vision Bladé presented of his defiant narrator? Rather than a choice between an authentic account of Cazaux's masculinity or a fake constructed by Bladé, what readers encounter in Cazaux's legend text and Bladé's ways of recording it is a conversation about place, time, and language that is colored by gender. This is no fixed portrait of what it meant for men of different classes at the time to be masculine. As Judith Butler writes: "Gender is a complexity whose totality is permanently deferred, never fully what it is at any given juncture in time" (1999, 22). Stories like "My Uncle from Condom" are not Cazaux's explanation of what it means to be a man but his discussion with Bladé of how men are in the world, how they react to revolutions, untrustworthy hosts, surprising fairies, or the persistence of folklore collectors.

In the text of "My Uncle from Condom," Bladé's unrecorded questions and prejudices seem to bump up against Cazaux's vision of how the world is. If, as Fox suggested (1987), gender operated in tandem with discourses about authenticity in the writings of folklorists, I have tried to show that the critique of masculinity in this legend text reveals more than just the regrettable misogyny of the intellectual history of the discipline. It also offers lessons about the contact between different social experiences of masculinity and the ways that even, or especially, a fraught relationship between two men from very different backgrounds depends on an unmentioned silence: the erasure of women's experience from this conversation, man to man.

NOTES

1. The translations from Bladé's writings are my own.

2. Nye writes that "although the language and empirical basis constituting what it meant to be a man changed radically [in the nineteenth century] with the production of new formal knowledge about the body, the primordial qualities of manliness exemplified in the noble gentleman were adopted with minimal revision by middle-class men. The instrumentality that facilitated this process of adaptation was a male code of honor that survived the destruction of the Old Regime in 1789 by accommodating its practices and usages to the unique sociability and legal arrangements of bourgeois civilization" (1993, 8).

3. [Bladé notes:] "I did, in fact, meet the abbé de Ferrabouc during my childhood in the vicarage of Saint-Mézard, in the *canton* of Lectoure (Gers), where he died as a very old man. The real name of this good priest was Herrebouc, which came from the lands of the old county of Fezensac, which his ancestors were lords of. During the Revolution, the abbé de Ferrabouc emigrated to Spain, and he lived for a long time in Córdoba. Need I add that he never mentioned a word of what my narrator told me, even if Cazaux said it believing it to be true?"

4. [Bladé notes:] "[Saint-Bertrand-de-Comminges is the] *chef-lieu* of the *canton* of the *département* of the Haute-Garonne, and is in the part of this department formed by the central Pyrenees."

5. [Bladé notes:] "[The valley of Aran is] a Spanish valley, next to France. It is the source of the river Garonne."

6. [Bladé notes:] "The top of the valley of the Ariège, which opens onto Spain and Andorra on the southern side."

7. [Bladé notes:] "Small region made up of the highest part of the Aude valley. Capcir was ceded to France by the Treaty of the Pyrenees at the same time as Vallespir, Conflent, and the French Cerdagne."

8.   [Bladé notes:] "'*No. Quiero delante comer una pierna del frayle.*' This is Castilian Spanish, but this is what the narrator said. In Catalan it would be: '*No. Vuy abant manja une cama del capella.*"

9.   [Bladé notes:] "June 24."

10.   When the antiheroine of this legend discovers her husband's magic flies, he allows her to use them to do the housework. The industrious flies send the now-idle woman mad by doing everything she asks of them, and the husband finally advises her to get rid of them, which she does. Considering that it is the only legend Cazaux told that explored a woman's role in any depth, it bears the marks of a considerable misogyny, suggesting that women need housework to remain happy.

8

Sexing the Turkey
Gender Politics and the Construction of Sexuality at Thanksgiving

LuAnne Roth

> *I love Thanksgiving turkey. It's the only time in Los Angeles that you see natural breasts.*
>
> Arnold Schwarzenegger

NORMAN ROCKWELL'S CLASSIC PAINTING, *Freedom from Want* (March 6, 1943), depicts the iconographic American Thanksgiving (see figure 8.1). As an apron-wearing woman sets the turkey platter down, the patriarch stands beside her at the head of the table, carving knife close at hand. The family members around the table look on with giddy anticipation. One man turns back, peering at us from the corner of the painting. Is he inviting us to the meal? Or is he hinting at something amiss about this beloved holiday? Nearly sixty years later, Gurinder Chadha's cinematic ode to American Thanksgiving, *What's Cooking?* (2000), likewise hints that things are not as they appear to be. The opening credits roll over an object that gradually comes into focus, while a trumpet plays a somber rendition of "The Star-Spangled Banner." The object resolves into a roast turkey, a man brandishing his carving knife over it. As the frame widens, the all-American nuclear family appears, smiling proudly around the patriarch, who is poised to carve the bird. As the last triumphant lines of the national anthem fade out, the image slides out of frame, revealing an advertisement for turkeys on the side of a Los Angeles Metro bus that is driving away.

Although "cultural institutions are visible," says Homi Bhabha, "the ideology behind them . . . is concealed" (1994, 172). Both *Freedom from Want* and *What's Cooking?* play with viewers' expectations. Despite the Thanksgiving meal's infamous soporific effect, these images suggest citizens

148

DOI: 10.7330/9780874218985.c008

Figure 8.1 "Freedom from Want" painting by
Norman Rockwell (1943). Oil on canvas. 116.2 x
90 cm. Norman Rockwell Museum, Stockbridge,
Massachusetts. Originally published in the March
6, 1943, issue of *The Saturday Evening Post.*

should be alert to and expose the ideological implications of even the most
beloved holidays.[1] In this vein, I examine contemporary examples of gender performativity around the Thanksgiving holiday in order to make visible the patriarchal ideology that operates. Here, I focus on Thanksgiving
moments found, by and large, within some sort of visual frame in the media
of everyday life (Balsamo 1995), including key scenes from television, film,
YouTube, and commercial advertisements as well as literary works.[2]

Thanksgiving represents "a day of intensified patriarchy" in the majority of American households, that is, when the division of labor between
males and females becomes more pronounced than usual (Pleck 2000, 42).
As women wash the dishes in the kitchen, and men listen to the football
game in the living room, it becomes clear that women have (often willingly)
given up their leisure and that both men and children benefit from this sacrifice.[3] This arrangement has not been entirely disadvantageous for women,
argues historian Elizabeth Pleck (2000). As women cook together to prepare
for Thanksgiving, they can prove their womanly skills and gain companion-
ship in the realm of the kitchen. Moreover, at the end of the meal, women
are appreciated once again for their culinary skills. Melanie Wallendorf and

Eric Arnould write: "Grateful aunts asked for a hostess's recipes; stuffed diners called out their compliments. In the recipes they chose, women remembered and honored a dead mother or other female relative. The act of using a mother's or grandmother's recipes was a way for women to make a powerful, loving connection with the dead" (1991, 25).

Notwithstanding any sense of empowerment the gendered division of labor affords, women often report feeling exhausted at the end of the day. In their study of American families, Wallendorf and Arnould found: "Although regarded as a day of rest by men, in most households Thanksgiving Day is a day of . . . physical labor for women." One-third of women in the study considered Thanksgiving to be a hurried day, while only one-sixth of men saw it this way. In the majority of families they observed, men were positioned to be served. In contrast, women begin preparations days before the feast—with such backstage work as coordinating with guests, procuring ingredients, cleaning the house, and preparing the food—and on Thanksgiving Day itself they busily attend to last-minute details. Nearly half of women reported that their major Thanksgiving Day activity involves cooking for others. One interviewee, Paula Lefkowitz, recalls of her Polish grandmother: "My grandma would always try to serve the food while everyone else was eating. We would always tell her to sit down, but she never seemed to listen" (1991, 25).

By the 1970s, during the "postsentimental era" (Pleck 2000, 39), more women held paying jobs and could devote less time to the feast. Therefore, men began to do more housework and cooking. If men *helped* at Thanksgiving, researchers emphasize that women continued to retain control over the feast. Fieldwork reports in 1989, for example, note that "men were not doing much of the cooking, but they were helping with the cleanup" (Pleck 2000, 39). Even in the households in which men assist, women still assume primary responsibility for the planning and preparation.

In many households, men offer symbolic labor, for example, taking the cooked turkey out of the oven, carrying it to the table, and carving it. In contrast to the "days of hidden labor that women put into ironing tablecloths, polishing silver, and molding gelatin salads," men's labor receives publicity and is recorded in photographs (Arlie Hochchiel, quoted in Wallendorf and Arnould 1991, 25–26; see also Freund 1991). In the iconographic Thanksgiving scene, the matriarch steps aside at the moment of high ritual drama, leaving room for the patriarch to present and carve the turkey. "For thousands of years," observes Margaret Visser, the roast beast "was placed before the family as a result of male enterprise and triumph; and men, with their knives, have insisted on carving it up . . . before the expectant and admiring crowd" (1991, 231; 1992). Borrowed from British

Christmas traditions, the turkey-carving ritual emerged as the American holiday's symbolic core. As the "cult of domesticity" spread throughout the United States during the nineteenth century, turkeys and turkey carving became compulsory at American Thanksgivings (Pleck 1999).

Victorian author Isabella Beeton reflects on the significance of the bird, writing in her 1861 *Mrs Beeton's Book of Household Management*: "A noble dish is the turkey, roast or boiled . . . and we can hardly imagine an object of greater envy than is presented by a respected portly *paterfamilias* carving, at the season devoted to good cheer and genial charity, his own fat turkey, and carving it well" (quoted in Hughes 2006, 148). The art of carving turkey, says Mrs. Beeton, involves "getting from the breast as many fine slices as possible; and all must have remarked the very great difference in the large number of people whom a good carver will find slices for, and the comparatively few that a bad carver will succeed in serving." Carving the roast turkey, therefore, becomes a lesson in managing resources.[4] "You could always tell a gentleman," concludes Beeton, "by the grace and style with which he apportioned a roast" (149).

Pleck notes that in the twentieth century, "men still carved the turkey, but increasingly in the kitchen rather than at the table . . . Since so few fathers taught their sons to carve, men had to learn from reading instructions in a cookbook." American magazines in the 1980s celebrated men skilled in "making turkey dressing and gravy, simmering giblets, peeling and mashing potatoes, and taking instruction from svelte grandmothers as to how to trim the edges of pie pastry" (2000, 149). "The man presents the 'hunted' bird (actually purchased in a supermarket after being raised in a feed pen)," Wallendorf and Arnould observe, "while the woman presents the gathered berries (from a can) and cultivated vegetables (also purchased in the supermarket)" (1991, 25).

In the majority of American families at the turn of the twenty-first century, the paterfamilias still holds the role of turkey carver. How that position is assigned within the family unit has yet to be adequately explored by scholars of the holiday. When successful, the ritual operates to reconstitute patriarchal ideology and a sense of *communitas*; the turkey becomes the flesh that unites. At other times, the ritual fails. For example, *Avalon* (directed by Barry Levinson, 1990) depicts one example of this contested ground. Set in Baltimore in the 1940s, the film follows the Krichinsky family's immigration and assimilation into American culture, including the extended family gathering annually to celebrate Thanksgiving. In the first Krichinsky Thanksgiving, the Polish-Jewish matriarch Eva (Joan Plowright) wonders about the origins of the holiday, saying to her female kin, "I don't understand this holiday, Thanksgiving. We're giving thanks to whom? All I'm saying is we had to get the turkey, and we had to kill it to say thanks. If it wasn't for this holiday we wouldn't have turkey. I don't eat turkey the rest of the year; why do I have to eat it now?" Several years later, one of the brothers, Gabriel (Lou Jacobi), arrives later than usual. Responding to the pleas of hungry children, the family starts eating without him. "The seemingly innocuous act of cutting the Thanksgiving turkey without waiting for Gabriel has dire consequences," writes Eric Goldman of this scene. When Gabriel arrives to find the carving already under way, he starts ranting, "You cut the turkey without me? You cut the turkey without me?" Storming out of the house, he starts a long-standing family feud. The once unfamiliar American holiday, adopted with some reluctance by the immigrants, becomes so engrained in one generation that deviation from the new tradition threatens to destroy family cohesion (2003, 115; see also *By the Light of the Silvery Moon* [directed by David Butler, 1953]).

In *Home for the Holidays* (directed by Jodi Foster, 1995), the turkey-carving ritual likewise fails to unite, as the Larsons compete ruthlessly about whose turkey will be more popular—Joanne's (Cynthia Stevenson) lean "nutri-turkey" or her mother's (Anne Bancroft) "traditional turkey." When the portly Mr. Larson (Charles Durning) cannot carve the traditional turkey because he is holding the knife upside down, his openly gay son Tommy (Robert Downey Jr.) takes over. Amid chaotic conversation, the camera focuses repeatedly on the knife and turkey to highlight Tommy's difficulty even using the sharp edge. Embarrassed, he blames his mother, asking if she has "welded it together." When the knife slips, the traditional turkey is flung onto the lap of Joanne, bearer of the nutri-turkey, covering her body with the fatty juices she abhors. With references to consumerism and "human cholesterol," the patriarch's bungled attempt to carve the turkey signifies unchecked American consumerism. Moreover, in a holiday legendary for causing closeted gay people discomfort (Pleck 2000, 19), Tommy's carving fiasco marks his nonheteronormative sexual orientation.[5] Evidently, the prerogative to carve the Thanksgiving turkey remains the patriarchal right of only *hetero*sexual males.

The patriarchal prerogative is similarly negotiated vis-à-vis the turkey-carving ritual in *Brokeback Mountain* (directed by Ang Lee, 2005). The film follows modern-day cowboys Jack Twist (Jake Gyllenhaal) and Ennis Del Mar (Heath Ledger), who meet during the summer of 1963 when hired to protect a flock of sheep on the titular mountain. Even while proclaiming themselves straight, the men fall in love and have a sexual encounter that sets into crisis their assumptions about sexual desire and masculinity (see

Figure 8.2. "Stud duck do the carving around here." *Brokeback Mountain.*

also Boone 2003, 461). Fearful of their fiercely homophobic communities, the men go their separate ways, marry women, and have children. The camera cuts to two juxtaposed meals occuring fourteen years later, illustrating how the threat of homosexuality hovers over the Thanksgiving meal.

In the first scene, which takes place in Childress, Texas, at the home of Jack and his wife, a close-up shot of the turkey expands to reveal Jack carrying the bird to the dining room. His father-in-law L.D. (Graham Beckel) stands as the turkey arrives, grabs the carving utensils out of Jack's hands, puffs out his substantial belly, and declares, "Stud duck do the carving 'round here." Jack responds submissively, "You bet, L.D. I was just saving you the trouble" (see figure 8.2). The camera cuts to Lureen (Anne Hathaway), who notices their son, Bobby (Jake Church), watching football instead of eating his soup. She threatens to turn off the television if he does not start eating, at which the boy makes a belligerent retort. "You heard your mama," Jack says firmly, backing up his wife. "You finish your meal, and then you can watch the game." Jack turns off the television and returns to the table. In response, L.D. sets down the carving knife. "Hell . . . we don't eat with our eyes," he growls. "Want your boy to grow up to be a man, don't you, darling? Boys should watch football." Turning the television back on, L.D. returns to the turkey. Annoyed, Jack responds: "Not until he finishes a meal that his mama took three hours fixing!" Turning off the TV set, Jack slaps it to punctuate his point. As he returns to the table, L.D. sets down the carving knife and heads for the television again. Exploding, Jack points aggressively and yells, "You sit down, you old son-of-a-bitch! This is *my* house, this is *my* child, and you are *my* guest. Now you sit down before I knock your ignorant ass into next week." The threat of violence causes L.D. to sit back down. Pleased, Lureen turns to Bobby and gestures at his food. Exasperated, Jack sighs, wipes his brow, and begins carving the turkey.

Gender is performed here in several ways: through the division of labor, through the turkey-carving ritual, and through the ritual of football. Significantly, all of these cultural forms involve narratives of territorial expansion and belief in American exceptionalism.[6] Like football and the western genre, both reactions to the industrial revolution, the turkey-carving ritual emerged during the height of the "ideology of domesticity" to counteract the feminizing influence of the domestic realm and to assert symbolically that men were in charge (Pleck 1999, 775–776). As such, theories about the western may be mapped onto the landscapes of both football and Thanksgiving's turkey-carving ritual. For example, Richard Slotkin's theory of "regeneration through violence" (1973, 5), a common narrative pattern in which the hero moves to the western frontier and enacts societal regeneration by use of violence, parallels the typical American Thanksgiving. Pleck describes the holiday in the 1920s: "Encamping in the living room, men seemed to find solace in an all-male group, after having participated in an event so female in ambience. One function of football, even enjoyed vicariously, was to reaffirm men's bonds with other men and their masculinity, to inject some manliness into the sentimentality. Sons, listening to the game with their fathers, were learning the rules of male sociability—and being weaned away from their mothers. Listening to football was an additional masculine element that followed the ritual of carving the turkey, man the gladiator side by side with man the hunter" (1999, 782–783). Regeneration through violence occurs in *Brokeback Mountain*. By becoming menacing (slapping the television, pointing aggressively, and threatening violence), Jack regains the turkey-carver role. His violent outburst temporarily establishes him as contender for "stud duck."[7]

The noise of a motor intrudes through a sound bridge, followed by a close-up of another turkey being carved at a Thanksgiving attended by Ennis. The meal takes place at the home of his ex-wife, Alma (Michelle Williams), and her new husband, Monroe (Scott Michael Campbell), in Riverton, Wyoming. Now the official patriarch of the family unit, Monroe sits at the head of the table and carves with an electric knife. Demoted from his former status as patriarch, Ennis sits on the side of the table, between the children, Alma Jr. and Jenny (Sarah Hyslop and Cayla Wolever). The conversation is awkward and strained. Alma Jr. asks her father to tell a story about his bronco-riding days. Throughout the next series of shots, the turkey is consistently framed in the foreground, and when Ennis concludes his short story the camera cuts again to Monroe, who switches on the knife to carve again. The camera zooms to a close-up of the knife cutting the turkey flesh, which closes the scene.[8]

Significantly, both of these Thanksgiving scenes open and close with the camera's focus on the turkey, foreshadowing that gendered power will be negotiated over its body. While there is no explicit contest over the patriarchal prerogative to carve the turkey in the second Thanksgiving scene, masculinity is still negotiated in other ways, for example, by juxtaposing the sport of bronco riding with that of figure skating, the televised sport watched by Monroe and the girls, and when the camera lingers (twice) on Monroe's use of an electric knife. Despite his possession of this phallic implement, these images suggest that his masculinity is compromised by his reliance on a power tool instead of his own strength.

THE SEXUAL TURKEY

"In the safer confines of the paterfamilias' house," writes Kathryn Hughes, "it is the breast—plump, sweet, maternal—that gets devoured" (2006, 150) (see figure 8.3). As a full character in the drama of Thanksgiving, the bird is anthropomorphized and gendered in American culture, and negotiations occurring over its body may prove to have implications for both turkeys and humans. Consider how the bird has become a fetish, a point made evident in "the elaboration of attention to live turkeys destined for the table" and representations of full-feathered toms that began to appear in the mid-nineteenth century (Siskind 2002, 48; Tuleja 1987). In fact, the turkey featured so prominently throughout the United States in November is the image of a male gobbler during the spring mating season, the tom in full display. Like a peacock, the tom erects his tail feathers, spreading them like a fan. In addition, his wattles swell, becoming more brightly colored. The tom also puffs out his feathers, drags his wings, and gobbles, in a visual and auditory display intended to lure the hens (Davis 2001, 29–30; Raisch 1990; A. F. Smith 2006, 127; Wolf Howl Animal Preserve 2009).[9] The adoption of the gobbler's sexual display as the national symbol of the holiday corresponds with a societal fascination with turkey sexuality (see "Weird Experiment #4: The Sexual Turkey" 2008).

Despite this cultural absorption, when writer Barbara Kingsolver actually tries her hand at domestic turkey breeding she encounters a lack of

Figure 8.3 Sexy Bikini Tanned Turkey gendered female. "How to Recipe for a Bikini Tanned Turkey by Dear Miss Mermaid." http://dearmissmermaid.com/turkey%20recipe.html, accessed 7/10/10

information about turkey mating behavior from poultry husbandry manuals. She complains: "The whole birds-and-bees business has been bred out of turkeys completely, so this complex piece of former animal behavior is now of no concern to anyone. Large-scale turkey hatcheries artificially inseminate their breeding stock. They extract the eggs in a similarly sterile manner and roll them into incubators, where electric warmth and automatic egg-turning devices stand in for motherhood. For the farmers who acquire and raise these hatchlings, the story is even simpler: fatten them as quickly as possible to slaughter size, then off with their heads. That's it" (2007, 320).

With this dearth of information, Kingsolver had to teach herself (and her turkeys) about turkey sexuality. "The first hen who'd come into season was getting no action from either of the two males," she recounts of her awkward exploration. "These guys [Tom and Bud Tom] had been fanning their tails in urgent mating display since last summer, but they directed the brunt of their show off efforts toward me, each other, or any sexy thing I might leave sitting around, such as a watering can. They really tried hard with the watering can. Lolita kept plopping herself down where they'd have to trip over her, but they only had eyes for some shiny little item. She sulked and I didn't blame her. Who hasn't been there?" (2007, 325–326).

In the wild, hens are attracted by the sound of gobbling. "Hens come to gobblers when they're ready," explains Roger Raisch, who has studied wild turkey mating behavior for years. "Then he'll stop gobbling and start strutting (the image we see at Thanksgiving). Sometimes they are together for days before she'll let him mate with her" (personal communication; see also 1990) (see figure 8.4). Kingsolver discovered that domestic hens are evidently just as fussy. She arranges for the birds to have a "honeymoon suite" inside the main barn (the distracting watering can removed). Identifying with Lolita, the author writes:

> She practically had to connect the dots for him—no bras to unhook, heaven be praised—but finally he started to get the picture. She crouched, he approached, and finally stopped quivering his tailfeathers to impress

Figure 8.4 Mating turkey decoys: "Breeding Tom" and
"Hot Hen," by Delta Industries. Photo courtesy of
http://TurkeyHuntingSecrets.com and Roger W. Raisch,
Copyright 1998-2012. http://www.turkeyhunting
secrets.com/store/store-decoys-delta-wildwillard.htm,
accessed 7/10/10

her. After all these many months, it took him a couple of beats to shift
gears from "Get the babe! Get the babe!" to "Oh-oh yess!" Inch by inch he
walked up onto her back. Then he turned around in circles several times,
s-l-o-w-l-y, like the minute hand of a clock, before appearing to decide on
the correct orientation. I was ready to hear the case for artificial insemination. But it looked now like he was giving it a go.

After all of this foreplay, actual turkey intercourse involves an act called a
"cloacal kiss," during which the male bird touches his cloaca to the female's.
Whether the female's eggs are fertilized depends on whether this cloacal kiss
is successful. After a paragraph explaining the biology of turkey reproduction, Kingsolver continues her story about Lolita and Tom.

I watched, I don't mind saying. Come on, wouldn't you? Possibly you
would not have stooped quite as low as I did for the better view, but geez,
we don't get cable out here. And this truly was an extraordinary event,
something that's nearly gone from our living world. For 99.9 percent of
domestic turkeys, life begins in the syringe and remains sexless to the end.
Few people alive have witnessed what I was about to see . . .
Paradise arrives when a fellow has kneaded his lady's erogenous wing
zones for a long, long time with his feet, until she finally decides her suitor
has worked himself up to the necessary fervor. Without warning, quick as

an eyeblink, she flips up her tail feathers and reaches upward to meet him. Oh, my gosh! I gasped to see it. (2007, 326–327)

Even before this startling attention to and identification with turkey sexuality, Kingsolver had been waxing poetic about the Thanksgiving meal: "I'm partial to the traditional menu. I love carving up Tom on the table, and then *revisiting him* throughout the following weeks in sandwiches, soups, and casseroles" (2007, 281; emphasis added). Given Kingsolver's obvious interest in the sex lives of turkeys, particularly Lolita's, this reference to "revisiting him" may, in fact, suggest more than just leftovers.

Whereas Kingsolver focues on turkey sexuality, a different sort of sexualization of the turkey body manifests in *What's Cooking?* From purchasing, thawing, and stuffing to presentation, the turkey becomes a full character, with numerous individuals who gaze at, wonder about, and lavish attention on the dead turkey that will become the centerpiece of the Thanksgiving meal. For example, the Avila family obsesses over whether the bird will be big enough to feed everyone, and the Williams women gather around the oven door, arguing over whether the flesh is too pink. Shots of women caressing, kissing, and patting turkeys further this reading of the turkey as fetish.[10] One version of the film's poster offers a gaggle of gazing women (see figure 8.5), with all major female characters framed by oven walls, as if the photo were taken from the stove's interior. Presumably, the women are checking to see whether the turkey has finished cooking. They smile knowingly, for this is no ordinary turkey—a handful of dynamite has been inserted into its anus! Substituting explosives for stuffing, the image foreshadows family dramas to erupt, yet the image of dynamite being shoved into the hole that was the turkey's anus/pelvis alludes to sexual encounters as well.

FROM PREPARATION TO PENETRATION

On the one hand, as previously mentioned, cultural representations of Thanksgiving—from advertisements and greeting cards to children's art—draw upon the symbol of the male turkey in full sexual display.[11] On the other hand, the gendering of turkeys in other visual media forms leans toward the feminine and the feminized. Consider a scene in *What's Cooking?* when Mrs. Seelig (Lainie Kazan) instructs her daughter's lover on the proper method of stuffing the turkey. "Make sure it goes all the way in the back," the matriarch says. Carla (Julianna Margulies) responds, "Hmm, that's my favorite part," with a wink and a smile at Rachel (Kyra Sedgwick). With these subtle gestures, the turkey is sexualized, and even coded as queer. The

Figure 8.5. A gaggle of gazing women on the DVD cover of *What's Cooking?*

reference to Carla's "favorite part" is echoed later with a turkey baster in front of the oven, her comic gesture foreshadowing an announcement that the lovers are pregnant. Referencing the so-called turkey-baster method of insemination (injecting donated sperm into the vagina), sexualization of the turkey body here signifies a loving lesbian reproductive act.

Further examples of the turkey being associated with the female body appear in an episode of television's *Friends*, "The One with the Thanksgiving

Figure 8.6a Scene from television's "Friends": Joey places a turkey carcass on his head. "The One With The Thanksgiving Flashbacks." 1998.

Figure 8.6b. Scene from television's "Friends": Monica places a turkey carcass on her head. "The One With The Thanksgiving Flashbacks." 1998.

Flashbacks" (directed by Kevin Bright, 1998). In a flashback to an earlier Thanksgiving, Joey (Matt LeBlanc) places the turkey over his head (in an attempt to scare Chandler [Matthew Perry]), but the ploy is foiled when Joey's head gets stuck inside the bird.[12] Trying to help Joey remove it, Monica (Courteney Cox) says to Phoebe (Lisa Kudrow), "Okay, you pull, and I'll open the legs as wide as possible." When Joey giggles at the double entendre, Monica rolls her eyes in disgust. Later, in another flashback, Monica puts her own head inside a turkey's pelvic cavity, then places a fez and large yellow glasses on the turkey head and mimics a striptease dance (in an effort to cheer up Chandler) (see figures 8.6a and b). If the turkey references a generalized female body in one scene, in the other it becomes an extension of Monica's female body (see also Bronner 2004; *Gallina Blanca* 1960; Williams-Forson 2006).[13]

John Currin's painting *Thanksgiving* likewise illustrates this conflation of turkey and female bodies (see figure 8.7). The painting features three blonde White women preparing a turkey (2003). Based on Currin's wife at three different ages, the women appear very birdlike. The one on the right arranges a bouquet of flowers, an act resembling nest making, while the one on the left tries to feed another with an empty spoon. The center figure cranes her neck, her mouth gaping open like a baby bird, while holding a phallic-shaped yam in her hand, the vegetable pointed, conveniently, at her pelvis. The painting, however, is about more than just sex.

Some have noted "suggestions of a secret and disturbing disarray just under the surface" (Adrian 2010, 1), for example, the woman holding the empty spoon wears a smock matching the translucent flesh of the raw turkey. Her full breasts, thin neck, and birdlike arms parallel the plump and naked-looking raw turkey, an image simultaneously titillating and repelling.

Figure 8.7 Currin's painting draws a visual parallel between the turkey and the bodies of the women. "Thanksgiving" by John Currin (2011), oil on canvas, 1729 x 1323 mm. Image courtesy of the Gagosian Gallery.

Moreover, she is positioned directly above the turkey, so that visually her body becomes one with the bird's body.[14] The third woman focuses on the pelvic cavity of the turkey, holding a grape in front of its hole.

If this painting represents art imitating real life, then it is worth considering the real-life Miss Drumstickz pageant, which occurs at the annual

Figure 8.9 "Pour Some Gravy on Me" parodies Def Leppard's "Pour Some Sugar on Me" (*Pour Some Gravy on Me* 2007).

Figure 8.8 *Miss Drumstickz pageant, 1953* (*Miss Turkey Trot / Miss Drumsticks Pageant* 2010).

Turkey Trot Festival in Yellville, Arkansas. For the competition, young women in swimsuits shave and oil their legs to a smooth and glossy splendor (see figure 8.8). Then, holding a cardboard cutout of a wild turkey male in full display over their torsos, they strut across the stage as the audience whistles and cheers at their high-heeled "drumsticks."[15] Similarly, in a YouTube video titled *Pour Some Gravy on Me* (2007) (see figure 8.9), which parodies Def Leppard's sexually suggestive song "Pour Some Sugar on Me," an animated turkey performs an exotic dance. She wears heart-shaped thong underwear and high-heeled stilettos. The lyrics of the song to which she dances are equally suggestive, including "Pour some gravy on me / And stuff me with stuff" and "C'mon, grease me up / Pour some gravy on me / I can't get enough."

The turkey stripper swings her ample buttocks to and fro while tassels jiggle from her pierced nipples. In parody of Jennifer Beals's infamous shower dance scene from *Flashdance* (directed by Adrian Lyne, 1983), the turkey stripper leans back in a chair and pulls a chord, releasing a pot of hot gravy to fall between her legs as the lyrics conclude: "I'm hot, good to eat / I'm the Thanksgiving feast / Yeah!" Both images and lyrics in this performance draw parallels between preparing/eating food and sexual acts. The stuffing and gravy in this trajectory allude to sex and its resulting secretions.[16] The turkey begging to be "eaten" here follows the patriarchal fantasy that women want to be "stuffed" have men ejaculate on them. Alternatively, the video suggests that the oppressed—whether objectified females or turkeys—want to be oppressed.

Another animated music video plays upon this fantasy of the sexually receptive turkey in *I Want to Stuff You* (2007) (a parody of the Exiles' hit song, "I Wanna Kiss You All Over"). Here, though, a man sings a love song to his "Butterbird" turkey:

> When I get home, babe,
> Turn the oven on.
> All day I've been thinking about you
> and it won't be long.
> Massage your skin so gently
> Don't make me beg.
> Gotta whip out my stuffing
> and spread your legs. MMMMM.
> I'm hungry.
> I'm hungry, babe.

At this point the camera zooms out to reveal the man with his head inside the turkey's pelvic cavity (as seen in the *Friends* episode). In case that isn't creepy enough, a living turkey head appears inexplicably on the turkey carcass to join in singing the last refrain, "I want to stuff you all over and over again . . . 'Til the night closes in." While the protagonist of this music video claims to massage the turkey's skin "so gently," the singer's hunger (aka sexual rapaciousness) takes center stage.

Each of these scenes positions the turkey body as a female waiting to be stuffed, basted, and otherwise penetrated. The symbolic slippage between women and meat in Western culture allows for images to be interpreted from a stance of human-centered male identification. From breasts to thighs, "the association between attractive human female bodies and delectable, attractive 'meat'" has been culturally constructed. An advertisement for a kitchen tool named "the turkey hooker" makes this point clear. Designed to move a hot cooked turkey from the roasting pan to the serving platter, the device hooks into the hole that was once the bird's neck. An accompanying image shows an anthropomorphized version of the turkey hooker in use, "a turkey in high-heeled shoes, one wing placed seductively, invitingly, behind her head, hints of breasts showing" (see figure 8.10), while the advertising copy reads: "an easy pick up from pan to platter" (Adams 1998, 67). Caricaturing a human prostitute, the "turkey hooker" dresses and poses seductively in order to be beheaded, defeathered, roasted, and eaten.[17] When viewed

Figure 8.10 Animated turkey from "The Turkey Hooker" advertisement
(Adams [1990] 2003:32).

through a feminist lens that attends to the cultural association between turkeys and women, such seemingly benign scenes are imbued with power
dynamics that hint at sexual violence. In fact, these dynamics of power and
domination play out similarly whether the turkey (or the human stuffing it)
is envisioned as male or female.

A blog about "The Turkey Man" demonstrates this point, referring to
a sexual fetish in which "a man feels sexual pleasure when he is treated like
the Thanksgiving turkey."

"The Turkey Man" is an extreme form . . . We didn't make this up. A
Turkey Man usually has a dominatrix dressed as a classic mothering house-
wife come to his home, where he has constructed a large oven out of usually cardboard or plywood. The Turkey Man then strips, leaving only his

Figure 8.11a Still from Eli Roth's "Thanksgiving" trailer: the title sequence of a knife stabbing a turkey.

socks (like the little paper booties on the turkey's feet), and crawls into the oven. The woman then describes to the man how she will baste, cook and eat him. Lord only knows where the meat thermometer ends up! Gobble gobble! (Ebb 2007)

To further elaborate on this theme of sexual domination, I focus next on a close reading of the faux movie trailer *Thanksgiving* (directed by Eli Roth, 2007). Released for the intermission section of *Grindhouse* (directed by Robert Rodriguez and Quentin Tarantino, 2007), the trailer exposes the deeper implications of the turkey-carving ritual in just three minutes of shocking visuals. The trailer begins quietly with Grandma (Liliya Malkina) whistling a tune to herself as she massages a raw turkey with a stick of butter. The subjective camera follows the killer's movement as he reaches for a large kitchen knife and closes in on Grandma, who turns and screams in horror.[18] Then the camera cuts away to the title shot, in which the stentorian voice-over (by director Roth) aligns the viewer with the turkey with such lines as, "This holiday season, prepare to have the stuffing scared out of you." The screen dissolves to red and cuts to a close-up image of a knife stabbing a roast turkey. Blood oozes out of its body, and the letters in the word "Thanksgiving" drip blood (see figure 8.11).

This sequence of shots draws attention to the violence inherent in Thanksgiving, a theme that persists throughout the rest of the trailer. For

Figure 8.11b Still from Eli Roth's "Thanksgiving" trailer: the roast turkey/man.

example, in the next scene, a cheerful Thanksgiving parade takes place in Plymouth, Massachusetts, where "the fourth Thursday in November is the most celebrated day of the year." A man dressed as a pilgrim helps costume a man dressed as a turkey-pilgrim, while another dressed as an Indian chief places the finishing touch of a turkey mask on the turkey-pilgrim. "The table is set / the festivities have begun," continues the narrator, "when an uninvited guest has arrived." At this, the camera cuts to a shot of another pilgrim—an imposter—zipping his black leather combat boots. "This year, there will be no leftovers," adds the voice-over. The killer pilgrim steps in front of the camera and swings his machete, chopping off the turkey's head with one swipe. After a prolonged shot of the head rolling gruesomely on the street and the crowd's frightened chaos, the camera cuts to the headless body of the turkey, which stumbles around and then falls to the street, as the title "Thanksgiving" drips blood once again. While these scenes challenge the myth of the first Thanksgiving by associating it with violence and death, what comes next shows us again the sexual side of this violence.[19]

The camera follows two teenagers stealing away for some hanky-panky in a school gymnasium. Giggling incessantly, the blond, pigtailed cheerleader does a striptease while jumping on the trampoline. Her boyfriend, wearing a letterman's jacket, watches eagerly from the side. As the voice-over warns, "White meat, dark meat, all will be carved," the cheerleader removes her shirt and bloomers, offering the camera several shots of her own "white meat" (see figure 8.11a). Suddenly the killer descends, muffling the boyfriend and yanking him out of the frame. Oblivious, the cheerleader continues her routine. She jumps up, spreading her legs into a straddle split. Viewers see the knife stabbed through the bottom of the trampoline. The camera dissolves from a close-up of the (erect) knife to a low-angle shot of the cheerleader's crotch, editing that makes the phallic knife appear to stab the girl. The camera cuts away to the now-familiar title shot of the knife stabbing a roast turkey that bleeds.[20]

After decapitating several teenage boys on Lover's Lane, the trailer finally returns to Grandma's house. Still alive, she opens the door to welcome the guests, while the voice-over commands us to "arrive hungry" and "leave stuffed." In the next shot, the family is gagged and bound. His face obscured by shadows, the killer unveils the huge platter on the table. Instead of a roast turkey, the "money shot" is a man's supine body—knees spread, feet bound, flesh roasted, and unknown objects protruding from his anus, revealing the double entendre of the voice-over's "leave stuffed." Viewers can assume the victim's head has been removed because they have already witnessed heads being removed in the previous scenes and because Thanksgiving turkeys tend to be served headless. Leaving no doubt, the camera tilts down to reveal a decapitated young man's head stuffed into an actual turkey's neck hole and an apple stuffed into his mouth. A reaction shot shows a guest vomiting, a scene followed by the narrator's closing words: "You'll come home for the holidays . . . in a body bag." At this, the trailer offers one last shocking glimpse of the aproned killer standing at the head of the table and copulating with the turkey's body (with the man's head attached).

During an interview, Roth explains how the Motion Picture Association of America Ratings Board made him remove the full frontal nudity in the cheerleader scene with scratching and clever editing. Gratefully, Roth remarks, "And, you know, they even let me keep the turkey sex, even though it's not really sex with a turkey. It's a cooked turkey, although it's not really a full turkey. I mean, someone having sex with a live turkey—that would be really gratuitous. I mean, it's someone having sex with a cooked turkey with a decapitated head on top of it, so it's more of a turkey/human hybrid, really" (quoted in Edwards 2007).

What does it mean to turn people into turkeys and then decapitate, dominate, stuff, and screw them? The spectacles of death in this trailer illuminate aspects of the Thanksgiving turkey and the rituals employed to kill it, "dress" it, and carve its body.[21] From the title shot of a knife stabbing a turkey and the bleeding "Thanksgiving" the trailer reminds us that violence is core to the holiday. Whether reel life or real life, for Karen Davis, this sort of cultural moment requires a process of scapegoating: "Modern industrial society has become so alienated from the food production process that people can easily forget that an animal had to be killed in order for the turkey to get to the oven," Davis argues. "Consequently, all kinds of articles, comics, jokes, and bizarre rituals crop up right before Thanksgiving, emphasizing the subjectivity of the bird. That way we can't miss the fact that someone—a turkey, not a turnip—had to be sacrificed for the feast" (2001, 120). While Slotkin's theory of "regeneration through violence" is useful in discussing how the turkey became the structuring metaphor of Thanksgiving (1973, 5), the theory falls short of addressing the apparent need for ritual reenactment. Freud's "repetition compulsion" may be usefully applied here. As a result of this psychological condition, an individual is unconsciously compelled to keep repeating a traumatic event—a process that extends beyond individual psyches to social psyches as well. In this trajectory, Thanksgiving's turkey-carving ritual operates as a sort of repetition compulsion to constitute familial and national subjectivity (Freud 1950; see also Sceats 2000, 40). This point is made in the "Pangs" episode of television's *Buffy the Vampire Slayer*, when Anya (a former vengeance demon) astutely remarks about the holiday: "To commemorate a past event, you kill and eat an animal. It's a ritual sacrifice—with pie."

The shocking stabbings and decapitations in Roth's *Thanksgiving* trailer and the decapitated stripper of *Pour Some Gravy on Me* go beyond sacrifice, reminding those brave enough to look about the violence associated with Thanksgiving (Davis 2001; Roth 2010; Siskind 2002). Moreover, these Thanksgiving scenes suggest a sexual process at play in the scapegoating ritual, highlighting America's preoccupation with the phallus as a source of power. The repeated shots of decapitation and penetration reveal a profound anxiety about castration and sexual violation at play in the holiday. By identifying the symbolic parallels between the knife and the phallus, other seemingly innocent scenes—especially close-up shots of knives carving the flesh of Thanksgiving turkeys—begin to take on new significance.

Returning to Rockwell's iconographic painting, perhaps this is what the man in the lower corner is trying to say—that things are not what they appear to be. On a basic level, patriarchy is a social system in which the family and society are ruled by men. Patriarchal ideology reinforces men as authority figures over women, children, and property (see de Beauvoir 1989; Bordo 1993; Friedan 1963). At Thanksgiving, gender is performed and reinforced as much through the division of labor as through football and the turkey-carving ritual. However, gender also comes into play as humans reflect on turkey sexuality. In the media examples described above, "sexing the turkey" involves a more general domination, whether chopping off its head, massaging it, stuffing it, cutting it, or eating it. If one of the central mechanisms of patriarchy is to disguise male domination as a natural phenomenon, then an interrogation of such Thanksgiving moments is crucial to expose the murky underbelly of the holiday. The turkey's flesh feeds more than individuals and families; it also feeds ideology. Such bizarre cultural moments—when the turkey is gendered, sexualized, and dominated—point to a profound cultural anxiety about masculinity, subjectivity, and nationhood, creating fissures in the ideology of Thanksgiving and suggesting that ultimately, the act of consumption may prove to be an act of aggression and sexual domination.

NOTES

1. Within decades, Rockwell's iconographic painting was being parodied (see Darkow 2007; Pleck 2000, 36; "Rockwell Rolls over in His Grave" 2008).

2. The title of this chapter, excerpted from a chapter of my doctoral dissertation (Roth 2010), plays upon the title of Anne Fausto-Sterling's *Sexing the Body: Gender Politics and the Construction of Sexuality* (2000).

3. Historically, while men and women occupied separate spaces on Thanksgiving, "it was easier for a woman to enter the living room where men were listening to the game than for a man to don an apron and help in the kitchen" (Pleck 1999, 782; see also Turner and Seriff 1993; B. Williams 1984).

4. Mrs. Beeton offers other skills for the aspiring middle class to maintain a respectable household, for example, raising children, balancing the books, subduing "the natives," and building bridges—"and she does it all with a turkey" (Hughes 2006, 231). The imperial "scope of domesticity" was also central to the mission of Sarah Josepha Hale, who opposed the women's rights movement as "the attempt to take woman away from her empire of home" (quoted in A. Kaplan 1998, 585). Domestication paralleled westward expansion, in Hale's worldview, so that "while Anglo-Saxon men marched outward to conquer new lands, women had a complementary outward reach from within the domestic sphere." Women "could be more effective imperialists," Hale argued, by "penetrating those interior feminine colonial spaces" (588). In this schema, the language of territorial expansion draws upon the language of sexual conquest (585). Similarly, as an allegory for territorial invasion, football ritually reenacts sexual conquest, "in which one male demonstrates his virility . . . at the expense of a male opponent" by feminizing him. As such, Alan Dundes argued that "victory entails some kind of penetration" (1997, 27). These processes of dominance and aggression shed light on the rituals of Thanksgiving.

5. Disgusted and covered in grease, the homophobic Joanne blurts out that Tommy has secretly married his life partner, accusing him of bringing shame to the family by kissing his spouse in public.

6. The marriage between football and Thanksgiving dates back to at least 1869 (Pope 1997, 54). The western genre and football developed concurrently as rituals of homecoming and turkey carving were being ushered into the Thanksgiving holiday. Once radio entered homes in the 1920s, football "threatened to overwhelm the domestic occasion." Some accused the game of being too violent and dangerous, a training ground for war, and a symbol of imperialism. It is hard to escape the irony of Thanksgiving as a *family* event when it is "punctuated by (mostly) men listening to a game noted for its aggressive body contact, warlike language, male bonding, and the ability of contestants to withstand pain" (Pleck 1999, 782). In this trajectory, the overtly masculine game expresses "territorial,

sexual, or economic conquest" (Lindquist 2006, 448), through its association with the master narrative of the "first Thanksgiving," in which the Pilgrims and Wampanoag Indians allegedly shared a harvest feast in 1621. Although the narrative is based on fiction, legend, and public relations rhetoric rather than historical fact, a plethora of institutions actively perpetuate this self-serving version of American history (Reese 2006). Historians have brought to the fore painful truths about relations between Wampanoag and Pilgrims, which were marred by distrust and betrayal. As such, like the western and football, the American Thanksgiving is linked to national imperialism and territorial expansion (Lindquist 2006, 448; see also Pope 1993, 73).

7.   Alternating shots of the two men are framed so that a glass of white wine (actually yellow in color) is positioned in the foreground. As each man returns from the television, the glass of yellow liquid is positioned directly below his crotch, framing that equates their power struggle to a pissing contest.

8.   Cultural critics have observed a process of "phallic appropriation" occurring in genres ranging from westerns and crime films to horror films. The gun in this schema becomes an extension of the western hero, assuming masculine and sexual meanings (e.g., Clover 1992). While there is no gun per se in *Brokeback Mountain*'s Thanksgiving sequence, knives operate here as phallic substitutes.

9.   Turkey males are said to be polygamous, mating with at least five females during the breeding season (Wolf Howl Animal Preserve 2009). Hunting-supply companies capitalize on this knowledge with the sale of life-size turkey decoys locked in intercourse. Sold separately, the three-dimensional "breeding tom" is designed to fit atop the "Delta Hot Hen Decoy." The advertisement closes with, "You haven't seen anything until you try this guy. The breeding pose drives gobblers wild to investigate and fight with the intruder tom. Used alone or in conjunction with a couple of Hot Hens, Feeding Hot Hens, and a Jake. The combination will lure in even the most stubborn toms" ("Supreme Breeding Tom" 1998).

10.   The dramatic turkey presentation montage is accompanied by a triumphant musical soundtrack and the sounds of "oohing" and "aahing" from family members.

11.   In addition to the male turkey adopted as the core symbol of the holiday, husbands are sometimes referred to as turkeys, the term denoting lazy, stupid, or insipid behavior— especially those husbands who sit in front of the television on Thanksgiving Day while their wives do all the work (Tuleja 1987). Worthless politicians are also referred to as turkeys, a point repeatedly made in political comics and even by presidents at the now-annual Presidential Turkey Pardoning Ceremony (see Davis 2001, 17–24; Fiskesjö 2003, 3; A. F. Smith 2006, 110–129).

12.   This *Friends* episode probably derives from a *Mr. Bean* episode ("Merry Christmas Mr. Bean"), in which the title character (Rowan Atkinson) loses his watch while stuffing the Christmas turkey. To retrieve it, he sticks his head inside the cavity and gets stuck just as his girlfriend arrives. I am indebted to Diane Tye for drawing attention to this lineage.

13.   All references to online videos appear in quotation marks without dates and should be searched in the filmography.

14.   Currin has described this painting as an allegory of his wife Rachel's pregnancy (see http://aphelis.net/thanksgiving-john-currin-2003/).

15.   In addition to the "Miss Drumstickz Pageant," one of the main attractions of the Turkey Trot Festival (since 1946) is the "turkey drop," in which live turkeys are thrown out of airplanes (*He's Mine* 2009; *Miss Turkey Trot* 2010).

16.   Consider a blog posting, *Why Women Hate Men*, a website that makes fun of Internet personal ads. Critiquing an ad, "Weasel" writes: "He's about as spontaneous as the ritual

preparation of a Thanksgiving Day turkey. Which, ironically, might make it easier for him to fuck you, because if he fucked you in a 4-inch pan lined with carrots and rotated you every thirty minutes, at least he'd know he was following the proper directions. But either way, I guarantee you his stuffing would somehow end up leaving you dry" ("Mr. Spontaneity" 2008).

17.   Other examples of turkeys eager to be eaten include: "Mr. Turkey" (sung to the tune of "Mr. Sandman"); "Turkey in Yo Belly Time"; "Stuff It Good" (sung to Devo's "Whip It"); "We Will Eat You" (sung to Queen's "We Will Rock You"); "The Turkey Song" (sung by Adam Sandler); and "Turkey Jive Thanksgiving."

18.   The trailer pays homage to John Carpenter's *Halloween* (1978), which implicates the audience in the crime by showing events from the killer's point of view.

19.   Roth recounts his inspiration for the trailer: "We grew up in Massachusetts and were huge slasher movie fans—and every November we were waiting for the Thanksgiving slasher movie. We had the whole movie worked out: A kid who's in love with a turkey, and then his father killed it, and then he killed his family and went away to a mental institution and came back and took revenge on the town" (quoted in Edwards 2007).

20.   This juxtaposition of shots makes the connection between knife and phallus— between the penetration of the knife into the turkey and the penetration of the phallic knife into human bodies. Roth credits generic expectations as influencing his decisions when he remarks: "If I don't exploit this girl I have failed as a *Grindhouse* director" (quoted in Edwards 2007).

21.   Consider the advice in "How to Dress and Clean a Turkey": "To gut a turkey, cut a slit from the end of the breast bone nearly to the vent (anus). Insert your fingers into the opening and gently pick up the large intestine. Then, with your other hand carefully cut a complete circle around the anus, which will free the intestine. Next, carefully reach inside the body cavity, find the gizzard and pull it out along with the intestines. Reach back in to remove the heart, lungs and liver. Finally, rinse the body cavity with fresh water" (Adele and Raisch 1998–2002).

9

Listening to Stories, Negotiating Responsibility

Exploring the Ethics of International Adoption through Narrative Analysis

Patricia Sawin

PARENTS WHO HAVE ADOPTED CHILDREN INTERNATIONALLY encounter all the usual delights and difficulties of raising a child. We can expect, additionally, to help our children mourn their lost birth family, struggle over identity formation because they are perceived as racially or ethnically different from their adoptive family, and possibly deal with aftereffects of early malnutrition, lack of medical care, or orphanage life. International adoptive parents like myself are also challenged to understand and explain our chosen path to forming a family, grappling with ethical disputes that those who bear the children they love and raise rarely encounter. Finding both popular and scholarly debates less helpful than I had hoped, as a folklorist I turn to stories told by those directly involved in international adoption. Drawing together folklorists' theories of narrative shaping and sharing with feminist ethicists' model for using stories to negotiate reciprocal responsibilities, I offer an approach to making ethical sense of international adoption that, I argue, more adequately takes its complexities into account.

While international adoption has become increasingly familiar and accepted in North America, public discourse provides inconsistent support to parents striving simply to create a stable family life and raise happy, healthy kids. Popular media, unsurprisingly, offer little help, since only extreme examples produce exciting news copy. One moment we are invited to admire Brangelina displaying their beautiful multiracial brood. The next, further rumors surface about Madonna's circumventing Malawian law in her

DOI: 10.7330/9780874218985.c009

son's adoption. Debate rages on blogs and call-in shows when a Tennessee woman abruptly puts her seven-year-old son on a plane back to Russia or when American evangelicals are caught taking a busload of children across the border from earthquake-stricken Haiti to the Dominican Republic. Most international adoptive parents have experienced these dichotomized discourses in interactions with strangers as well as family members. We squirm at the praise that casts us as self-sacrificing saviors, rather than simply parents, of that "lucky baby." Yet we are stung by unbidden criticism of our family composition based on, depending upon the politics of those we encounter, scarcely veiled racism, a conviction that White parents are unfit to nurture children of color (see National Association of Black Social Workers 2011), or an assumption that international adoption is inevitably exploitative and corrupt.

International adoption is also hotly debated in the legal and social science literatures. In the last few years anthropologists and historians, many of whom are adoptive parents themselves, have begun to provide nuanced, ethnographically informed analyses of particular situations (e.g., Anagnost 2000; Dubinsky 2010; Fonseca 2005; Johnson 2005; Kim 2010; Leinaweaver 2007; Seabrook 2010; Ward 2011; Yngvesson 2010). Those who articulate a firm position pro or con—like adoption advocate legal scholar Elizabeth Bartholet and adoption critics historian Laura Briggs and anthropologist Jessaca Leinaweaver—argue in starkly dichotomized terms. Frustratingly, they tend to talk past each other, using key terms with divergent valences and finessing their own lapses in logic. And the United Nations, as the primary arbiter of the terms under which adoption between countries can be arranged, via the Convention on the Rights of the Child and the Hague Convention on Protection of Children and Co-operation in Respect of Intercountry Adoption (intended to "protect children and their families against the risks of illegal, irregular, premature or ill-prepared adoptions abroad" [Hague Conference on Private International Law 2011]), sometimes offers clarification but at other times seems to use its mandate for reform to halt international adoption altogether.

Advocates tend to emphasize children's needs: "Children's most fundamental human rights include the right to a nurturing family which is often available only through international adoption" (Bartholet 2010, 91). They stake their claims in psychological and developmental terms that can write birth parents out of the picture: "Human beings need parental care for a prolonged period to survive physically and to develop mentally and emotionally. Even the best institutions fail to provide the care that infants and young children need" (94). Critics insist that we see international adoption not as an individual matter but rather as one facet of a global system of "stratified reproduction" (Colen 1995, 78) wherein wealth and privilege influence "who is normatively entitled to refuse childbearing, to be a parent, to be a caretaker, to have other caretakers for their children, to give nurture or to give culture (or both)" (Ginsberg and Rapp 1995, 3). Briggs and Diana Marre question, "Who is normatively entitled to expect of others that they will engage in biological reproductive functions for them, while they retain the 'right' to be the providers of the child's nurture and culture?" (2009, 17).[1] Critics likewise remind us that "plenary adoption," in which the child's connection to his or her birth family is legally expunged, lies at one extreme of a range of child-sharing arrangements (Briggs and Marre 2009; see also Saltzman 2009; Yngvesson 2004). They record how local forms of temporary fosterage can be overwhelmed by international models that assume permanent placement as the norm and label parents unfit if they are even briefly unable to provide for their children (Leinaweaver 2007). In so doing, however, critics privilege parental rights and avoid not only questions of the "best interests of the child" but even the suggestion that children could have needs or rights distinct from those of their parents, an especially controversial suggestion of the Convention on the Rights of the Child.

UNICEF offers clarification in urging use of the term *children without parental care* rather than the emotionally loaded and imprecise *orphan*. In emphasizing that children may be "deprived of their first line of protection—their parents" permanently *or temporarily* for various reasons, and in stressing how long it may take to reunite children with their parents after war or natural disaster, they insist that children "without parents" are not necessarily appropriate for adoption (UNICEF 2011a). The Convention on the Rights of the Child specifically requires signatories to "recognize that inter-country adoption may be considered as an alternative means of a child's care, if the child cannot be placed in a foster or an adoptive family or cannot in any suitable manner be cared for in the child's country of origin" (article 21b). The key adoption-related provisions—that "the best interests of the child shall be the paramount consideration" (article 21) and that states shall take measures to "prevent the abduction of, sale of, or traffic in children" (article 35) and to "combat the illicit transfer and non-return of children abroad" (article 11)—are crucial underpinnings for ethical international adoption. However, a number of rights intended to protect minority and refugee populations from national neglect sound, when applied to international adoption, like ways of promulgating issues important to adults, ethnic groups, or nations *as if they were* children's rights. Children require parental care, but do they require the care of their birth parents? Children require a national identity and the rights it confers, but surely it is adults who care that particular children continue their birth parents' nationality (UNICEF 2011b, articles 7, 8, and 9).

Advocates can seem naive about how international adoption occurs in practice or the real difficulties of enforcing national or international law in the countries from which most adoptees come. Bartholet insists that "there is no real need to buy or kidnap children, since there are so many millions of desperate, impoverished birth parents incapable of caring for their children, and so many millions of orphaned and abandoned children." But that does not necessarily refute the accusation that "adoption facilitators wrongfully take babies by paying money to induce birth parents to surrender, and even by kidnapping" (2010, 96). Critics, however, base a wholesale condemnation of international adoption on unproven assertions, arguing—without adducing concrete evidence—that past crimes in which members of right-wing Latin American militaries murdered, disappeared, or imprisoned leftists and adopted their children or sold them for adoption have established conditions in which criminal gangs continue to traffic in children (Briggs 2006; Briggs and Marre 2009; 11–12; Dubinsky 2010; 107–108). And the Hague Convention provisions that require central state authorities to accredit all those involved in the care, evaluation, and placement of adoptees (Hague Conference on Private International Law 2011, articles 6–11) provide national governments the self-justifying opportunity to insist that the government itself and its employees are neither corruptible nor liable to engage in adoption for profit, an assertion that those who have dealt with governments in the global South often contest.

Amid these conflicting claims, where might one find ethical guidance? I propose feminist philosopher Margaret Urban Walker's "ethics of responsibility" (1998, 78; see also Bloom and Sawin 2009). Her model requires, however, that parties negotiate their relative responsibilities with each other. Scholarly critics and advocates are at such cross-purposes that I hesitate to apply Walker's approach to their interaction. Paradoxically, it is easier to envision a conversation that might support ethical negotiation among those who live daily with international adoption—adoptive parents, adopted children, and the families of children adopted by others.[2] Much of this conversation is admittedly partial and mediated. Adoptive and birth parents rarely communicate face-to-face, and the voices of those we must only provisionally characterize as "relinquishing" mothers (given the connotation of voluntary action) are especially scarce, available only in fragments or via intermediaries. Still, members of all three groups are seeking to communicate their experiences and to learn about those of the others by whatever means available, which inspires me to see what Walker's model and an extension elaborated by Ofelia Schutte (2000) might reveal. Perspectives drawn from folklorists' study of personal narrative—especially work based on Mikhail Bakhtin's (1981, 1986) observations on the shaping of stories for particular audiences and Amy Shuman's (2005) critique of the claims made for stories transported far from their original tellers—will help us recognize when speakers are talking to each other (or not), perhaps even when they are (or are not) negotiating in good faith, and how we might inure ourselves to inevitable silences. This combination of feminist and folkloristic perspectives can frame a workable ethical understanding of international adoption and keep us from being immobilized by inevitable ambiguity.

AN ETHICS OF RESPONSIBILITY

A feminist ethics, Walker argues, requires members of an "epistemic community" to commit to understanding the collective grounds of their moral knowledge (1998, 58) and "account[ing] to each other for their identities, relationships, and values that define their responsibilities" (61). In contrast, any nonnegotiable ethical ideal (a "theoretical-juridical model" [53]) functions within a patriarchal, hierarchical system that devalues socially variable lives, reinforces existing privilege, and excludes deeper insights into lived realities, emotional contexts, complex human relations, and systemic social inequality (54–55). So people working together in good faith can develop expectations for relative behavior that are actually more moral (because more specific and more flexible) than following any preconceived standards. "Being held responsible in certain ways, or being exempted or excluded from responsibility of certain types or for certain people," constitutes an "ethics of responsibility" (78). Members of an epistemic community aim to become "morally reliable" for one another (117) and to achieve "nongeneric accountability" (115) appropriate to their respective situations, needs, and capacities. Schutte, additionally, advocates the moral benefits of allowing oneself to be "decentered" through openness to someone with divergent experience and social position. "The breakthrough in the concept of understanding *the other*," she argues, "occurs when one combines the other as different from the self with the acknowledgment of the self's decentering that results from the experience of such differences . . . Interpersonal and social interactions marked by cultural (as well as sexual, racial, and other kinds of) difference allow us to reach new ethical, aesthetic, and political ground" (2000, 48).

The experience of international adoption clearly requires adoptive parents and adopted children to reimagine their identities, but can those seeking a collective ethics work out relative responsibilities and new identities without everyone engaging in face-to-face dialogue? Those whose rights presumably conflict, birth parents and adoptive parents, rarely interact. Postcolonial feminist scholars would likely insist that reliance on text rather than encounter leaves too much to the imaginations of the economically and racially privileged adoptive parents, empowering them to put words into other people's mouths (Mohanty 2003) and believe self-serving projections of birth parents' experiences (Spivak 1988). Walker's model, however, emphasizes flexibility and encourages participants to revisit earlier solutions, which one can argue is happening as more adoptive parents seek contact with birth families or means to learn about and to alleviate oppressive conditions in children's birth countries. Furthermore, a folkloristic perspective argues that birth parents could never realistically tell adoptive parents a single definitive story that would resolve all ethical dilemmas, which is precisely why the ethics of responsibility meshes so well with folklorists' understanding of the complex dynamics of sharing stories.

STORIES AND ETHICS

Working out decisions and expectations about the ethical conduct of international adoption not through rancorous debate, but through sympathetic conversation, would allow all involved to tell their stories and negotiate their claims. While one might want to hear from many others, including adoption facilitators and authors of national and international law, in this essay I focus on the stories told by those most intimately concerned: adoptive parents, adoptive children, and birth families.

Insights about storytelling articulated by folklorists and linguistic anthropologists offer guidance for making sense of these consequential narratives. Foundational in this work was Bakhtin's argument that every utterance is formed in response to prior statements and in anticipation of the ways interlocutors will understand, report, and transform what they hear (1986). A story, like an individual word, necessarily "tastes of the contexts in which it has lived its socially charged life" (1981, 293). The contextual approach to folklore study, emphasizing interpretation of narrative texts in their cultural, social, and historical setting, is a congruent and converging development (Bauman 1986; Kirshenblatt-Gimblett 1975). Deborah Tannen argues that words spoken in one context and reported by the listener in another are grossly misunderstood if perceived and responded to as the words of the original speaker (1989, 101). Shuman questions the assumption that telling and retelling stories creates meaning and, ultimately, mutual understanding, noting that "the farther stories travel from the experiences they recount, the more they promise" (2005, 1), yet "storytelling is pushed to its limits both by the use of a particular story beyond the context of the experience it represents and by the use of a personal story to represent a collective experience" (3). Stories are crucial for making sense of experience, but recipients must think critically about their origins, circulation, transformation, and intended audience and the claims they are being used to bolster in current contexts. Not only is access to the single true story impossible; there is no such original to grasp.

Adoptive Parents' Stories. I begin with the stories with which I am most familiar, those adoptive parents tell to each other and potential adopters, and those they tell to their children. Adopters or those who are contemplating the possibility avidly trade accounts of the process. By sharing hard-won knowledge and recounting arcane details, obstacles, and missteps, parents offer resources and establish expertise. I recall listening eagerly to recently returned parents' advice about which hotel to choose in Guatemala City and how to remain calm during the nerve-wracking visa process at the U.S. embassy. Later, I enjoyed playing the expert, describing my vain effort to stop a county official from putting whiteout on a notarized document in order to warn those still "in the paper chase" about mistakes that would force them to repeat time-consuming steps. These accounts can be a lifeline for parents preparing for, or stuck midway in, the adoption process and are shared on listservs and blogs as well as in person. Among successful adoptive parents they establish bonds and substitute for mothers' rite-of-passage stories about giving birth, verifying the new parent as one who has done the hard things necessary to bring a new member into the family. Notably, however, adoptive parents shape these stories almost entirely for others within their privileged category, with little apparent thought of how they might sound to those who have relinquished children under difficult circumstances. And in depicting a process that can be bewildering, exhausting, and enraging, adoptive parents position themselves as those with morality on their side and with rights to children born in another country to other parents, while often situating the legal systems intended to safeguard children's and birthparents' human rights and civil liberties as the enemy.

A remarkably influential subset of parent-to-parent stories, shorthand comparative national characterizations, offer apparently authoritative advice to prospective parents facing the strange task of selecting from which country to adopt.[3] The reliability of blanket claims describing an entire culture in a phrase might seem questionable, but for those with little knowledge they can have a determinative influence. These are metonyms of narrative (Kalčik 1975), abbreviated references that imply but rarely inquire into more extensive accounts of what has transpired in particular countries. Korea, for instance, has a reputation as a good place to adopt from—efficient, honest, first-world medical system, healthy babies. In addition, a sense of Koreans as prejudiced against "mixed-blood" children, although primarily relevant to those fathered by U.S. servicemen half a century ago, still gives Korean adoption a superior ethical cachet.

When I was seeking to adopt, I heard (although I cannot recall from whom, confirming the tenacity and unaccountability of these floating stories) that I should avoid India because of AIDS and Russia because of fetal alcohol syndrome. Cambodia had recently closed amid accusations of illegal activity by an American adoption agency. Guatemala was apparently ideal since, I was told, babies were placed with decently paid foster mothers to ensure their health, and the process was cleaner than in the past, with DNA tests required to prevent illegal abductions. I asked acquaintances familiar with Guatemala for advice and got conflicting reports. One woman recently returned from a trip to Guatemala reported the disapproval of adoption expressed by the nuns at the Guatemalan orphanage where she had volunteered. One of the nuns claimed that "a lawyer will just pay a prostitute to have a baby for any American who wants to adopt." Conversely, an NGO worker who had spent several years in Guatemala insisted that the nuns' attitude sprang from competition between the Catholic church, which runs orphanages in Guatemala, and Protestant denominations that promote adoption.

China generally tops the moral hierarchy, given the clear story about baby girls dumped in orphanages because of the government's one-child policy (which strikes feminists and conservatives alike as a draconian infringement upon individual rights) and a cultural system that demands sons to perpetuate the family. Yet the very demand for Chinese babies encouraged China to establish more stringent requirements for adoptive parents, including weight limits and restrictions on single women (the latter evidently aimed at blocking lesbians from adopting). A clear attraction of China is that adoptive parents can imagine themselves allies of Chinese women forced to relinquish their children by a heartless national bureaucracy rather than by poverty or even through fraud. I doubt, however, that American parents consider the ease with which they stereotype a Communist state as evil or recognize the cultural background of their own outrage at the Chinese legislation of family size, which *is* legal within that governmental system.[4] For Guatemala, the legendary machismo and irresponsibility of Guatemalan men serves as analogous justification (Dubinsky 2010, 124), giving American parents a villain to blame and a way to position themselves as supporters of women or rescuers of babies.

This shifting moral hierarchy can produce smugness about one's own choice and judgmental impressions of others'. The first time historian Karen Dubinsky recounted her adoption experience in an academic lecture, for example, an audience member holding her own (apparently) internationally adopted infant challenged, "But really, why on earth did you choose Guatemala?" (2010, 103). What deters one person may, however, motivate another. I chose Guatemala partly because I had spent time there and felt comfortable returning, but I was also impelled by a developing critical awareness that Guatemala and the United States had been linked for more than a century by agribusiness and industry looking for cheap labor and by U.S. support for totalitarian regimes bent on keeping that labor available and tractable. As beneficiary of my government's exploitative and violent policies, I reasoned, I bore more direct responsibility for the conditions that might make cause a Guatemalan woman to relinquish her infant than for those in China or Kazakhstan, the two other countries then open to a single woman of my age. Critics could instead see my adoption as an extension of the pattern of exploitation, but I report my motivation as an example of parents' thinking, based on the stories they grasp at crucial junctures.

In terms of Walker's ethical model, in telling these stories adoptive parents serve as an epistemic community. But we do so almost exclusively for each other, justifying our choices only relative to other adopters and mostly blocking awareness of the stories and claims of birth parents, except in self-congratulatory ways. The availability of simplified stories supplied by other parents and adoption agencies may keep potential adopters from sensing a need to research the situations that make individuals and countries allow their children to be adopted. In Shuman's terms, these partial characterizations of the child's birth country have been carried too far from their source to reliably support the authority attributed to them. As Emily Noonan argues, parent discourse reveals how globalization is understood and negotiated at the level of the family (2007). In the early stages, parents may indeed leave unchallenged a pervasive sense that denizens of wealthy countries are the unproblematic, deserving recipients of the products that flow to us from the global South.

Recall, however, that Walker insists that certain people can (at least temporarily) be relieved of certain responsibilities. Parents often come to the decision to adopt only after struggling with infertility, mourning the lack of a partner with whom to conceive, or debating whether to add their own biological progeny to the world's population. Stories that assist in identifying a child and getting her or him home are arguably the only accounts that the adoptive parents' own internal family-building story of disappointment, frustration, search, and hoped-for success can reasonably accommodate—at least during the adoption process and in the early years of family consolidation.

Once adoptive parents are more secure in our own identities and ability as parents, we are often more able to take on formerly intolerable responsibilities. For years we have known that we finesse complicated and imperfectly known histories when we assure our children, "Your birth parents loved you but were not able to raise you." We recognize that the "adoption story" that others urged us to document for our children as a substitute for a birth story (Larsen 2007, 52) and the pictures of a fancy hotel as "the place where our family began" are not fully satisfying for them or us. So we set out, belatedly, to learn more about the political and economic history of our child's birth country, to raise money and contribute to efforts to improve the situation of families like the one from which our child came, or even to try to find our child's birth family, hoping to hear their stories and possibly establish a relationship. Indeed, an emerging story genre is the one we find on the *American Family: Just Your Typical American Family . . . Sorta* blog, in which the mother/author recounts finding one daughter's birth family in China and her emotions as they arrange phone calls and plan for a visit to the village where she was born (*American Family* 2012).

Children's Stories. As internationally adopted children reach adulthood, many communicate with each other about common concerns, creating blogs, artworks, and memoirs, and sharing their stories with filmmakers and scholars. A full account of this ongoing process is beyond the scope of this chapter; I highlight emerging trends. It might be expected that adopted children may suffer trauma and that adoptive parents may or may not understand or deal well with children's need to mourn their loss of birth family and to be reassured that their current parents will not abandon them (Eldridge 1999). Issues vary as much by generation as by birth country—consider the difference between a Korean adoptee forty years ago, the only Asian in a White community, whose adoptedness was never discussed, and my daughter, who regularly plays with a group of adopted Guatemalan kids, adores her fictive "big sisters," one from Cambodia, one from China, and encounters other international adoptees in almost any public gathering. Overall, I am struck by how variable and complex adoptees' reactions are.

A vociferous minority, like those who write blogs under the screen names "Transracial Abductee" and "Bastardette," lash out with vituperative condemnation of international adoption, calling it "a racist system of forced assimilation and brainwashing" (*Transracial Abductees* 2011; *Daily Bastardette* 2011). These adoptees invest in naturalized notions of family composition and birth culture that adoptive parents see themselves as progressively transcending. It would be difficult for any adoptive parent not to react defensively, and these writers seem interested in blasting adoption advocates and rallying those who share their anger rather than talking with anyone with a different perspective. But I would love to understand what led them to this tragic pass. I dare to suggest that honest conversation in a broader epistemic community might help these bereft and angry adult adoptees understand and be understood as well as help parents learn how to support other adoptees in working out an identity that accommodates two (or more) places, cultures, and families.

In contrast, many adoptees either find no pressing need to delve into their origins or affirm their primary identity as a member of the community in which they were raised. The nine-year-old granddaughter of friends, whose parents arranged for them to live in Guatemala for six months, declared to her grandmother upon their return, "I'm a Carrboro [North Carolina] girl, *not* a Guatemala girl!" although she might reconsider someday. A majority of adoptees are evidently stretched in positive ways as well as challenged by the need to reconcile the two facets of their identity. The Korean adoptees studied by Eleana Kim affirmed that their experience neither vilifies nor vindicates the practice of which they were the subjects (2010). Even among those who decided to spend extended periods in Korea, few said they felt alienated from the (usually European) cultural identity with which they had been raised. Even egregious cases of deception can produce positive results. Nelson Ward de Witt, who learned as a teenager that his birth mother was a murdered Salvadoran guerrilla and that his grandmother had sought him for years, reports that developing relationships with his Salvadoran family brought him closer to his American parents and brother and has turned both himself and his adoptive mother into memoirists, exploring his birth mother's decisions (de Witt 2011a, 2011b; Ward 2011). In the context of an epistemic community, adoptees might narrate their lives to make different claims relative to either family, but these honest, emerging self-characterizations—formulated first to help the adoptee make sense of his or her own experience—offer a clear story to which others can respond.

Birth Families' Stories. Walker's model of narrative sharing and negotiation would require that all members of the adoption triad have reliable access to each others' developing life accounts. Yet the stipulations of plenary adoption combined with distance and fear (on the part of stigmatized birth parents, adoption coordinators reluctant to have their methods scrutinized, and adoptive parents) mean that most adoptive parents and adopted children have only generalized or speculative knowledge of birth parents' stories, and only a few birth parents have knowledge of the child after their separation.

The few birth parents whose stories make it onto the Internet or occasionally into the news are precisely those whom adoptive parents pray are not their own child's original families, those seeking to retrieve children abducted and sold for adoption. Adoptive parent organizations like Guatadopt.com publicize these accounts and call for the return of kidnapped children, although critics might dismiss this as attempting to bolster what those opposed to international adoption see as a nonexistent distinction between voluntary and involuntary relinquishment. It remains difficult, however, to extrapolate the pervasiveness of fraud or abduction from limited examples. Dubinsky, for example, conveys credible reports of Guatemalan intermediaries between birth parents and adoption lawyers pressuring and manipulating pregnant women (2010, 118). Yet she also argues that scandal stories peopled by predictable figures—profiteering lawyer, desperate, deserted pregnant young woman, older friend who offers help to a girl in trouble only to take advantage of her—easily take disproportionate hold on audience imaginations (2010, 100–103).

A few classic texts expressing birth mothers' feelings have been available for at least a decade, and more are appearing. Korean adoptees have the touchstone collection of letters, *I Wish for You a Beautiful Life,* that birth mothers at the Ae Ran Won "home for unwed mothers" were encouraged to write to process their grief (Dorow 1999). The mothers write directly to their children, often explaining their decision to let the child be adopted, but especially declaring, "My dear son, please remember that I will always love you very much. I also want you to remember that you are my son and are very important to me" (17). Dana Sachs recounts the heartrending stories of Vietnamese mothers who sent beloved children abroad during the 1975 Operation Babylift (2010). Chinese journalist Xinran published the collection *Message from an Unknown Chinese Mother: Stories of Loss and Love* (2011), which provides more complex accounts of the interaction of tradition, old landownership laws favoring males, and the one-child policy in individual lives and recounts the heartbreak and even suicide of mothers forced to relinquish daughters. Barbara Yngvesson quotes a letter that a Colombian birth mother included in her son's adoption dossier, although it tells nothing specific about her reasoning except that "I do not want him to lack what he needs or to suffer" (2010, 1–2).

Adopted children and adoptive parents form an eager audience for these accounts, a key reason that I see the beginnings of an epistemic community in this mediated space of books and blogs. But presumably for now most of the communication from birth parents is one way, except in rare instances where adoptive families seek out and find birth families. And birth parents, resigned to the already enforced separation, write almost exclusively to their children or perhaps in protest against government policies or cultural strictures that prevented them from keeping those children. We can sense implicitly what they would ask of adoptive parents for the children—to love them and give them a "better life" (however the birth parent might conceptualize that). But these texts give them little opening to express what they might ask of adoptive parents for *themselves*.

Trying to make sense of our own child's situation, adoptive parents piece together stories of birth parents we never met from whatever fragments of information were conveyed by intermediaries. The Guatemalan adoption lawyer with whom I worked sent photos from the day my daughter's birth mother put her in the care of the woman who would foster her until the adoption was complete.[5] In retrospect, I realize that these were intended to prove that the child was not stolen—the woman holding the baby appears to be the same one in the photocopy of the birth mother's national ID card in the adoption dossier. But what am I to make of this young woman's modest pink turtleneck or her apparently calm demeanor? When the foster mother put my daughter into my arms, she made a point of telling me that the birth mother had not cried when she relinquished the baby. Mindful of Tannen's warnings about reported speech (or, in this case, reported lack of communication), how should I interpret this assertion? It seems suspicious, too convenient for encouraging me to believe that the birth mother did not want the baby I so desired. It emphasizes the foster mother's caring nature, since she sobbed when it was time to leave the baby with me. And supposing that the birth mother did not cry, what might that mean? That she was relieved? That she was too proud to let the foster mother see her cry? That she was traumatized and numb? I cannot know, though I can encourage other adoptive parents at least to ask these hard questions.

Still, fragmentary evidence tells little about nuanced, conflicted lives. As Dubinsky notes, "In public discussions, birth mothers are caricatured as victims or villains and thus rendered mute . . . Does adoption enhance or foreclose on reproductive alternatives for Guatemalan women? . . . The full story of transnational adoption is simply unknowable until the conversation includes birth mothers" (2010, 125). Fortunately, increasing numbers of adoptive families are searching for and finding birth families, often with the help of in-country intermediaries who recognize an opportunity to do well-remunerated work while filling a pressing need. From the accounts of paid searchers and families who have searched successfully, adoptive parents are starting to get answers to the kinds of questions we would like to ask of birth families. When children were not given up voluntarily, as in the army's separation of children from murdered leftist parents during the civil wars in Latin America, grandparents have been indefatigable in their search (Ward 2011). Paid searchers appear sensitive to the risks to a birth mother whose neighbors or current partner may not know that she once gave up a child, yet report that only a tiny percentage of birth families refuse the opportunity to reconnect (M. Jones 2007). They *do* want to be found. And reunion reports do not suggest that birth families blame adoptive parents who have lovingly raised the child, nor that they usually demand the child's return.

Yet what would birth families ask of adoptive parents, if given the chance? Some are content simply with knowing that their child is safe and well provided for; others want to enter into an ongoing relationship. Some will refuse any money from the adoptive family, while others will accept or request support for their other children or themselves. Some will even ask if the adoptive family can take in another child to give her or him the same chances (M. Jones 2007). Yet I have also heard of an instance in which the birth family rebuffed the adoptive family's attempts to assist another daughter with her education, marrying her off at fifteen, presumably because they could not really imagine the life of the adopted child even after meeting her in person. Birth mothers are likely to share feelings that adoptive parents find it hard to hear; "Beatriz told us that she was deeply depressed for a year after the adoption was finalized. She got through her pain by turning to God," reports journalist Elizabeth Larsen (2007). The pervasive sense from accounts of birth families reunited with adopted children is that they are pleased that adoptive parents have given the children what their birth parents hoped for: education, health care, and opportunity. Yet we are still far from the point where birth parents can engage not only with the fait accompli of a past adoption but with recommendations for future policy.

Following Shuman, we recognize the moral benefit of giving birth families the opportunity to communicate directly and repeatedly with the parents who adopted their children (2005). Yet a Bakhtinian perspective also emphasizes that when adoptive parents or children or researchers manage to talk with birth parents, the stories they might tell are also inevitably shaped for the current audience and circumstances. It is not possible to recapture perfectly the life and motivations of a birth mother at the time she relinquished her child, nor of any other party to the adoption at a prior stage. Teachers at the Guatemalan Spanish school where I studied when my daughter was a toddler doted on her and smiled at me, apparently regarding the adoption as a positive development. Yet on our last day the school director informed me that he had assisted adoptees searching for their Guatemalan birth families. "Bring your daughter back in twenty years," he urged, "and I'll help you look, but be prepared to hear stories completely different from the ones you've been told." I am eager to help my daughter search, perhaps even sooner, but must remind myself and teach her that no single story will tell us the whole truth.

ANALYSIS AND REFLECTIONS

This essay proposes a framework, based on the feminist ethics of Walker and Schutte and on Bakhtinian narrative theory, to help those directly involved in international adoption move toward negotiating appropriate relative responsibilities. Walker's nongeneric accountability asks all participants in the epistemic community to be honest about the privileges from which they benefit, generous about their resources and capabilities, and reasonable but not self-abnegating about their needs. Each person must respect the contributions others are currently able to make, although that does not preclude challenging others or oneself to do more or think differently.

This as yet fledgling epistemic community would presumably agree that those already parenting internationally adopted children must prioritize raising the particular child who has become ours and fulfilling our commitment to enable that young person to realize his or her potential. In an earlier exploration of the ethics of international adoption I concluded, "Or maybe next week we'll just work on eating with a spoon" (Sawin 2005). Some might hear this as a flip cop-out, but for me that remark still captures our primary—and absorbing—responsibilities to the children we made a promise to parent. Yet it is incumbent upon adoptive parents, given our relatively privileged position, to take the lead in establishing a functioning epistemic community in which differently situated actors may eventually converse and, meanwhile, to draw upon the available evidence to envision what others involved in international adoption might expect of us. In order to make an effective level of mutual communication possible, adoptive parents must, in my view, tackle four substantial and, for many, unanticipated challenges.

Those of us who have already adopted must, to begin, find the time and energy to learn more about the complicated political histories of our children's birth countries and other sending countries and not content our-selves with festive cultural practices appropriate to share with our young children. Scholarly critics of culture camps may not appreciate what goes on in these specialized epistemic communities, where adoptive parents assured of a sympathetic ear explore moral anxieties and share strategies for tack-ling medical and learning challenges common to children from particular countries. Still, to the extent that such gatherings and other "birth culture" resources emphasize purely "celebratory representations of cultural differ-ence," they "make invisible the historical events and political and economic structures that shape understandings of race, ethnicity, and difference" (Anagnost 2000, 391). They may effectively deprive adoptees of crucial information about the conditions that led to their separation from their first family.

As a corollary, adoptive parents must consider the stories we share with potential adopters, resisting the inclination to exaggerate our expertise or let our accounts of the search for a child eclipse imperfectly known sto-ries of birth families and emerging stories of adopted children. Likewise, we must refuse to let a sense of psychic connection with birth families, however sincerely felt, obscure actual power relationships. Susan Barrett and Carol Aubin, for example, write, "Feminists who adopt internationally are in a unique position to further the active connection among women of varying cultures . . . We, ourselves, are inextricably bound to another woman who gave birth to the children we raise" (1990, 134–135). For once I agree with Transracial Abductee, who calls this "self-indulgent wish-ful thinking" (2011).

Further, I urge adoptive parents to capitalize on Schutte's vision of allowing ourselves to be "decentered." Early in our children's lives we must focus on incorporating them and making them feel securely part of the fam-ily, emphasizing their similarities to us. But as they inevitably differentiate themselves, we can revel in and celebrate their distinctiveness, rather than "simply taking the decentering [we] might experience in the light of the other's differences as a deficit in [our] control over the environment" (2000, 48). When families, schools, religious congregations, sports teams, scout troops, and communities as a whole embrace as their own children who are "visibly different," what is visible as difference shifts. When those children fulfill expected roles in Western, middle-class families—loving their par-ents, learning from them, carrying on family culture (Zelizer 1994)—yet do not also perpetuate the biological inheritance of those who raise them, the notion of family shifts. Thoughtful adoptive parents can scarcely help but have their own sense of identity and of who belongs to/with whom "decentered" by the long-term relationship with a child whom they love unconditionally, yet who always in some ways asserts his or her persistent difference. Likewise, learning that our family happiness is inextricable from complicated and tragic events half a world away will not be comfortable, but we can appreciate the possibility for intellectual and ethical growth.

The next logical ethical step for most adoptive families will be to search for the birth family or for as much information as can be garnered about their specific history. I acknowledge that this is a tall order. Even the most adventurous adoptive parents imagine locating their child's birth family with a mixture of hope and dread (*American Family* 2012; M. Jones 2007; Larsen 2007; Ward 2011), and few anticipated that adoption might require them to build relationships with an unknown extended family. Not every parent will have the emotional or financial resources to pursue this kind of knowledge, nor will every child wish for or even tolerate it. Not all searches will succeed, although some individuals are discovering that even ostensibly impossible searches in China, where children must be abandoned anonymously and illegally, can prove successful (*American Family* 2012). Other countries may eventually follow Korea in welcoming adoptees back and opening adoption records (Kim 2010). We are barely on the threshold of figuring out how to converse and connect with birth families different from us in culture, language and, most dauntingly, education and class, but the process of writing this chapter has convinced me that we must plunge into that unknown.

For those considering adopting internationally, the parallel requirement is to give up the "privileged innocence" whereby families evince little curiosity about the circumstances under which their child comes to them (Dubinsky 2010, 124) and to insist upon greater transparency and more complex, if painful, stories from adoption agencies. Adoptive parents need to acknowledge from the beginning the ways we are implicated as beneficiaries of the imbalanced global economic system, precisely because that challenges our implicit sense of entitlement to the world's poor children. Whatever struggles we have faced in our own journey to parenthood, we cannot treat birth families like global storks dropping into our laps babies of whose source we remain blissfully ignorant. Thus we need to insist upon information about and, ideally, contact with birth families at the time of adoption. Ultimately, we must move toward Yngvesson's visions of open international adoption (2010, 115) and even cross-cultural co-parenting (2004, 221–223). Adopted children are most likely to thrive with secure roots in both families. Stable connections with birth families provide adoptive parents a personal conduit for learning about and acting to remedy the forces that separate children from their original families. International adoption is (crassly put) a consumer-driven process, so if adoptive parents pursue contact with birth parents and demand that fuller knowledge be a condition of adopting, policies will change and the practice of (re)connecting with birth families will become more commonplace and guided by clearer expectations on all sides.

I ask a lot of adoptive parents, believing that our children and their birth parents would ask these things of us. Yet the ethics of nongeneric accountability allow us some leeway. We should be hopeful but realistic about what we as individuals and as a group can accomplish and recognize that change takes time. Many adoptive parents are already responding to their sense of others' needs and their consequent ethical duties: supplying adopted children's requirements for knowledge about their birth countries by organizing culture camps; raising money to build schools in their child's birth country; publishing pro-adoption legal articles and opinion pieces; heading a research institute on adoption issues; or doing the ethnographic and historical research that advances and challenges our understandings.[6] I honor, and urge others to honor, all of these efforts, even those one finds imperfect or misguided, as the contributions that those with particular perspectives and abilities are currently able to make. Crucially, I believe, adoptive parents must resist debilitating defensiveness about our particular adoption, recognizing that we acted in good faith to provide a loving home for a child, that we will never know everything about the circumstances under which she or he came to us, and that international adoption almost certainly offers children greater emotional and material support and greater opportunities to grow up healthy and educated than if they had remained in their birth country as poor, out-of-wedlock, or over-quota children. Nongeneric accountability likewise surely excuses adoptive parents exhausted by the demands of raising an infant or attending to a child with special needs from leading the move toward systemic improvement. Happily, too, important parts of this work will be done by others: by the anthropologists and historians who provide access to more complex stories; by intermediaries within sending countries, who can talk to birth parents in ways we cannot; and ultimately by our children as they forge their own paths and make their own decisions about what and who they need to know to form their evolving identities. But adoptive parents will need to rise to many unanticipated challenges, exercising courage, compassion, and humility. If we truly appreciate the privilege of raising, loving, and being loved by children born to and separated from other parents, I believe we can find the energy to participate in the full epistemic community of which our children make us members.

NOTES

Thanks to Leslie Rebecca Bloom, Emily Noonan, Riki Saltzman, Bron Skinner, and the editors of this volume for constructive feedback on earlier versions of this essay.

1. Receiving the greatest number of international adoptees from 1980 to 2004 were the United States, Spain, France, Italy, Canada, the Netherlands, Sweden, Norway, Germany, Switzerland, Denmark, Belgium, Australia, and Finland. Sending the most children to the United States during that period were China, Russia, Guatemala, South Korea, Kazakhstan, Ukraine, India, Haiti, Ethiopia, and Colombia (Selman 2009).

2. In this essay I do not distinguish among adopted children given up by single birth mothers (as is common in Korea and Guatemala), those from families with two parents forced by poverty or state policy to put the child in an orphanage (as in South America and China), and those whose parents are dead but whose grandparents search for them (as in Latin America during the civil wars), so I use "birth families" and "birth parents" interchangeably.

3. Instead of preparing to raise whatever child results from a pregnancy, you have to make choices about how far you are able to travel, how long you are willing to wait, how much you can afford to pay, what cultural background you are willing to grapple with, and more or less what your child will look like.

4. Adoption scholars offer more nuanced characterizations—not yet well known enough to impact U.S. public attitudes—of the Chinese situation. First, the state did have a well-considered rationale for its birth-limitation policy; unless the birth rate decreased it could not create economic development fast enough to provide schooling and social support for the expected number of children. Second, the one-child policy was applied with some flexibility depending on local politics. Third, some Chinese parents adopted abandoned children despite penalties. And fourth, urban parents in China increasingly express a desire for a daughter rather than a son (Anagnost 2000; Johnson 2005).

5. Legally in Guatemala at that time, the birth mother relinquished the child to the lawyer arranging the adoption, who employed the foster mother.

6. See references respectively for Heritage Camps for Adoptive Families (2011); Sustainable Schools International (2012); Bartholet (2010); Pertman (2000); and Anagnost (2000); Briggs (2006); Briggs and Marre (2009); Dubinsky (2010); and Johnson (2005).

10

"What's under the Kilt?"
Intersections of Ethnic and Gender Performativity

Diane Tye

ONE DAY IN LATE 2004 MY HUSBAND, PETER, a bagpiper, and I, a folklorist, opened our in-boxes to discover a photograph shared by Barbara and David P. Mikkelson at the contemporary legend website Snopes.com. Later titled "Crown Jewels" (see figure 10.1), the group shot reportedly documented Queen Elizabeth II's November 2004 visit to the First Battalion of the Argyll and Sutherland Highlanders in Canterbury, England, to present medals to the unit commemorating its tour of duty in Iraq. The humor in the photo was supplied by Colonel Simon West, seated front and center beside a prim Queen Elizabeth. West was wearing a wide smile and not much else . . . as his kilt stretched across his knees clearly showed. For the next few days the picture generated discussion among our networks of folklorists and pipers. Some scrutinized the photo closely. Was it digitally modified to be more revealing than the original? Did Colonel Simon West know what he was doing? Could it be true? Some saw the photograph as an unfortunate mistake but others immediately understood it as a prank, either on the part of the colonel or at his expense. Most kilt wearers preferred the latter explanation: they suspected Colonel West's stance was intentional and that he was using humor to protest the closure of his battalion as part of a controversial regional amalgamation of Scottish regiments.[1]

As they shared their interpretations, our friends linked the picture and the narratives it prompted to other humorous representations of kilted men in song, contemporary legend, local legend, joke, personal experience narrative, and a growing body of cyber humor comprised of digitally altered images or "photoshops" (see Frank 2009) generated by software

DOI: 10.7330/9780874218985.c010

Figure 10.1 Circulated photo of Colonel Simon West and his Battalion during Queen Elizabeth II's 2004 visit.

editing programs like Photoshop, and websites such as *Worth 1000* (www. worth1000.com) that offer sophisticated instruction on photo editing. Circulated through the Internet as obvious visual jokes or as hoaxes posing as actual news, photoshops have emerged alongside older expressive forms, like joke cycles and photocopy lore, as an important vehicle of humorous political critique (Ellis 2003; Frank 2004). They offer a humorous take on world events from the terrorist attack on the World Trade Center and the devastation of Hurricane Katrina to the actions of elected officials. The photo of West fits into this genre, for although the Mikkelsons were unable to determine if West intentionally posed or if the photo of him was manipulated from the beginning, different versions published in British newspapers the *Daily Mail* and the *Mirror* offer evidence of doctoring. They concluded that "either the *Daily Mail*'s picture was edited for decency's sake, or someone took the original photo and digitally added some extra naughty bits" (Mikkelson and Mikkelson 2004).

Visual cyber humor represents a sizable subset of bawdy humor about men in kilts; a Google image search in December 2010 for "men in kilts" produced over 69,500 hits, which included many examples of male kilt wearers going "regimental style,"[2] that is, without underwear, and (apparently) inadvertently exposed by a gust of wind or a wrong move. Although it is impossible to determine if a decontextualized example, circulated by an email or Facebook link, is staged joke, hoax, or "blooper," certainly some are contrived, as in fact the photo of West may be. However, out of the many examples of exposed men in kilts that circulate on the Internet, it is reasonable to assume that some document accidental situations. As I will explore, the *un*clear intent of this humor parallels the kilt's own ambiguity as a multivalent signifier of ethnicity, gender, and sexuality and, significantly, it opens up these areas for consideration at a time when ideas of masculinity and manhood are being challenged, deconstructed, and redefined (see Kimmel and Messner 2012). With the help of members of Newfoundland's City of St. John's Pipe Band, I reflect on some of the messages about ethnicity and sexuality conveyed by "What's under the kilt?" humor. Here I draw on recorded interviews I conducted in fall 2007 with five band members as well as email correspondence from several others. Because sexual orientation is relevant to this discussion, I note that everyone I consulted self-identified as heterosexual.

PLAYING (WITH) SCOTTISHNESS

Through the streets in my kilt I go
All the lassies cry, "Hello!
Donald, where's your troosers?" (Stewart 1989)

According to the *Oxford English Dictionary*, *kilt* is Middle English and originated in the mid-fourteenth century as a verb in the sense of "tuck up around the body." It has Scandinavian connections, being related to the Danish *kilte,* meaning "tuck (up)" and the Old Norse *kilting,* meaning "a skirt." The use of *kilt* as a noun dates to the mid-eighteenth century, but the history of the garment itself stretches back at least two centuries earlier to the end of the sixteenth century. Originally the "great kilt" was a full-length garment, the upper part of which could serve as a cloak. The bottom half eventually developed into the small, or walking kilt (similar to today's modern kilt).

How the kilt became one of the most familiar markers of Scottishness is a matter of debate (see Trevor-Roper 2008), but its complex story brings together elements of Scottish culture, popular resistance, official military dress, and romantic nationalism. The kilt has been associated with Highland Scottish resistance since the British government attempted to exercise control over Scotland in 1746 through its Disarming Act (see Gibson 1998). The act prohibited the wearing of Highland clothing, including the kilt. Although the act was repealed in 1782, it has been the subject of romantic retellings since (e.g., the 1995 movies *Braveheart* and *Rob Roy*), so that the kilt is now linked not only to Scottish history but to the cultural oppression the Scots suffered at the hands of the English. Members of the British army's Highland regiments who had adopted tartan and kilts as part of their uniform were exempted from the Disarming Act, and after the act's repeal, these elements became even more widespread within the British military. As a result, other contemporary associations stem from the kilt's military connections. After the revocation of the Disarming Act, Highland Societies were created, encouraging both the playing of Highland music and the wearing of Highland dress. King George IV's visit to Scotland in 1822 further strengthened the kilt's position as a symbol of patriotism rather than rebellion. Sir Walter Scott and the Highland Societies celebrated the occasion with much tartan and pageantry that promoted the widespread wearing of Highland dress (Dunbar 1981, 79).

The kilt's adoption and evolution outside Scotland is equally complicated. In my home province of Nova Scotia, Premier Angus L. Macdonald adopted Scottishness as the provincial identity during the second quarter of the twentieth century (McKay 1992, 8), even though some historians argue that neither the Scots settlers nor their descendents actually wore kilts (see Dunbar 1981, 13). By the 1950s, the Nova Scotia provincial government promoted what historian Ian McKay has termed "merry tartanism" (1992, 34) in an effort to sell the province to visitors. They adopted an official provincial tartan and installed a kilted piper at the border to welcome tourists. For some Nova Scotians, the kilt was also a complex expression of "critical nostalgia" (Cashman 2006) in that its evocation of earlier times represented a critique of modernity.

In geographical locations where Scottish ancestry is not promoted, arguably meanings are more convoluted still. In these contexts, the kilt can be read as a performance of Scottish "ethnic drag." Drawing on Homi Bhabha's notion of mimicry (1994) and Judith Butler's concept of gender performativity (1999), Katrin Sieg coined the term *ethnic drag* to refer to "not only cross-racial casting on stage, but more generally, the performance of 'race' as a masquerade." She continues, "As a crossing of racial lines in performance, ethnic drag simultaneously erases and redraws boundaries posturing as ancient and immutable . . . As a technique of estrangement, drag denounces that which dominant ideology presents as normal, and inescapable, without always offering another truth" (2002, 2). Although Sieg was thinking of race, her comments apply equally to displays of ethnicity.

Take the experience of wearing a tartan kilt in Newfoundland, a province that constructs itself as English and Irish. It is something members of the City of St. John's Pipe Band do every time they perform. Established in the mid-1970s, this is still Newfoundland and Labrador's only pipe band more than thirty-five years later. Although the band presents itself as Scottish, playing Scottish tunes and wearing Scottish tartan kilts, most members do not have Scottish ancestry. Membership has fluctuated, peaking at approximately two dozen and ebbing at less than half that number; when Simon West's picture circulated in late 2004, there were about twelve active members (nine men and three women). At that time, one piper was of Scottish birth, but only a few of the others could claim even distant Scottish roots. Rather, most pipers and drummers were graduates of the provincial cadets' band program who simply wanted an opportunity to continue playing.

The vast majority of people who make up the band's local audiences have no Scottish connections either. The province's small population of Scottish descent is located on Newfoundland's west coast, an eight- or ten-hour drive from the capital city, where the band is based. The band receives annual financial support from the City of St. John's, for which it is named, presumably to ensure the availability of pipe music for municipally sponsored events. Although the band is regularly engaged to "pipe in" curlers at a tournament, participants on a pub crawl, members of a head table, or mourners at a funeral, it has difficulty securing performance gigs. In a city with little Scottish heritage, this band is not recognized by residents as their own, as was evidenced a few years ago when the band applied to play at the annual St. John's Folk Festival and was refused.

A member of a Scottish pipe band is by definition an anomaly in a city and province that heavily promote themselves as Irish; he or she is certainly not conceived of as part of the folk culture. And yet, as Caitlin Fry (2007, 2) observed in Australia, "Scottishness is simply not exotic enough to be regarded as 'ethnic.'" A Scottish kilt may symbolize cultural identification in Scotland itself or in places where it creates a feeling of kinship among individuals of Scots descent, such as Nova Scotia (see Crane, Hamilton, and Wilson 2004, 680). But to wear a kilt in St. John's is to perform a form of "reconstructed ethnicity," a term Dean MacCannell uses to refer to "the kinds of ethnic identities which have emerged in response to the pressures of tourism" (1984, 377). He writes:

> *Reconstructed ethnicity*, is the maintenance and preservation of ethnic forms for the entertainment of ethnically different others . . . The new reconstructed ethnic forms are produced once almost all the groups in the world are located in a global network of interactions and they begin to use their former colorful ways both as commodities to be bought and sold, and as rhetorical weaponry in their dealings with one another, suddenly it is not just ethnicity anymore, but it is understood as rhetoric, as symbolic expression with a purpose or a use-value in a larger system. This is the basis for a distinctive form of modern alienation, a kind of loss of soul. (385)

MacCannell paints a bleak picture, noting that relationships between tourists and ethnic locals are at best perfunctory: "Any social relationship which is transitory, superficial and unequal is a primary breeding ground for deceit, exploitation, mistrust, dishonesty, and stereotype formation . . . When the touristic definition of an ethnic group or community prevails, the group is frozen in an image of itself *museumized*. The group becomes a *thing*" (388).

Today most Euro North Americans would recognize dressing in a costume using blackface as inappropriate except for a very few circumstances—such as, for example, when White actors play the title character in Shakespeare's *Othello* or when White singers do the title role in Verdi's opera *Otello*. Employing and/or parodying markers of Scottish identity in a performance of ethnic drag is less problematic, however. In 2006, two years after the photo of Simon West began making its rounds, the Nova Scotian brewery Alexander Keith's continued the long history of stereotyping Scottish ethnicity in a series of popular television ads featuring an angry, stingy Scot. More recently, Scotts Miracle-Gro's 2012 television ads parodied a blustery Scot, sometimes accompanied by his dog Haggis, teaching his neighbors about proper lawn care. Arguably, the depictions in these ads build on the earlier success of comedian Mike Myers and his memorable Scottish characters like Stuart MacKenzie, the stern father in *So I Married an Axe Murderer* (1993) and Fat Bastard, the obese henchman in the second and third Austin Powers movies: *Austin Powers: The Spy Who Shagged Me* (1999) and *Austin Powers in Goldmember* (2002). These are just a few examples, but it is safe to say that the number of Scottish caricatures in contemporary popular culture eclipses that of many other ethnic groups and that Scots are one of the few ethnic groups still joked about publicly.

Although the visibility of Scottish ethnic caricatures and the acceptability of laughing at Scots ethnicity undoubtedly heighten the play factor when members of the City of St. John's Pipe Band perform, in the Newfoundland context, the kilt is not only a marker of Scottishness, it is an indicator of difference. Recent analyses of mummering traditions in Newfoundland demonstrate that the social meanings of blackface in the province drew on both popular constructions of race and ideas about strangers to create a culturally specific expression of otherness (see Best 2008). Similarly, I would argue that when a man wears a tartan kilt in Newfoundland, he is an indicator of otherness as well as a representative of Scottish ethnicity. Band members report being stared at by nearly everyone they meet as well as being stopped, and sometimes verbally harassed, by strangers passing by on foot or in cars. Of course I am not suggesting that it is only in Newfoundland that wearing a kilt attracts attention. One piper I spoke with, who has worn a kilt in cities across two continents, finds that it is only at Highland Games (where characteristically nearly all the male participants, and often a significant percentage of the audience, are in kilts) that he escapes special notice. In all other contexts he draws interest. Although more common in Scotland than other places, the kilt brings looks even on the streets of Edinburgh, where, he says: "People will stare at you because you're either a tourist or you're in the theater or doing a show." The kilt may cue spectacle, but this reference to Scottish tourism both emphasizes how its meanings shift depending on the context and points to its complexity as a sign.

PLAYING (WITH) SEX/UALITY

"The young man joins the Royal Army, and after basic training he comes home on leave in his highland uniform. This first evening in the family parlor, his mother takes him aside and says, 'Son, if you're going to be a soldier, you're going to have to learn to sit like a lady'" (Alex 2004).

Writing as both researcher and member of a Scottish bagpipe band in Australia, Caitlin Fry is quick to characterize the kilt as a "powerful symbol of masculinity, connecting the wearer with constructions of the Scottish Highlander, who embodies aspects of masculinity: toughness, stoicism, courage and embracing a life outdoors" (2007, 8). Fry argues:

The activities undertaken by men while wearing kilts are congruent with masculinity. Men wear the kilt at the football, when out to attract a partner, when getting married, when playing loud and powerful bagpipes, to compete in the "strong men" competitions at Highland Gatherings, where they lift and throw heavy objects. The practicalities of wearing the kilt also emphasize masculinity. The kilt must be strapped on, not buttoned, tied or zipped . . . The kilt is designed for a male body, in particular the fit, young male body of the army . . . It emphasizes an ideal male form, but does not hang so well on a body that transgresses this body type: women, older men and the overweight. (8–9)[3]

As Fry's comments suggest, female bagpipers have not presented a serious challenge to the kilt's masculine identification. Discussion on the subject of women's dress in an online forum for bagpipe players reflects a diversity of uniform choices (Dunsire 2001). After World War II, the number of women pipe bands increased, and while some issued their members a kilt, kilt jacket, and sporran, more often they chose a feminized version of a kilt or skirt. For example, the Canadian Women's Army Corps Pipe

Band, established in 1943, adopted a jacket, military skirt, and no sporran (Cape n.d.). From the 1970s, with the decline of all-women bands and the increased integration of women into co-ed bands that began as all-male organizations, many female pipers have worn the same clothing as their male counterparts, which often consists of a kilt jacket, kilt, and sporran.

Despite the kilt's well-established masculine associations, male kilt wearers experience persistent challenges to their masculinity and repeated requests for clarification concerning their performances of it. The majority of kilt-related humor supports the claim that "the most fascinating and powerful element of wearing the kilt is not the garment, but rather what is underneath" (C. Fry 2007, 10). Some members of the City of St. John's Pipe Band reported being asked the question "What's under the kilt?" "*all* the time." One admits, "I don't know what it is about it. The women love it. They try to lift up under your kilt. They're very open about it." Other band members echo this when they describe how a man's appearance in a kilt signals a time for play. It is as if when a man wears a kilt, everyone's gender identity is called into question. On these occasions, the sense of personal liberation often associated with disguise is either extended or transferred to those female spectators who respond by laughing and asking flirtatiously, "What's under the kilt?" (see Ray 2005, 238).

As Helga Kotthoff explains, "keying"—in this case laughter and a playful tone—is central to conversational humor: "Keying is a process, which regulates the particular reality and coherence relations of utterances . . . In humor the relationship to reality is loosened and special inferences are needed to create 'sense in nonsense,' to use Freud's expression . . . Loosening the relationship between statement and reality means widening the possible scope of imagination. Laughter particles in utterances are important keying markers; they often index that a text is to be interpreted as humorous" (2006, 7). The kilt wearer shifts the context from spectacle to carnival for, as Bakhtin argues, the two are closely related. The exchange that follows invites participation (1968, 7) and temporarily suspends hierarchical order. The question "What under the kilt?" conforms to what Bakhtin describes as "a special type of communication impossible in everyday life" that is "frank and free, permitting no distance between those who came in contact with each other and liberating etiquette and decency imposed at other times" (10).

Based on the female challenge "What's under the kilt?" I would argue, contra Fry, that the kilt is not read uniformly as "the only male garment left unconquered by women" (2007, 1). Rather, for some it more closely approximates female than male attire. By extension, my research with kilt wearers shows that to look like a woman is apparently read by some women as an invitation to treat a man as they themselves are treated. In fact, Fry herself notes that for a man to wear a kilt in public is to become "collective 'property'" (11). Members of the City of St. John's Pipe Band shared experiences that support this view, not only describing how they negotiated verbal harassment but also detailing physical assaults that ranged from a female passerby putting her hand, uninvited, under one's kilt to more organized efforts. One piper describes, "With digital cameras people will, there's a double team thing . . . You get set up. Somebody's, 'I'm really interested in that tie. Is that a regimental tie?' And then of course the partner will go around with a camera and [*whistles, demonstrating person taking picture up under kilt*]."[4] Another piper, a physician, describes encountering coercion that is almost impossible to resist:

> I've often worn kilts to say the Health Care Corporation Gala for the Miller Centre, instead of wearing a tux . . . And . . . sometimes [I've] even been set up. So you know, someone, they would say, 'Now come over. Now listen, this girl wants to ask you a question. If you'll let her find out what's under your kilt, we'll donate to the foundation' . . . And of course you go over there . . . It depends. [Sometimes you let her look because] five hundred is money. Five hundred bucks going to the foundation is [a big donation].

The men's experiences confirm Caitlin Fry's observation that "while literature about dress and gender places emphasis on the visual, many do not simply observe a kilt; they approach and interact with the kilt-wearer" (2007, 11). Significantly, it seems that the question is not asked of women (see 11–12; Ray 2005, 237).

Historically, women have been socialized to be the appreciative recipients of jokes rather than joke tellers, so that when they adopt the medium of sexual humor, they are assuming what Regina Barreca terms "bad girls' humor": "Bad Girls say what they think. This is particularly important because what the Bad Girl says out loud is usually the same thing that everybody else is thinking but is too ashamed to admit. This is often at the heart of women's humor—the ability to say out loud what nobody thought a girl was allowed to think, let alone say" (1991, 49). As women turn the tables on men, they physically show what it means to be read as sexually available because of one's clothing. Their performances might be interpreted as a mimicry of how men more often regard and approach women's bodies. Just as Homi Bhabha understands colonial mimicry to be "the desire for a reformed, recognizable Other, *as a subject of a difference that is almost the same, but not quite,*" women's mimicry exaggerates the usually (but not always) more distanced male gaze and transforms it into verbal and/or physical aggression. It demonstrates the complexities that Bhabha identifies as "the sign of a double articulation" and "complex strategy of reform, regulation and discipline, which 'appropriates' the Other as it visualizes power" (1994, 86).

In some contexts, the women's joking takes on a teasing quality that builds commonality between a woman and a man perceived to be dressed like one. As Jennifer Hay writes, "Humor can challenge existing boundaries, attempt to set new ones, or create or maintain boundaries by making an example of someone present" (2000, 724). The reversal can be a time of education, showing men what it feels like to be under the gaze and even under threat. But the boundaries between acceptable behavior and sexual harassment are fluid where jokes are concerned (Kotthoff 2006, 17). Hay notes, "Some teasing primarily reinforces solidarity and expresses rapport, whereas other teases serve primarily to maintain the power of the teaser" (2000, 720). Whatever the humor's intent, however, it can open up normally unspeakable topics for discussion: "Once speakers agree that they are engaging in humorous interaction, conversational postulates can be violated without interfering with communication . . . Socially unspeakable topics can more readily enter the discourse, because the ambiguity of the humor mode allows them to be talked about in disguised and deniable form" (Crawford 2003, 1420). Characteristic of studies that show women's talk and humor to be subversive and challenging of larger societal discourse regarding gender and sexuality (e.g., see Coates and Jordan 1997; Crawford 2003), women's humorous question "What's under your kilt?" takes advantage of one of those "in-between spaces" that Bhabha identifies as crucial in the articulation of difference (1994, 1). The question takes both men and women out of their patriarchally constructed roles, exploring other social constructions of what it means to be either sex/gender, in an expression that arguably both confirms conventional femininity in its flirtatiousness and serves as a site of resistance to it in its forwardness.

Male audience members sometimes read, or pretend to read, the kilt either as a statement of homosexuality or as a mark of the cross-dresser. For example, a middle-aged piper in the City of St. John's Pipe Band recalled a gig he played in the bar district of St. John's when he was ridiculed: "We played with [the band] Abbey Road . . . [during] the George Street Festival . . . so myself and Jack are standing off to the side and . . . there's this great big gronk behind us. You could hear, 'Queers wearing skirts. Look at the queers wearing skirts.'" Another piper, in his twenties, recounted playing in the closing ceremonies of an ice stadium that had been a fixture in the city for fifty years. As the band played its way out of the building, a male spectator yelled, "Nice fucking skirt!" The drummer reports being "ready to put down the drum and go after him." A third band member, now in his forties, reported encountering even more taunting when he was younger: "I remember before I was driving or if I didn't have the car that night, I'd walk to curling club or whatever and if you'd meet another bunch of high school students then they are given to asinine comments." Onlookers assert hegemonic masculinity (Connell 2005) by distancing themselves through homophobic comments from the man whose dress displays visual ambiguity. When men position themselves against homosexuality, they adopt, as Deborah Cameron argues, a "kind of discursive strategy [that] is not only *about* masculinity, it is a sustained performance *of* masculinity" (1997, 590)

PERFORMING HEGEMONIC MASCULINITY IN A KILT

Attacks clothed in humor are difficult to respond to (see Greenhill et al. 1993; Kotthoff 2006, 13), and many male kilt wearers report opting to stay within the play frame when probed about what's under their kilt. Most band members have a stock answer; in fact, new kilt wearers are sometimes supplied with a selection of quick one-line replies such as "Shoes and socks" (see *Miss Cellania* 2010) because as the handbook *So You're Going to Wear a Kilt!* advises, whatever underwear is actually chosen, "you must never admit you are wearing pants under the kilt. This is part of the mystique" (J. C. Thompson 1989, 98). One of the younger men in the St. John's band responds with "Not a thread," while a longtime piper reports, "I have a standard line that I use . . . when anyone asks, 'What do you wear under the kilt?' . . . I always turn it around: 'So you're asking what's worn under the kilt?' So, of course they say yes and I say, 'There's nothing worn under the kilt. It's all in good working order.'" He goes on to explain the effectiveness of this response: "[The answer] is standard. It's relatively polite. People smile at it. And you don't ruin anyone's fun really and you just go away." The humorous reply, or wisecrack, disciplines the woman who oversteps her bounds at the same time as its one-upmanship elevates the teller's status, a function that some researchers have identified as being more important to men than women (Hay 2000, 733).

Some of the male pipers and drummers describe feeling uncomfortable when drunken women in the audience try to grope under their kilt or when pranks are pulled with cameras. One piper comments, "The practice of having the throwaway cameras on the tables [at weddings is] disastrous.

Especially—I mean, guys will pick them up themselves and *woh ooh* [mimics taking picture under kilt]." However, the band members often turn to humor to right any power imbalance and assert their hegemonic masculinity. A male kilt wearer can be the target of a prank with a camera, but he can also turn the tables. As another piper jokes, "When the bride starts to recognize [band members by what's under their kilts], then you've got problems." He pretends to be looking at wedding pictures with the bride when they come to a photo of a man's genitals that she identifies as Peter: "'How do you know that is Peter?' [The bride answers,] 'Oh, I recognize the tartan in the background [and] the mole at three o'clock.'" The close of his joke erases any question surrounding the kilt wearer's "real" performance of masculinity, and the humor is targeted where it should be in any good patriarchal joke: at the real (biological) woman. Margaret Wetherell and Nigel Edley remind us that hegemony is not automatic but involves contest and constant struggle; male dominance must be continually reasserted at the expense of women and the alternative forms of masculinities it subordinates and marginalizes (1999, 336). While humorous exchanges that equate a man in a kilt with a woman or identify him as homosexual may create opportunities for straight men to rethink power dynamics around gender and sexual orientation, those chances generally seem not to be taken up.

The retorts build on a larger complex of humor depending on this kind of reversal. For example, a well-known folksong that now has countless parodies on YouTube describes the experience of a drunken Scotsman when two women can't resist looking under his kilt as he lies passed out on the street:

> As a gift they left a blue silk ribbon tied onto a bow
> Around the bonnie star the Scots kilt did lift and show . . .
> Now the Scotsman woke to nature's call and stumbled towards the trees
> Behind the bush he did lift his kilt and gawks at what he sees
> And in a startled voice he says to what's before his eyes
> ["]Oh lad I don't know where you've been but I see you've won first prize."
> ("Dying Request" n.d.)

The humor assures, just like the comeback, that "nothing is worn under the kilt" as well as that "everything is in working order." In fact, some of the band members argue that women read the kilt primarily as an indication of sexual availability rather than ambiguity and that this interpretation can be to their advantage if they are heterosexual single men. For example, one of the pipers says he likes to think of the kilt as "eight yards of chick magnet" and prides himself on once picking up a girl when he piped at a funeral. Like the jokes, he transforms the kilt; it is not a feminine skirt but a tool of masculine bravado. He concludes, "That's why you wear a kilt—because you can swagger in it. It's a garment given to swaggering."

Much of the kilt-related humor that band members of the City of St. John's Pipe Band share among themselves reaffirms hegemonic, heterosexual masculinity. For example, walking kilted down the streets of St. John's requires a certain amount of confidence, but one piper claims, "The musical instrument is primary and the costume is secondary." Although his comment suggests that the kilt is almost inconsequential to a piper, he also intimates that this casual attitude is expected and that it distinguishes pipers from other male kilt wearers, like Scottish country dancers, for example, for whom he suggests "the kilt would be a big thing, a primary thing." On the other hand, he argues that pipers don't give the kilt a second thought; they are comfortable because other band members are similarly dressed: "You have your uniform on." Stories of comfort level sometimes separate kilt wearers from those outside the band, as shown in the narrative one band member tells of a friend who fell asleep in his kilt after a night of drinking. He snuggled down and pulled the kilt up around his shoulders for warmth . . . much to the dismay of the cleaners who arrived at the barracks in the morning.

Jokes and pranks teach young men how to move, and apropos of Simon West, how to sit in a kilt, for as a younger drummer in the St. John's band comments, "I know from experience that it is quite possible to have your little man showing and not know it." Successfully maneuvering in a kilt represents a rite of passage, for in contrast to the mother's advice to her son in the well-known joke above, the men actually sit any way but like ladies, with their legs spread open and kilts anchored in between. Knowing where to sit, how to sit, what underwear to wear, or how to march long distances without underwear all mark the experienced kilt wearer. The inexperienced—young men who perch on the side of a chair only to be flipped backward by their friends, those who lose underwear during a march, or those who are badly chafed by the tartan—become the brunt of joke and stories.

How well one wears a kilt helps establish one's place in the band's hierarchy. Misdemeanors are long remembered and, once recorded in the band annals, are difficult to shake. Former band members continue to live on in reputation. For example, the City of St. John's band still comically refers to a former piper who, as one band member put it, "blew too hard and a certain sphincter didn't hold and he was wearing his kilt and it was obvious down the leg and he got his name labeled to that act." A more recent narrative concerns a drummer who, as the story goes "had his shower, puts on his kilt and goes out and comes back after six hours of hard marching and realizes, 'Oh, I left my towel on underneath my kilt.'" While this story is particularly popular among the pipers in that it builds on an "inside" tradition of sharing disparaging narratives about drummers, the drummer at the center of the story also enjoys telling it on himself. Certainly his polished delivery indicates he has told it often.

These few examples illustrate humor's conservative and disciplinary functions. As Christie Davies writes concerning the ethnic joke, people often turn to humor to define themselves in terms of who they are not: "Jokes are told about the members of a group that is recognizably similar and who, to the joke-tellers look like themselves as seen in a distorting mirror" (1998, 12–13). Assuring the world and themselves that "nothing is worn," the men argue that despite any appearances to the contrary, as might be suggested by the kilt's ambiguity, their performance should be read as hegemonic; they are "real men."

COUNTER/HEGEMONIC PERFORMANCES

Much "What's under the kilt?" humor shared by male members of the band constitutes part of irreverent "lad" culture. Paul Fussell has written about the rise of "lads" in World War I, a designation characterized by its warmth (as opposed to "men," which Fussell argues was largely neutral and "boys," which was a little warmer term) as well as its erotic, homosocial overtones (2000, 282). The *Oxford English Dictionary Online* echoes these connections in its definition of "lad" as "informal[,] a boy or young man (often as a form of address) . . . a group of men sharing recreational, working, or other interests." Echoing the focus on homosociality, Celeste Ray sees an emphasis of public ritual at Scottish heritage celebrations like Highland Games to be egalitarian male bonding (2005, 240). She argues that these kinds of public rituals exert a "public patriarchy . . . characterized by public domain processes that are simultaneously patriarchal (hierarchical domination by men) and fratriarchal (collective domination by men)" (241). "What's under the kilt?" humor also operates simultaneously as homosocial and hypermasculine expression for, as the *Oxford English Dictionary Online* indicates, yet another meaning of "lad" is "a man who is boisterously macho in his behavior or actions, especially one who is interested in sexual conquest." Whoever—male or female—may be the attraction of the kilt wearer's sexual interest, as Caitlin Fry points out, the kilt covers but also can quickly expose "unbridled virility at the flick of a hem" (2007, 10).

There is an affectionate rebelliousness to the lad, as the pipers in the St. John's band revealed when they described selecting pieces of music with subtexts: a retreat chosen to play for an unpopular politician or "The Clumsy Lover" selected for a wedding. This defiance might take the form of purposefully positioning a kilt at an opportune moment to expose what is underneath, as band members speculate was the case with Colonel Simon West. To make people laugh is to momentarily have control of the situation, and Simon West's kilt, riding above his knees, photoshopped or not, shows the world that he has not been co-opted—and, by extension, nor have members of his regiment. The photo, taken in the throes of the controversial amalgamation of the Scottish regiments, may well protest the demise of the First Battalion of the Argyll and Sutherland Highlanders. Perhaps this was West's intention, as members of the St. John's band believe, or it may express the viewpoints of others who later engaged in some creative photoediting. In a military structure that allows little if any room for contestation of official decision making, jokes may be particularly valuable as a vehicle for protest. Rebellious humor provides momentary freedom from the constraints of social convention, or what Michael Billig terms "a moment of transcendence" (2005, 208), when power relations can be temporarily inverted without lasting consequences (Crawford 2003, 1420).

MULTIPLE READINGS

The ambiguity of the kilt is suited to humorous discourse, which is itself characterized by ambiguity, paradox, multiple interpretations of reality, and partially resolved incongruity. Elliott Oring writes: "Jokes are highly ambiguous forms of communication. Jokes are grounded in a system of relations that are 'appropriately incongruous' and thus to some extent self-contradictory. The techniques of jokes would be rejected were they employed in logical argument. Jokes are a species of play, and messages lodged within the play frame are often obscure. Even when particular ideas raised by a joke can be precisely identified, the position of the joke teller with respect to these ideas may be uncertain. Consequently, jokes are not transparent and their messages may not be simple, clear, or unambiguous" (2003, 59). While joking about those in power may provide a much-appreciated outlet for frustration and even create a temporary reversal, it does not bring about permanent transformation (see Billig 2005, 212). In fact, some analysts see the primary benefit of rebellious humor to be for the joke teller rather than any larger group or cause (Wetherell and Edley 1999, 350). Far from being transformative, rebellious constructions of masculinity may still function to reproduce male power (Crawford 2003, 1423).

Meanings behind "What's under the kilt?" humor are multifaceted, sometimes contradictory, and support what Wetherell and Edley describe as "a multiplicity of hegemonic sense-making" (1999, 351). The kilt introduces a play frame that invites carnavalesque behavior by individuals—male kilt wearers as well as female and male spectators—engaged in accomplishing a wide variety of identity positions (352). Ray contends that "Scottish-American men are exploring the 'plurality of masculinities' modeled by forefathers and from which to draw a sense of male identity . . . They are also submitting themselves, in ritual and dress, as objects to the gaze of women and other men." Although Ray suggests that putting patriarchy and masculinity "on a pedestal" reflects changes in the power of gender identities (2005, 257), I would argue that jokes directed toward, or told by, male kilt wearers do not have either immediately transformative or lasting consequences; at best they open up a space to explore hegemonic masculinity and to challenge power structures that support it. Conversely, much "What's under the kilt?" humor supports hegemonic performances of ethnicity and gender; its challenges to official culture are easily contained. As Billig argues, "Far from subverting the serious world of power, the humor can strengthen it . . . The more we laugh and the more we imagine ourselves to be daringly free in the moments of our laughter, the more we are complying with the demands of the so-called free market. And the more we reveal ourselves captive to the demand that we possess a naughty sense of humor" (2005, 212). Simon West's kilt, resting above his knees, may register serious objections to the closure of his regiment; it can be read as a sign that even though regiment members obey orders, they have not been silenced. At the same time, the humor reasserts male authority: the man in a skirt is a man.

NOTES

Thank you to Peter Latta and other members of the City of St. John's Pipe Band who shared their kilt-wearing experiences with me. Of course I take full responsibility for all interpretations, which may or may not be shared by band members. An earlier version of this chapter was presented to the American Folklore Society, Quebec City, October 2007, and I benefited from the discussion and questions generated at that time. Thanks to Heather King for first forwarding the photo of Simon West to me, Ben Staple for his research assistance, and Pauline Greenhill for her close reading and helpful suggestions.

1. Protest against the amalgamation of the regiments was led by an organization called Save the Scottish Regiments. In December 2004, over 2,000 campaigners marched through Edinburgh to express their opposition (see BBC News 2004). Six years later, feelings were

still running high when Lieutenant General Sir Alistair Irwin's appointment as president of the Royal British Legion Scotland drew criticism. Scotland's most senior soldier until his retirement in 2006, Irwin wrote a paper for the army's executive board that proposed the abolition of single-battalion regiments for a large regional formation ("Veterans 'Lose Faith' in Poppy Charity Chief" 2010).

2. The practice of not wearing underwear under a kilt was adopted by military regiments and crossed over to civilians. The question of what one should wear under a kilt is a perennial one. In November 2010 it surfaced again and in response, Brian Wilton, director of the Scottish Tartans Authority, advised wearing underwear for reasons of hygiene and decency (Mclaughlin 2010).

3. Of course, contra Caitlin Fry, not all women's bodies are uniform, and not all older men are unfit. Further, many Canadian private girls' schools have adopted kilts as part of their uniform.

4. See Caitlin Fry (2007, 12) for an Australian example of this.

11

"Composed for the Honor and Glory of the Ladies"

Folklore and Medieval Women's Sexuality in The Distaff Gospels

Theresa A. Vaughan

Night 1, chapter 21

> "If a woman wants to know for certain whether her husband is betraying her, she must watch to see if he spends a full lunar month without approaching her: then, if she suspects him, it is certainly not without reason."
>
> Gloss. "This gospel is true," said Maroie Ployarde, "because, for more than three lunar months, Jan Ployard, my husband, has not done anything, as if I am the kind of woman to put up with that!" (Jeay and Garay 2006, 97)

*T*HE *D*ISTAFF *G*OSPELS (*LES EVANGILES DES QUENOUILLES*), a fifteenth-century French manuscript, presents a series of about 230 items of folklore—beliefs, sayings, and remedies—within a frame narrative.[1] It shares this structure, linking loosely related stories in the context of a sequence of tellings, with more famous works from the Middle Ages, including Chaucer's *The Canterbury Tales* and Boccaccio's *Decameron*. In the most commonly read version of *The Distaff Gospels*, the so-called Paris Manuscript,[2] a clerk agrees to spend six successive nights recording the "gospels" of older women and the responses of those who gather to hear and discuss the important knowledge being taught. Each night, one woman is appointed a "doctoresse," or teacher, in a setting deliberately imitating a male-centered classroom. The doctoresse proclaims a statement from an authoritative source, in this case popular belief. These ideas gain respectability by being referred to as "gospels," but the ironic tone mocks both the women and the ecclesiastical tradition. The students—the

DOI: 10.7330/9780874218985.c011

other women present—comment upon and affirm the statement in the "gloss"[3] through their own experience or that of others. The clerk assigns each proclamation a chapter, as if it were a selection of a biblical text.

The distaff, used to spin thread, refers both to a tool that the women employ during their gatherings and to women's domains in general.[4] Until the industrial age, spinning was a common daily occupation for women of most social classes in their spare time, a task that could be undertaken when sitting, standing, or even walking. Thus, the name of the collection, *The Distaff Gospels*, refers to the world of women in general on the basis of their common occupation, the spinning of wool or flax into thread that would be eventually woven into cloth.[5]

Although respectful to the women in their presence, the often-bemused clerk frequently mocks them and distances himself from their "gospels" when he records them. While the text itself, and the frame narrative in particular, can be placed within the antifeminist tradition of medieval writing (or at least the *querelle des femmes*),[6] it nevertheless records women's popular beliefs, sayings, and remedies. Though ostensibly written by a man, the clerk, who often finds humor in mocking silly, domineering, and oversexed old women, the folklore itself, found in the gospels as opposed to the glosses, is neither misogynistic nor male dominated. Instead it likely represents folklore about women and possibly even by women, embodied in women who are fully strong-willed, intelligent, and sexual beings, commenting upon and influencing their lives. For example, the women discuss a typical sexual remedy:

Night 2, chapter 1

> "I tell you, as true as the gospel, that when a woman wants to be well loved by her husband or her lover, she must give him catnip to eat: he will be so much in love with her that he will not rest until she is close to him."
>
> Gloss. "This is true," said Burghe Fauvele, "because I did that with my husband and I prepared a salad with it. But that love lasted only six weeks and this is why I think that it must be repeated often." (Jeay and Garay 2006, 103)

Or, in the case of a condemnation of men who beat women:

Night 5, chapter 14

> "If a woman's throat itches, it is a sign of good news, that she will soon have a good meal at a wedding or a churching feast.[7] But if her head is itching, it is a bad sign because she could be beaten by her husband."

Gloss. Perrette Longues Tettes said that when a man who has beaten his
wife in the past has an itchy throat, it is a sign that he will be hanged. (167)

Most scholars consider the traditions in the *Gospels* to more or less accurately reflect fifteenth-century folklore. *The Distaff Gospels'* contents concern
women, whose actual daily issues may be discerned in them. It is thus likely
that they reflect women's folklore, and they may in some instances actually
come from women. In contrast, Gretchen Angelo (2003) and Madeleine
Jeay (1982) presume that the quotations attributed to the gathered women
in the glosses were inserted by the male author or authors for misogynistic
comic effect. Literature of the time period was nearly always male authored,
and the glosses' comments mirror the language of other contemporary fictional works by men. In particular, they resemble the comic literature that
often plays upon stock characters like the oversexed old woman and the
weak and cuckolded man—figures medieval people apparently found amusing. Nevertheless, Laura Doyle Gates (1997), among others, argues that
even in the glosses, with their obvious female caricatures, irrepressible old
women with strong opinions and identities emerge. In that sense, though
the glosses may have been intended for comic effect, misogyny is not the
only trope that is present.

There are multiple editions of *The Distaff Gospels*. Originally written and
published in French as *Euvangiles des queneules (Les évangiles des quenouilles*
in modern French), it has also appeared in English, Dutch, and German
versions as well as an Occitan adaptation. No modern English translation
existed until recently when Jeay and Kathleen Garay published a critical edition and English translation in 2006. There are two complete early manuscripts in French: the shorter, anonymous Chantilly version, likely written
sometime before 1474,[8] and the longer but more widely read Paris version,
probably written sometime in the late 1480s. The latter, commonly attributed to Fouquart de Cambray, Anthoine du Val, and Jean d'Arras, is the
most frequently published and translated. Although the gospels and folklore
in the Chantilly and Paris texts are similar, the latter has the best-developed
frame narrative, glosses, and added examples. However, most scholars see it
as the more overtly misogynist (e.g., Angelo 2001, 25; Jeay and Garay 2006,
26–27; Small 2009, 232).

Between 1482 and 1490, no fewer than five different printings from
two publishing houses in France came out, indicating the text's popularity.
The first English translation, circa 1510, by Wynkyn de Worde in London,
also went through several editions and sold well (Jeay and Garay 2006, 27).
The original intended audience for the manuscripts is not entirely clear, but

evidence suggests that they were written for the Burgundian court rather than for scholarly or ecclesiastical consumption (Angelo 2003, 86). Given their target readership of aristocratic courtiers, it is not surprising that these manuscripts were written in vernacular French rather than in Latin. The incunabula[9] and later print works, illustrated with standard woodcuts, were for the less well-to-do.

Most folklore in the manuscripts comes from the regions of Flanders and Picardy (Krueger 1988, 943). In *Savoir faire: Une analyze des croyances des "Evangiles des quenouilles"* (1982), Jeay makes a convincing case that the folklore collected and contained within *The Distaff Gospels* is not merely the creation of the manuscript authors. Quite a number of the beliefs in *The Distaff Gospels* also appear in *Le Folk-lore de France* by Paul Sébillot, (2006) a four-volume collection of nineteenth-century traditions published from 1904 to 1907, with emphasis on material from northern France. Jeay argues that the presence of similar or even identical beliefs nearly four centuries later indicates the authenticity of those found in *The Distaff Gospels*. She contends that beliefs, sayings, and remedies from the fifteenth century could survive in recognizable form into the nineteenth century, given the rather conservative nature of folklore. This assertion has been accepted in subsequent works (see L. D. Gates 1997; Morris 1988).[10] Feminist academics who have examined and analyzed *The Distaff Gospels* over the past twenty years (e.g., Angelo 2001; L .D. Gates 1997; Jeay 1982; Phillips 2007), concentrate largely on antifeminist literature and the querelle des femmes; on the contrast between orality and literacy (the women representing orality, the male scribe representing literacy); and on scholarly versus popular literature. While the conclusions they have reached vary, some argue that the voices of the women are negated by the mocking gaze and words of the scribe (Angelo 2003), while others contend that both male and female voices can be heard in this text. The latter suggest that women's voices cannot be completely silenced by the clerk or the misogynistic tone set by the male authors (L. D. Gates 1997). The comic characters themselves, while humorous and likely the invention of the male author or authors, display an admirable irrepressibility that cannot be termed wholly misogynistic in character. In addition, such critics point out that the work's comic nature allows the women's voices, even those within the narrative frame, to take on a joyful and laughing essence (Perfetti 2003, 114–115).

While modern scholars link this type of text to misogynistic traditions or to related genres such as the *fabliaux*,[11] and portions of the work unquestionably criticize women and femininity, *The Distaff Gospel*'s authors most likely imitated the typical literature produced by male clerks for comic effect. University clerks compiled collections of misogynist, often humorous stories for use by priests in their sermons and other preaching. Such works formed part of their intellectual training. "When we look closely at these male-authored texts, however, we find that clichés about women's talkativeness, excessive libido, and deceitfulness are played with, reversed to charge men with the same faults, or reconfigured in ways that make trouble with easy antifeminist essentialism" (Perfetti 2003, 2–3).

To analyze the text as a whole, including the Chantilly manuscript and most especially the Paris manuscript, we must consider it on a number of levels. Folklore in the form of beliefs, sayings, and remedies from oral tradition lies at its core. Circumscribing that material, the narrative frame must be understood within the emerging vernacular literary tradition of the time, drawing from the both the ecclesiastical and scholastic perspectives. The use of the ecclesiastical seats the format within the realm of aristocratic, rather than more popular works, as upper-class audiences would have received training in the ecclesiastical tradition, while the middle class would not. The manuscript authors play with these different traditions from the church and the academy to comic effect, as I demonstrate below.

Little work on *The Distaff Gospels* published to date has taken ethnological or folkloristic approaches to it beyond noting evidence of its folklore's authenticity. Instead, most scholars explore the text within the literary tradition. Jeay's work offers one notable exception, particularly *Savoir faire* (1982). In it, Jeay (also the translator of a modern French version of the *Evangiles* [1985]) first demonstrates the authenticity of the folklore by working backward, primarily from the work of Sébillot, mentioned above.[12] She then proceeds to a structuralist analysis of the *Gospels'* traditions, using, among others, the article "Brown County Superstitions: The Structure of Superstition" by Alan Dundes (1961). Jeay is, without a doubt, the foremost modern authority on the *Evangiles*. However her attempt to fit these folk beliefs into a structuralist framework produces an analysis that some American scholars find less successful than it might be (Morris 1988). American folklorists have not found beliefs and superstitions[13] particularly amenable to structuralist methodology. Even Dundes's abovementioned work does little more than discuss the definition of superstition and broadly classify the beliefs he collected into the categories of signs, magic, and conversion superstitions.

Another quasi-structuralist, or at least classificatory, attempt to analyze the lore in the *Evangiles* was undertaken by Anne Paupert in *Les fileuses et le clerc: Une étude des "Evangiles de quenouilles"* (1990). In it, she supports Jeay's assertion that the *Gospels'* folklore is authentic by comparing it with similar beliefs from later periods and extrapolating backward through time. It seems clear, then, that the text represents the rural popular culture of Flanders and Picardy, particularly as it pertained to women's experiences of marriage, childbirth, and child care, and to their folk remedies. It also demonstrates that the aristocratic or elite culture of the day was sufficiently removed from rural life by this point that a collection of such rural lore would be interesting and amusing for its intended aristocratic audience. The bulk of Paupert's book classifies beliefs (Jeay 1993, 1107). Neither Jeay nor Paupert incorporates much English-language folklore scholarship in their analyses, and the reader familiar with the latter literature may experience a disconnect between it and what the two scholars set out to accomplish. Thus, analysis in French of the *Distaff Gospels* can be fruitfully supplemented from the perspectives of English-language folklore studies.

While being mindful of the difficulty of pinpointing the exact cultural context for these beliefs, feminist scholarship on women's folklore offers a useful mode of analysis. As much groundbreaking work (see Farrer 1986; Greenhill and Tye 1997; Hollis, Pershing, and Young 1993; Jordan and Kalčik 1985; Radner 1993) has demonstrated, women's folklore can be subversive, enhance female-centered relationships, and express a worldview and concerns that are and were unique but interdependent with the traditions of the culture as a whole. For example, in studying a body of nineteenth-century local legends recorded by Mary Katzman Lawson, a writer and newspaper editor from Preston, Nova Scotia, folklorist Diane Tye (2002) compares stories Lawson composed based on legends told to her by her mother and published as a series in her newspaper, the *Provincial*, with later revisions that were shaped by a male editor and published as an official community history. The early narratives that draw directly on oral tradition express a female-centered worldview; they reflect multiple viewpoints and take up difficult subjects, including domestic violence. In contrast, the later versions concentrate more heavily on the "facts," draw on public documents such as court records rather than oral testimony, and create a linear narrative of progress and respectability. Tye's work represents just one approach to the examination of historic traditions.

It can sometimes be difficult to sort out the relationship between folklore and text in the Middles Ages (Peck 2007, 100). A considerable body of scholarship addresses the interplay among folktale, myth, and legend in medieval literature, but less has been said about the place of folk belief in the literary tradition. With respect to the *Gospels*, the distinction manifests between the ideas of the elite, relatively urbanized, educated audience at whom the book is aimed and the beliefs of the rural peasant women who proclaim their "gospels" on each successive night. We should keep in mind, however, that while an aristocratic audience may have found peasants, and especially old peasant women, amusing in part due to class differences, at this point in history there was no romantic glorification of peasant life. Such a view, associated with the nineteenth-century social evolutionary theories of British and British-influenced folklore and anthropology, dates to centuries after the *Gospels* were published. Medieval aristocratic people would likely have thought of peasants as simple and unsophisticated, but would not have seen them as representing some earlier phase of sociocultural development. As anthropologist Stanley Jeyaraja Tambiah (1990) has argued, the scientific orientation that radically altered Western worldviews was absent in medieval Europe. We cannot assign scientific meaning, or lack thereof, in the modern sense to medieval belief. Analyzing magic, the supernatural, and folk belief presented in *The Distaff Gospels*, we must allow for a different way of thinking about the world.

Medieval ideas about the beliefs of rural women would have been influenced by the twin strands of authority that privileged the writings of antiquity, on the one hand, and the traditions of the church on the other. Although fifteenth-century Italy was going through significant intellectual evolution, the development of humanism, and the reexamination of religious ideas, the world of Flanders—that of the *Gospels*— would have been less influenced by these trends.[14] The text's humor comes not from the "bad science" of the women speaking but from the much older tradition of misogyny inspired partly, but certainly not entirely, by ecclesiastical literature. It made women into men's intellectual inferiors, ruled by their sexual appetites,[15] and it contrasted elite and peasant cultures or, perhaps, literate and oral cultures (Angelo 2001; Loyson 2004).

By the end of the fifteenth century, women like Hildegard of Bingen, Christine de Pizan, and Heloise, to name some of the best known, sought to become part of the intellectual and ecclesiastical writing traditions (Blamires 1992; Dinshaw and Wallace 2003). And others, like the aristocratic Marie de France, influenced the vernacular tradition of literature and poetry (Dinshaw and Wallace 2003). However, the female characters in *The Distaff Gospels* express their beliefs and customs within a framework that knowingly acknowledges and mocks scholasticism and theological debate, juxtaposing the male, educated tradition with the oral tradition of the uneducated women. The male clerk who records their pronouncements in both the Chantilly and Paris manuscripts, and comments on the women's beliefs in the Paris manuscript, makes it clear that he distances himself from them. For example, on the fourth night, after a lively session that would be followed by the women throwing themselves a party, the clerk writes: "I was sorry not to have another man's company so that I might have laughed with him because, truly, their ways were very strange and, as far as I could tell, they seemed to think that, from now on, the world should be ruled and governed by their constitutions and chapters" (Jeay and Garay 2006, 155). Or, following the fifth night, "After my farewell, I took my leave and went to rest since my head was empty because of their senseless talk that my mind had quite failed to grasp" (173). Finally, at the conclusion of the *Gospels*, the author writes, "You, my lords and ladies, who will read or have read this short treatise, consider it as a pastime for idle moments; don't give any consideration to anything which has been written, if you please, and don't look for any benefit, essential truth or good lesson. Instead, consider that it has been written to demonstrate the frailty of those who gossip in this way when they are together" (189).

The literate male writer seeks to detach himself both from the actual knowledge contained within the "gospels" and from the women themselves. Possibly he fears that his association with them might weaken his reputation by showing that he identifies overmuch with the culture of women, thus calling into question his masculinity. Dismissing women's conversation as "gossip" is a long-held strategy for disempowering women's words (Kousaleos 1999; Weigle 1982). Thus the clerk mocks the women both for the sake of humor and to show that what they say doesn't actually carry the weight of truth (L. D. Gates 1997, 17). It has also been suggested that perhaps these beliefs, because they were not church sanctioned and thus possibly were associated with heresy or witchcraft, needed to be soundly repudiated in the text so that the author(s) would not come under suspicion by the authorities (Shaus 2006, 266).

From this point forward, I will refer to the Paris manuscript only. The doctoresses who preside over each of the six nights of instruction and proclamation of their gospels deserve some mention, as they help to set the stage for what will follow. On the first night, Monday, we meet Dame Ysengrine du Glay (Ysengrine the Joyous). Ysengrine, sixty-five, has been married five times and has taken several lovers. A midwife, she fears that her younger husband will be unfaithful. Midwives had a poor reputation, especially since the delivery of children had become the purview of the medical establishment after the founding of the university system in the 1100s. Midwives were increasingly viewed as merely superstitious old women rather than legitimate medical practitioners (Jeay and Garay 2006, 79). Medieval people found the character of the oversexed old woman or widow amusing, and they are common in French fabliaux and comic literature (Karras 2005, 81). From the point of view of the church, widows who could not remain chaste were encouraged to remarry. "The church followed the lead of male scholars (and poets) who suggested that women's sexual appetites were voracious and, once unleashed, difficult to manage" (Hanawalt 2003, 60). The church viewed women, generally associated with sexual appetite and lack of control, as temptations to men until the age at which they had lost their beauty and attractiveness and were found to be merely comical. That did not mean, however that women didn't actually enjoy sex into their later years—the *Gospels* suggests that many of them did.

The subsequent nights feature Transeline du Croq (Transeline the Hooker), age sixty, skilled at divination and the concubine of a priest; Abonde du Four (Abonde of the Oven), a corpulent retired prostitute; Sebile des Mares (Sibyl of the Swamps) from Vaud, aged fifty-seven and associated with heresy and witchcraft; Gomberde la Faee (Gomberde the Sorceress), still with a strong sex drive but married to a man who doesn't want sex as much as she; and Berthe de Corne (Berthe the Horny), about eighty and secretly trained by her father, a doctor, implying that she practiced medicine, which was generally illegal for women to do at this point in the medieval period (Jeay and Garay 2006).

These women, fitting the literary comic stereotype of oversexed old women who may also be dabbling in witchcraft, are presented for the amusement of members of the elite audience, who saw themselves in radically different terms. Elite women were expected to marry in order to preserve family titles and property rights but were not normally portrayed as wantonly sexual. Aristocratic women, according to tradition, had greater control of their desires and behavior than did peasants. Their only alternative to the socially acceptable role of chaste wife was to participate in the courtly love of Marie de France, whereby they were objects of adoration but out of reach to knights. They were expected to have more self-control than peasant women had (Shahar 2003, 126).

Within the *Gospels*, however, we see a more nuanced picture of women and their knowledge. For example, the lore of the first night, led by Ysengrine du Glay, highlights gender conflict between men and women, particularly within marriage. For example:

Night 1, chapter 1

> "And in this regard, and for my first chapter, I say that it is as true as the gospel that the man who wrongfully wastes the possessions that come to him from his wife, without her permission and against her wishes, will answer for this before God, as if he had committed a theft."

> Gloss. On this chapter an old woman called Griele, wife of Jehan Joquesus, said that indeed the husband who acts as described in this chapter is sent to purgatory for wicked husbands after dying in a vat of brimstone, if he has not carried out his penance in this world by making donations to the sick. (Jeay and Garay 2006, 81)

This chapter refers to the customs of marriage dowry, which vary over the medieval period and from place to place. Generally speaking, by the later Middle Ages, women would bring a dowry into the marriage and would also receive a dower, a gift of land or property, from the husband's family. Ostensibly, women were supposed to retain some control over both the dower and dowry, and would retain rights to both if widowed (see Amt 2010, 44–45). In some places, women legally operated businesses independently of their husbands or male relatives. Widows who had retained sizable assets from one or more previous marriages became attractive candidates for remarriage (Shahar 2003, 237–239). According to law, husbands were supposed to secure permission from their wives to use these assets—although in practice this did not always happen.[16] In most locations, her resources could not be used to pay her husband's debts, for example, without her permission. The gospel pronounced by Ysengrine du Glay, and confirmed by Griele, assigns a harsh quasi-spiritual punishment (burning in molten rock) to men who go against their wives' wishes regarding use of their property.

Other examples from the first evening address this and other problems that wives encounter in marriages. Night 1, chapter 2 decries men who do not follow the advice of their wives. Chapter 3 asserts that men who beat their wives will never obtain the mercy of the Virgin Mary. Chapter 4 indicates that men who take actions without informing their wives are worse than thieves (Jeay and Garay 2006, 83). Chapter 5 echoes chapter 1, expanding condemnation to men who squander household resources, even if not from the wives' assets (83, 85). In chapter 18, we find that husbands are to blame when they, or their wives, stray sexually (95).

Among the other examples from the first night, we find divinatory and instructional advice pertaining to marriage, although typically the women's response in the gloss reflects social commentary:

Night 1, chapter 6

> "A young woman who wishes to know the name of her future husband should stretch out the first thread which she has spun that day at her door and then find out the name of the first man to pass by—she can be certain that this will be the name of her husband."

> Gloss. To this, one of the gathering, Geffrine, wife of Jean le Bleu,
> stood up and said that she has proven this from her own experience and
> that this very thing happened to her—she curses the moment that she met
> the man who has now lost all his bloom and good looks and who was such
> a poor lover that he did nothing but sleep. (Jeay and Garay 2006, 85)

The gospel here states a fairly typical divination technique for deter-
mining a future husband's name. Many such methods exist in cultures
worldwide, including dropping an apple peeling, the shape of which forms
the letter that will begin the name of one's husband, or leaving the written
letters of the alphabet facedown in a basin of water overnight; the one facing up in the morning similarly signifies (Opie and Tatem 1989, 276). The
gloss, in this case, reflects the common medieval literary trope of the husband who cannot perform sexually, although it is not unrealistic to imagine
a woman being dissatisfied with her husband's loss of attractiveness and sex
drive. The medieval reader would have found amusing the juxtaposition of
the tired old man, no longer virile, with the sexually potent old woman.

Other examples from the first night that involve methods of divination
or supernatural consequences include the following: the tenth gospel states
that a young woman who drinks milk boiled in a frying pan or earthen pot
will find that it will rain on her wedding day, and that her husband will be ill
tempered. In the twelfth gospel, we find that if a young virgin woman marries an equally inexperienced young man, their first child will be "simple"
(Jeay and Garay 2006, 89). In chapter 16, the woman who eats the last
cherry while with her suitor will be the last to marry—although the wording
implies that eating the last cherry is some sort of game (93). As the epigraph
shows, the twenty-first chapter advises that a woman who suspects her husband of cheating on her should see if he goes at least one lunar month
without approaching her sexually—if this happens, then her suspicions are
grounded (97). Another method of detecting a straying husband is found in
chapter 25: if a woman loses her garter in the middle of a street, it is a sure
sign that her husband (or lover) is cheating (95).

The subsequent evenings also feature folklore that pertains to women.
I have chosen only those examples that relate directly to sexuality and/or
gender roles. Sayings suggest that a man who offers his mistress a knife as a
New Year's gift will cool the love between them (night 2, chapter 20, Jeay
and Garay 2006, 117); that a man who is mounting a horse should not
accept any sword or piece of equipment from his wife or he will be unable
to use it when necessary (night 3, chapter 20, 135); that a married man who
has an affair with a married woman will never enter heaven (night 4, chapter

7, 143); and that a man who has kissed the altar after Mass must not kiss any woman other than his wife for the following week (night 4, chapter 8, 143, 145). All constrain men but implicate women, as they have consequences for a man's wife or lover. I note particularly that night 4, chapter 7 is in keeping with many of the sayings of the first night, in that a man who betrays his wife will find spiritual consequences for his misbehavior.

Spells, remedies, and divination are also included. A woman should feed her husband or lover catnip in order to increase his sexual desire for her (night 2, chapter 1, Jeay and Garay 2006, 101, 103). A woman who fears she is being ridden by an incubus[17] at night should place an oak stool in front of the fire so the incubus will sit down on it and be unable to get up (night 2, chapter 10, 109). If a woman places a walnut leaf picked just before nones[18] on midsummer's night in her husband's or lover's left shoe, he will love her passionately (night 4, chapter 23, 153). If a woman makes a soup from herbs picked just before dawn on midsummer's night and feeds it to her beloved, he will love her and will never leave her (night 5, chapter 1, 159). If a woman wishes to avoid being beaten by her husband, she should put his shirts under the altar on a Friday celebration of the Passion,[19] then have him wear one on Sunday. He will be sweet and loving (night 5, chapter 2, 161). If a woman has an itchy head, it is a sign that she may be beaten by her husband (night 5, chapter 14, 167). White fever (lovesickness) can be worse than other fevers but can be cured with a soup made in St. George's vessel (night 6, chapter 6, 177, 179).[20]

Most of these beliefs have to do with love and sexuality. One specifically addresses the issue of domestic violence. In each case, women attempt to exert control over uncertainties that affect their well-being. The sexuality and behavior of others concern women in their own lives, but desires for one's own gratification or safety can be difficult to impose on others. Divination, spells, and remedies help women control uncertainty and make men (and incubi!) conform to their wills.

Several sayings and proverbs concern incest taboos, including that a man who initiates sex with his commother[21] will not go to heaven unless his godson does penance for both of his godparents (night 4, chapter 3, Jeay and Garay 2006, 141). Incest taboos relate to the forbidden or darker side of sexuality. In this case, the church's rules prohibiting sex between even non–blood kin godparents of the same child could be troublesome. If the community were small, the practice of naming multiple godparents could limit the number of licit sexual partners. Note here, however, that there is no open disagreement with church law but rather an implicit assertion that it would be the man, rather than the woman, who would initiate illicit sex.

The *Gospels* also include sayings and proverbs regarding the sexual lives of men and women of the church. Clergy who have intercourse with nuns or other women religious will die in pain and with an erect penis (night 4, chapter 4, Jeay and Garay 2006, 141, 143). A woman who remains the mistress of a priest until her death is the "devil's mount," and will not achieve salvation (night 4, chapter 5, 143). If a priest or friar has sex with a married woman, he cannot be granted forgiveness unless the husband grants it first (night 4, chapter 6, 143). Two levels of discourse work here. The clerical or ecclesiastical tradition condemns sexual activity on the part of clergy. The popular tradition, however, acknowledges their frequent engagement in illicit sex. Perhaps straddling both traditions, women as well as men are condemned for the practice. We are faced by a contradiction, however, when we learn that Transeline du Croq, the leader of the second night, "retired and became the concubine of the priest in town who heard her confession night and day, which is why all her neighbors treated her with great reverence" (103). Oversexed clergy are present in fabliaux, and in *The Distaff Gospels* women both enjoy their ministrations and condemn them for their sins.

The above reflect women's belief and knowledge. But within the glosses, the author of the Paris manuscript increases his manuscript's comedic impact. For example:

Night 4, chapter 18

> "When a woman has a cock which is slow and shy, she should give him garlic to eat and rub its crest with it, and it will be stronger and sturdier and also better at exercising its rights over the hens."
>   Gloss. "If someone could find the herb which revives shy husbands," said Marotte Ridee, "I would give my shirt and even beg for my bread."
> (Jeay and Garay 2006, 151)

The prescription of garlic to improve the health and performance of a rooster is traditional. However, the gloss adds a humorous twist by depicting one of the women, Marotte Ridee, as old but still quite eager for sex.

Folklorists are at a disadvantage in interpreting the folklore presented in *The Distaff Gospels*. We cannot see it performed in its original context, and an artificial framing narrative intervenes from a male point of view. Even the examples of folklore, though probably authentic to the time period, may or may not have been collected from women to begin with; we simply have no evidence either way. Virtually all folklore from the Middle Ages and later periods encounters the same problems, rendering it somewhat difficult to ascribe modern feminist interpretations. The bulk of work in feminist folkloristics dates to the 1970s and later and has concentrated primarily, although certainly not exclusively, on contemporary cultures (Greenhill, Tye, and Cantú 2009, xxiv–xxv). Despite work on medieval folklore by medievalists and folklorists, the overlap between medieval studies and contemporary folkloristics is still less than it might be, particularly in the area of feminist scholarship (Lindahl, McNamara, and Lindow 2002, xix–xxii; Sautman, Conchado, and Di Scipio 1998, 1–17).

Nevertheless, presuming at least some of its material as women's own traditions, the beliefs and customs found in *The Distaff Gospels* demonstrate that women had many of the same domestic concerns as they do today. They wanted their voices to be heard in the marital relationship and beyond. They wanted control over their own resources, or at least consultation in their use. They faced the challenges of domestic violence and its avoidance. They wanted satisfying sex lives and attentive partners. They were sometimes concerned about the fidelity of their husbands and lovers. They were curious about whom they would marry, and wanted some control over their future health and welfare and that of their husbands and children. Traditional forms of expression held great importance for women, who had no access to channels of formal decision making (Greenhill and Tye 1997; Radner 1993). All of these concerns are expressed through the religious beliefs and cultural norms of their time, and all remain common to women today.

The complications of interpreting this lore in its specific cultural context should not prevent us from appreciating that the women it quotes and comments on were not silent, asexual creatures. Our ability to see medieval women as sexual beings has been hindered by the incorrect modern assumption that medieval Europe, largely under the sway of a church that had since the time of its fathers propounded a negative view of sexuality and of sexual intercourse, rendered women silent on the subject of sex (Karras 2005, 18). Instead, while medieval life had very strict gender definitions and restrictions on acceptable behavior, medieval people talked about sex in a way we might today find rather straightforward and surprising (19). According to Ruth Mazo Karras, the medieval era was also a world in which, it can be safely assumed, a large number of men and women ignored the writings of ecclesiastical and scholarly men about the problems of sexual intercourse and the virtues of chastity (21). Or, if there were not a total disregard for church teachings, it was a world in which people chose to have illicit sex regardless of the spiritual consequences of their acts. Thus, according to Judith M. Bennett, rural medieval people were by no means abstaining from sex outside marriage: "Although medieval records seldom illuminate the sexual experience of rural dwellers, no contemporary sources lend any credence to the view that preindustrial sexual relations were either uncreative or particularly unpleasurable for women . . . Manorial fines for illicit sexual intercourse and illegitimate births also testify to both the extent of sexual activity and the pleasure of women; with so many births in the countryside attributed to unmarried women, it is hard to suppose that most women viewed sexual intercourse as an unpleasant marital obligation" (1987, 102–103). The women of *The Distaff Gospels* certainly show no shame about their sexual nature. We should also keep in mind that the modern Euro–North American conception that women are naturally shy and reticent about sex is actually a product of nineteenth-century Victorian England, not of the Middle Ages.

The setting of *The Distaff Gospels* imagined by its male authors imitates the scholarly setting for humorous effect. It is not unreasonable to assume, however, that women—particularly among themselves—talked freely about sex and their dissatisfaction with men in general or with specific male husbands and lovers—just as many do today. Even if the *Gospels'* authors played up the bawdiness of the women's conversation for comic value, as is entirely likely, the fact remains that most of these folkloric texts were probably collected from women or reflect women's speech and beliefs.

In *The Distaff Gospels*, women attempt to exercise some control over domestic violence, which was apparently common in the Middle Ages. Even though French fabliaux parody the violent and/or aggressive wife (Shahar 2003, 78), just as current apologists for misogynist violence solemnly intone that "women can be abusive too," the *Gospels* show women's concern about their husbands beating them. Women were considered their husbands' property in many locations. Thus, it was lawful for a man to beat his wife, short of severe injury, in order to correct her behavior. A woman could ask for a separation from her husband, but given women's limited ability to support themselves financially in much of Europe, economic realities forced many to return home (Ward 2002, 49). While the idea of domestic violence could be the subject of comic relief, it was normally the husband as victim that medieval people found amusing, because he had been displaced from his usual role as spiritual and physical head of the household.

We also see women, stereotypically consigned to the realm of the physical, applying their knowledge of church teachings and of the consequences of sin to the men who betray them—whether sexually, materially, or relationally. The women of *The Distaff Gospels* want to have control over their lives, their property, and their decisions. Those glosses written by men may parody and exaggerate women's dissatisfactions for comic relief or to distance the authors from heretical ideas, but the actual gospels themselves show a reasonable human expectation for respect and fidelity. And although the joke of the oversexed elderly woman is an old one, going back to the ancient world, the *Gospels* show that women expected sexual satisfaction. They fully inhabited their bodies while also being engaged in the spiritual world. They tried to control their milieu in the way that humans deprived of socially sanctioned power always have, through beliefs, divination, and folk remedies.

Endeavoring to understand medieval women's lives through folklore alone is fraught with pitfalls, just as trying to understand medieval women's lives exclusively through the writing of men leaves an incomplete picture, to say the least. Legal documents, such as court records, give a glimpse of women as they both used and were subject to the legal system. The relatively small volume of written material, largely from aristocratic women of the time, gives some picture of the daily lives and concerns of upper-class, literate women. But few texts offer the intimate view of the lives of peasant women that the *Gospels* delivers. I have argued, concurring with Lisa Perfetti (2003) and L. D. Gates (1997), that their narrative framing does not wholly stifle women's voices and experiences. I have further contended that we actually can tell something about medieval women's lives and desires from the folklore in *The Distaff Gospels*, especially the relatively unadulterated gospels spoken by the doctoresses. Despite a great separation of time and culture, medieval women are recognizable to their counterparts today in that they also desired happiness and some measure of control over their lives. The author of the Paris manuscript of *The Distaff Gospels* may have been speaking tongue-in-cheek when he dedicated the work to the "honor and glory of the Ladies," but perhaps there is more truth to that dedication than he intended.

NOTES

The author wishes to thank Liz Locke and Jean Roselius for their excellent suggestions for initial improvement of the text. Pauline Greenhill and Diane Tye have patiently aided in the further development of this chapter. All translations from modern French are the author's own, while the translations of *The Distaff Gospels* are the work of Jeay and Garay (2006). I am most grateful to these two scholars for making this text available to the English-speaking world. Any mistakes and shortcomings that remain are the author's alone.

1.　I use the term *folklore* in its most literal sense, to refer to items of traditional lore that originate with a folk group, in this case French women of the era.

2.　Located in the Bibliothèque nationale de France, BnF fr. 2151.

3. The gloss, (*glose*), responds to the speaker who reported the gospel. Typically the gloss in *The Distaff Gospels* agrees with the content and offers evidence of the gospel's truth or an elaboration upon it.

4. The distaff was ubiquitous; "distaff side" is also a common reference to women within a family or in general. In France, "tomber en quenouilles" (to fall into distaffs) meant that power moved into the hands of women—such as a monarchy passing to a queen (L .D. Gates 1997, 15).

5. While spinning was nearly always done by women, the weaving of the thread could be most commonly done by men or women, depending on local custom.

6. The *querelle des femmes* refers to the literary tradition, primarily in medieval Latin and early modern French, Italian, and Spanish texts, of rhetorically asserting either the superiority or inferiority of women. Many important works in this tradition were written by clerics, but others contributed, including some women authors such as Christine de Pizane (Bock 2002, 1–8).

7. A "churching" celebrated a woman returning to the church building after childbirth. In the Middle Ages, a woman who had given birth was considered impure until she had undergone this ritual, performed outside the door of the church. Only afterward could she enter. The period of time between childbirth and churching varied, but forty days was common. The practice likely derived from Jewish purity laws. Women would often hold a celebration with their female friends marking this event (Orme 2001, 31–33).

8. Located in the Musée Condé (manuscript 654) (Jeay and Garay 2006, 23).

9. Incunabula, works made using moveable type, were produced prior to about 1500, the very earliest period of printed, rather than handwritten, documents in Europe.

10. However, folklorists Carl Lindahl, John McNamara, and John Lindow caution against confusing an instance of folklore with earlier or later examples because folklore itself changes over time (2002, xix).

11. Fabliaux, comical short tales originally found in northeastern medieval France, relate a deception that leads to unintended results. They are often bawdy or scatological in tone (Chatten 2002, 126–128).

12. For example, in *The Distaff Gospels*, night 2, chapter 21, we find, "Anyone who can ride a bear the distance of nine paces without faltering will be immunized against nine kinds of sickness" (Jeay and Garay 2006, 119). Compare to Sébillot's "It is said that those who have courage, have mounted a bear and have no more fear. Women like this who fear nothing, have no doubt mounted [a bear]" (2006, 3:46).

13. Folklorists generally avoid the term *superstition* because of its distancing effects and tendency to refer to the beliefs of another that the person labeling them does not share. The term *belief* better captures the intention behind such ideas (Mullen 2000).

14. Nevertheless, many of the significant changes of the Italian Renaissance had their roots in the thirteenth and fourteenth centuries, and so would not have been wholly foreign to the people of Flanders and Picardy.

15. See, for example, St. Jerome's "Against Jovinian," fourth century AD (Amt 2010, 18–19).

16. A husband's use of her assets without consent could, however, be used as legal grounds for a separation or annulment—in practice somewhat difficult as not all courts allowed a woman to bring suit or to testify without the consent of her husband or the support of another respectable man (Shahar 2003, 86).

17. An incubus, a male demon said to "ride" or have sex with women at night, sometimes causes pregnancy. The female counterpart is a succubus (Leach and Fried 1972, 515–516).

18.   "Nones" relates to the hours of divine offices, used to tell time throughout the medieval period. Though nones were normally held in midafternoon, Jeay and Garay note that this reference refers to the time just before dawn on midsummer's night (2006, 153).

19.   During the week, different days were assigned to commemorate different events. Beginning with Tertullian, an early church father and prolific writer of the second and third centuries, Friday commemorates the Passion of Christ (New Advent 2009).

20.   This remedy might make a veiled reference to syphilis, as St. George was thought to protect his faithful against the disease, and "making soup" was sometimes used as a metaphor for sexual intercourse (Jeay and Garay 2006, 179).

21.   A commother is a female godparent to the same child. During some points in the Middle Ages, children were given numerous male and female godparents in order to solidify community social and economic bonds. The church frowned upon the practice (see Orme 2001, 201–204).

12

"Just Like Coming to a Foreign Country"
Dutch Drag on a Danish Island

Anne B. Wallen

IN THE CLASSIC DANISH CRIME COMEDY *The Olsen Gang on the Track,* the bumbling thief Kjeld refers to the journey from central Copenhagen across a bridge to the island of Amager as being "just like coming to a foreign country" (*Olsen-banden på sporet,* directed by Erik Balling, 1975). While Kjeld's summation of Amager as somehow "foreign" is typical of Danish attitudes to the island, for many it has an even more decidedly unfavorable reputation. Known as Shit Island, northern Amager hosted the dumping site for Copenhagen's "night soil" in the late nineteenth century (Housted 2002, 44). When I moved to Amager in 2008, I was aware of these stereotypes but quickly began to understand the place as something of a microcosm of modern Denmark, as it includes densely populated urban areas, a large international airport, a Red Cross asylum center, nature preserves, and farmland. At its northern tip, where I lived, the 95.3-square-kilometer teardrop-shaped island is part of Copenhagen (*Den Store Danske* 2009–2012), while the southern end includes areas devoted to agriculture and two large protected natural areas used for recreation and grazing livestock (Lumby 2010).

An aspect of Amager culture that surprised me was the presence of a significant community that referred to itself as "Dutch," and whose relationship with the island demonstrates the persistence of ethnic and gender categories in a society generally known for its equality. The town of Store Magleby at the island's southern end is known as Dutch Village and is the site of a museum that preserves the cultural heritage of a group of people who immigrated to Denmark nearly 500 years ago. The community's Amager Museum is only meters from the runways of the airport that is now one of the main sites of immigration to Denmark. Much of the contentious

DOI: 10.7330/9780874218985.c012

debate about immigration and integration in contemporary Denmark centers on those who are euphemistically referred to as being of "other ethnic background than Danish." The Danish adjective *anden* used in these situations can mean "second," "other," or "different," depending on context; the phrase focuses on the population in question while simultaneously asserting Danish as an ethnic identity. Commonly used in news media and by police when describing unidentified criminal suspects, it codes for non-White, not just non-Danish. Similarly, the term *bilingual* is used in educational contexts to refer to children with immigrant backgrounds, highlighting language as a marker of otherness.

On Amager, the presence of the local community that self-identifies as Dutch complicates issues of immigration by performing different narratives about gender, integration, and national identity than those seen among either contemporary newcomer groups or the native Danish ones. In this chapter, I draw on advertising, commemorative texts, newspaper and government reports, and publications from Museum Amager to trace the development of the "Amager Dutch" tradition. I begin by considering the rich historical perspective before examining its performance in contemporary Denmark and then reflecting on how national heritage, gender, and immigration are discussed in the context of this particular group.

The journey from the Danish parliamentary building Christiansborg in central Copenhagen to the thatched roofs and brightly painted farm buildings of Store Magleby is an easy thirty-five-minute bus ride, but in many ways it is indeed like a journey to a foreign land, and into the past. From the seventeenth century onward, the village was a regular destination for the royal family and members of court during the Shrovetide carnival, *fastelavn*. Dressed in refined versions of the Sunday-best clothing of the local farmers, the royal court, including foreign ambassadors, rode out to Store Magleby in carriages to witness traditional rituals such as the barbaric practices of mounted riders trying to "knock the cat from the barrel" and "pull the head off the goose" as well as the more tame "egg dance" (Hjorth 1986, 12–20). The events were so popular that several times the Amager peasants were also invited to the royal residence in Copenhagen to perform their carnival games out of season, and Queen Sophie Amalie (1628–1685) had her portrait painted in a costume frequently described as inspired by Amager costumes (26).

In twenty-first-century Denmark, the Amager costume is still seen on special occasions in Store Magleby, particularly for a harvest festival Sunday in September and for carnival events in late winter. Of course there is nothing unusual about local traditions being preserved in this way, but the twist

in this case is the continued emphasis on tracing these traditions and costumes not to Danish peasant history but to a group of Dutch farmers who
immigrated to Amager in the early sixteenth century at the behest of King
Christian II. Yet even as it looks back to a centuries-old Dutch heritage,
the Amager Dutch community is above all else an extremely locally oriented Danish one. For much of the first decade of the twenty-first century,
Denmark's center-right government aligned with the anti-immigration,
nativist Danish People's Party to curtail immigration, resulting in "measures
so strict that Denmark has been reprimanded by international courts and
human rights agencies" (Klausen 2009, 152).[1] In the context of the current
European-wide anxiety about non-Western and especially Muslim immigration, calls to preserve national heritage are common.

I see the case of the Amager Museum and the preservation of rituals
and traditions linked to sixteenth-century Dutch immigration as an unusual
example of immigration's place within Danish heritage. The Dutch population kept itself relatively isolated for an exceptionally long period of time,
preserving its own court system, language, and church until the early nineteenth century, and its particular dress until as recently as the early twentieth
century. The website for the Amager Museum states, "After 480 years, there's
still something special about being 'Dutch' on Amager" (Museum Amager
2012a).[2] To outsiders, however, it seems incredible that the Dutch could
maintain this "special" status for so long, or that the distinctions between
Danes and Dutch could really be preserved for nearly five centuries. Clearly
the Dutch did intermarry and integrate with the Danes, their court system
and special church privileges eventually did come to an end, and their language has all but disappeared. The Dutch peasants thus represent a uniquely
privileged community that continued to be marked as different for centuries
after their arrival.

The situation raises questions about immigration and integration, ethnicity and nationality when differences between groups are minimal, and
the sands of time have become deep. Not only are the languages of Denmark
and Netherlands closely related, but even eighteenth-century physiogno-
mists would have been hard pressed to construct physiological (what they
would have considered racial) differences between the populations. The two
countries also have had a long-standing special relationship in terms of cultural exchange, with the Netherlands in particular exercising strong influences on Danish culture; a two-volume study outlining this centuries-long
exchange, with contributions by some of Denmark's leading scholars, was
published while both countries were occupied by Nazi forces (Fabricius,
Hammerich, and Lorenzen 1945).

Adding an almost absurd element, English speakers unfamiliar with the cultures often confuse the Dutch and Danish as well as Denmark, Holland, and the Netherlands. Actual similarities between the countries and their inhabitants do manifest: the Netherlands and Denmark are both low-lying, flat countries in northern Europe; both have strong social welfare systems and old constitutional monarchies; and both populations maintain historic affinities for bicycles, windmills, and blue and white porcelain. Nonetheless, these two different nations are separated geographically by no less a neighbor than Germany. The Nazi occupations of the Netherlands and Denmark are indeed just one milestone in their respective complicated histories with Germany; in the case of Denmark, in 1776 the kingdom enacted its first citizenship law as part of an effort to stem German influence in government positions.

What remains of the ancient immigration is the term *Dutch*. Not so much an identification with the contemporary Netherlands, it preserves and reconstructs a past through signs and practices that maintain the profile of the almost mythological Dutch immigrant. No one can trace ancestry back to the original Dutch immigrants, or even to the immediate generations afterward. Church records did not then exist, and any personal documents that the first generations of Dutch immigrants might have had with them would have been lost in one of the many fires that ravaged the settlement in the seventeenth and eighteenth centuries. The physiology, specifically the skin color, of the Dutch meant that they could figuratively disappear into the surrounding Danish population. Identification with the Amager Dutch today is thus entirely by choice, but it exists simultaneously with identification with Danishness. The continued use of Dutch given names, the participation in traditions coded Dutch, and the use of the Amager Dutch folk costume serve to reinforce this choice.[3] These practices are usually accompanied by explanations that serve both as reminders for locals and as mediators for outsiders.

The most visible of these practices is the use of the traditional Amager Dutch costume, which constitutes an unusual example of ethnic drag. Although the "crossing of racial lines in performance" is central to Katrin Sieg's concept of ethnic drag (2002, 3), in this particular case, a focus on ethnicity occurs beyond racial considerations. Given the Whiteness of both the Dutch and the Danes, Dutch drag on Amager emphasizes other aspects of ethnicity by demonstrating what Sieg calls "ethnic competence," which is primarily "based on knowledge and performance" rather than on "biological concepts of 'race'" (117). This is not to say, however, that Amager Dutch drag does not also continue to focus on boundaries between people.

The continual references to the Amager Dutch community's history as "immigrants" constructs them as distinct from the Danes, even as their Whiteness and their long history in Denmark elide connections to today's immigrant populations.

The Amager Dutch were successful enough in what Pauline Greenhill has described as "the creation and maintenance of boundaries between themselves and other people" (1994, 12) that they were able to develop a culture separate enough from Danish culture that a popular film like *The Olsen Gang on the Track* could jokingly refer to it as being like a "foreign country." While Sieg sees one of the primary motivations for contemporary German performances of ethnic drag as lying in a desire to be aligned with "the victims and avengers of genocide, rather than its perpetrators and accomplices," different considerations are at stake for the Amager Dutch (2002, 13). I believe that part of the motivation can be traced to a desire to counter Amager's low status in contemporary Denmark by harkening to a time when the Amager Dutch enjoyed greater privileges. The separateness of Amager that is mocked by other Danes is embraced and portrayed as a positive force in this scenario.

Given that both modern Denmark and the Netherlands prize their reputations for gender equality, I see a further paradox in the ways that the Amager Dutch community also maintains a gender-disparate image. According to the Human Development Report published by the United Nations in 2010, the Netherlands is the most gender-equal country in the world; number two is Denmark (United Nations Development Program 2010, 156). The gendered aspects of these performances have implications in light of the role that the perception of gender inequality among immigrant populations plays in immigration and integration debates. For example, Karen Margrethe Dahl and Vibeke Jakobsen document in their study on gender, ethnicity, and integration in Denmark that not only is the latter—particularly in terms of education and employment—hampered by the traditional gender roles of the immigrants themselves, it is also hindered by discrimination from employers and educators based on "stereotyped understandings of gender and ethnicity" (2005, 8–9). The geographical situation of these performances on Amager, basically next door to the airport and an asylum center, and also only about fifteen kilometers from Parliament's home of Christiansborg, puts the Amager Dutch at the heart of Danish immigration, though they are far removed from the experience of other, more recent immigrant populations.

HISTORIC BACKGROUND—FOUNDATION NARRATIVE

The specific details about exactly when, why, and even how many Dutch immigrants came to Denmark in the early sixteenth century are not certain, though local historians have done their best to establish some semblance of a foundation narrative from the sources available. In these stories, King Christian II invited Dutch farmers to Denmark and gave them rights to the island of Amager, either because of their ability to provide superior vegetables to the court or so that they could teach their superior agricultural techniques to the Danish peasants (Frandsen 2002, 7). A royal charter from 1521 outlines the rights of the Dutch peasants, including the specific guarantees that the immigrants would be allowed to maintain Dutch traditions and customs and even to be exempt from the corvée work required of Danish peasant tenant farmers (Hjorth 1986, 9–10). The Danish peasants of Amager were forcibly removed to Zealand, though they began to return under King Frederik I.[4] In 1547 King Christian III granted the Dutch rights to Store Magleby in exchange for promising to keep their farms tidy, maintain their Protestant faith, pay 300 marks in annual rent, and provide the court with root vegetables and onions (10).

The privilege of landownership granted the Dutch immigrants meant that they could distinguish themselves agriculturally from Danish farmers, who were forced to operate under tenant and open-field systems that focused on grain production, with vegetables and other crops being produced only for their own use. In contrast, the Dutch farmers could rotate crops and focus on raising vegetables, which they were able to sell at a good profit in the nearby capital (Abrahamsen 1964, 6), and Amager became known as Copenhagen's Kitchen Garden (Thurah and Kaae 1968, n.p.). It is in direct relation to the Dutch success with agriculture that their dress also became well known. Though it is impossible to know exactly what sort of clothes the original Dutch immigrants wore and how they differed from those the Danish peasants were wearing, it is clear that, with time, the Dutch intentionally developed distinctive clothing as part of the literal marketing of their products in Copenhagen (Frandsen 2002, 7). The women's dress was regarded as particularly interesting, with its "splendid colors and rich decoration" (Hjorth 1986, 10). However, these clothes were not necessarily of value to people outside the Amager Dutch community; Birte Hjorth describes how the clothes of an Amager Dutch woman who married a Danish man from the town of Sundbyøster (also on Amager) were taken back to Store Magleby to be sold after her death, as they would fetch a better price there (19).

This background information makes clear how the Dutch immigrants were not only truly privileged, particularly compared to their Danish neighbors, but also clearly recognized as a distinct group. Eighteenth-century scholar Laurids de Thurah reports that the Amager Dutch referred to themselves as "the King's Amagers," and indeed, the place-name became so bound to the Dutch peasants that many writers are careful to refer to the island's Danish residents as Amager Danes.[5] From the earliest texts to those from the early twenty-first century, the persistence of Dutch language and customs is remarked upon. For example, the Dutch were allowed to maintain their own judicial system until 1821, and a kind of Low German-Dutch creole was used in the Store Magleby church and schools until around the same time. Several texts attest that aspects of the language continued to be used through the nineteenth century, and that Dutch lexical influences could be found in the local Danish dialect until the mid-twentieth century (Thurah and Kaae 1968, n.p.).

THE ISLAND OF AMAGER

As discussed above, Amager has low prestige within the region, is the brunt of jokes as Shit Island, and is generally coded as a place very foreign and/or distinct from the capital. Geographical street names also add to the sense of distance from Denmark. On the island's north end, for example, street names include Swedish provinces and German cities and states, other European countries, and North American locales, while streets in the south end refer to African countries. Dutch cities are, however, reserved for the area directly west of Store Magleby and south of the airport.

One of the world's oldest civil airports, Copenhagen's deserves some special attention here. Today, Denmark's only land border is with Germany, which, as a fellow member of the Schengen Area, has very minimal border controls. Given the relatively low number of travelers who enter the country at one of its 130 harbors, Copenhagen Airport is in effect the most important gateway to the country from so-called third countries, that is, those not part of the European Union or the Nordic Passport Union (Ministeriet for Flygtninge, Indvandrere og Integration 2008, 3). In 2012, 23.3 million passengers used Copenhagen airport, over eight times more than Denmark's second international airport (Copenhagen Airports n.d.a; Billund Airport 2013). At the time of its construction in 1925, the airport was named after the nearby village of Kastrup, but it was also close to the village of Maglebylille, which was slowly eaten up by the ever-expanding runways and taxiways until most of the village was razed in 1969 (Jansen 2002, 201).

More recently, the airport worked with the local community in preservation projects. In 2002 Copenhagen Airports A/S sold a historic farmstead to Museum Amager, contributing a deed of gift that made the purchase possible (Københavns Lufthavne 2003). The farmstead, known as Fadersminde (Father's Memory), had previously been used for training at the airport, but these activities were being moved to another historic building—the Vilhelm Lauritzen terminal from 1939, a major example of Nordic functionalist architecture that is now a listed building (Copenhagen Airports n.d.b). In a single night in 1999, the entire 2,600-ton, 110-meter-long building was moved across the runways on "50 steel reinforcing structures supported by connected flatbed trucks (744 wheels) with reciprocal height adjustment" to an area next to what remains of Maglebylille, just north of Store Magleby, where it was restored and now functions "as a terminal for special VIP arrivals" (Iversen n.d.). But these preservation efforts are not the only examples of refunctioning and reuse at the airport; the airport is also well known for refurbishing its runways and taxiways with materials recycled from the old runways (COWI 2010).

With so much going on in this contained environment, it is not surprising that the island today has a kind of identity crisis. Airport recycling initiatives and the Shit Island nickname are also tied to the fact that most of Copenhagen's waste management is still based on the island (see R98 2010). Similarly, a debate has emerged recently about renaming the old Dump Road to something less unsavory. While some commentators argue against this as a whitewashing of the island's history, proponents of the change feel that such names are an embarrassment for the island and do not reflect the significance of its current role in Denmark (see Levinsen 2010 and Dueholm 2010). For example, Amager has played host to significant international events, such as the 2009 International Olympic Committee session and the 2009 United Nations Climate Change Conference, both of which took place at Bella Center on the island's western side.

A fall 2009 ad campaign by Amagerbanken, founded as a local bank in 1903, seems to flout the island's negative connotations by projecting it as completely independent (*Politiken* 2011b).[6] Campaign posters depict a stylized map of the island, floating independently, with no sign of the rest of Copenhagen, any of Sjælland, or the bridge, built in 2000, that crosses the sound to connect Amager to Malmö, Sweden (see figure 12.1). The absence of references to the rest of Copenhagen or Denmark, moreover, highlights Amager's and the bank's status as distinct from Denmark's largest bank, Danske Bank (literally Danish Bank), whose headquarters are—of course—in central Copenhagen.

Matching Amagerbanken's usual logo colors, the illustrated island is overwhelmingly green, as though it were heavily wooded, with illustrations

Figure 12.1 Amagerbanken's 2009 ad campaign shows the island of Amager as
detached from the rest of Denmark, but also highlights how it is a microcosm for the
country. The Amager Dutch figure is most visible on the airplane's tail fin.

of island landmarks and institutions popping out from between cartoon-
ish trees, while other sites and major streets are marked in light gray. The
sites included emphasize the noteworthy cultural activities and institutions, including the distinctive spiral tower of Our Savior's Church, the

humanities campus of Copenhagen University, the Copenhagen Opera House, the headquarters of the Danish Broadcasting Corporation, Field's Shopping Center, and the airport. On the now-defunct website portion of the campaign, aimed at clients aged eighteen to twenty-eight, a video featured a young woman who speaks at length about Amager's attractions, but who also somewhat defensively adds in a fashionable mix of Danish and English, "Amager will never be totally trendy, I know, and thank you very much, but Amager is *my* island" (Amagerbanken 2010). Just as the campaign's spokeswoman claims Amager as her own, so too is the map colonized by silhouette images of the bank's logo—a man in characteristic historic Amager Dutch clothing, holding a basket of vegetables in one hand and a measuring cup in the other (Amagerbanken 2011). The figures on the island correspond approximately to the locations of Amager Bank branches, while other figures can be seen in the space around the island engaging in "travel": riding in a hot-air balloon, windsurfing, and emblazoned on the tail fin of an airplane making its landing approach to Copenhagen Airport.

According to the website, the logo is based on the old seal of the Store Magleby *schout* (a local administrator) first developed in the late 1600s and used until the system was abolished in 1821. It was adapted by the bank for its emblem in 1906 to symbolize its "good business sense and local knowledge as well as the island's historic background as the royal pantry" (Amagerbanken 2011). While the seal and the original version of the logo showed an Amager man in everyday work clothes, the 1973 and 1978 restylizations (as well as the 1930s sculptural relief on the bank's main building at the north end of Amager on which they are based) put him in the festival clothes reserved for married men's use at major religious holidays and special occasions such as weddings (Møller 1996, 56). The costume features very wide, knee-length pants, a black jacket, a red scarf, and an unusual, almost disc-shaped, large, fuzzy blue hat called a *floshat* (Hjorth 1996, 48–51).

This change codes the figure more clearly as "Dutch," as this hat was the most distinctive aspect of the Amager Dutch costume. Books on the subject take pains to explain the hat's origins in the headgear of sixteenth-century Dutch sailors, and its use among the Amager Dutch is presented as evidence of their continued ties to the Netherlands, since a proper blue floshat had to have been produced there. Hjorth, for example, writes that contact with the Netherlands was maintained via trade and sailing, made possible by the close proximity of the important fishing and shipping town of Dragør, only a couple of kilometers from Store Magleby (1996, 26).

But this change also amounts to a dressing up, as the combination of festival clothes with the props of work—vegetables and the measuring cup—is incongruous. Moreover, the male figure is misleading, since it was primarily women who sold the goods at market. The choice can be attributed to a reliance on traditional gender roles in which men are connected with finances. The logo draws upon two of the best-known aspects of the Amager Dutch—their farming and their unusual clothing—and combines them in a single image meant to demonstrate the bank's attachment to Amager. Yet however tied to the island's history the image is meant to be, it still required explanation for the bank's modern clients; the logo is explained at length in both Danish and English on the website, suggesting that the origins of the figure and his hat are not common knowledge. Ironically, Store Magleby is obscured on the Amagerbanken map by the ad's text; the Amager Dutch figure is present everywhere on the island, but his home is rendered invisible and inconsequential.

AMAGER MUSEUM

While the Amager Dutch man in Amagerbanken's logo references a distant, imagined past, the south end manifests the present-day use of Amager Dutch costumes in Store Magleby. An analysis of selections from the February 2010 members' newsletter of the Museum Amager gives a picture of contemporary costume use as well as of traditional activities, particularly carnival (Museum Amager 2010b). As noted above, the large blue floshat was the standout element of Amager Dutch men's clothing traditions. Illustrations of the Amager Dutch carnival depict the practitioners of the games wearing clothes not unlike those on the Amagerbanken logo, including the hat. This costume is also represented, along with a woman's festival costume, in the logo for the Amager Museum. But according to Lisbeth Møller, when it became impossible to get new blue floshat from the Netherlands in the 1840s, the Amager Dutch began switching over to black cylinder top hats (1996, 132). This substitution is typical of the many incremental changes over the centuries to the traditions that are still labeled Dutch, even as they are both separated from the Netherlands and clearly integrated into the Danish setting. The newsletter's cover features a color photograph of two men on horseback, wearing black pants, vests, top hats, and broad-sleeved white shirts: the Amager Dutch men's costume as it was known in the nineteenth century, minus the jacket, which would have been cumbersome while riding or performing the carnival games (140–141).

Each man is also carrying a large Danish national flag, known as Dannebrog, which according to legend fell from heaven to support the Danish king in battle in 1219, though its earthly existence is first documented from the late fourteenth century. Inge Adriansen describes how in the nineteenth century the flag underwent a transformation from symbol of the monarchy and of state authority to a popular symbol of unity in the face of national challenges, particularly in relation to the country's German neighbors (2003, in particular 127–172). An 1807 illustration of Dannebrog's use by the "Dutch peasants on Amager" at carnival is one of the earliest known examples of private use (133). Today, the flag is used in a variety of private contexts—such as on birthday cakes and Christmas trees—that may be surprising to non-Danes (or non-Scandinavians) (171). At the time when the Amager Dutch began using Dannebrog, Denmark was an absolute monarchy, yet the peasants used this royal symbol as a festival decoration. The Danish flag's adoption by people who were identified and who self-identified as Dutch is also remarkable because even today it is understood to indicate the group's self-image as "a legitimate part of Danish society" (127). The situation reveals the extent to which the allegedly Dutch festival has become a Danish one.

Tellingly, there is no caption for the image of the riders with Dannebrog on the newsletter's cover; unlike the users of Amagerbanken, the periodical's readership is privy to the costume's pedigree. In fact, in the entire section "Carnival," the word *Dutch* is never mentioned. Instead, the text focuses on the tradition's longevity, claiming its practice "since the 1600s" and "for generations." The very names Store Magleby and Amager are sufficient for the in-group readers to make the connection to the Dutch community (Museum Amager 2010a). As is common in "display events"[7] of ethnic heritage in North America, carnival is presented as pleasurable not only to take part in but also to observe. In an entry on a carnival "preparation" day, performers and their activities are described in the present tense: "The barrel painter decorates the carnival barrel according to local, historical tradition. The saddle-maker inspects and repairs the horse's '*snekketøj*' [shell-decorated tack]. The horse's mane and tail are braided and decorated with ribbon. The boys decorate their bicycles for their own 'carnival-ride.'" Potential spectators are exhorted to "also experience two small girls being dressed as carnival brides" (13–14).

Not only is the Dutch background of the activities not mentioned, neither are the activities explained. The uncommon term *snekketøj* is marked by quotation marks as being unusual, but it is not defined. What exactly is the boys' "own 'carnival-ride'"? Why are the girls dressed up as brides, and what does it have to do with carnival? Pictures show the children in costumes that seem to be miniature versions of the nineteenth-century festival costume, suggesting the common carnival motif of role inversion (young-old), but the lack of exposition underscores the exclusivity of the arrangement. To find out about it, it is implied, your presence at the event is required. In this way, the tourist spectators who venture to Store Magleby are enlisted in the preservation of its heritage. As much as the museum strives to educate potential visitors from outside the immediate vicinity about local history, the event is also in many ways a small-town phenomenon that requires insider knowledge.

The main event of carnival in Store Magleby, however, is known nationwide in Denmark, if in different variations. "Knocking the cat from the barrel" was one of the attractions of the historic Amager Dutch carnival. A living cat was put in a barrel suspended between two poles, and mounted riders would take turns striking the barrel with a special bat until it broke and the cat fell out. Opinions are divided as to the origins of this *fastelavnsridning* (carnival-riding) ritual, with some claiming that it originated with the Amager Dutch, and others saying that it was known elsewhere in Denmark and southern Sweden before their arrival, but it was in any case practiced in many areas through the nineteenth century (Bregenhøj and Larsen 2007, 256–274). With time, the cat was removed from the equation, replaced in some instances with candy. Today this tradition is still called "knocking the cat from the barrel" but is mostly performed by children on foot in motley costumes who take turns striking the barrel, almost like a piñata. The Store Magleby organization Friendship Circle, however, today claims to carry out the most historically authentic performance. There, the men—and only men—still ride horses in a full gallop toward the (empty) barrel, with honors going to the one who knocks the final bit of the barrel from the rope it is attached to. They all wear the same clothes as the men on the newsletter cover described above, giving the event a visual uniformity and emphasizing the historical, traditional nature of the event.

Whether the ritual has Dutch or Danish origins, the self-identified Amager Dutch at the Amager Museum are now the most visible guardians of this heritage, though there are other sites at which it is performed. In nearby Dragør, pre-Lenten festivities began in 1890 as masked parades and carnival riding, sometimes on water, with costumes and decorations that were "fantastic and comic." In 1970 a Dragør carnival organization was formed to arrange carnival riding in Dragør as a "true copy" of the practice in Store Magleby, "but with a single exception—in Dragør the riders are of both genders" (Dragør Kommune n.d.). Images from the Dragør municipality website and from local newspapers show that the women who participate in the ritual strive to emulate the visual uniformity of the male Store Magleby riders, dressing in the same costumes, pulling long hair back and covering it with the top hat. In 2010 the winner of the Dragør carnival riding was a woman named Ane Mette Wieder, who had also been crowned

"barrel king" twice previously (Bjørton 2010). A list of competition win-
ners from 1970 to 2014 on the organization's website shows that women
have won the "barrel king" title fourteen times (Dragør Fastelavnsforening
n.d.). Both the male-gendered costumes and the use of the term *barrel king*
underscore the ritual's reliance on traditional gender roles, despite this organization's explicit desire to allow women to participate. These contestants
are thus performing a double drag: as "Dutch" and as men.[8]

Other articles in the Museum Amager newsletter give additional insights
into the gendered aspects of the community's heritage performance. Such
a clear traditional division of male and female performance and work is
unusual in Denmark, a country that generally prides itself on a gender
equality, which is (as indicated above) often presented as a contrast to immigrant populations. One article focuses on four members from the "core" of
the Amager Museum's volunteer corps—"four spry gals" (Jansen and Jansen
2010, 16–18). The word translated as "gal" is usually used affectionately to
refer to girls or young women, but can also carry an implication of unmarried women who "behave immorally, despicably or loosely" (*Den Danske
Ordbog* n.d.). This use to describe mature women is clearly not intended to
be insulting but rather to be jovial; yet to some degree it also reinforces a
traditional perception of women and women's contributions to the performances as less serious and more childlike, especially in contrast to the role
of the mighty barrel king."

While the women's drag implicates ethnicity, they also perform a kind
of time-travel drag that returns them to traditional gender roles of past centuries. Each of the four women profiled has special tasks at the museum
that, as the title demonstrates, are heavily gendered domestic activities:
baking, sewing, flower arranging, and weaving. The women are described
as having these interests outside of their connection to the museum—the
seamstress and weaver are educated in these professions. Each profile makes
explicit the woman's connection not only to the museum but also to Store
Magleby and Amager. Only one is identified as being from somewhere else;
she is immediately noted as coming from the island of Bornholm, and it is
by virtue of her expertise as a weaver that she has joined the community.
The other profiles make references to family members and to childhood
memories that signify the women's deeper roots in the community. The
Amager costume features prominently in many of the reminiscences; for
example, one woman was inspired to refurbish her aunt's old costume. Each
woman makes a statement about the museum's presence in her thoughts or
her efforts to be there at every opportunity, reflecting its role in her daily life
and her strong identification with it.

AMAGER DUTCH AND OTHER IMMIGRANTS

Though the museum also features changing exhibitions and is particularly well known for its summer enactment of a working farm circa 1900, the permanent exhibitions focus on "the history of the Dutch immigration to Denmark in the 16th century and their descendants' life and culture" (Museum Amager 2012a). This emphasis on the Amager Dutch as immigrants is carried over in a variety of texts, and when the website refers to "being 'Dutch' on Amager" as "something special," it shows that there is still a claim that the group has an identity distinct from being just Danish. The Amager Dutch are of course also—or even principally—Danish, but their self-identification with the "Dutch" supplements the Danishness rather than excluding or being precluded by it.

The many references to the history of the "immigrants" and "immigration" to Amager make that group unusual in that it is closely identified both with the Danish island and with a separate point of origin—not autochthonous, despite centuries of residence. The justification for the claims to the island, and more specifically the village of Store Magleby, comes not only from the royal invitation and charters but also from the group's solidarity and fidelity to its origins. The museum website maintains that a sense of "fellowship" is "still here," not only via the festivals and organizations "but through an ingrained consciousness that the Dutch have stood together through centuries" (Museum Amager 2012b.).

The desire to compare the Dutch to contemporary immigration is likewise present in the museum's texts and projects. One of its stated themes is "cultural encounters," related in the newsletter's summary of the 2009 annual report to the development of a project called "Welcome?" (Bager 2010, 5). The project's website calls it an ongoing collaboration being developed by Amager Museum with the Danish Immigration Museum, Museum Lolland-Falster, and the Dragør Local Archive. The results—a Web exhibition, traveling exhibition, and educational materials—will examine "integration across time as seen through three historical examples of invited immigration—the Dutch immigration to Amager in the 1500s, the Polish labour migration around the year 1900 and the immigration of Turkish guest workers in the 1960s and 70s." The goal is "to learn more about integration as a social process—not least in light of contemporary debate" (Danish Immigration Museum 2012). A somewhat similar miniseries and Web project from the educational branch of the public television station DR in 2003 used the Dutch as the starting point on its timeline of Danish immigration history. The website stressed that "Denmark has always been a destination for immigration" and sought to emphasize that debates about "foreign cultures, foreign languages, foreign clothing—foreign people" are not a recent source of controversy (DR 2004).

Though the "Welcome?" project's results were unavailable when this chapter was written, it is worth noting that its point of departure quite literally questions how "welcome" immigrants can be. The title's question mark casts doubt on the sincerity of the invitation and the welcoming reception for the immigrants, in both the short and long terms. The historical distance and dearth of primary sources on the 1521 Dutch immigration make comparison to the more recent groups difficult at best. But the project website suggests an attempt to emphasize the ongoing presence of Dutch identity while the community is also held up as an example of successful integration. Pictures on the website refer to each of the three groups under consideration; the Poles and Turks are represented by pictures of adults at work, but the Dutch by a recent color photograph showing two young girls in folk costume, shot from behind. This gesture softens the historical gap with an inversion, representing the oldest immigrant group with the youngest "immigrants"—and arguably also by its association with girls, not boys or men—but also suggests a model whereby traditions can be maintained and passed on to future generations. Ultimately, in the case of the Amager Dutch, these traditions become local, Danish traditions.

A newsletter article entitled "Let the Food Speak" shows an attempt to put the Amager Dutch story into a constellation with a different type of contemporary immigration to Denmark. A museum project sponsored by the Danish Cultural Heritage Board called Stove-side Conversations—The Meal across Cultures had four cooks from the museum's volunteer corps meeting with asylum seekers housed at the Red Cross Center in nearby Kongelunden. The project focused on the cross-cultural phenomena of food and food preparation rather than on "the immediate barriers like language, culture and religion." According to the article, the asylum seekers learned something about both Danish history and, "not least," Amager's history, as well as being able to share some of their own culture with the museum volunteers (Ravn 2010, 12).

Claus Ravn writes that the story of the Dutch immigration to Amager has parallels to contemporary immigration, "especially when it comes to influence on food culture" (2010, 12). But he does not elaborate on what these parallels are or on what food was prepared. The only nationality mentioned other than Danish is Dutch; we do not know what the asylum seekers eat or where they come from. In fact, the Red Cross Center at Kongelunden is a special location; 150 of its 250 spots are for those "who need care beyond the care provided for all asylum seekers." A large number have psychiatric illnesses and physical disabilities, including some who are "seriously disabled survivors of torture" (Roure 2009, 8; see also Frivilig i Dansk Røde Kors n.d.). Even if the participants in these "stove-side conversations" did not come from among the most special cases, the contrast between them and the invited, successful immigrants from 500 years ago could hardly be greater.

Though the museum's volunteers appear to be making a sincere effort to promote cross-cultural understanding and to welcome the asylum seekers, the cheerful focus on trite, superficial similarities—that the Dutch and the asylum seekers both came to Denmark from other countries and both have cultural food traditions—offers little in the way of reflective or critical examination of the challenges that immigrants currently experience. As described by Sieg, "The sharing of food evokes the multicultural food fair, that arch cliché of capitalist pluralism" (2002, 138) and simultaneously again displays the tendency of Dutch drag to rely on traditional gender roles; most of those in the photographs accompanying the article are women. There is no mention of the extraordinary privileges enjoyed by the Dutch over their Danish neighbors, nor of the fact that the Dutch were linguistically, religiously, and physiologically more similar to the Danes than are the majority of contemporary immigrants, 67 percent of whom are of non-Western backgrounds (Ministeriet for Flygtninge, Indvandrere og Integration 2009, 7). While the article and the museum's projects seem optimistic about the benefits of "cultural encounters," contemporary Danish integration policy debate, as in many European countries, has shifted "towards an increasingly assimilationist rhetoric" in which immigrants are expected to absorb quickly into Danish society (Klausen 2005, 69). Denmark's former minister of integration Søren Pind repeatedly stated that he does not like to use the term *integration*, preferring *assimilation* (*Information* 2011). The activities that work to preserve the nearly 500-year-old Amager Dutch heritage, while emphasizing the group's immigration history, stand in stark contrast to the demands on newcomers.

Nonetheless, Amager Dutch remains an identity that can be assumed and performed on special occasions, and one that is regarded as worth preserving, along with old Amager farms like Fadersminde, Vilhelm Lauritzen's 1939 airport terminal, and even, when occasion calls for it, traditional gender roles. Yet as much as participation in Amager Dutch activities is voluntary, it seems unlikely that someone with "other ethnic background than Danish" could join them as anything except an outside observer. The proximity of Sudanvej (Sudan Way) to Doorn Allé (Doorn Avenue), and Tunisvej (Tunis Way) to Tilburg Allé (Tilburg Avenue—Doorn and

Tilburg are Dutch cities) at the island's south end offers a vision of immigrant coexistence that belies how far it really is from Christiansborg or even Store Magleby to Kongelunden. The busy flight patterns overhead and the steady drone of airplane engines are a constant reminder of the comings and goings of would-be immigrants, but the "welcome?" that awaits them is, at best, ambivalent.

NOTES

1.   Anders Fogh Rasmussen stepped down as prime minister to become secretary-general of NATO in 2009; he was replaced by Lars Løkke Rasmussen (no relation), who in September 2011 lost a reelection bid to the Social Democrat Helle Thorning-Schmidt, who became the country's first female prime minister.

2.   Museum Amager is made up of three exhibition locations: Amager Museum, Dragør Museum, and Mølsteds Museum, at three different sites in Dragør municipality. Note the potential for confusion due to the close similarity of the names of the Amager Museum and the overarching institution, which has been known as Museum Amager since 2008.

3.   The reportedly high number of people with Dutch names in Dragør municipality is frequently cited as evidence of the continued Dutch influence there. Examples of such names are given to back up the claim, as on Museum Amager's website (Museum Amager 2012b).

4.   The Danish island of Sjælland, known in English as Zealand, is the largest island in Denmark and the one on which Copenhagen is located; it is not to be confused with the Dutch (!) province of Zeeland, or even with New Zealand, which is named after the Dutch province.

5.   Island residents were traditionally known by the appellation *amager* (plural *amagere*). Danish pronunciation is famously indistinct, and *Amager* is often colloquially written as "Ama'r" to reflect it. In recent years, however, residents have been called *amagerkaner*— the inserted "kan" syllable is stressed—in what the dictionary *Den Danske Ordbog* (n.d.) calls a "joking imitation" of the word for American, *amerikaner*. This usage is so common that the dictionary actually lists *Amager* as "rare." While the older form, identical to the island's name, emphasized the residents' connectedness to it, the newer one humorously suggests that they are as removed from other Copenhageners or Danes as Americans.

6.   The bank suffered in the global financial crisis and collapsed on February 8, 2011, and in July of that year BankNordik bought most of it (*Politiken* 2011a).

7.   Roger D. Abrahams writes that a display event "provides *the* occasion whereby a group or community may call attention to itself" by presenting a prepared performance for an audience (1987, 181).

8.   See the chapter "Morris: An 'English Male Dance Tradition,'" in Greenhill (1994, 64–125) for a discussion of another tradition embroiled in a gender-authenticity dispute.

13

Encountering Ghost Princesses in *Sou shen ji*
Rereading Classical Chinese Ghost Wife Zhiguai *Tales*

Wenjuan Xie

GHOST PRINCESS/WIFE NARRATIVES, A GROUP OF classical Chinese *zhiguai* tales, offer much material for gendered analysis. The rather fluid genre of zhiguai, literally meaning writing/recording (*zhi*) supernatural/strange tales (*guai*), "appeared in the form of collections of relatively short pieces of anomalous and supernatural events, and took the factor of *guai* as the basic generic feature" (Kao 1985, 4). In the Chinese context, "supernatural" refers primarily to the types of reality depicted rather than to the mode of representation employed. That is, most zhiguai creators held a strong belief that the paranormal events they detailed actually happened; they regarded their works as records rather than fancies. Such narratives are classical (*wenyan*) in language, not because they are canonical or ancient. Classical Chinese, associated with formal occasions and institutions such as education, legislation, official documents, and literature, had vocabularies and styles different from the oral language in everyday use. Vernacular Chinese (*baihua*) became widely used in literary forms only near the very end of the late imperial China.

As a genre, zhiguai dates to the Six Dynasties (220–589 CE), when the earliest extant collection, *Sou shen ji* (*In Search of the Supernatural: The Written Record*, circa 350 CE), was compiled by the court historian Gan Bao (?–360 CE). This assemblage was imitated by later zhiguai authors[1] in both style and theme, thereby establishing a new genre of Chinese literature. The Six Dynasties zhiguai author-compliers invariably ascribed these time-honored tales to folk traditions that they had perceived "with [their] own

DOI: 10.7330/9780874218985.c013

eyes and ears" (Gan 1979, 2). Like folktales in the West, the zhiguai narratives contain stories associated with vernacular culture and reflect popular belief systems. At the same time, the genre exemplifies interactions between folk and bureaucratic culture.

According to Karl S. Y. Kao's typology, zhiguai tales can roughly be classified into six types: (1) about portents and omens, where irregularities in the natural order comprise signs with cosmological significance; (2) about necromantic communion, relating manifestations of ghosts and spirits and their communication with humans; (3) about animistic phenomena, recording nonhuman creatures and objects and their interactions with people; (4) about communion with transcendent beings, exploring manifestations of fairies and deities and their trafficking with human beings; (5) about thaumaturgical phenomena, including manifestations of magic feats and transformations associated with *fang-shi* (necromancers) and Daoist practitioners; and (6) about retributive phenomena, mainly about divine vengeance and miracles related to the Buddhist faith and native Chinese beliefs (1985, 4–6). Though zhiguai are not exactly equivalent to Western folktales, both offer a "juxtaposition of various collective conceptions of the world" that reflect cultural ideologies and shape culture (Gramsci 1999, 134). Furthermore, both Western folktales and zhiguai function as what Alan Dundes calls "a mirror of culture" that provides the "autobiographical ethnography" of the people (2007, 55). According to Dundes, folk ideas constitute the underlying assumptions of culture that are the building blocks of a worldview. Thus, through identifying patterns, one can construct "how each of the ideas is related to the total worldview of that culture" (1971, 96).

In this essay, rather than investigate the whole corpus of zhiguai, my focus is on a specific zhiguai subgenre that falls between the second and fourth types in Kao's classification: ghost princess/wife tales. These narratives resemble the Western fairy tale in structure and narrative more than in themes and dramatis personae, as I shall demonstrate. Among the 454 tales recorded in *Sou shen ji*, 24 tales in volume 16 deal with ghosts. Four relate romances between a living male and a ghost princess and two deal with deadly sex into which female ghosts entice men. The rest record nonerotic trafficking between humans and ghosts, such as ghosts soliciting help in dreams, ghosts cheating humans, and humans tricking ghosts. Though tales of ghost princesses/wives might not be significant in number, they display a notable pattern. Typically, they revolve around three steps: the human male hero's encounter with the ghost princess, their marriage ceremony (or married life), and the return of the hero to the human world and the return of the heroine to her ghost world.

To a certain extent, these four romances form a tale type—a prototype for more developed later adaptations and imitations, exerting an enduring influence in later production both within and outside zhiguai tradition. They can be seen particularly in the more mature Tang Dynasties (618–907 CE) romances, in independent Chinese operas in the Song (960–1279 CE) and Yuan Dynasties (1271–1368 CE), in the massive corpus of the Ming and Qing (1368–1644 CE) *biji* (notebook) fictions, and ultimately in Chinese modern fiction and contemporary films. The fantasy of a sexual—occasionally erotic in later texts—encounter with a ghost woman resurfaces in various forms throughout Chinese literary tradition and functions as an integral part of Chinese cultural identity. The persistent images of a ghost princess/wife point to a particular pattern of imagination in Chinese culture produced by the interactions of various cultural elements: the belief in ghosts, the philosophy of yin and yang, the custom of marrying the dead, the institutions of kinship and marriage, and different social views of success for men and women. Images of ghost princesses/wives present a fascinating and frequently explored character type. Like the handsome prince or the helpful animal in European tales, they have secured a niche in the Chinese literary imagination.

From the mid-1980s on, selections and complete collections of well-known zhiguai have been translated into Western languages, though they did not receive significant academic attention until the late 1990s. Recent research primarily focuses on zhiguai collections from late imperial China, such as *The Discourse on Foxes and Ghosts: Ji Yun and Eighteenth-Century Literati Storytelling* (Chan 1998), *Alien Kind: Foxes and Late Imperial Chinese Narrative* (Huntington 2003), and *Phantom Heroine: Ghosts and Gender in Seventeenth-Century Chinese Literature* (Zeitlin 2007). There has been little discussion of the earlier zhiguai tradition, the collections that flourished in the Six Dynasties as represented by *Sou shen ji*. The only monograph on classical zhiguai I located, *Classical Chinese Supernatural Fiction: A Morphological History* (Zhao 2005), limits its discussion to a descriptive morphological survey of zhiguai and leaves the task of interpretation untouched. My goal here is to offer a female-centered interpretation of these tales.

An intriguing aspect of gender in the ghost princess/wife zhiguai tales lies in the fact that although presentations of women and sexuality are often pronounced, the genre has been a male-dominated tradition. Dramatically different from the Western fairy-tale tradition (e.g., see Harries 2001 and Seifert and Stanton 2010), few if any Chinese collections were compiled or written by women; the historic production, circulation, and consumption of the zhiguai have always been restricted to male (court) literati. No female tellers or authors are mentioned in the literary sources that I located (Kao 1985; Li 1984, 1993, 1997; Lu 1963b; and Zhao 2005). As Kao observes, not only zhiguai but the literary activity as a whole in the Six Dynasties period "was conducted mostly within circles of closely related men of let-ters, including sovereigns, members of the royal houses, and their ministers, usually scholar-officials" (1985, 17).

Notwithstanding the challenges of applying Western-based theory to a body of non-Western narratives, Bengt Holbek's *Interpretation of Fairy Tales* provides a valuable starting point. In his study, based on Danish wonder tales but widely generalized, Holbek observed notable thematic and stylistic differences between "masculine" and "feminine" tales (1987, 161), which he defines as the narrative's "two genders" (406). According to Holbek, tale gender can be decided according to two criteria (though he failed to clarify whether one only or both would be required): the gender of the protagonist who plays an active role in major moves of the tale, and the gender of the protagonist who is of a lowborn origin (161, 417). That is, if the two main characters in a tale are a lowborn young male (LYM) and a highborn young female (HYF), and/or the male is active in moves while the female passive, then the tale has a masculine gender. Conversely, if the heroine is a lowborn young female (LYF) and the hero a highborn young male (HYM), and/or the female is active while the male passive, the tale is feminine. Holbek's binary argument becomes problematic especially when he proposes to regard the tales as "a means of collective daydreaming" in the sense that "they depicted a true world, i.e., the world as it should be" (406). He emphasizes that daydreaming should not be understood in a pejorative sense but as a gender-neutral fantasy that reflects the pursuit of an ideal world by the common folk collectively, regardless of gender.

My doubts about the validity of Holbek's binary paradigm and the legit-imacy of drawing a correspondence between the protagonist's origin and his/her role in the moves aside, there remains the disturbing contradiction between his gendered tale types and the nongendered worldviews he argues that the tales project. On the one hand, Holbek argues, fairy tales are collec-tive, "composite dreams in which 'his' and 'her' dreams were intertwined" that appeal to both sexes; he seems to blur and minimize gender distinctions among tales. On the other hand, he admits "a marked agreement between the sex of the storyteller and the 'gender' of the tale" and that "a tale may be rendered differently depending on whether it is told by a woman or a man" (1987, 434), demonstrating that gender matters and makes a difference in shaping the tales' content. Holbek remains ambiguous on the issue of how the sex of the tale-teller/creator would influence the gender of the tales and the construction of gendered dreams. If the tales are gendered in terms of both the narrative and the narrator, it is reasonable to conjecture that the dreams and worlds they project, and their attractions, should be gendered accordingly.

Given the male authorship but often female-centered content of the Chinese zhiguai, I take Holbek's work only as a point of departure. To better elucidate the gendered specificity of the tradition, I address the following questions: What is the role of sex, gender, and sexuality in the ghost princess tales? How are feminine and masculine genders constructed? What are the male anxieties, dreams, and perceptions projected? How is the narrative shaped by a male perspective, from a male viewpoint, and for a male audience? How are femininity and masculinity differently conceived? Is it possible for the "masculine" tales, which have historically excluded women from participating in production and circulation, to reflect a holistic worldview that appeals to both genders, or rather, can we identify in them a tendency to see the world in male-biased terms? And ultimately, what can the tales tell us about the potential and limitations of the male perspective?

IMAGINING THE OTHER: WOMEN, GHOSTS, AND GHOST WIVES

In Western folktales Rapunzel lives imprisoned in a tower, Cinderella near the cinders, and Snow White in a deathlike sleep. In the end, each is rescued by a Prince Charming who comes forward to ask for her hand. By comparison, heroines in Chinese zhiguai are much less fortunate. They die prematurely before marriage, wait in their tomb for years, and sometimes leave their burial place for a working-class or peasant man's room at midnight before they can find a man to marry and have sex with. The corpse bride makes the hero extremely rich, bears him a child, and then, only then, vanishes from the human world and rests in peace underground. Tale 395 in *Sou shen ji*, "The Ghostly Wedding Nights," relates a story of this kind:

> There once was a man named Hsin Tao-tu in Lung-hsi Commandery who, in his travels to seek learning, arrived at a place some four or five *li*[2] outside the city of Yung-chou. There he came upon a large dwelling, and at its gate stood a woman in dark clothing. Tao-tu approached to beg a meal, and the woman in dark garb went inside to call her mistress—one Ch'in-nü. The latter summoned Tao-tu, and he entered that many-storied building to find Ch'in-nü sitting on a couch against the west wall. Tao-tu announced his name and surname, and when the formalities were over, he was directed to the east couch to be seated.

A meal was assembled in no time, and when Tao-tu had eaten, Ch'in-nü spoke to him: "I am the daughter of King Min of Ch'in and was given in marriage to one of the royal clan of Ts'ao. Unhappily, before the marriage was consummated, I died. That was twenty-three years ago, and I have lived alone in this great house since then. Now that you have appeared, it is my wish that we become husband and wife."

Three days and three nights passed before the woman spoke her thoughts. "You are a living human and I am a ghost. It is only because we have a predestined relationship in our past that we have been allowed to spend these three nights together. But we could not be united for long without great calamity befalling us. Our three tender nights are hardly enough to express deep feelings, yet here it is time for you to fly. I wonder what I should give you, sir, as a token of our sweet days?"

So saying, she ordered a coffer brought forth from behind the bed and opened [it]. Out of it she drew a golden pillow, which she gave to Tao-tu to remember her by. When [the] sad parting and tearful leave-taking were finally done, she ordered the dark-clothed woman to see Tao-tu to the gate.

He had scarce taken several steps when the great dwelling disappeared and a tomb stood in its place. Tao-tu hastened out of that mausoleum and looked to find that at least the golden pillow he carried in his bosom had not altered.

He soon reached the country of Ch'in and there put the golden pillow up for sale. Just at that time the Queen of Ch'in was on an eastern tour and seeing Tao-tu offering a golden pillow for sale, she was curious and ordered that it be shown her. She asked Tao-tu where he had obtained it and he told her the whole story.

When the Queen heard him, she wept uncontrollably. However, having some lingering doubts, she dispatched her men to the grave site to have the coffin exhumed and opened. All funerary articles were in place save only the golden pillow. Opening the princess's shroud, it appeared that there had indeed been conjugal congress. Then did the Queen of Ch'in believe all.

"My daughter is possessed of a special sanctity," she sighed. "Dead these twenty-three years, she was yet able to consort with a living human and made him my real son-in-law."

With that she had Tao-tu appointed her Commandant-escort, gave him a horse and chariot worked in gold, and bade him return to his own country.

For this reason, ever afterward people call a son-in-law "Commandant-escort" (*fu-ma*). Even the royal son-in-law is today titled "Commandant-escort." (Gan 1996, 195–196)

The first point at issue is whether the ghost's female gender is arbitrary or has deeper cultural connotations. *Sou shen ji* does not lack tales about ghosts, but only female ghosts are associated with unions with living beings. Male ghosts materialize as baleful spirits specializing in frightening children and pestering human communities (e.g., tale 376); engaging in discussion with living males and convincing the latter of the existence of ghosts (tale 378); as a guard who warns a human about the limit of his life (tale 379); or requesting a human to take better care of his coffin (tale 383). No male ghost has sexual and/or marital relations with a living female. Only one option organizes the personae in a romance between a ghost and a living human in *Sou shen ji*: a female ghost and a living male. The prototype of female ghosts with erotic connotations in *Sou shen ji* later transforms into what Anthony C. Yu calls tales of "the amorous ghost." The term is Yu's translation of *qing-gui*, the title of a chapter in *Qingshi* (History of Love), an anthology of tales by Feng Menglong (1574–1645), another master of the ghost narrative. As Yu has noted, none of the thirty-eight ghost romance tales included in that chapter concerns a male ghost; instead, there is this persistent pattern of a "normal" human protagonist and "the incredibly beautiful, sensual and sometimes virtuous figure of another realm" (1987, 429).

This distinct feminization of the ghost in zhiguai and the consequent creation of the sexual ghost-encountering tradition wherein the female sex predominates should be understood as a male Chinese literary and cultural artifact. Male characters are humans; female characters are ghosts. This objectification of the female sex as the other points to a male-centered perspective, not only in ghost wife tales but also in a wide range of stories about other kinds of alien wives in zhiguai—serpents, foxes, or other animal-spirit wives. In her study of the fox-wife zhiguai tales, Rania Huntington arrives at the similar observation that "the supernatural romance in the classical tale remained primarily a pleasure for male readers" in that "the romance is viewed only from the male and human side" (2003, 288). Projected in tale 395 is the duality of man as the self and woman as the other that has cross-culturally stigmatized the perception of gender. This binary also echoes critical concerns that Simone de Beauvoir raises in her canonical feminist work *The Second Sex*: "why woman has been defined as the other" and "what have been the consequences from man's point of view" (1989, xxv).

The association of women with the other, in the alien form of a ghost, originates from the application of the binary concepts of yin and yang to gender characteristics in customary Chinese thought. Traditionally, the yin element is associated with the dark, death, the earth, cold, femininity, and wives. In contrast, the yang represents light, life, heaven, warmth, masculinity, and husbands. Within this oppositional pair, the yin-female and yang-male pattern is conveniently adapted to conceptualize the relation between ghost and human: the ghost is to the living as female is to male, as wife is to husband, and as yin is to yang. A ghost identity attaches to members of the female sex due to their common yin element, while the human identity is reserved for males based on their association with yang.

Viewed further in the light of the analogy between the yin-yang hierarchy and the gender hierarchy in family and social realities in the Six Dynasties, the mechanism behind the creation of a ghost wife in the male imagination can be revealed. According to the influential philosophical text *Chunqiu fanlu*, attributed to the Han Confucian scholar Dong Zhongshu, yang is venerable and yin base. The hierarchy of yang and yin is thought to determine the gender hierarchy: "*Yang qi*[3] is warm while *yin qi* is cold; *yang qi* gives while *yin qi* takes away; *yang qi* is benevolent while *yin qi* is criminal; *yang qi* is lenient while *yin qi* is severe; *yang qi* is caring while *yin qi* is hateful; *yang qi* gives life while *yin qi* kills . . . The husband is *yang* and the wife is *yin* . . . The Way of *yin* is devoid of anything that acts on its own" (2003, 166, 168).

From the Han period on, the hierarchical yin-yang/feminine-masculine analogy and yang-venerable/yin-base associations have permeated intellectual discourses, especially those concerning the wife's role in gender relations. The relationship between husband and wife portrayed in later texts almost exclusively assumes this decidedly gendered form, as illustrated in "The Ghostly Wedding Nights." The female ghost zhiguai romance tale also participates in perpetuating the subordination of yin and elevation of yang in that the ghost, as the female virgin, because of her untimely premarital death, has to rely on a living male to fulfill her social role—to be a wife. For the dead female soul to be able to rest underground, it must be married off.

Chinese people have long believed in the existence of ghosts, and the concept of marrying the ghost in zhiguai has deep cultural origins (see Campany 1991). Arranging marriages for the dead has been a custom in China since the eleventh century BCE, and is still practiced in some regions. The custom of arranging marriages between a dead soul and a living person is not so strictly gendered that the dead must be female and the living male. The ritual of *Minghun* or *Youhun*, for marrying the dead, first became popular in the West Zhou Dynasty (1097–771 BCE). For instance, *Jiashang* (marrying the dead) was recorded in a chapter, "*Meishi* (The Matchmaking)," in a supposedly third-century BCE ritual text, *Zhouli* (The Rites of the Zhou Dynasty), with the annotation by Zheng Kangcheng (127–200 CE)[4] that it was "for those who died under nineteen years old" (Ruan 2009, 1581). Another detailed description of the possible ritual reference for these tales can be found in a less known Jin or Yuan Dynasty (1153–1368 CE) ritual manual called *The Secret Burial Classic of the Great Han Dynasty* (*Dahan yuanling mizang jing*). Its section "*Minghun yili pian* (Rite of Marrying the Dead)," translated by the zhiguai scholar Judith Zeitlin, offers the following rationale for the practice:

> With Heaven and Earth, there is the intermingling of *yin* and *yang*; with humankind, there is the relationship between husband and wife. In life, a couple shares a coverlet; in death, they share a coffin. But sometimes after a man has undergone the capping ceremony for coming of age, he dies before taking a wife; and sometimes after a woman has undergone the hair pinning ceremony to mark her maturity, she dies before being married off. Because it is not permitted to omit the "grand burial" for ancestors, in such cases, a marriage is made between two "pure souls" (*zhen hun*) to keep them from becoming lonely ghosts. (2007, 34)[5]

Drawing also on the yin-yang thought, this manual nevertheless justifies the marriage between two pure souls by the complementary, rather than hierarchical, nature of the yin and yang. Zeitlin regards marrying a female soul and marrying a male soul as not distinguished in their priority but equally prominent in ritual practices. In contrast, in zhiguai tales, references to marrying a female soul far outnumber those to marrying a male soul and, as discussed above, they are the only ghost marriage tales recorded in *Sou shen ji*. In fact, in *Sou shen ji*, those tales[6] where the ritual framework is referred to exclusively belong to the ghost wife tale type, revealing a male-centered structuring perspective. In later collections of tales of ghost romances, ritual frameworks are usually less evident. Rather, later author-compliers often foreground either the great love between humans and ghosts that transcends life and death, the humanization of the female ghosts through reacquisition of human status, or the sexual parasitism and prey that a ghost temptress might inflict on the human male.

In *Sou shen ji*'s male-biased habit of conceptualizing the world, the ghost identity becomes eternally attached to the female other, the yin gender, while the self, the yang gender, can be dissociated from a ghostly connotation. As a result, in the zhiguai ghost romance tales, the male sex—representing and represented by the identity of the narrator—is invariably maintained as the absolute yang while the female sex is at the mercy of male imagination. The ghost marriage theme *becomes* gendered in male production, to the extent that it is culturally unimaginable to think of a male counterpart for the ghost Princess Ch'in-nü. This character remains nameless in that *Ch'in-nü*, meaning a girl/daughter of the State Ch'in, is only an indicator of her origin and gender. No named male would wait in the lonely underground world for twenty-three years before detaining a living passerby to set his soul at peace through sex. The reversal of a male ghost prince marrying a humble human female simply has never been employed.

What complicates the gender constructions in the example tale is that the concept of the yin and yang here does not necessarily or exclusively correspond to the paradigms of the feminine and the masculine. Despite his yang identity, the human male protagonist demonstrates characteristics and features that are usually attributed to the feminine personality and to women, such as passivity, inferiority, and disenfranchisement in power relations. In contrast, the female, despite being a kind of super-yin wherein her yin gender is compounded with her yin ghost identity, displays strong masculine attributes: she is active, superior, and enfranchised in terms of power. In "The Ghostly Wedding Nights," Princess Ch'in-nü initiates in proposing sex, which—in the Chinese culture that forbids premarital sex—is often referred to using the euphemism of "becom[ing] husband and wife." She retains the active part in sending Tao-tu away in a timely fashion and giving him the golden pillow. She comes from a royal origin and would have married into the same royal clan had she not died young. She thus defies her feminine categorization while simultaneously occupying it. In contrast, her husband Tao-tu remains passive, invited to the communion, offered sex, given the token, questioned by the queen, and ultimately recognized as the royal son-in-law. A poor man who has to beg for meals along his journey, he has little power before being assimilated into the royal family through his sex with the ghost princess. Yet he ultimately triumphs.

Returning to Holbek's division of "masculine" and "feminine" tales, it becomes problematic to apply the two criteria he proposes when attempting to assign a tale gender to "The Ghostly Wedding Nights." If we consider who plays the active role and enacts the central moves, the tale is feminine. If we judge by the combination of the main characters, it becomes a masculine tale, linking the lowborn young male (Hsin Tao-tu) to the highborn young female (Princess Ch'in-nü). The discrepancy occurs because the worldview Holbek posits assumes a fixed dichotomy of female and male that corresponds to the feminine and masculine. Such a mapping of a fixed relationship between sex and gender has been extensively contested by contemporary feminists. For example, as Judith Butler argues:

> Taken to its logical limit, the sex/gender distinction suggests a radical
> discontinuity between sexed bodies and culturally constructed gen-
> ders . . . The presumption of a binary gender system implicitly retains the
> belief in a mimetic relation of gender to sex whereby gender mirrors sex or

is otherwise restricted by it. When the constructed status of gender is theo-
rized as radically independent of sex, gender itself becomes a free-floating
artifice, with the consequence that *man* and *masculine* might just as easily
signify a female body as a male one, and *woman* and *feminine* a male body
as easily as a female one. (1999, 6)

In our tales, the male protagonists' gender appears more feminine than
masculine; they are passive, powerless, inferior, marginalized, silent, and
obedient. In contrast, the princesses are independent, active, superior, awe-
inspiring, driven by unabashed sexuality, and manipulative, thus subverting conventional gender attributes ascribed to women in ancient patriarchal
China. This seeming reversal of traditional stereotypes—female with masculine attributes and male with feminine attributes—further complicates
the gender associations of the tale.

However, I would like to argue that it is precisely within this ambiguity
that the implied male perspective can be detected. One of the reasons the
gender of the tale is difficult to pin down is because male-centered aspi-
rations are obscured in the conceptualization of a subversive supernatural
princess, possessing ghostly subjectivity and agency. The problem is that her
power is imagined by male narrators and exists only in an imaginary realm.
Her desires are merely projections of those of human men. Her action
comes from male fantasy, her speech prescribed by the male author, and her
supernatural identity constructed in the interest of men. Thus, within the
male-dominated zhiguai tradition, encounters with ghost princesses mainly
project male desires. The gendered body of the ghost functions not only as
a space for male literary imagination of the other but also as the location
where patriarchal and heterosexual institutions perpetuate the fixation of
the gender hierarchy.

MARRYING THE GHOST PRINCESS:
WHOSE HAPPY-EVER-AFTER?

Tale 396, "The Princess of Sui-yang and Scholar T'an," in *Sou shen ji* offers
another example of the ghost princess/wife tale type. This story resembles
the previous one in terms of narrative, persona, and theme. Yet many notable differences emerge. A further examination of the elements manifested
in this tale highlights other crucial aspects of the male-centeredness in constructing the ghost princess zhiguai tale type. The tale recounts:

A certain scholar T'an of the Han dynasty was forty years old and still
unmarried. He was deeply moved by reading the *Book of Odes*. Once,
around midnight, a young woman of some fifteen or sixteen years,

beautiful and elegantly attired—utterly without equal in the empire—came to him and offered to be his in marriage.

"However," said she, "I am unlike other humans, and you must never see me by lamp- or torchlight for three years. When that time is past, it will be possible to do so."

She became his wife and bore him a son. But after two years he could scarcely bear it longer. One night, when he had seen her to bed, he secretly brought a torch and shone it on her. Above the waist she was covered with flesh as an ordinary human; below her waist was only a skeleton.

His wife awoke and spoke: "You have betrayed me. I was going to become fully human—oh, why could you not have waited just one more year before exposing me to flame-light?"

T'an apologized, but she tearfully insisted she could stay no longer: "I know I must discontinue our marriage rituals forever, but I have great concern for my son and fear you two may not be able to sustain yourselves when I am gone. If you will follow me now, I will leave you a gift."

T'an followed her as she led him to a beautifully decorated mansion and a room which housed many unusual objects. From among them she chose a pearl-studded robe and gave it to him, saying: "This you may use to support yourselves." Then she tore a piece of material from T'an's garments and kept it when he left.[7]

T'an took the robe to the marketplace, and the household of the Prince of Sui-yang bought it for ten million coppers. The Prince recognized the robe: "This belonged to my daughter! What is it doing in the marketplace? Her tomb must have been violated!" Thereupon he had T'an arrested and beaten. T'an told the entire truth, but the Prince was inclined to disbelieve him. He inspected his daughter's tomb and all was complete as before. He had the coffin taken out and there, pinched under the lid, was a piece of cloth.

When the Prince called T'an's son to him, he saw the lad did greatly resemble his daughter and finally believed the story. He summoned T'an and richly rewarded him, acknowledging him as his son-in-law. The boy he made a Gentleman-page in his court. (Gan 1996, 196–197)

Unlike tale 395, in this narrative, the ghost princess of Sui-yang (who, like Princess Ch'in-nü, is known only by a place association, not a proper name) approaches the scholar T'an at midnight, instead of inviting him to her tomb-palace. The scene of their ghostly encounter is not the underground world but the human world. Rather than detaining the living male for their wedding nights, the princess of Sui-yang transgresses into the human world in her pursuit of marriage, seeking reattainment of a human body. She chooses to conceal her ghost identity and cohabits with scholar T'an with the only condition that she should not be looked at by lamplight. However, T'an breaks the taboo, so the princess leaves him. Yet, quite unexpectedly, what T'an receives for his breach is not punishment but excessive reward. Though he loses his ghost wife, he is left with a human male heir and a pearl robe, which brings him greater fortune and power.

T'an's loss of a wife is compensated by the miraculous acquisition of a new social status as the royal son-in-law. In contrast, the princess recedes quickly from the tale; her fate is no longer significant, as long as her royal identity is recognized and safely transferred to the male human. In this light, the ghost princess functions as no more than a medium for her human husband to access the power embodied in her royal identity. At a deeper level, at the core of the traffic between the human man and the ghost woman lies the triangular relation among them and her patriarchal clan. The ghost princess's role is to mediate between her husband and her family so as to facilitate a patrilineal transfer of power and "male homosocial desire," to borrow Eve Kosofsky Sedgwick's term (1985, 21). The female sex of the ghost body becomes the signifier of social power. What matters fundamentally is not the sex, gender, or human/ghost aspects of her identity but the possibility of power and status acquisition for the male human that her social status ensures. For the male producer and consumer of zhiguai tales, the encounter with a ghost princess projects the coalition of the desires for sex and for power, thus exhibiting a concern for male well-being only.

Desires projected in tales often stem from a sense of lack. As Holbek observes of fairy-tale wish fulfillment, "The loss of the sources of satisfaction in actual life forces the desires into acceptance of compensation in imaginative tales" (1987, 268). Steven Swann Jones writes that fairy tales "help us to recognize and cope with typical problems and anxieties that we encounter in life. All of these issues may be regarded as of paramount interest to audience members who are trying to . . . answer life's enduring and perplexing questions" (2002, 20). However, in Chinese ghost princess/wife tales, the compensation is imagined and the dreams and worldviews they project all stem from men's perspectives. Echoing this view, Chinese scholar Yu Rujie argues that the (male) desires often transmitted into zhiguai narratives manifest because of what he designates as the "creation-compensated repression" symptomatic of Chinese literati. According to Yu Rujie, zhiguai, as a genre less censored than other high orthodox forms, is less constrained by conventions and morals. It is possible for heroes in zhiguai to transgress and transcend the social reality; hence, the genre provides "the best form for Chinese literati to write about sex and sexuality" (1991, 52). As the iconic Chinese cultural critic Lu Xun humorously notes, "The Spanish sing under the windows of young girls to win their love . . . However[,] scholars in our country . . . always say how the girls come to lure [men]" (1963a, 27). Viewed in this light, the ghost princess becomes an imaginary agent for Chinese literati to actualize real-life desires in a miraculous and effortless way.

In the Six Dynasties, arranged marriages, mostly within the same social class, dominated. Particularly in this era, society was stratified into two classes: the upper *shi* and the lower *shu*. The former were foremost in all aspects of life—politics, economy and culture—and their dominance in society formed a special political system of *menfa zhengzhi* (politics of prominent clans) (see Tian 1989, 330–362). In ancient Chinese society, marriage was decided based on social and political considerations rather than emotion and sexual drives. It then represented the most important way for one family to connect with another and enlarge its own power and influences. Thus, marriage between the upper shi class and the lower shu class was very rare. Many lower-class men could not marry at all due to social constraints. For some, marrying into a shi clan offered a shortcut to enter the power group. It compared positively to studying for more than ten years with the slim chance of passing the civil exams, as the story of scholar T'an shows. Thus, it is not surprising that all ghost wife zhiguai tales end with the living male getting promoted and his family line being accepted into the upper class. This change of the hero's identity through marriage is critical to understanding the implied male perspective that shapes "The Princess of Sui-yang and Scholar T'an" as decisively masculine in concern and interest.

Yet this masculine tale departs from Holbek's LYM-HYF definition in that the hero is no longer young. Scholar T'an is in his forties when the princess pays him the nocturnal visit. What we have here is marriage between a lowborn older male and the HYF. This misalliance, in terms of age difference, social distance, and life-death boundary, indicates a lopsided conceptualization of womanhood and manhood from a male perspective. Princess Sui-yang's beauty is highlighted from the outset; she is "a young woman of some fifteen or sixteen years, beautiful and elegantly attired—utterly without equal in the empire." Yet the tale relates nothing regarding what scholar T'an looks like. All we know is that he is forty years old (which is very old for marriage at his time), still unmarried (which can only be explained by his lower socioeconomical status), and reading *Book of Odes* (a collection of ancient poetry and songs with strong erotic connotations). To sum him up, scholar T'an is a poor old bachelor who badly needs and desires to get married, which renders him less an individual than a type, or a stereotype, of a special community of lower-class males excluded from the marriage institutions and power structures in the hierarchical society.

The ghost princess demonstrates directly oppositional qualities: she is young, beautiful, and rich. She is the one who initiates in the romance. She is also the one who is betrayed by her spouse. She is fertile and bears her old husband a male heir, the lack of which would be not only a shame but a disaster for a male within the patriarchal Chinese family system. She takes it as her responsibility to provide sufficient financial aid to her husband and boy child before she leaves the human world. She expects her living relatives will exhume her tomb to verify her marriage with scholar T'an, so she wisely takes a piece of his clothing as the evidence. She sacrifices herself and brings about the happily-ever-after life for her human husband and son. In other words, she represents the most idealized womanhood man can conceive, especially when opposed to the overshadowed image of her husband.

If, as shown in this tale, the ghost princess owns everything and her husband nothing at all, what then motivates the ghost princess to marry the scholar? What can she gain from the marriage? To what degree can the tale thereby appeal to a female reader? The first question directs us to another detail in this tale, that is, the literary hypothesis that female ghosts can reacquire a human identity through living with a human male. This idea is also developed from the yin-female and yang-male analogy. According to the traditional Chinese yin-yang cosmological thought, two fundamental elements, or energy (*qi*), are needed for the genesis of the universe and everything living in it: the yang qi and the yin qi. Again, to cite the Han philosopher Dong Zhongshu's theory: "*Yang qi* is warm while *yin qi* is cold; *yang qi* gives while *yin qi* takes away; . . . *yang qi* gives life while *yin qi* kills" (2003, 166). As mentioned before, the ghost/female is the yin while the human/male the yang, so my conjecture follows that by living with the human male (the super-yang), the female ghost (the super-yin) will regain the yang qi, that is, the energy for generating a new life. However, to be able to assume human shape again, Princess Sui-yang has to take in enough yang qi without her ghost identity being discovered. This is why from the start she insists on a three-year period during which scholar T'an may not look at her by lamplight. The ghost princess, though superior to the scholar in other aspects, has to rely on his male yang qi to obtain her own human identity. This dependence of the ghost on the human projects and reinforces the hierarchical relations between female and male, wife and husband, as viewed from a male perspective. For this reason, the sense of fulfillment for the female ghost, which is imagined by the male zhiguai authors in the first place, is essentially denied through scholar T'an's breach of the taboo. If the tales could be seen as dreams, they are the dreams of men only; and in these dreams, the happily-ever-after utopia is reserved for the heroes only, while the ghost princess/wife heroines invariably recede back into their dark world underground.

In this zhiguai tale type, it seems that death has freed women from social conventions and empowered them to act upon their own desires. Both Princess Ch'in-nü and Princess Sui-yang appear to be outside patriarchal regulation. They choose their partners, propose marriage, and relinquish their human partner at their own will. They are seen as dominant figures in these tales. However, the female sex never participates in the image-creating process. Women's desires are merely projections of those of human men and their agency comes from male fantasy. Their speech is prescribed by the male author and their identity constructed in the interest of men. They are the creation-objects, and men are the creator-subjects. Their female subjectivity and agency are devoid of their own intentions; they are shadows reflecting the dreams of others. Within the male-dominated zhiguai tradition, women function primarily as a symbol, a substitute, and an idea. The world these tales depict is mainly for men; it is the world as it should be for them.

NOTES

1.   Most notably Feng Menglong (1993); Hong Mai (1985); Liu Yiqing (1988); Niu Zengru (1985); Pu Songling (2006); Qu You (1981); Tao Qian (1981); Yuan Mei (1986). In accordance with conventions for Chinese names, the surname is first, followed by the given name.

2.   A traditional Chinese unit of distance, li has varied considerably over time but now has a standardized length of 500 meters, or half a kilometer.

3.   Also *chi* or *ch'i*, often translated as "energy flow," originally as a conceptualization of the pair of energy flows that motivates the universe. In Chinese philosophy the term later refers to an active principle generating and sustaining any living thing in the universe.

4.   He is also known as Zheng Xuan, a prominent annotator, Confucian scholar, and philosopher in the early Han Dynasty, best known for his annotation of Confucian classics and *Shijing* (Book of Odes), the earliest collection of poetry and songs. His annotations had been used as official textbooks for civil exams for centuries.

5.   See the originals in Yao et al. (1986, 8199:19a) and Hu et al. (1992, vol. 1, no. 15, 155).

6.   In tale 397, "Lu Chong," ritual protocols are more explicitly emphasized. The marriage is formally arranged by the deceased fathers of the couple, and the girl's given name, Wen-hsiu, is interpreted retrospectively as a phonological anagram for spirit marriage, "You-hun," thereby inserting a specific reference to the practice into the text. On the other hand, in tales 395 and 396, the ritual apparatus is absent, but the goal of marrying off a lonely female spirit is clearly achieved; thus, there is a symbolic fulfillment of womanhood through marriage and sex.

7.   This story is reminiscent of ATU 425, "The Search for the Lost Husband" tale type series, particularly 425B, "Son of the Witch," formerly "The Disenchanted Husband." In the latter, however, it is the groom, not the bride, who is enchanted and the bride, not the groom, who breaks a prohibition. Further, the narrative ensures the restoration of the couple's relationship by the actions of the bride, who accomplishes impossible tasks to ensure that she and her husband are reunited.

Bibliography

Abrahams, Roger. 1983. *The Man-of-Words in the West Indies: Performance and the Emergence of Creole Culture.* Baltimore: Johns Hopkins University Press.

Abrahams, Roger. 1987. "An American Vocabulary of Celebrations." In *Time out of Time: Essays on the Festival,* edited by Alessandro Falassi, 173–183. Albuquerque: University of New Mexico Press.

Abrahamsen, Povl. 1964. *Hollænderbyen. Kort Beskrivelse. Udsent til Store Magleby Sogn af udsmykningsfondet ved Store Magleby Kirke.* Copenhagen: n.p.

Ackroyd, Peter. 1979. *Dressing Up: Transvestism and Drag: The History of an Obsession.* New York: Simon and Schuster.

Adams, Carol J. 1998. "Eating Animals." In *Eating Culture,* edited by Ron Scapp and Brian Seitz, 60–75. Albany: State University of New York Press.

Adele, Nadine, and Roger Raisch. 1998–2002. "How to Dress and Clean a Turkey." Accessed April 30, 2011. http://www.turkeyhuntingsecrets.com/library/libindex -lists-dress.htm.

Adrian, Kim. 2010. "John Currin's *Thanksgiving.*" Accessed June 20, 2012. http://www .foodcultureindex.com/2010/10/john-currins-thanksgiving.html.

Adriansen, Inge. 2003. "Nationale symboler i Det Danske Rige." Vol. 1 of *Fra fyrstestat til nationalstater.* Copenhagen: Museum Tusculanum.

Alex. 2004. "Crown Jewels on Display." *The Museum of Hoaxes* (blog). November 28. Accessed May 20, 2012. http://www.museumofhoaxes.com/hoax/weblog/comments /1573.

Alleman, Jeanne. 1930. *Un d'Artagnan de plume: Jean-François Bladé.* Paris: Plon.

Allen, Graham. 2000. *Intertextuality.* London: Routledge.

Amagerbanken. 2010. *Basickort.* Accessed July 28, 2011. http://www.basickort.dk.

Amagerbanken. 2011. Accessed March 23, 2011. http://www.amagerbanken.dk/. Site discontinued.

American Family: Just Your Typical American Family . . . Sorta. 2012. "Finding Chinese Birthparents." Accessed April 11, 2014. http://web.archive.org/web/201308 23102506/http://american-family.org/finding-chinese-birthparents/.

Amt, Emilie. [1992] 2010. *Women's Lives in Medieval Europe: A Sourcebook.* New York: Routledge.

Anagnost, Ann. 2000. "Scenes of Misrecognition: Maternal Citizenship in the Age of Transnational Adoption." *Positions* 8 (2): 389–421. http://dx.doi.org/10.1215 /10679847-8-2-389.

Anatole, Christian. 1985. "Une vocation en suspens: Bladé auteur de nouvelles." In *Jean-François Bladé, 1827–1900: Actes du Colloque de Lectoure, 20 et 21 Octobre 1984,* edited by Jean Arrouye, 11–16. Béziers: Centre international de documentation occitane.

Ancelet, Barry Jean. 1989. *Capitaine, Voyage ton Flag: The Traditional Cajun Country Mardi Gras.* Lafayette: University of Southwestern Louisiana.

Ancelet, Barry Jean. 2001. "Falling Apart to Stay Together: Deep Play in the Grand Marais Mardi Gras." *Journal of American Folklore* 114(453): 144–153.

Andreasen, Eyðun. 2010. "The Seal Woman." Accessed November 22, 2010. http://www .stamps.fo.Default.aspx?ID=1131&PID=ProductID=PROD30.

Angelo, Gretchen. 2001. "Author and Authority in the *Evangiles des quenouilles*." *Fifteenth Century Studies* 26:21–41.

Angelo, Gretchen. 2003. "Creating a Masculine Vernacular: The Strategy of Misogyny in Late Medieval French Texts." In *The Vulgar Tongue: Medieval and Postmedieval Vernacularity*, edited by Fiona Somerset and Nicholas Watson, 85–98. University Park: Pennsylvania State University Press.

Arājs, K., and A. Medne. 1977. *Latviešu pasaku tipu rādītājs/The Types of the Latvian Folktales*. Riga: Zinātne.

Arrouye, Jean, ed. 1985a. In *Jean-François Bladé, 1827–1900: Actes du Colloque de Lectoure, 20 et 21 Octobre 1984*, edited by Jean Arrouye, 5–10. Béziers: Centre international de documentation occitane.

Arrouye, Jean, ed. 1985b. *Jean-François Bladé, 1827–1900: Actes du Colloque de Lectoure, 20 et 21 Octobre 1984*. Béziers: Centre international de documentation occitane.

Ashliman, D. J. 2000. "The Sealskin." Accessed November 9, 2010. http://www.pitt.edu /~dash/type4080.html#sealskin.

Assaf, Francis. 2003. "L'impossible souveraineté: Le roi-prétexte dans les contes de madame d'Aulnoy (1690–1698)." *Biblio* 17(145): 267–275.

Bacchilega, Cristina. 1997. *Postmodern Fairy Tales: Gender and Narrative Strategies*. Philadelphia: University of Pennsylvania Press.

Bacchilega, Cristina, and John Rieder. 2010. "Mixing it Up: Generic Complexity and Gender Ideology in Early Twenty-first Century Fairy Tale Film." In *Fairy Tale Films: Visions of Ambiguity*, edited by Pauline Greenhill and Sidney Eve Matrix, 23–41. Logan: Utah State University Press.

Bager, Maibritt. 2010. "Årsberetning for Amager Museum 2009." *Museum Amager: Medlemsblad for Museumsforeningerne*, no. 1 (February), 4–6.

Bakhtin, M. M. 1968. *Rabelais and His World*. Translated by Helene Iswolsky. Cambridge, MA: MIT Press.

Bakhtin, M. M. 1981. *The Dialogic Imagination*, edited by Michael Holquist. Translated by Caryl Emerson and Michael Holquist. Austin: University of Texas Press.

Bakhtin, M. M. 1986. "Problems of Speech Genres." In *Speech Genres and Other Late Essays*, edited by Carol Emerson and Michael Holquist, translated by Vern W. McGee, 60–102. Austin: University of Texas Press.

Baldwin, James. 1985. "Here Be Dragons." In *The Price of the Ticket: Collected Nonfiction, 1948–1985*, 677–90. New York: St. Martin's/Marek.

Balsamo, Anne. 1995. "Forms of Technological Embodiment: Reading the Body in Contemporary Culture." In *Cyberspace/Cyberbodies/Cyberpunk*, edited by Mike Featherstone and Roger Burrows, 215–238. Thousand Oaks, CA: Sage. http://dx.doi.org /10.4135/9781446250198.n13.

Barchilon, Jacques. 1975. *Le conte merveilleux Français de 1690 à 1790: Cent ans de féerie et de poésie ignorées de l'histoire littéraire*. Paris: Librairie Honoré Champion.

Barreca, Regina. 1991. *They Used to Call Me Snow White . . . but I Drifted: Women's Strategic Use of Humor*. New York: Penguin Books.

Barrett, Susan, and Carol Aubin. 1990. "Feminist Considerations of Intercountry Adoptions." *Women & Therapy* 10(1–2): 127–138. http://dx.doi.org/10.1300/J015 v10n01_12.

Bartholet, Elizabeth. 2010. "International Adoption: The Human Rights Position." *Global Policy* 1(1): 91–100. http://dx.doi.org/10.1111/j.1758-5899.2009.00001.x.

Bauman, Richard. 1971. "Differential Identity and the Social Base of Folklore." *Journal of American Folklore* 84(331): 31–41. http://dx.doi.org/10.2307/539731.

Bauman, Richard. 1972. "Belsnickling in a Nova Scotia Island Community." *Western Folklore* 31(4): 229–243. http://dx.doi.org/10.2307/1498220.

Bauman, Richard. 1975. "Verbal Art as Performance." *American Anthropologist* 77:290–311.

Bauman, Richard. 1986. *Story, Performance, and Event: Contextual Studies in Oral Narrative*. Cambridge: Cambridge University Press. http://dx.doi.org/10.1017/CBO9780511620935.

Bauman, Richard, and Charles L. Briggs. 2003. *Voices of Modernity: Language Ideologies and the Politics of Inequality*. Cambridge: Cambridge University Press. http://dx.doi.org/10.1017/CBO9780511486647.

Baxter, Sarah. 2009. "Women Are Victors in 'Mancession': Gender Roles Are Being Rewritten in America as Men Bear the Brunt of Job Losses." *Sunday Times,* June 7.

BBC News. 2004. "Protest over Merger of Regiments." December 18. Accessed May 20, 2012. http://news.bbc.co.uk/2/hi/uk_news/scotland/4106465.stm.

Beck, Ervin. 1989. "Rhymes." In *Global Anabaptist Mennonite Encyclopedia*, vol. 5, edited by Cornelius J. Dyck and Dennis D. Martin, 774–775. Scottdale, PA: Herald.

Bederman, Gail. 1995. *Manliness and Civilization: A Cultural History of Gender and Race in the United States, 1880–1917*. Chicago: University of Chicago Press. http://dx.doi.org/10.7208/chicago/9780226041490.001.0001.

Beeton, Isabella. 1861. *Mrs Beeton's Book of Household Management*. London: S.O. Beeton.

Behar, Ruth. 1995. "Introduction: Out of Exile." In *Women Writing Culture*, edited by Ruth Behar and Deborah A. Gordon, 1–29. Berkeley: University of California Press.

Bella, Leslie. 1992. *The Christmas Imperative: Leisure, Family and Women's Work*. Halifax: Fernwood.

Ben-Amos, Dan. 1971. "Toward a Definition of Folklore in Context." *Journal of American Folklore* 84(331): 3–15. http://dx.doi.org/10.2307/539729.

Benbow, Heather Merle. 2007. "Ethnic Drag in the Films of Doris Daqrrie." *German Studies Review* 30(3): 517–536.

Bendix, Regina. 1997. *In Search of Authenticity: The Formation of Folklore Studies*. Madison: University of Wisconsin Press.

Benedikz, B. S. 1973. "Basic Themes in Icelandic Folklore." *Folklore* 84(1): 1–26. http://dx.doi.org/10.1080/0015587X.1973.9716492.

Bennett, Gillian. 1999. *Alas Poor Ghost: Traditions of Belief in Story and Discourse*. Logan: Utah State University Press.

Bennett, Jessica, and Jesse Ellison. 2010. "Women Will Rule the World: Men Were the Main Victims of the Recession. The Recovery Will Be Female." *Newsweek,* July 6.

Bennett, Judith M. 1987. *Women in the Medieval English Countryside: Gender and Household in Brigstock before the Plague*. Oxford: Oxford University Press.

Benson, Peter. 2008. "Good Clean Tobacco: Philip Morris, Biocapitalism, and the Social Course of Stigma in North Carolina." *American Ethnologist* 35(3): 357–379. http://dx.doi.org/10.1111/j.1548-1425.2008.00040.x.

Bergen, Jake. 2005. "The Brumtop." In *Halbstadt Heritage*, edited by Dave Sawatzky, 389–390. Altona: Friesens.

Berry, Wendell. 1991. "The Problem of Tobacco." In *Sex, Economy, Freedom and Community: Eight Essays*, 53–68. New York: Pantheon Books.

Best, Kelly. 2008. "'Making Cool Things Hot Again': Blackface and Newfoundland Mummering." *Ethnologies* 30(2): 215–248. http://dx.doi.org/10.7202/019953ar.

Bettelheim, Bruno. 1976. *The Uses of Enchantment: The Meaning and Importance of Fairy Tales*. New York: Knopf. http://dx.doi.org/10.1037/e309842005-008.

Bhabha, Homi K. 1994. *The Location of Culture.* New York: Routledge.

Billig, Michael. 2005. *Laughter and Ridicule: Towards a Social Critique of Humour.* London: Sage.

Billund Airport. 2013. "2012 / Billund Airport." Accessed April 15, 2014. http://www.bll. dk/om-lufthavnen/statistikker/2012.

Birberick, Anne. 2005. "Changing Places: d'Aulnoy's *Le nouveau gentilhomme bourgeois.*" In *Intersections,* edited by Faith E. Beasley and Kathleen Wine, 285–292. Tübingen: Gunter Narr Verlag.

Bird, Sharon R. 1996. "Welcome to the Men's Club: Homosociality and the Maintenance of Hegemonic Masculinity." *Gender & Society* 10(2): 120–132. http://dx.doi.org /10.1177/089124396010002002.

Bjørton, Hanne. 2010. "Ane slagtede tønden for tredje gang." *Amagerbladet,* February 16. Accessed August 16, 2012. http://dinby.dk/dragoer/ane-slagtede-toenden-for-tredje-gang.

Bladé, Jean-François. 1861. "Les sources de l'histoire de la Gascogne et les manuscrits de l'Abbé Daignan du Sendat." *Bulletin du Comité d'histoire et d'archéologie de la province ecclésiastique d'Auch* 2:417–436.

Bladé, Jean-François. 1862. Dissertation sur les chants heroiques des Basques. *Revue d'Aquitaine et du Languedoc* 7:137–144, 189–194, 224–231.

Bladé, Jean-François. 1869. *Études sur l'origine des Basques.* Paris: A. Franck.

Bladé, Jean-François. 1881. *Poésies Populaires de la Gascogne.* 3 vols. Paris: Maisonneuve et cie.

Blamires, Alcuin ed. 1992. *Women Defamed and Women Defended: An Anthology of Medieval Texts.* Oxford: Clarendon Press.

Bladé, Jean-François. 1885.*Contes populaires de la Gascogne.* Paris: Aubéron, 2008.

Bloom, Leslie Rebecca, and Patricia Sawin. 2009. "Ethical Responsibility in Feminist Research: Challenging Ourselves to Do Activist Research with Women in Poverty." *International Journal of Qualitative Studies in Education* 22(3): 333–351. http:// dx.doi.org/10.1080/09518390902835413.

Bock, Gisela. 2002. *Women in European History.* Translated by Allison Brown. Malden, MA: Blackwell.

Boone, Joseph A. [1995] 2003. "Vacation Cruises; or, The Homoerotics of Orientalism." In *Feminist Postcolonial Theory: A Reader,* edited by Reina Lewis and Sara Mills, 460–488. Cambridge: MIT Press.

Bordo, Susan. 1993. *Unbearable Weight: Feminism, Western Culture and the Body.* Berkeley: University of California Press.

Bourguet, Marie-Noëlle. 1976. "Race et folklore: L'image officielle de la France en 1800." *Annales: Histoire, Sciences Sociales* 31(4): 802–823. http://dx.doi.org/10.3406/ahess .1976.293750.

Bourke, Angela. 1999. *The Burning of Bridget Cleary.* Harmondsworth: Penguin.

Brandes, Stanley H. 1980. *Metaphors of Masculinity: Sex and Status in Andalusian Folklore.* Philadelphia: University of Pennsylvania Press.

Brandth, Berit, and Marit S. Haugen. 2005. "Doing Rural Masculinity—From Logging to Outfield Tourism." *Journal of Gender Studies* 14(1): 13–22. http://dx.doi.org/10.108 0/0958923042000331452.

Bregenhøj, Carsten, and Hanne Pico Larsen. 2007. "Masks and Mumming Traditions in Denmark." In *Masks and Mumming in the Nordic Area,* edited by Terry Gunnell, 189–274. Uppsala: Kungl. Gustaf Adolfs Akademien för svensk folkkultur.

Briggs, Charles L., and Richard Bauman. 1992. "Genre, Intertextuality, and Social Power." *Journal of Linguistic Anthropology* 2(2): 131–172. http://dx.doi.org/10.1525/jlin .1992.2.2.131.

Briggs, Laura. 2006. "Making American Families: Transnational Adoption and U.S. Latin America Policy." In *Haunted by Empire*, edited by Ann Laura Stoler, 344–365. Durham, NC: Duke University Press. http://dx.doi.org/10.1215/9780822387992 -014.

Briggs, Laura, and Diana Marre. 2009. "Introduction: The Circulation of Children." In *Transnational Adoption: Global Inequalities and the Circulation of Children*, edited by Diana Marre and Laura Briggs, 1–28. New York: New York University Press.

Brocklebank, Lisa. 2000. "Rebellious Voices: The Unofficial Discourse of Cross-Dressing in d'Aulnoy, de Murat, and Perrault." *Children's Literature Association Quarterly* 25(3): 127–136. http://dx.doi.org/10.1353/chq.0.1336.

Bronner, Simon J. 1998. *Following Tradition: Folklore in the Discourse of American Culture.* Logan: Utah State University Press.

Bronner, Simon J. 2004. "'This Is Why We Hunt:' Social-Psychological Meanings of the Traditions and Rituals of Deer Camp." *Western Folklore* 63(1–2): 11–61.

Bronner, Simon, ed. 2005. *Manly Traditions: The Folk Roots of American Masculinities.* Bloomington: Indiana University Press.

Brown, W. Norman. 1927. "Change of Sex as a Hindu Story Motif." *Journal of the American Oriental Society* 47:3–24. http://dx.doi.org/10.2307/593238.

Burke, Carol. 2004. *Camp All-American, Hanoi Jane, and the High-and-Tight: Gender, Folklore, and Changing Military Culture.* Boston: Beacon.

Burke, Kenneth. 1973. *The Philosophy of Literary Form: Studies in Symbolic Action.* Berkeley: University of California Press.

Burke, Peter. 1978. *Popular Culture in Early Modern Europe.* New York: New York University Press.

Burley Tobacco Growers Co-operative Association. 1991. *The Producer's Program: Fifty Golden Years and More.* Lexington: Burley Tobacco Growers Co-operative Association.

Butler, Judith. 1988. "Performative Acts and Gender Constitution: An Essay in Phenomenology and Feminist Theory." *Theatre Journal* 40(4): 519–531. http://dx.doi.org /10.2307/3207893.

Butler, Judith. 1993. *Bodies That Matter: On the Discursive Limits of "Sex."* New York: Routledge.

Butler, Judith. [1990] 1999. *Gender Trouble: Feminism and the Subversion of Identity.* New York: Routledge.

Butler, Judith. 2001. "Doing Justice to Someone: Sex Reassignment and Allegories of Transsexuality." *GLQ: A Journal of Lesbian and Gay Studies* 7(4): 621–636. http:// dx.doi.org/10.1215/10642684-7-4-621.

Butler, Judith. 2004. *Undoing Gender.* New York: Routledge.

Cahill, Susan. 2010. "Through the Looking Glass: Fairy-tale Cinema and the Spectacle of Femininity in *Stardust* and *The Brothers Grimm*." *Marvels & Tales: Journal of Fairy-Tale Studies* 24(1): 57–67.

Cameron, Deborah. 1997. "Performing Gender Identity: Young Men's Talk and the Construction of Heterosexual Masculinity." In *Language and Masculinity*, edited by Sally A. Johnson and Ulrike Hanna Meinhof, 47–64. Oxford: Blackwell.

Campany, Robert F. 1991. "Ghost Matter: The Culture of Ghosts in Six Dynasties *Zhiguai*." *Chinese Literature: Essays, Articles, Reviews* 13:15–34.

Cantú, Norma E., Pauline Greenhill, and Rachelle H. Saltzman. 2009. "Women Folklorists." In *Encyclopedia of Women's Folklore and Folklife*, edited by Liz Locke, Theresa A. Vaughan, and Pauline Greenhill, lix–lxix. Westport, CT: Greenwood.

Cantú, Norma E., and Olga Nájera-Ramírez. 2002. *Chicana Traditions: Continuity and Change.* Urbana: University of Illinois Press.

Cape, Janet. n.d. "The Canadian Women's Army Corps Pipe Band." Accessed March 10, 2013. http://www.cwacband.com.

Caplow, Theodore. 1982. "Christmas Gifts and Kin Networks." *American Sociological Review* 47(3): 383–392. http://dx.doi.org/10.2307/2094994.

Caplow, Theodore. 1984. "Rule Enforcement within Visible Means: Christmas Gift Giving in Middletown." *American Journal of Sociology* 89(6): 1306–1323. http://dx.doi.org/10.1086/228017.

Cardigos, Isabel. 2006. *Catalogue of Portuguese Folktales*. Helsinki: Academia Scientiarum Fennica.

Carr, Edward R. 2008. "Men's Crops and Women's Crops: The Importance of Gender to the Understanding of Agricultural and Development Outcomes in Ghana's Central Region." *World Development* 36(5): 900–915. http://dx.doi.org/10.1016/j.worlddev.2007.05.009.

Carver Carpasso, Ruth. 1987. "Madame D'Aulnoy and the Comedy of Transformation." *Papers on French Seventeenth Century Literature* 14(27): 575–588.

Case, Sue-Ellen. 1988/1989. "Toward a Butch-Femme Aesthetic." *Discourse (Berkeley, Calif.)* 11(1): 55–73.

Cashman, Ray. 2006. "Critical Nostalgia and Material Culture in Northern Ireland." *Journal of American Folklore* 119(472): 137–160. http://dx.doi.org/10.1353/jaf.2006.0016.

Chan, Tak-hung Leo. 1998. *The Discourse on Foxes and Ghosts: Ji Yun and Eighteenth-Century Literati Storytelling*. Honolulu: University of Hawai'i Press.

Chatten, Nicola. 2002. "Fabliau." In *Medieval Folklore: A Guide to Myths, Legends, Tales, Beliefs and Customs*, edited by Carl Lindahl, John McNamara, and John Lindow, 126–128. New York: Oxford University Press.

Chauvin, Victor. 1904. *Bibliographie des ouvrages Arabes our relatifs aux Arabes publiés dans L'Europe chrétienne de 1810 à 1885*. Liège: H. Vaillant-Carmanne.

Cheal, David. 1988. *The Gift Economy*. New York: Routledge.

Chiaramonte, Louis. 1969. "Mumming in 'Deep Harbour': Aspects of Social Organization in Mumming and Drinking." In *Christmas Mumming in Newfoundland: Essays in Anthropology, Folklore, and History*, edited by Herbert Halpert and G. M. Story, 76–103. Toronto: University of Toronto Press.

Chodorow, Nancy. 1978. *The Reproduction of Mothering: Psychoanalysis and the Sociology of Gender*. Berkeley: University of California Press.

Chornoboy, Eleanor. 2007. *Faspa with Jast: A Snack of Mennonite Stories Told by Family and Guests*. Sanford, MB: Interior.

Clarke, Donald. 2010. "A Lovely Nowhere." *Irish Times*, February 19. Accessed May 14, 2011. http://www.irishtimes.com/newspaper/features/2010/0219/1224264785151.html.

Clary Lemon, Jennifer. 2010. "'We're Not Ethnic, We're Irish!': Oral Histories and the Discursive Construction of Immigrant Identity." *Discourse & Society* 21(1): 5–25. http://dx.doi.org/10.1177/0957926509345066.

Clover, Carol. 1992. *Men, Women and Chainsaws: Gender in the Modern Horror Film*. Princeton: Princeton University Press.

Coates, Jennifer, and Mary E. Jordan. 1997. "Que(e)rying Friendship: Discourses of Resistance and the Construction of Gendered Subjectivity." In *Queerly Phrased: Language, Gender, and Sexuality*, edited by Anna Livia and Kira Hall, 214–232. Oxford: Oxford University Press.

Cocchiara, Giuseppe. 1981. *The History of Folklore in Europe*. Translated by John McDaniel. Philadelphia: Institute for the Study of Human Issues.

Cohan, Steven. 1995. *Screening the Male: Exploring Masculinities in Hollywood Cinema*. London: Routledge.

Colapinto, John. 2000. *As Nature Made Him: The Boy Who Was Raised as a Girl*. Toronto: HarperCollins.

Colen, Shellee. 1995. "'Like a Mother to Them': Stratified Reproduction and West Indian Childcare Workers and Employers in New York." In *Conceiving the New World Order: The Global Politics of Reproduction*, edited by Faye Ginsburg and Rayna Rapp, 78–102. Los Angeles: University of California Press.

Collins, Patricia Hill. [1990] 2000. *Black Feminist Thought: Knowledge, Consciousness and the Politics of Empowerment*. New York: Routledge.

Connell, R.W. 1987. *Gender and power: Society, the Person, and Sexual Politics*. Sydney, Australia: Allen, Mercer and Urwin.

Connell, R. W. [1995] 2005. *Masculinities*. Berkeley: University of California Press.

Copenhagen Airports. n.d.a. "Strategy." Accessed April 15, 2014. http://www.cph.dk/en /about-cph/profile/Strategy/.

Copenhagen Airports. n.d.b. "Guide to art and architecture." Accessed April 15, 2014. http://www.cph.dk/en/about-cph/profile/Facts-about-CPH/Art-and-architecture /Guide-to-art-and-architecture/.

Courtès, Guy, and Michel Bordes. 1985. "Les origines de J.-F. Bladé et ses séjours à Lectoure." In *Jean-François Bladé, 1827–1900: Actes du Colloque de Lectoure, 20 et 21 Octobre 1984*, edited by Jean Arrouye, 59–70. Béziers: Centre international de documentation occitane.

COWI. 2010. *Airports and aviation*. Accessed April 28, 2011. http://www.cowi.com/menu /service/bridgetunnelandmarinestructures/documents/021-1500-010e-10c_airports.pdf.

Crane, Tara Christopher, Jean A. Hamilton, and Laurel E. Wilson. 2004. "Scottish Dress, Ethnicity, and Self-Identity." *Journal of Fashion Marketing and Management* 8 1): 66–83. http://dx.doi.org/10.1108/13612020410518709.

Crawford, Mary. 2003. "Gender and Humor in Social Context." *Journal of Pragmatics* 35(9): 1413–1430. http://dx.doi.org/10.1016/S0378-2166(02)00183-2.

Crenshaw, Kimberlé W. 1991. "Mapping the Margins: Intersectionality, Identity Politics, and Violence against Women of Color." *Stanford Law Review* 43(6): 1241–1299. http://dx.doi.org/10.2307/1229039.

Cromwell, Jason. 1999. "Passing Women and Female-Bodied Men: (Re)Claiming FTM History." In *Reclaiming Genders: Transsexual Grammars at the Fin de Siècle*, edited by Kate More and Stephen Whittle, 34–61. London: Cassell.

Currin, John. 2003. *Thanksgiving*. Image courtesy of the Gagosian Gallery. Accessed December 1, 2010. http://aphelis.net/thanksgiving-john-currin-2003/.

d'Aulnoy, Marie Catherine Baronne. 1998. *Contes II, contes nouveaux ou Les Fées à la mode*, edited by Philippe Hourcade. Paris: Société des textes français modernes.

Dahl, Karen Margrethe, and Vibeke Jakobsen. 2005. *Køn, etnicitet og barrier for integration. Fokus på uddannelse, arbejde og foreningsliv*. Copenhagen: Socialforskningsinstitutet.

Daily Bastardette. 2011. Accessed April 11, 2014. http://www.dailybastardette.com.

Daniel, Pete. 1980. *Breaking the Land: The Transformation of Cotton, Tobacco, and Rice Cultures since 1880*. Urbana: University of Illinois Press.

Danish Immigration Museum. 2012. "Welcome?" Accessed July 4, 2012. http://www.danishimmigrationmuseum.com/index.php?page=udstilling.

Darkow, John. 2007. *Thankful We're Not Jayhawks*. Cartoon in *Columbia Tribune*'s Darkow Tiger Series. Accessed July 20, 2010. http://archive.columbiatribune.com/Darkow /EatEmUpTigers.asp.

Davies, Christie. 1998. *Jokes and Their Relation to Society*. New York: Mouton de Gruyer. http://dx.doi.org/10.1515/9783110806144.

Davis, Karen. 2001. *More Than a Meal: The Turkey in History, Ritual, and Reality*. New York: Lantern Books.

Dawkins, R. M. 1953. *Modern Greek Folktales.* Oxford: Clarendon.

de Beauvoir, Simone. [1949] 1989. *The Second Sex.* Translated by H. M. Parshley. New York: Vintage.

de Certeau, Michel, Dominique Julia, and Jacques Revel. 1986. "The Beauty of the Dead: Nisard." In *Heterologies: Discourse on the Other,* translated by Brian Massumi, 119–136. Minneapolis: University of Minnesota Press.

de Witt, Nelson Ward. 2011a. *Ana's Miracle: A Family Blog.* Accessed July 10, 2011. http://www.anasmiracle.com.

de Witt, Nelson Ward. 2011b. "Identifying Nelson/Buscando a Roberto: Nelson Ward de Witt's Documentary Film." Accessed July 10, 2011. http://www.identifyingnelson.com.

Defrance, Anne. 1998. *Les contes de fées et les nouvelles de Madame d'Aulnoy (1690–1698).* Geneva: Librairie Droz.

Dégh, Linda. 2001. *Legend and Belief: Dialectics of a Folklore Genre.* Bloomington: Indiana University Press.

Dégh, Linda, and Andrew Vázsonyi. 1971. "Legend and Belief." *Genre (Los Angeles, Calif.)* 4:281–304.

DeGraff, Amy Vanderlyn. 1984. *The Tower and the Well.* Birmingham, AL: Summa.

Dekker, Rudolf M., and Lotte C. van de Pol. 1997. *The Tradition of Female Transvestism in Early Modern Europe.* New York: St. Martin's.

Den Danske Ordbog. n.d. Accessed April 27, 2011. www.ordnet.dk/ddo.

Den Store Danske. Gyldendals åbne encyklopædi. 2009–2012. S.v. "Amager." Accessed July 4, 2012. http://www.denstoredanske.dk/index.php?title=Danmarks_geografi_og_historie /Danmarks_geografi/K%C3%B8benhavn/Amager.

Dinshaw, Carolyn, and David Wallace, eds. 2003. *The Cambridge Companion to Medieval Women's Writing.* New York: Cambridge University Press. http://dx.doi.org/10.1017 /CCOL052179188X.

Dong, Zhongshu. 2003. "Excerpt from *Chunqiu fanlu.*" [Luxuriant Gems of the Spring and Autumn] In *Images of Women in Chinese Thought and Culture: Writings from the Pre-Qin Period to the Song Dynasty,* edited by Robin Wang and translated by Mark Csikszentmihalyi, 162–169. Indianapolis: Hackett.

Dorow, Sara. 1999. *I Wish for You a Beautiful Life: Letters from the Korean Birth Mothers of Ae Ran Won to Their Children.* St. Paul, MN: Yeong and Yeong.

Doss, Cheryl R. 2002. "Men's Crops? Women's Crops? The Gender Patterns of Cropping in Ghana." *World Development* 30(11): 1987–2000. http://dx.doi.org/10.1016 /S0305-750X(02)00109-2.

Doty, Alexander. 2000. *Flaming Classics: Queering the Film Canon.* New York: Routledge.

Douglas, Mary. 1966. *Purity and Danger: An Analysis of Concepts of Pollution and Taboo.* London: Routledge and Kegan Paul. http://dx.doi.org/10.4324/9780203361832.

Downing, Charles. 1972. *Armenian Folk-Tales and Fables.* London: Oxford University Press.

Dozon, Auguste. 1881. *Contes Albanis.* Paris: Ernest Leroux.

DR. 2004. "Indvandringens historie – tidslinje." Accessed January 1, 2009. http://www .dr.dk/indvandring/index3.asp. Site discontinued.

Dragør Fastelavnsforening. n.d. "Tøndekonger gennem tiden." Accessed April 15, 2014. http://www.123hjemmeside.dk/DragoerFastelavnsforening/20487696.

Dragør Kommune. n.d. "Fastelavn i Dragør – Lokalarkiv." Accessed March 23, 2011. http://www.dragoer.dk/page1221.aspx.

Dubinsky, Karen. 2010. *Babies without Borders: Adoption and Migration across the Americas.* New York: New York University Press.

Dueholm, Lars Berg. 2010. "Respekt for amagerkanerne." *Jyllands-Posten Debat.* Accessed May 14, 2011. http://jyllands-posten.dk/opinion/breve/ECE4328824/respekt-for -amagerkanerne/.

Dugaw, Dianne. 1989. *Warrior Women and Popular Balladry, 1650–1850*. New York: Cambridge University Press.

Duggan, Anne E. 1998. "Feminist Genealogy, Matriarchy, and Utopia in the Fairy Tale of Marie-Catherine d'Aulnoy." *Neophilologus* 82(2): 199–208. http://dx.doi.org/10.1023/A:1004257511857.

Dundes, Alan. 1961. "Brown County Superstitions: The Structure of Superstition." *Midwestern Folklore* 11(1): 25–56.

Dundes, Alan. 1964. "Text, Texture and Context." *Southern Folklore Quarterly* 28:251–265.

Dundes, Alan. 1971. "Folk Ideas as Units of Worldview." *Journal of American Folklore* 84(331): 93–103. http://dx.doi.org/10.2307/539737.

Dunbar, John Telfer. 1981. *The Costume of Scotland*. London: B.T. Batsford.

Dundes, Alan. 1978. "Into the Endzone for a Touchdown: A Psychoanalytic Consideration of American Football." *Western Folklore* 37(2): 75–88. http://dx.doi.org/10.2307/1499315.

Dundes, Alan. 1997. "Traditional Male Combat: From Game to War." In *From Game to War and Other Psychoanalytic Essays on Folklore*, 25–45. Lexington: University of Kentucky Press.

Dundes, Alan. [1969] 2007. "Folklore as a Mirror of Culture." In *The Meaning of Folklore: The Analytical Essays of Alan Dundes*, edited by Simon J. Bronner, 53–66. Logan: Utah State University Press.

Bob Dunsire Bag Pipe forums. Accessed March 10, 2013. http://forum.bobdunsire.com/forums/.

"Dying Request." n.d. Accessed November 20, 2010. http://www.jeepcorner.com/karlsxj/thescotsman.mp3. Site discontinued.

Ebb, Zoetica. 2007. "Fear the Turkey Man." *Coilhouse,* November 22. Accessed August 21, 2012. http://coilhouse.net/2007/11/fear-the-turkey-man/.

Edwards, Gavin. 2007. "Online Exclusive: Horror Film Directors Dish about *Grindhouse* Trailers." *Rolling Stone*, April 19. Accessed October 10, 2009. http://archive.today/um86O.

Eggerz, Solveig. 2008. *Seal Woman*. Denver: Ghost Road.

Eichler, Margrit, and Jeanne Lapointe. 1985. *On the Treatment of the Sexes in Research*. Ottawa: Social Sciences and Humanities Research Council of Canada.

Ekins, Richard, and Dave King, eds. 1996. *Blending Genders: Social Aspects of Cross-dressing and Sex-changing*. London: Routledge.

Eldridge, Sherrie. 1999. *Twenty Things Adopted Kids Wish Their Adoptive Parents Knew.* New York: Random House (Dell).

Ellis, Bill. 2003. "Making a Big Apple Crumble: The Role of Humor in Constructing a Global Response to Disaster." In *Of Corpse, Death and Humor in Folklore and Popular Culture*, edited by Peter Narváez, 35–80. Logan: Utah State University Press.

Ellis, Carolyn. 2004. *The Ethnographic I: A Methodological Novel about Autoethnography*. New York: Altamira.

Ellis, Carolyn, and Arthur Bochner. [1994] 2000. "Autoethnography, Personal Narrative, Reflexivity: Research as Subject." In *Handbook of Qualitative Research*, 2nd ed., edited by Norman K. Denzin and Yvonna S. Lincoln, 733–768. Thousand Oaks, CA: Sage.

Epp, Marlene. 2008. *Mennonite Women in Canada: A History*. Winnipeg: University of Manitoba Press.

Epp-Tiessen, Esther. 1982. *Altona: The Story of a Prairie Town*. Altona, MB: D.W. Friesen and Sons.

Epstein, Julia, and Kristina Straub, eds. 1991. *Body Guards: The Cultural Politics of Gender Ambiguity*. New York: Routledge.

Escott, Colin, and Martin Hawkins. 1980. *Sun Records, The Brief History of the Legendary Record Label.* New York: Quick Fox.

Fabricius, Knud, L. L. Hammerich, and Vilhelm Lorenzen, eds. 1945. *Holland-Danmark. Forbindelserne mellem de to lande gennem tiderne.* Copenhagen: Jespersen og Pios Forlag.

Faludi, Susan. 1999. *Stiffed: The Betrayal of the American Man.* New York: William Morrow.

Faris, James C. 1969. "Mumming in an Outport Fishing Settlement: A Description and Suggestions on the Cognitive Complex." In *Christmas Mumming in Newfoundland: Essays in Anthropology, Folklore, and History,* edited by Herbert Halpert and G. M. Story, 128–144. Toronto: University of Toronto Press.

Farrer, Claire R., ed. [1975] 1986. *Women and Folklore: Images and Genres.* Prospect Heights, IL: Waveland.

Farrer, Peter. 1996a. Female Attire: Male Experiences of Cross-dressing—Some Historical Fragments." In *Blending Genders: Social Aspects of Cross-dressing and Sex-changing,* edited by Richard Ekins and Dave King, 9–26. London: Routledge.

Farrer, Peter. 1996b. "120 Years of Male Cross-dressing and Sex-changing in English and American Literature." In *Blending Genders: Social Aspects of Cross-dressing and Sex-changing,* edited by Richard Ekins and Dave King, 123–132. London: Routledge.

Faust, M. 2010. "Filmmaker Neil Jordan Talks about His New Film, *Ondine.*" *Artvoice,* June 23. Accessed May 14, 2011. http://artvoice.com/issues/v9n25/film_feature.

Fausto-Sterling, Anne. 2000. *Sexing the Body: Gender Politics and the Construction of Sexuality.* New York: Basic Books.

Fecskó, Edina. 2008. "Psychoanalytic Interpretations of the Film Adaptations of 'Little Red Riding Hood.'" In *Words and Images on the Screen: Language, Literature, Moving Pictures,* edited by Ágnes Pethö, 300–313. Newcastle: Cambridge Scholars in Publishing.

Feintuch, Burt. 2003. "Introduction: Eight Words." In *Eight Words for the Study of Expressive Culture,* edited by Burt Feintuch, 1–6. Urbana: University of Illinois Press.

Feng, Menglong. [1611?] 1993. *Qingshi* [History of Love], Edited and annotated by Zhanzhan waishi. Shanghai: Shanghai guji chubanshe.

Ferrell, Ann K. 2012a. "Doing Masculinity: Gendered Challenges to Replacing Burley Tobacco in Central Kentucky." *Agriculture and Human Values* 29(2): 137–149. http://dx.doi.org/10.1007/s10460-011-9330-1.

Ferrell, Ann K. 2012b. "'It's Really Hard to Tell the True Story of Tobacco': Stigma, Tellability, and Reflexive Scholarship." *Journal of Folklore Research* 49(2): 127–152. http://dx.doi.org/10.2979/jfolkrese.49.2.127.

Firestone, Melvin M. 1969. "Mummers and Strangers in Northern Newfoundland." In *Christmas Mumming in Newfoundland: Essays in Anthropology, Folklore, and History,* edited by Herbert Halpert and G. M. Story, 62–75. Toronto: University of Toronto Press.

Firestone, Melvin M. 1978. "Christmas Mumming and Symbolic Interactionism." *Ethos (Berkeley, Calif.)* 6(2): 92–113. http://dx.doi.org/10.1525/eth.1978.6.2.02a00020.

Fiskesjö, Magnus. 2003. *The Thanksgiving Turkey Pardon, the Death of Teddy's Bear, and the Sovereign Exception of Guantánamo.* Chicago: Prickly Paradigm.

Fonseca, Clauda. 2005. "Patterns of Shared Parenthood among the Brazilian Poor." In *Cultures of Transnational Adoption,* edited by Toby Alice Volkman, 142–161. Durham, NC: Duke University Press. http://dx.doi.org/10.1215/9780822386926-006.

Fox, Jennifer. 1987. "The Creator Gods: Romantic Nationalism and the En-Genderment of Women in Folklore." *Journal of American Folklore* 100(398): 563–572. http://dx.doi.org/10.2307/540913.

Francis, E. K. 1955. *In Search of Utopia: The Mennonites in Manitoba.* Glencoe, IL: Free Press.

Frandsen, Karl-Erik. 2002. "Indledning." In *Amager*, edited by Karl-Erik Frandsen, Inger Kjær Jansen, and Lis Thavlov, 7–41. Copenhagen: Nyt Nordisk Forlag Arnold Busck.

Frank, Russell. 2004. "When the Going Gets Tough, the Tough Go Photoshopping: September 11 and the Newslore of Vengeance and Victimization." *New Media & Society* 6:633–658.

Frank, Russell. 2009. "The *Forward* as Folklore: Studying E-mailed Humor." In *Folklore and the Internet: Vernacular Expression in a Digital World*, edited by Trevor J. Blank. All USU Press Publications, paper 35. Accessed December 6, 2010. http://digital commons.usu.edu/usupress_pubs/35.

Frankenberg, Ruth. 1993. *White Women, Race Matters: The Social Construction of Whiteness*. Minneapolis: University of Minnesota Press.

Franklin, Sarah. 2006. "The Cyborg Embryo: Our Path to Transbiology." *Theory, Culture & Society* 23(7–8): 167–187. http://dx.doi.org/10.1177/0263276406069230.

Freud, Sigmund. [1920] 1950. *Beyond the Pleasure Principle*. [Jenseits des Lustprinzips]. Translated by James Strachey. New York: Liveright.

Freund, Hugo Allen. 1991. "Celebrating the American Thanksgiving: An Experience-Centered Approach to Meaning Formation in a New England Family." Ph.D. diss., University of Pennsylvania.

Friedan, Betty. 1963. *The Feminine Mystique*. New York: Norton.

Friend, Craig Thompson, ed. 2009. *Southern Masculinity: Perspectives on Manhood in the South Since Reconstruction*. Athens: University of Georgia Press.

Friesen, John. 2001. "Reinländer Mennonite Settlement on the West Reserve." In *Old Colony: Mennonites in Canada, 1875 to 2000*, edited by Delbert F. Plett, 3–19. Steinbach: Crossway.

Friesen, Victor Carl. 1988. *The Windmill Turning: Nursery Rhymes, Maxims, and Other Expressions of Western Canadian Mennonites*. Edmonton: University of Alberta Press.

Frivilig i Dansk, Røde Kors. n.d. "Center Kongelunden – Dansk Røde Kors." Accessed April 28, 2011. http://frivillig.drk.dk/sw39772.asp.

Frow, John. 2006. *Genre*. London: Routledge.

Fry, Caitlin. 2007. "Built for the Kilt: Gendered Constructions of What 'Real Men' Wear. Paper Delivered as Part of King Power." Paper presented at the Designing Masculinities Symposium, Royal Melbourne Institute, August 16–17. Accessed April 5, 2014. http://erwinkompanje.files.wordpress.com/2013/04/caitlin-fry-kilt.pdf.

Fry, Rosalie K. 1959. *Secret of the Ron Mor Skerry*. Boston: E. P. Dutton.

Fussell, Paul. 2000. *The Great War and Modern Memory*. Oxford: Oxford University Press.

Gan, Bao. [350?] 1979. *Sou shen ji, Edited and annotated by Wang Shaoying*. Beijing: Zhonghua Shuju.

Gan, Bao. 1996. *In Search of the Supernatural: The Written Record*. Translated by Kenneth J. DeWoskin and James Irving Crump. Stanford: Stanford University Press.

Gates, Henry Louis, Jr. 1985. "'Writing 'Race' and the Difference It Makes." *Critical Inquiry* 12(1): 1–20. http://dx.doi.org/10.1086/448318.

Gates, Laura Doyle. 1997. "Distaff and Pen: Producing the *Evangiles des quenouilles*." *Neophilologus* 81(1): 13–20. http://dx.doi.org/10.1023/A:1004248127559.

Gaunt, Kyra D. 2006. *The Games Black Girls Play: Learning the Ropes from Double-Dutch to Hip-Hop*. New York: New York University Press.

Geertz, Clifford. 1980. "Blurred Genres: The Refiguration of Social Thought." *American Scholar* 49(2): 165–180.

Genette, Gerard. 1997. *Paratexts: Thresholds of Interpretation*. Translated by Richard Macksey. Cambridge: Cambridge University Press. http://dx.doi.org/10.1017/CBO978 0511549373.

Gibson, John G. 1998. *Traditional Gaelic Bagpiping, 1745–1945.* Edinburgh: NMS; Montreal: McGill-Queen's University Press.

Giffney, Noreen, and Myra J. Hird, eds. 2008. *Queering the Non/Human.* Burlington, VT: Ashgate.

Ginsberg, Elaine K. 1996. "Introduction: The Politics of Passing." In *Passing and the Fictions of Identity,* edited by Elaine K. Ginsberg, 1–18. Durham, NC: Duke University Press. http://dx.doi.org/10.1215/9780822382027-001.

Ginsberg, Faye D., and Rayna Rapp. 1995. "Introduction: Conceiving the New World Order." In *Conceiving the New World Order: The Global Politics of Reproduction,* edited by Faye D. Ginsburg and Rayna Rapp, 1–18. Los Angeles: University of California Press.

Girard, René. 1965. *Deceit, Desire, and the Novel: Self and Other in Literary Structure.* Translated by Yvonne Freccero. Baltimore, MD: Johns Hopkins University Press.

Glassie, Henry. 1995. "Tradition." *Journal of American Folklore* 108(430): 395–412. http://dx.doi.org/10.2307/541653.

Goffman, Erving. 1959. *The Presentation of Self in Everyday Life.* New York: Anchor Books.

Goldman, Eric A. 2003. "Avalon and Liberty Heights: Toward a Better Understanding of the American Jewish Experience through Cinema." *American Jewish History* 91(1): 109–127. http://dx.doi.org/10.1353/ajh.2004.0028.

Goldstein, Diane. 2004. *Once upon a Virus.* Logan: Utah State University Press.

Goldstein, Diane. 2007. "Scientific Rationalism and Supernatural Experience Narratives." In *Haunting Experiences: Ghosts in Contemporary Folklore,* edited by Diane E. Goldstein, Sylvia Grider, and Jeannie Banks Thomas, 60–78. Logan: Utah State University Press.

Gramsci, Antonio. [1950] 1999. "Observations on Folklore." In *International Folkloristics: Classic Contributions by the Founders of Folklore,* edited by Alan Dundes, 131–136. Lanham, MD: Rowman and Littlefield.

Greenhill, Pauline. 1994. *Ethnicity in the Mainstream: Three Studies of English Canadian Culture in Ontario.* Montreal: McGill-Queen's University Press.

Greenhill, Pauline. 1995. "'Neither a Man Nor a Maid': Sexualities and Gendered Meanings in Cross-dressing Ballads." *Journal of American Folklore* 108(428): 156–177. http://dx.doi.org/10.2307/541377.

Greenhill, Pauline. 1997. "'Who's Gonna Kiss Your Ruby Red Lips': Sexual Scripts in Floating Verses." In *Ballads into Books: The Legacies of Francis James Child,* edited by Tom Cheesman and Sigrid Rieuverts, 225–235. Bern: Peter Lang.

Greenhill, Pauline. 2002. "Folk and Academic Racism: Concepts from Morris and Folklore." *Journal of American Folklore* 115(456): 226–246.

Greenhill, Pauline. 2008. "'Fitcher's [Queer] Bird': A Fairy Tale Heroine and Her Avatars." *Marvels & Tales* 22(1): 143–167.

Greenhill, Pauline. 2009. "Folklore about Women." In *Encyclopedia of Women's Folklore and Folklife,* edited by Liz Locke, Theresa A. Vaughan, and Pauline Greenhill, xxxv–xlvii. Westport, CT: Greenwood.

Greenhill, Pauline. 2010. *Make The Night Hideous: Four English-Canadian Charivaris.* Toronto: University of Toronto Press.

Greenhill, Pauline. 2013. "'I Wish You Were a Maid': Transgender Imagination in Newfoundland Ballads." In *Songs of People on the Move,* edited by Thomas A. McKean, 211–223. Trier: Wissenschaftlicher Verlag Trier.

Greenhill, Pauline. 2014. "'If I Was a Woman as I Am a Man': Transgender Imagination in Newfoundland Ballads." In *Changing Places: Feminist Essays in Empathy and Relocation,* edited by Valerie Burton and Jean Guthrie, 172–198. Toronto: Inanna.

Greenhill, Pauline, Kjerstin Baldwin, Michelle Blais, Angela Brooks, and Kristen Rosbak. 1993. "25 Good Reasons Why Beer Is Better than Women and Other Qualities of the Female: Gender and the Non-seriousness of Jokes." *Canadian Folklore Canadien* 15(2): 51–67.

Greenhill, Pauline, Anita Best, and Emilie Anderson-Grégoire. 2012. "Queering Gender: Transformations in 'Peg Bearskin,' 'La Poiluse,' and Related Tales." In *Transgressive Tales: Queering the Grimms*, edited by Kay Turner and Pauline Greenhill, 181–205. Detroit: Wayne State University Press.

Greenhill, Pauline, and Anne Brydon. 2010. "Mourning Mothers and Seeing Siblings: Feminism and Place in *The Juniper Tree*." In *Fairy Tale Films: Visions of Ambiguity*, edited by Pauline Greenhill and Sidney Eve Matrix, 116–136. Logan: Utah State University Press.

Greenhill, Pauline, and Sidney Eve Matrix, eds. 2010. *Fairy Tale Films: Visions of Ambiguity*. Logan: Utah State University Press.

Greenhill, Pauline, and Peter Narváez. 2002a. "Afterword: The *Journal of American Folklore* and Americanist versus Canadianist Traditions." *Journal of American Folklore* 115:283–292.

Greenhill, Pauline, and Peter Narváez. 2002b. "Introduction: Folklore in Canada." *Journal of American Folklore* 115(456): 116–128. http://dx.doi.org/10.1353/jaf.2002.0014.

Greenhill, Pauline, and Diane Tye, eds. 1997. *Undisciplined Women: Tradition and Culture in Canada*. Montreal: McGill-Queen's University Press.

Greenhill, Pauline, Diane Tye, and Norma Cantú. 2009. "Women's Folklore." In *Women's Folklore and Folklife*, edited by Liz Locke, Theresa Vaughan, and Pauline Greenhill, xxiv–xxv. Westport, CT: Greenwood.

Grimm, Jacob and Wilhelm. 2003. *The Complete Fairy Tales of the Brothers Grimm*, 3rd ed, edited and translated by Jack Zipes. New York: Bantam.

Gubar, Susan. 1997. *RaceChanges: White Skin, Black Face in American Culture*. New York: Oxford University Press.

Haase, Donald. 1999. "Yours, Mine, Ours? Perrault, the Brothers Grimm, and the Ownership of Fairy Tales." In *The Classic Fairy Tales*, edited by Maria Tatar, 353–364. New York: Norton.

Haase, Donald. 2003. "Framing the Brothers Grimm: Paratexts and Intercultural Transmission in Postwar English-Language Editions of the *Kinder- und Hausmarchen*." *Fabula* 44(1): 55–69. http://dx.doi.org/10.1515/fabl.2003.010.

Haase, Donald. 2010. "Decolonizing Fairy Tales." *Marvels & Tales* 24(1): 17–38.

Hague Conference on Private International Law. 2011. "The *Hague Convention of 29 May 1993 on Protection of Children and Co-operation in Respect of Intercountry Adoption*." Accessed May 19, 2011. http://www.hcch.net/index_en.php?act=text.display&tid=45.

Halberstam, Judith. 1998. *Female Masculinity*. Durham: Duke University Press.

Halberstam, Judith. 2008. "Animating Revolt/Revolting Animation: Penguin Love, Doll Sex and the Spectacle of the Queer Nonhuman." In *Queering the Non/Human*, edited by Noreen Giffney and Myra J. Hird, 265–281. Burlington, VT: Ashgate.

Halpert, Herbert, and G. M. Story, eds. 1969. *Christmas Mumming in Newfoundland: Essays in Anthropology, Folklore, and History*. Toronto: University of Toronto Press.

Hanawalt, Barbara. 2003. "Widows." In *The Cambridge Companion to Medieval Women's Writing*, edited by Carolyn Dinshaw and David Wallace, 58–69. New York: Cambridge University Press. http://dx.doi.org/10.1017/CCOL052179188X.005.

Handelman, Don. 1984. "Inside-Out, Outside-In: Concealment and Revelation in Newfoundland Christmas Mumming." In *Text, Play, and Story: The Construction and Reconstruction of Self and Society*, edited by Edward M. Bruner, 247–277. Washington, DC: American Ethnological Society.

Handler, Richard, and Jocelyn Linnekin. 1984. "Tradition, Genuine or Spurious." *Journal of American Folklore* 97(385): 273–290. http://dx.doi.org/10.2307/540610.

Hannon, Patricia. 1993. "A Politics of Disguise: Marie-Catherine D'Aulnoy's 'Belle-Etoile' and the Narrative Structure of Ambivalence." In *Anxious Power: Reading, Writing, and Ambivalence in Narrative by Women*, edited by Carol J. Singley and Susan Elizabeth Sweeney, 73–89. Albany: State University of New York Press.

Harries, Elizabeth Wanning. 2001. *Twice upon a Time: Women Writers and the History of the Fairy Tale*. Princeton: Princeton University Press.

Harris, Dan. 2010. "Recession Prompts Gender Role Reversal: Failing Economy Challenges Convention: Male Nurses, Stay-at-Home Dads." ABC World News (online). 4 May. Accessed January 7, 2011. http://abcnews.go.com/Business/story?id=7497859&page=1.

Harris, Jason Marc. 2009. "Perilous Shores: The Unfathomable Supernaturalism of Water in 19th-Century Scottish Folklore." *Mythlore* 28(1–2): 5–25.

Harris, Trudier. 1995. "Genre." *Journal of American Folklore* 108 430): 509–527. http://dx.doi.org/10.2307/541658.

Harris-Lopez, Trudier. 2003. "Genre." In *Eight Words for the Study of Expressive Culture*, edited by Burt Feintuch, 99–120. Urbana: University of Illinois Press.

Hay, Jennifer. 2000. "Functions of Humor in the Conversations of Men and Women." *Journal of Pragmatics* 32(6): 709–742. http://dx.doi.org/10.1016/S0378-2166(99)00069-7.

Haydock, Nikolas A. 2002. "Arthurian Melodrama, Chaucerian Spectacle, and the Waywardness of Cinematic Pastiche in *First Knight* and *A Knight's Tale*." In *Film and Fiction Reviewing the Middle Ages*, edited by Tom Shippey and Martin Arnold, 5–38. Cambridge: D. S. Brewer.

Heiniger-Casteret, Patricia. 2004. "Jean-François Bladé, un folklorista-contaire." In *Contes e cants: Les recueils de littérature orale en pays d'oc, XIXe et XXe siècles*, edited by Claire Torreilles and Marie-Jeanne Verny, 59–78. Montpellier: Centre d'Estudis Occitans.

Heiniger-Casteret, Patricia. 2009. "Une collecte chez Jean-François Bladé." In *La voix occitane*, edited by Guy Latry, 599–614. Bordeaux: Presses Universitaires de Bordeaux.

Heritage Camps for Adoptive Families. 2011. "Celebrating Adoption." Accessed July 4, 2011. http://www.heritagecamps.org/.

Herzog, Dagmar. 2009. "Syncopated Sex: Transforming European Sexual Cultures." *American Historical Review* 114(5): 1287–1308. http://dx.doi.org/10.1086/ahr.114.5.1287.

Hird, Myra. 2004. "Chimerism, Mosaicism and the Cultural Construction of Kinship." *Sexualities* 7(2): 217–232. http://dx.doi.org/10.1177/1363460704042165.

Hird, Myra. 2006. "Animal Transex." *Australian Feminist Studies* 21(49): 35–50. http://dx.doi.org/10.1080/08164640500470636.

Hjorth, Birte. 1986. *Fastelavn i Hollænderbyen*. Dragør: Foreningen "Vennekredsen.

Hjorth, Birte. 1996. "Den tidlige Amagerdragt." In *Amagerdragterne—Deres Historie Og Brug*, edited by Birte Hjorth, Dirch Jansen, and Lisbeth Møller, 11–51. Dragør: Dragør Kommune.

Hodne, Ørnulf. 1984. *The Types of the Norwegian Folktale*. Oslo: Universitetsforlaget.

Holbek, Bengt. 1987. *Interpretation of Fairy Tales*. Helsinki: Academia Scientiarum Fennica.

Hollis, Susan Tower, Linda Pershing, and M. Jane Young, eds. 1993. *Feminist Theory and the Study of Folklore*. Chicago: University of Illinois Press.

Hong, Mai. [1161–1172] 1985. *Yijian zhi* [Tales from Yijian]. Beijing: Zhonghua shuju.

Hooker, Jessica. 1990. "The Hen Who Sang: Swordbearing Women in Eastern European Fairytales." *Folklore* 101(2): 178–184. http://dx.doi.org/10.1080/0015587X.1990.9715792.

hooks, bell. 1990. "Marginality as Site of Resistance." In *Out There: Marginalization and Contemporary Cultures*, edited by Russell Ferguson, Martha Gever, Trinh T. Minh-ha, and Cornel West. 341–344. Cambridge: MIT Press.

hooks, bell. [1984] 2000. *Feminist Theory: From Margin to Center.* 2nd ed. London: Pluto.

Horstman, Dorothy. 1986. *Sing Your Heart Out, Country Boy.* Nashville: Country Music Foundation.

Hotchkiss, Valerie R. 1996. *Clothes Make the Man: Female Cross Dressing in Medieval Europe.* New York: Garland.

Housted, Erik. 2002. "Sundbyerne—Porten Til Amager." In *Amager,* edited by Karl-Erik Frandsen, Erik Housted, Inger Kjær Jansen, and Lis Thavlov, 43–148. Copenhagen: Nyt Nordisk Forlag Arnold Busck.

Howells, Robin. 1997. "Pleasure Principles: Tales, Infantile Naming, and Voltaire." *Modern Language Review* 92(2): 295–307. http://dx.doi.org/10.2307/3734803.

Hu, Jingdao, Yaoting Chen, Wengui Duan, and Wanqing Lin, eds. 1992. *Zangwai daoshu* [Taoist Collections outside the Canon]. Chengdu: Bashu shushe.

Hufford, Mary T. 1992. *Chaseworld: Foxhunting and Storytelling in New Jersey's Pine Barrens.* Philadelphia: University of Pennsylvania Press.

Hughes, Kathryn. 2006. *The Short Life and Long Times of Mrs. Beeton.* New York: Knopf.

Huizinga, Johan. 1950. *Homo Ludens: A Study of the Play-Element in Culture.* Boston: Beacon.

Huntington, Rania. 2003. *Alien Kind: Foxes and Late Imperial Chinese Narrative.* Cambridge, MA: Harvard University Asia Center.

Hutcheon, Linda. 2002. *The Politics of Postmodernism.* 2nd ed. London: Routledge.

Hymes, Dell. 1975a. "Breakthrough into Performance." In *Folklore: Performance and Communication,* edited by Dan Ben-Amos and Kenneth S. Goldstein, 11–74. The Hague: Mouton. http://dx.doi.org/10.1515/9783110880229.11.

Hymes, Dell. 1975b. "Folklore's Nature and the Sun's Myth." *Journal of American Folklore* 88(350): 345–369. http://dx.doi.org/10.2307/538651.

Information. 2011. "Pind: Vi er i en dybfølt kulturkamp." Accessed March 30, 2011. http://www.information.dk/telegram/261765.

Iversen, Charlotte. n.d. "Copenhagen Airport: The Night the Terminal Took Off Across the Runways." *1001 Stories of Denmark.* Accessed April 28, 2011. http://www.kulturarv.dk/1001fortaellinger/en_GB/copenhagen-airport/stories/newest/1/the-night-the-terminal-took-off-across-the-runways.

Jansen, Inger Kjær. 2002. "Tårnby Kommune." In *Amager,* edited by Karl-Erik Frandsen, Erik Housted, Inger Kjær Jansen, and Lis Thavlov, 149–236. Copenhagen: Nyt Nordisk Forlag Arnold Busck.

Jansen, Inger, and Dirch Jansen. 2010. "Fire raske tøser [Four spry gals]." *Museum Amager* 3 (February): 16–18.

Järv, Risto. 2005. "The Gender of the Heroes: Storytellers and Collectors of Estonian Fairy Tales." *Folklore (Tartu)* 29:45–60.

Jeay, Madeleine. 1982. *Savoir faire: Une analyse des croyances des "Evangiles des quenouilles" (XVe siècle).* Montreal: Editions CERES.

Jeay, Madeleine. 1985. *Les evangiles des quenouilles: Critical Edition Translated into Modern French.* Paris: J. Vrin.

Jeay, Madeleine. 1993. "Review: Paupert (Anne) Les fileuses et le clerc. Une etude des *Evangiles des quenouilles.*" *Revue belge de philologie et d'histoire. Belgisch Tijdschrift voor Philologie en Geschiedenis* 71(4): 1105–1107.

Jeay, Madeleine, and Kathleen Garay. 2006. *The Distaff Gospels: A First Modern English Edition of Les evangiles des quenouilles.* Peterborough, ON: Broadview Editions.

Johnson, Kay. 2005. "Chaobao: The Plight of Chinese Adoptive Parents in the Era of the One-Child Policy." In *Cultures of Transnational Adoption,* edited by Toby Alice Volkman, 117–141. Durham, NC: Duke University Press. http://dx.doi.org/10.1215/9780822386926-005.

Jones, Christine. 2003. "Phèdre Meets the Transvestite Heroine: Fantastic Variations on Classical Themes." *Papers on French Seventeenth Century Literature* 30(59): 379–395.

Jones, Maggie. 2007. "Looking for Their Children's Birth Mothers." *New York Times Magazine,* October 28, 46(L).

Jones, Michael Owen. 1984. "Introduction to the Special Section, Works of Art, Art as Work, and the Arts of Working—Implications for Improving Organizational Life." *Western Folklore* 43(3): 172–178. http://dx.doi.org/10.2307/1499898.

Jones, Steven Swann. 2002. *The Fairy Tale: The Magic Mirror of Imagination.* New York: Routledge.

Jordan, Rosan, and Susan Kalčik, eds. 1985. *Women's Folklore, Women's Culture.* Philadelphia: University of Pennsylvania Press.

Kalčik, Susan. 1975. "' . . . Like Ann's Gynecologist or the Time I Was Almost Raped': Personal Narratives in Women's Rap Groups." In *Women and Folklore: Images and Genres,* edited by Claire R. Farrer, 3–11. Austin: University of Texas Press.

Kao, Karl S.Y., ed. 1985. *Chinese Tales of the Supernatural and the Fantastic: Selections from the Third to the Tenth Century.* Bloomington: Indiana University Press.

Kaplan, Amy. 1998. "Manifest Domesticity." *American Literature* 70(3): 581–606. http://dx.doi.org/10.2307/2902710.

Kaplan, Steven L., ed. 1984. *Understanding Popular Culture: Europe from the Middle Ages to the Nineteenth Century.* New York: Mouton. http://dx.doi.org/10.1515/9783110854305.

Karras, Ruth Mazo. 2005. *Sexuality in Medieval Europe: Doing unto Others.* New York: Routledge.

Kim, Eleana J. 2010. *Adopted Territory: Transnational Korean Adoptees and the Politics of Belonging.* Durham, NC: Duke University Press. http://dx.doi.org/10.1215/9780822392668.

Kimmel, Michael. 2000. *The Gendered Society.* New York: Oxford University Press.

Kimmel, Michael. [1997] 2006. *Manhood in America: A Cultural History.* New York: Free Press.

Kimmel, Michael S., and Michael A. Messner, eds. [1988] 2012. *Men's Lives.* 9th ed. Boston: Allyn and Bacon.

Kingsolver, Barbara. 2007. *Animal, Vegetable, Miracle: A Year of Food Life.* New York: Harper Collins.

Kirshenblatt-Gimblett, Barbara. 1975. "A Parable in Context: A Social Interactional Analysis of Storytelling Performance." In *Folklore, Performance, and Communication,* edited by Dan Ben-Amos and Kenneth Goldstein, 105–130. The Hague: Mouton. http://dx.doi.org/10.1515/9783110880229.105.

Klassen, Doreen. 1989. *Singing Mennonite: Low German Songs among the Mennonites.* Winnipeg: University of Manitoba Press.

Klausen, Jytte. 2005. *The Islamic Challenge: Politics and Religion in Western Europe.* Oxford: Oxford University Press.

Klausen, Jytte. 2009. *The Cartoons That Shook the World.* New Haven: Yale University Press.

Københavns Lufthavne. 2003. "Copenhagen Airports A/S Sells Preservation-Worthy Farmstead to the Amager Museum." December 2. Copenhagen Airports press release.

Kodish, Deborah. 1987. "Absent Gender, Silent Encounter." *Journal of American Folklore* 100(398): 573–578. http://dx.doi.org/10.2307/540914.

Kotthoff, Helga. 2006. "Gender and Humor: The State of the Art." *Journal of Pragmatics* 38(1): 4–25. http://dx.doi.org/10.1016/j.pragma.2005.06.003.

Kousaleos, Nicole. 1999. "Feminist Theory and Folklore." *Folklore Forum* 30(1–2):19–34.

Krueger, Roberta L. 1988. "Review: Madeleine Jeay, *Les évangiles des Quenouilles.*" *Speculum* 63(4): 943–945. http://dx.doi.org/10.2307/2853567.

Kurdovanidze, Teimuraz. 2000. *The Index of Georgian Folktale Plot Types.* Tbilisi: Merani.

Lafforgue, Pierre, ed. 1995. *Les contes du vieux Cazaux.* Eglise-Neuve d'Isaac: Fédérop.

Lafont, Robert, and Christian Anatole. 1970. *Nouvelle histoire de la littérature occitane.* Paris: Presses Universitaires de France.

Lanclos, Donna M. 1996. "A Case Study in Folktale Analysis: AT 514, 'The Shift of Sex,' in Hispanic Societies." *Pacific Coast Philology* 31(1): 68–87. http://dx.doi.org /10.2307/1316770.

Larrieu-Duler, Mary. 1981. "La vie de société depuis la Révolution." In *Deux siècles d'histoire de Lectoure, 1780–1980*, 97–111. Lectoure: Syndicat d'initiative.

Larsen, Elizabeth. 2007. "Did I Steal My Daughter? The Tribulations of Global Adoption." *Mother Jones* 32(6): 52–59.

Laurent, Donatien. 1989. *Aux sources du Barzaz-Breiz: La mémoire d'un peuple.* Douarnenez: ArMen.

Lavergne, Adrien. 1904. *Jean-François Bladé: Notice biographique.* Auch: Cocharaux.

Lawless, Elaine. 2001. *Women Escaping Violence: Empowerment through Narrative.* Columbia: University of Missouri Press.

Leach, Edmund. 2000. "Animal Categories and Verbal Abuse." In *The Essential Edmund Leach*, edited by Stephen Hugh-Jones and James Laidlaw, 1:322–343. New Haven: Yale University Press.

Leach, Maria, and Jerome Fried, eds. [1949] 1972. *Funk and Wagnalls Standard Dictionary of Folklore, Mythology, and Legend.* New York: Harper San Francisco.

Leavy, Barbara Fass. 1994. *In Search of the Swan Maiden: A Narrative on Folklore and Gender.* New York: New York University Press.

Legros, Elisée. 1962. "Un examen de la classification internationale des contes dans sa second revision." *Dialectes belgo-romans* 19(2): 77–115.

Lehning, James. 1995. *Peasant and French: Cultural Contact in Rural France during the Nineteenth Century.* Cambridge: Cambridge University Press. http://dx.doi.org /10.1017/CBO9780511528897.

Leinaweaver, Jessica B. 2007. "On Moving Children: The Social Implications of Andean Child Circulation." *American Ethnologist* 34(1): 163–180. http://dx.doi.org/10 .1525/ae.2007.34.1.163.

Lemire, Elise. 2002. *"Miscegenation": Making Race in America.* Philadelphia: University of Pennsylvania Press.

Levinsen, Jakob. 2010. "En duft af Amager." *Jyllands-Posten.* Accessed May 10, 2011. http://blogs.jp.dk/levinsenlive/2010/05/12/en-duft-af-amager/.

Li, Jianguo. 1984. *Tangqian zhiguai xiaoshuo shi.* [History of *Zhiguai* before the Tang Dynasty] Tianjin: Nankai University Press.

Li, Jianguo. 1993. *Tangwudai zhiguai chuanqi xulu.* [History of *Zhiguai* and *Chuanqi* in the Tang and Five Dynasties] Tianjin: Nankai University Press.

Li, Jianguo. 1997. *Songdai zhiguai chuanqi xulu.* [History of *Zhiguai* and *Chuanqi* in the Song Dynasty] Tianjin: Nankai University Press.

Lindahl, Carl, John McNamara, and John Lindow. 2002. Preface to *Medieval Folklore: A Guide to Myths, Legends, Tales, Beliefs and Customs*, edited by Carl Lindahl, John McNamara, and John Lindow, xix–xxii. New York: Oxford University Press.

Lindquist, Danille Christensen. 2006. "'Locating' the Nation: Football Game Day and American Dreams in Central Ohio." *Journal of American Folklore* 119(474): 444–488. http://dx.doi.org/10.1353/jaf.2006.0046.

Liu, Yiqing. 1988. *Youming lu* [Tales of Darkness and Light], edited and Annotated by Zheng Wanqing. Beijing: Wenhua yishu chubanshe.

Lloyd, Timothy C., and Patrick B. Mullen. 1990. *Lake Erie Fisherman: Work, Identity and Tradition.* Urbana: University of Illinois Press.

Lochner, Jim. 2010. "The Wonderful World of the Brothers Grimm: Supplemental Liner Notes." *Film Score Monthly* 13(4). http://www.filmscoremonthly.com/notes /fsmcd1304_notes.pdf.

Locke, Liz, Theresa A. Vaughan, and Pauline Greenhill, eds. 2009. *Encyclopedia of Women's Folklore and Folklife.* Westport, CT: Greenwood.

Loewen, Royden. 1983. "Blumenort: A Changing Community, 1874–1982." Master's thesis, University of Manitoba.

Loewen, Royden. 1999. *Family, Church and Market: A Mennonite Community in the Old and New Worlds, 1850–1930.* Urbana: University of Illinois Press.

Loewen, Royden. 2006. *Diaspora in the Countryside: Two Mennonite Communities and Mid-Twentieth-Century Rural Disjuncture.* Toronto: University of Toronto Press.

Loomba, Ania. 1998. *Colonialism/Postcolonialism.* New York: Routledge.

Lott, Eric. 1993. *Love and Theft: Blackface Minstrelsy and the American Working Class.* New York: Oxford University Press.

Lovelace, Martin J. 1980. "Christmas Mumming in England: The House-Visit." In *Folklore Studies in Honour of Herbert Halpert: A Festschrift,* edited by Kenneth S. Goldstein and Neil V. Rosenberg, 271–281. St. John's: Memorial University of Newfoundland.

Loyson, Kathleen. 2004. *Conversation and Storytelling in Fifteenth- and Sixteenth-Century French Nouvelles.* New York: Peter Lang.

Lu, Xun. 1963a. *Lu Xun quanji* [The Complete Works of Lu Xun]. Vol. 4. Beijing: Renmin wenxue chubanshe.

Lu, Xun. 1963b. *Lu Xun quanji* [The Complete Works of Lu Xun]. Vol. 8. Beijing: Renmin wenxue chubanshe.

Lumby, Elisabeth. 2010. "Ferie-Køer På Vestamager." *Amager Bladet.* Accessed May 18, 2011. http://dinby.dk/dragoer/ferie-koeer-paa-vestamager.

Lunbeck, Elizabeth. 1994. *The Psychiatric Persuasion: Knowledge, Gender and Power in Modern America.* Princeton: Princeton University Press.

Lundell, Torborg. 1983. "Folktale Heroines and the Type and Motif Indexes." *Folklore* 94(2): 240–246. http://dx.doi.org/10.1080/0015587X.1983.9716283.

MacAulay, John M. 1998. *Seal-Folk and Ocean Paddlers: Sliochd nan Ròn.* Cambridge: White Horse.

MacCannell, Dean. 1984. "Reconstructed Ethnicity: Tourism and Cultural Identity in Third World Communities." *Annals of Tourism Research* 11(3): 375–391. http:// dx.doi.org/10.1016/0160-7383(84)90028-8.

Macías-González, Víctor Manuel. 2007. "Masculine Friendships, Sentiment, and Homoerotics in Nineteenth-Century Mexico: The Correspondence of José María Calderón y Tapia, 1820s–1850s." *Journal of the History of Sexuality* 16(3): 416–435. http:// dx.doi.org/10.1353/sex.2007.0068.

Magliocco, Sabina. 2004. *Witching Culture: Folklore and Neo-paganism in America.* Philadelphia: University of Pennsylvania Press.

Malone, Bill. 1998. "Honky-Tonk Music." In *The Encyclopedia of Country Music,* edited by Paul Kingsbury, 245–246. New York: Oxford University Press.

Marcus, Greil. 1982. *Mystery Train: Images of America in Rock 'n' Roll Music.* New York: E. P. Dutton.

Mark, Vera. 1991. "Cultural Pastiches: Intertextualities in the Moncrabeau Liars' Festival Narratives." *Cultural Anthropology* 6(2): 193–211. http://dx.doi.org/10.1525/can .1991.6.2.02a00050.

Marshall, Alison. 2011. *The Way of the Bachelor: Early Chinese Settlement in Manitoba.* Vancouver: University of British Columbia Press.

McGuirk, Paul. 2010. "*Ondine* (Neil Jordan, 2009)." *Estudios Irlandeses* 5:243–246.

McKay, Ian. 1992. "Tartanism Triumphant: The Construction of Scottishness in Nova Scotia, 1933–1954." *Acadiensis* 21(2): 5–47.

McKelway, Doug. 2010. "'Mancession' Threatens American Dream." *Fox News*. December 9. Accessed January 7, 2011. http://www.foxnews.com/politics/2010/12/09 /mancession-threatens-american-dream/.

Mclaughlin, Simon. 2010. "True Scots Kilt Wearers Up in Arms." Accessed December 6, 2010. http://news.carrentals.co.uk/true-scots-kilt-wearers-up-in-arms-34224958 .html.

Messner, Michael A. 1995. *Power at Play: Sports and the Problem of Masculinity*. Boston: Beacon.

Mikkelson, Barbara, and David P. Mikkelson. 2004. "Crown Jewels." Accessed April 4, 2014. http://www.snopes.com/photos/risque/queen.asp.

Mills, Margaret. 1985. "Sex Role Reversals, Sex Changes, and Transvestite Disguise in the Oral Tradition of a Conservative Muslim Community in Afghanistan." In *Women's Folklore, Women's Culture*, edited by Rosan A. Jordan and Susan J. Kalcik, 187–213. Philadelphia: University of Pennsylvania Press.

Ministeriet for Flygtninge, Indvandrere og Integration. 2009. *Tal og fakta: befolkningsstatistik om indvandrere og efterkommere*.

Ministeriet for Flygtninge, Indvandrere og Integration. 2010. "Danmarks flerårige program for perioden 2007–2013." *Ny i Danmark*. Accessed July 31, 2011. http://www .nyidanmark.dk/NR/rdonlyres/2B8903E9–18E7–4131-B7EF-CA5095CD65F2/0 /Danmarks_fleraarige_20072013.pdf. Site discontinued.

Miss Cellania. 2010. Accessed November 30, 2011. http://www.misscellania.com /miss-cellania/2006/6/18/under-the-kilt.html. Site discontinued.

Mitchell, Jane Tucker. 1978. *A Thematic Analysis of Mme. D'Aulnoy's Contes de Fees*. University, MI: Romance Monographs.

Mohanty, Chandra Talpade. 2003. *Feminism without Borders: Decolonizing Theory, Practicing Solidarity*. Durham, NC: Duke University Press. http://dx.doi.org/10.1215 /9780822384649.

Møller, Lisbeth. 1996. "Amagerdragter i 1800-tallet—Deres sammensætning og brug." In *Amagerdragterne—Deres Historie Og Brug*, edited by Birte Hjorth, Dirch Jansen, and Lisbeth Møller, 52–145. Dragør: Dragør Kommune.

Morris, Matthew W. 1988. "Review: "Madeleine Jeay, *Savoir faire: Une analyse des croyances des 'Evangiles des Quenouilles' (XVe siècle)*." *Speculum* 63(1): 178–181. http://dx.doi .org/10.2307/2854360.

Morrison, Craig. 1996. *Go Cat Go! Rockabilly Music and Its Makers*. Urbana: University of Illinois Press.

"Mr. Spontaneity." 2008. Posted by Weasel, August 13. Accessed July 30, 2010. http:// whywomenhatemen.blogspot.ca/2008/08/mr-spontaneity.html.

Mullen, Patrick B. 1984. "Hillbilly Hipsters of the 1950s: The Romance of Rockabilly." *Southern Quarterly* 22(3): 79–92.

Mullen, Patrick B. 2000. "Belief and the American Folk." *Journal of American Folklore* 113(448): 119–143. http://dx.doi.org/10.2307/541285.

Mullen, Patrick B. 2008. *The Man Who Adores the Negro: Race and American Folklore*. Urbana: University of Illinois Press.

Museum Amager. 2010a. "Fastelavn på Amagermuseet." *Museum Amager: Medlemsblad for museumsforeningerne* [Museum Amager: Newsletter for museum members], February 3, 13–14.

Museum Amager. 2010b. *Museum Amager: Medlemsblad for museumsforeningerne* [Museum Amager: Newsletter for museum members]. February 3.

Museum Amager. 2012a. "Amagermuseet." Accessed July 4, 2012. http://www.museum amager.dk/index.php?option=com_content&view=article&id=3&Itemid=3.

Museum Amager. 2012b. "Den hollandske indvandring." Accessed July 4, 2012. http://www.museumamager.dk/index.php?option=com_content&view=article&id=36&Itemid=35.

Narváez, Peter, and Martin Laba. 1988. "Introduction: The Folklore-Popular Culture Continuum." In *Media Sense: The Folklore-Popular Culture Continuum*, edited by Peter Narváez and Martin Laba, 1–8. Bowling Green, OH: Bowling Green State University Popular Press.

National Association of Black Social Workers. 2011. *Preserving Families of African Ancestry:Background and Significance*. Accessed June 29, 2011. http://c.ymcdn.com /sites/nabsw.org/resource/collection/0d2d2404-77eb-49b5-962e-7e6fadbf3d0d /Preserving_Families_of_African_Ancestry.pdf?hhSearchTerms=%22Preserving+and+ Families+and+African+and+Ancestry%22.

New Advent. 2009. "Liturgical Week." In *The Catholic Encyclopedia*. Accessed April 4, 2014. http://www.newadvent.org/cathen/15575b.htm.

Newton, Esther. 1972. *Mother Camp: Female Impersonators in America*. Englewood Cliffs, NJ: Prentice-Hall.

Newton, Judith, and Judith Stacey. 1995. "Ms. Representations: Reflections on Studying Academic Men." In *Women Writing Culture*, edited by Ruth Behar and Deborah A. Gordon, 287–305. Berkeley: University of California Press.

Niu Zengru. 1985. *Xuanguai lu* [Tales of the Mysterious and Strange], edited and annotated by Jiang Yun and Song Ping. Shanghai: Shanghai guji chubanshe.

Nodelman, Perry. 1988. "Children's Literature as Women's Writing." *Children's Literature Association Quarterly* 13(1): 31–34. http://dx.doi.org/10.1353/chq.0.0264.

Noonan, Emily J. 2007. "Adoption and the Guatemalan Journey to American Parenthood." *Childhood* 14(3): 301–319. http://dx.doi.org/10.1177/0907568207079211.

Norton, Rictor. 2002. "A Critique of Social Constructionism and Postmodern Queer Theory, Sexual Orientation." Updated June 19, 2008. Accessed April 17, 2014. http://www.rictornorton.co.uk/social10.htm.

Noyes, Dorothy. 2003. "Group." In *Eight Words for the Study of Expressive Culture*, edited by Burt Feintuch, 7–41. Urbana: University of Illinois Press.

Nye, Robert. 1993. *Masculinity and Male Codes of Honor in Modern France*. Oxford: Oxford University Press.

Ó Gialláin, Diarmuid. 2000. *Locating Irish Folklore: Tradition, Modernity, Identity*. Cork: Cork University Press.

Opie, Iona, and Moira Tatem. 1989. "Names, Divination with." In *A Dictionary of Superstitions*, edited by Iona Opie and Moira Tatem, 276–277. New York: Barnes and Noble Books.

Oring, Elliott. 2003. *Engaging Humor*. Urbana: University of Illinois Press.

Orme, Nicholas. 2001. *Medieval Children*. New Haven: Yale University Press.

Ortner, Sherry B. 1974. "Is Female to Male as Nature is to Culture?" In *Woman, Culture, and Society*, edited by Michelle Z. Rosaldo and Louise Lamphere, 66–78. Stanford: Stanford University Press.

Oxford Dictionary Online. Accessed November 30, 2010. http://www.oxforddictionaries.com.

Papachristophorou, Mariléna. 2002. *Sommeils et veilles dans le conte merveilleux grec*. Helsinki: Academia Scientiarum Fennica.

Parsons, Elsie Clews. 1923. *Folk-lore from the Cape Verde Islands, Part I*. Cambridge, MA: American Folk-lore Society.

Paton, Lucy Allen. 1907. "The Story of Grisandole: A Study in the Legend of Merlin." *PMLA* 22(2): 234–276. http://dx.doi.org/10.2307/456828.

Paupert, Anne. 1990. *Les fileuses et le clerc: Une étude des "Evangiles des quenouilles"*. Paris: Champion-Slatkine.

Peck, Russel A. 2007. "Folklore and Powerful Women in Gower's 'Tale of Florent.'" In *The English "Loathly Lady" Tales: Boundaries, Traditions, Motifs*, edited by S. Elizabeth Passmore and Susan Carter, 100–145. Kalamazoo, MI: Medieval Institute Publications.

Perfetti, Lisa. 2003. *Women and Laughter in Medieval Comic Literature*. Ann Arbor: University of Michigan Press.

Perry, Mark J. 2010. "The Great Mancession of 2008–2009." Testimony to the House Ways and Means Committee. 17 June. Accessed January 7, 2011. http://www.aei.org/article/society-and-culture/race-and-gender/the-great-mancession-of-2008-2009/.

Pertman, Adam. 2000. *Adoption Nation: How the Adoption Revolution Is Transforming America*. New York: Basic Books.

Petersen, Anker Eli. 2006. "Sælkvinden." Accessed November 4, 2010. http://heimskringla.no/wiki/S%C3%A6lkvinden.

Petkau, Irene Friesen, and Peter A. Petkau. 1981. *Blumenfeld: Where Land and People Meet*. Winkler, MB: Blumenfeld Historical Committee.

Pettitt, Tom. 1995. "Customary Drama: Social and Spatial Patterning in Traditional Encounters." *Folk Music Journal* 7(1): 27–42.

Philip, Neil. 2003. *Horse Hooves and Chicken Feet: Mexican Folktales*. New York: Clarion Books.

Phillips, Susan E. 2007. *Transforming Talk: The Problem with Gossip in Late Medieval England*. University Park: Pennsylvania State University Press.

Pic, François. 1985. "Essai de bibliographie de l'oeuvre imprimée de J.-F. Bladé." In *Jean-François Bladé, 1827–1900: Actes du Colloque de Lectoure, 20 et 21 Octobre 1984*, edited by Jean Arrouye, 147–190. Béziers: Centre International de Documentation Occitane.

Pleck, Elizabeth H. 1999. "The Making of the Domestic Occasion: The History of Thanksgiving in the United States." *Journal of Social History* 32(4): 773–789. http://dx.doi.org/10.1353/jsh/32.4.773.

Pleck, Elizabeth H. 2000. *Celebrating the Family: Ethnicity, Consumer Culture, and Family Rituals*. Cambridge, MA: Harvard University Press.

Politiken. 2011a. "Amagerbanken skifter navn." October 24. Accessed June 5, 2012. http://politiken.dk/erhverv/ECE1430102/amagerbanken-skifter-navn/.

Politiken. 2011b. "Nu er Amagerbanken officielt konkurs." February 8. Accessed March 23, 2011. http://politiken.dk/erhverv/ECE1189617/nu-er-amagerbanken-officielt-konkurs/.

Pooley, William. 2012. "Can The 'Peasant' Speak? Witchcraft and Silence in Guillaume Cazaux's 'The Mass of Saint Sécaire.'" *Western Folklore* 71(2): 93–118.

Pope, Steve W. 1993. "God, Games, and National Glory: Thanksgiving and the Ritual of Sport in American Culture, 1876–1926." *International Journal of the History of Sport* 10(2): 242–249. http://dx.doi.org/10.1080/09523369308713827.

Pope, Steve W. 1997. *Patriotic Games: Sporting Traditions in the American Imagination, 1876–1926*. Cambridge: Oxford University Press.

Postic, Fañch. 1997. "Le beau ou le vrai, ou la difficile naissance en Bretagne et en France d'une science nouvelle: La littérature orale (1866–1868)." *Estudos de literatura oral* 3:97–123.

Power, Nicole Gerarda. 2005. *What Do They Call a Fisherman? Men, Gender, and Restructuring in the Newfoundland Fishery*. St. John's: Institute of Social and Economic Research.

Pratt, Mary Louise. 1992. *Imperial Eyes: Travel Writing and Transculturation*. New York: Routledge.

Preston, Cathy Lynn. 2004. "Disrupting the Boundaries of Genre and Gender: Postmodernism and the Fairy Tale." In *Fairy Tales and Feminism: New Approaches*, edited by Donald Haase, 197–212. Detroit: Wayne State University Press.

Pu, Songling. [1680] 2006. *Strange Tales from a Chinese Studio*, edited and translated by John Minford. London: Penguin.

Qu, You. [1378?] 1981. *Jiandeng xinhua* [New Tales under the Lamplight], edited and annotated by Zhou Lengjia. Shanghai: Shanghai guji chubanshe.

Quimby, Karin. 1995. "*She Must Be Seeing Things Differently*: The Limits of Butch/Femme." In *Lesbian Erotics*, edited by Karla Jay, 183–195. New York: New York University Press.

R98. 2010. "R98—Danish: Koncessionens ophør." *R98*. Accessed July 28, 2011. http://www.r98.dk/dk/hjemmeside/om_r98/koncessionens_ophoer/. Site discontinued.

Rachamimov, Alon. 2006. "The Disruptive Comforts of Drag: (Trans)Gender Performances among Prisoners of War in Russia, 1914–1920." *American Historical Review* 111(2): 362–382. http://dx.doi.org/10.1086/ahr.111.2.362.

Radner, Joan Newlon, ed. 1993. *Feminist Messages: Coding in Women's Folklore*. Chicago: University of Illinois Press.

Radner, Joan N., and Susan S. Lanser. 1993. "Strategies of Coding in Women's Cultures." In *Feminist Messages: Coding in Women's Folklore Culture*, edited by Joan N. Radner, 1–29. Urbana: University of Illinois Press.

Rafferty, Terrence. 2010. "Neil Jordan's Possible World of the Impossible." *New York Times*, May 28. Accessed May 14, 2011. http://www.nytimes.com/2010/05/30/movies/30jordan.html.

Rainer, Peter. 2010. "Colin Farrell Plays a Feisty Irish Fisherman in *Ondine*, a Modern-Day Fairy Tale with a Twist." *Christian Science Monitor*, June 4. Accessed May 14, 2011. http://www.csmonitor.com/The-Culture/Movies/2010/0604/Ondine-movie-review.

Raisch, Roger. 1990. *Turkey Hunting Secrets*. West Des Moines, IA: American Heritage.

Ravn, Claus. 2010. "Lad maden tale" [Let the Food Speak]. *Museum Amager*, no. 3. (February), 12.

Ray, Celeste. 2005. "Bravehearts and Patriarchs. Masculinity on the Pedestal in Southern Scottish Heritage Celebration." In *Transatlantic Scots*, edited by Celeste Ray, 232–262. Tuscaloosa: University of Alabama Press.

Raymond, Janice. 1979. *The Transsexual Empire: The Making of the She-Male*. New York: Teachers' College Press.

Rea, Steven. 2010. "A Mermaid Tale with a Bit of Darkness." *Philadelphia Inquirer*, June 11. Accessed May 14, 2011. http://articles.philly.com/2010-06-11/entertainment/24998600_1_mermaid-annie-folk-tale.

Reese, Debbie. 2006. "Those Thanksgiving Lesson Plans." Accessed October 1, 2010. http://americanindiansinchildrensliterature.blogspot.ca/2006/11/those-thanksgiving-lesson-plans.html.

Reimer, Margaret Loewen. 1983. *One Quilt, Many Pieces*. Waterloo: Mennonite Publishing Service.

Rich, Adrienne. 1980. "Compulsory Heterosexuality and Lesbian Existence." In *Women, Sex and Sexuality*, edited by Catharine R. Stimpson and Ethel Spector Person, 62–91. Chicago: University of Chicago Press.

Rieti, Barbara. 2008. *Making Witches: Newfoundland Traditions of Spells and Counterspells*. Montreal: McGill-Queen's University Press.

Ritchie, Anne Thackeray. 2003. *The Fairy Tales of Madame D'Aulnoy*. Honolulu: University Press of the Pacific.

Rivers, Caryl, and Rosalind C. Barnett. 2011. "'Mancession' Focus Masks Women's Real Losses." *Women's eNews*, April 11, 2014. http://womensenews.org/story/equal-payfair-wage/110503/mancession-focus-masks-womens-real-losses.

Robertson, Margaret. 1982. "The Symbolism of Christmas Mummering in Newfoundland." *Folklore* 93(2): 176–180. http://dx.doi.org/10.1080/0015587X.1982.9716237.

Robertson, Margaret. 1984. *The Newfoundland Christmas House-Visit. Canadian Centre for Folk Culture Studies Paper 49.* Ottawa: National Museums of Canada.

Robidoux, Michael A. 2001. *Men at Play: A Working Understanding of Professional Hockey.* Montreal: McGill-Queen's University Press.

Rockwell, Norman. 1943. *Freedom from Want. Saturday Evening Post,* March 6. Accessed August 22, 2012. http://arthistory.about.com/od/from_exhibitions/ig/american_chronicles/aonr_dia_09_09.htm.

"Rockwell Rolls over in His Grave: *Freedom from Want* Parodies." 2008. Posted by "B2," November 24. Accessed April 13, 2011. http://tonermishap.blogspot.com/2008/11/rockwell-rolls-over-in-his-grave.html.

Roediger, David R. 1991. *The Wages of Whiteness: Race and the Making of the American Working Class.* London: Verso.

Romaine, Suzanne. 1994. *Language in Society: An Introduction to Sociolinguistics.* New York: Oxford University Press.

Rosenberg, Neil V., ed. 1993. *Transforming Tradition: Folk Music Revivals Examined.* Urbana: University of Illinois Press.

Rosin, Hannah. 2010. "The End of Men: How Women are Taking Control—Of Everything." *Atlantic,* July–August. Accessed April 14, 2014. http://www.theatlantic.com/magazine/archive/2010/07/the-end-of-men/308135/.

Roth, LuAnne. 2010. "Talking Turkey: Visual Media and the Unraveling of Thanksgiving." Ph.D. diss., University of Missouri.

Rotundo, E. Anthony. 1994. *American Manhood: Transformations in Masculinity from the Revolution to the Modern Era.* New York: Basic Books.

Roure, Martine. 2009. "Final Report of the Committee on Civil Liberties, Justice and Home Affairs on the Delegation to Denmark." European Parliament, Committee on Civil Liberties, Justice and Home Affairs, 2004–2009.

Ruan, Yuan, ed. [1815–1816] 2009. *Shisan jing zhushu* [Commentaries to the Thirteen Classics]. Vol. 2. Beijing: Zhonghua shuju.

Rubin, Gayle. 1984. "Thinking Sex: Notes for a Radical Theory of the Politics of Sexuality." In *Pleasure and Danger,* edited by Carole Vance, 267–319. London: Routledge and Kegan.

Sachs, Carolyn E. 1983. *The Invisible Farmers: Women in Agricultural Production.* Totowa, NJ: Rowman and Littlefield.

Sachs, Dana. 2010. *The Life We Were Given: Operation Babylift, International Adoption, and the Children of War in Vietnam.* Boston: Beacon.

Sacks, Harvey. 1995. *Harvey Sacks: Lectures on Conversation.* Vols. 1 and 2, edited by Gail Jefferson. Oxford: Blackwell. http://dx.doi.org/10.1002/9781444328301.

Salles-Loustau, Jean. 1985. "Le chant des sirènes: La part de Bladé." In *Jean-François Bladé, 1827–1900: Actes du Colloque de Lectoure, 20 et 21 Octobre 1984,* edited by Jean Arrouye, 191–202. Béziers: Centre international de documentation occitane.

Saltzman, Rachelle H. 2009. "Adoption." In *Encyclopedia of Women's Folklore and Folklife,* edited by Liz Locke, Theresa A. Vaughan, and Pauline Greenhill, 4–6. Westport, CT: Greenwood.

Santino, Jack, ed. 1994. *Halloween and Other Festivals of Death and Life.* Knoxville: University of Tennessee Press.

Sautman, Francesca Candé, Diana Conchado, and Giuseppe Carlo Di Scipio, eds. 1998. *Telling Tales: Medieval Narratives and the Folk Tradition.* New York: St. Martin's.

Sawatzky, Harry Leonard. 1971. *They Sought a Country: Mennonite Colonization in Mexico.* Berkeley: University of California Press.

Sawin, Patricia E. 2001. "Transparent Masks: The Ideology and Practice of Disguise in Contemporary Cajun Mardi Gras." *Journal of American Folklore* 114(452): 175–203.

Sawin, Patricia. 2004. *Listening for a Life: A Dialogic Ethnography of Bessie Eldreth through Her Songs and Stories.* Logan. Utah State University Press.

Sawin, Patricia. 2005. "Mother and Baby in Search of a Story: Negotiating Multiple Discourses of International Adoption." Paper presented at the Annual Meeting of the American Folklore Society, Atlanta, October 19–22.

Sax, Boria. 1998. *The Serpent and the Swan: The Animal Bride in Folklore and Literature.* Blacksburg, VI: MacDonald and Woodward.

Sceats, Sarah. 2000. *Food, Consumption and the Body in Contemporary Women's Fiction.* Cambridge: Cambridge University Press. http://dx.doi.org/10.1017/CBO978051148 5381.

Schlossberg, Linda. 2001. "Introduction: Rites of Passing." In *Passing: Identity and Interpretation in Sexuality, Race, and Religion,* edited by María Carla Sánchez and Linda Schlossberg, 1–12. New York: New York University Press.

Schneider, Rebecca. 1997. *The Explicit Body in Performance.* London: Routledge. http://dx.doi.org/10.4324/9780203421079.

Schroeder, Jac. 1999. *Landscapes of My Life: Memoirs.* Kamloops: Privately printed.

Schutte, Ofelia. 2000. "Cultural Alterity, Cross-Cultural Communication, and Feminist Theory in North-South Contexts." In *Decentering the Center: Philosophy for a Multicultural, Postcolonial, and Feminist World,* edited by Uma Narayan and Sandra Harding, 47–66. Bloomington: Indiana University Press.

Seabrook, John. 2010. "The Last Babylift: Adopting a Child in Haiti." *New Yorker,* May 10, 44–67.

Sébillot, Paul. [1906] 2006. *Le Folk-lore de France.* 4 vols. Chestnut Hill, MA: Adamant Media.

Sedgwick, Eve Kosofsky. 1985. *Between Men: English Literature and Male Homosocial Desire.* New York: Columbia University Press.

Segalen, Martine. 1983. *Love and Power in the Peasant Family: Rural France in the Nineteenth Century.* Translated by Sarah Matthews. Chicago: University of Chicago Press.

Seifert, Lewis C. 1996. *Fairy Tales, Sexuality, and Gender in France, 1690–1715: Nostalgic Utopias.* Cambridge: Cambridge University Press. http://dx.doi.org/10.1017/CBO9780511470387.

Seifert, Lewis C., and Domna C. Stanton. 2010. *Enchanted Eloquence: Fairy Tales by Seventeenth-Century French Women Writers.* Toronto: Iter.

Selby, Emily F., and Deborah P. Dixon. 1998. "Between Worlds: Considering Celtic Feminine Identities in *The Secret of Roan Inish.*" *Gender, Place and Culture* 5(1): 5–28. http://dx.doi.org/10.1080/09663699825304.

Selman, Peter. 2009. "The Movement of Children for Transnational Adoption: Developments and Trends in Receiving States and States of Origin, 1998–2004." In *Transnational Adoption, Global Inequalities and the Circulation of Children,* edited by Laura Briggs and Diana Marre, 32–51. New York: New York University Press.

Senjak, David. 1997. "Can a Fujiyama Mama Be the Female Elvis? The Wild, Wild Women of Rockabilly." In *Sexing the Groove: Popular Music and Gender,* edited by Sheila Whiteley, 137–167. London: Routledge.

Shahar, Shulamith. 2003. *The Fourth Estate: A History of Women in the Middle Ages.* Rev. ed. Translated by Chaya Galai. New York: Routledge. http://dx.doi.org/10.4324/9780203407882.

Shaus, Margaret. 2006. "Evangiles des quenouilles." In *Women and Gender in Medieval Europe: An Encyclopedia,* edited by Margaret Shaus, 266. New York: Routledge.

Shuman, Amy. 2005. *Other People's Stories: Entitlement Claims and the Critique of Empathy.* Urbana: University of Illinois Press.

Sider, Gerald M. 1976. "Christmas Mumming and the New Year in Outport Newfoundland." *Past & Present* 71(1): 102–125. http://dx.doi.org/10.1093/past/71.1.102.

Sieg, Katrin. 1998. "Ethnic Drag and National Identity: Multicultural Crises, Crossings, and Interventions." In *The Imperialist Imagination: German Colonialism and Its Legacy,* edited by Sara Friedrichsmeyer, Sara Lennox, and Susanne Zantop, 295–319. Ann Arbor: University of Michigan Press.

Sieg, Katrin. 2002. *Ethnic Drag: Performing Race, Nation, Sexuality in West Germany.* Ann Arbor: University of Michigan Press.

Sieg, Katrin. 2004. *The Ambivalence of Antifascist Rhetoric: Victims, Artists, and the Masses in Elfriede Jelinek's "Stecken, Stab und Stangl."* New German Critique 92 Spring-Summer: 123–140.

Sims, Martha C., and Martine Stephens. 2005. *Living Folklore: An Introduction to the Study of People and Their Traditions.* Logan. Utah State University Press.

Singer, Barnett. 1983. *Village Notables in Nineteenth-Century France: Priests, Mayors, Schoolmasters.* New York: State University of New York Press.

Siskind, Janet. [1992] 2002. "The Invention of Thanksgiving: A Ritual of American Nationality." In *Food in the USA: A Reader,* edited by Carole M. Counihan, 41–58. New York: Routledge.

Slater, Maya. 1982. "Madame d'Aulnoy and the Adult Fairy Tale." *Newsletter of the Society for Seventeenth Century French Studies* 4(1): 69–75. http://dx.doi.org/10.1179/c17.1982.4.1.69.

Slotkin, Richard. 1973. *Regeneration through Violence: The Mythology of the American Frontier, 1600–1860.* Norman: University of Oklahoma Press.

Small, L. D. 1975. "Traditional Expressions in a Newfoundland Community: Genre Change and Functional Variability." *Lore and Language* 2(3): 15–18.

Small, Susan. 2009. "Review: Madeleine Jeay and Kathleen Garay, *The Distaff Gospels: A First Modern English Edition of 'Les evangiles des quenouilles.'*" *University of Toronto Quarterly* 78(1): 232–233. http://dx.doi.org/10.1353/utq.0.0361.

Smith, Andrew F. 2006. *The Turkey: An American Story.* Chicago: University of Illinois Press.

Smith, Anna Marie. 1995. "The Regulation of Lesbian Sexuality through Erasure: The Case of Jennifer Saunders." In *Lesbian Erotics,* edited by Karla Jay, 164–179. New York: New York University Press.

Snell, Will, and Greg Halich. 2007. *"Tobacco Economies in the Post-Buyout Era": 2007 Kentucky Tobacco Production Guide,* edited by Kenny Seebold. Lexington: Cooperative Extension Service, University of Kentucky College of Agriculture.

Somerville, Siobhan B. 2000. *Queering the Color Line: Race and the Invention of Homosexuality in American Culture.* Durham, NC: Duke University Press.

Spitzer, Nicholas R. 2003. "Monde Creole: The Cultural World of French Louisiana Creoles and the Creolization of World Cultures." *Journal of American Folklore* 116(459): 57–72. http://dx.doi.org/10.1353/jaf.2003.0014.

Spivak, Gayatri C. 1988. "Can the Subaltern Speak?" In *Marxism and the Interpretation of Culture,* edited by Lawrence Grossberg and Gary Nelson, 271–313. Chicago: University of Illinois Press.

Staliūnas, Darius. 2007. *Making Russians: Meaning and Practice of Russification in Lithuania and Belarus after 1863.* New York: Rodopi.

Staples, Terry. 2008. "Brothers Grimm in Biopics." In *The Greenwood Encyclopedia of Folktales and Fairy Tales,* edited by Donald Haase, 142–144. Westport, CT: Greenwood.

Steed, Virgil S. 1947. *Kentucky Tobacco Patch*. Indianapolis: Bobbs-Merrill.

Stewart, Andy. [1961] 1989. "Donald Where's Your Troosers?" EMI Top Rank.

Stone, Kay F. 1997. "Difficult Women in Folktales: Two Women, Two Stories." In *Undisciplined Women: Tradition and Culture in Canada*, edited by Pauline Greenhill and Diane Tye, 250–265. Montreal: McGill-Queen's University Press.

Stone, Sandy. 1991. "The 'Empire' Strikes Back: A Posttransexual Manifesto." In *Body Guards: The Cultural Politics of Gender Ambiguity*, edited by Julia Epstein and Kristina Straub, 280–304. New York: Routledge.

Stryker, Susan. 2004. "Transgender Studies: Queer Theory's Evil Twin." *GLQ: A Journal of Lesbian and Gay Studies* 10(2): 212–215. http://dx.doi.org/10.1215/10642684-10-2-212.

Stryker, Susan, and Stephen Whittle, eds. 2006. *The Transgender Studies Reader*. New York: Routledge.

Stull, Donald D. 2009. "Tobacco Is Going, Going . . . but Where?" *Culture & Agriculture* 31(2): 54–72. http://dx.doi.org/10.1111/j.1556-486X.2009.01021.x.

"Supreme Breeding Tom and Collapsible Turkey Decoy." 1998. Accessed October 5, 2010. http://www.turkeyhuntingsecrets.com/store/store-decoys-delta-wildwillard.htm.

Sustainable Schools International. 2012. Accessed June 10, 2012. http://www.sustainableschoolsinternational.org/.

Szwed, John F. 1969. "The Mask of Friendship: Mumming as a Ritual of Social Relations." In *Christmas Mumming in Newfoundland: Essays in Anthropology, Folklore, and History*, edited by Herbert Halpert and G. M. Story, 104–118. Toronto: University of Toronto Press.

Taft, Michael. 1997. "Men in Women's Clothing: Theatrical Transvestites on the Canadian Prairie." In *Undisciplined Women: Tradition and Culture in Canada*, edited by Pauline Greenhill and Diane Tye, 131–138. Montreal: McGill-Queen's University Press.

Taggart, James M. 1997. *The Bear and His Sons: Masculinity in Spanish and Mexican Folktales*. Austin: University of Texas Press.

Tambiah, Stanley Jeyaraja. 1990. *Magic, Science, Religion and the Scope of Rationality*. New York: Cambridge University Press.

Tangherlini, Timothy. 1994. *Interpreting Legend: Danish Storytellers and Their Repertoires*. New York: Garland.

Tannen, Deborah. 1989. *Talking Voices: Repetition, Dialogue, and Imagery in Conversational Discourse*. Cambridge: Cambridge University Press.

Tao, Qian. 1981. *Soushen houji* [A Sequel to *Sou shen ji*], edited and annotated by Wang Shaoying. Beijing: Zhonghua shuju.

Tatar, Maria. 1999. *The Classic Fairy Tales*. New York: Norton.

Thanksgiving. 2003. By John Currin, oil on canvas, 1729 x 1323 mm. Accessed October 5, 2010. http://www.gagosian.com/shop/john-currin-2.

Thiessen, Jack. 2003. *Mennonite Low German Dictionary/Mennonitisch-Plattdeutsches Wörterbuch*. Madison: Max Kade Institute for German-American Studies.

Thomas, Jeannie B. 1995. "Pickup Trucks, Horses, Women, and Foreplay: The Fluidity of Folklore." *Western Folklore* 54(3): 213–228. http://dx.doi.org/10.2307/1500348.

Thomas, Jeannie B. 2003. *Naked Barbies, Warrior Joes, and Other Forms of Visible Gender*. Urbana: University of Illinois Press.

Thomas, Jeannie B. 2007. "The Usefulness of Ghost Stories." *In Haunting Experiences: Ghosts in Contemporary Folklore*, edited by Diane E. Goldstein, Sylvia Grider, and Jeannie Banks Thomas, 25–59. Logan: Utah State University Press.

Thompson, J. Charles. 1989. *So You're Going to Wear a Kilt! All You Want to Know about Tartan Dress*. 3rd ed. Glasgow: Lang Syne.

Thompson, Stith. 1946. *The Folktale*. New York: Holt, Rinehart and Winston.

Thomson, David. 1980. *The People of the Sea: A Journey in Search of the Seal Legend.* Washington, DC: Counterpoint.

Thurah, Laurids de, and Harry Kaae. 1968. "Amager Og Saltholm." In *Amager Og Saltholm.* Copenhagen: Rosenkilde og Bager.

Thurston, Herbert. 1910. "St. Joan of Arc." In *The Catholic Encyclopedia*, vol. 8. New York: Robert Appleton.

Tian, Yuqing. 1989. *Dongjin menfa zhengzhi.* [Politics of Prominent Clans in East Jin Dynasty] Beijing: Beijing University Press.

Tiger, Lionel. 1969. *Men in Groups.* London: Nelson.

Titon, Jeff Todd. 1980. "The Life Story." *Journal of American Folklore* 93(369): 276–292. http://dx.doi.org/10.2307/540572.

Titon, Jeff Todd. 2003. "Text." In *Eight Words for the Study of Expressive Culture*, edited by Burt Feintuch, 69–98. Urbana: University of Illinois Press.

Toews, Julius G. 1977. "Traditional Pastimes." In *Mennonite Memories: Settling in Western Canada*, edited by Lawrence Klippenstein and Julius G. Toews, 300–305. Winnipeg: Centennial.

Tosches, Nick. 1982. *Hellfire: The Jerry Lee Lewis Story.* New York: Delacorte.

Traimond, Bernard. 1985. "L'authenticité chez Bladé." In *Jean-François Bladé, 1827–1900: Actes du Colloque de Lectoure, 20 et 21 Octobre 1984*, edited by Jean Arrouye, 219–231. Béziers: Centre International de Documentation Occitane.

Transracial Abductees. 2011. "What Is This Shit? An Introduction." Accessed May 20, 2011. http://archive.is/CUuD6.

Trevor-Roper, Hugh. 2008. *The Invention of Scotland. Myth and History.* New Haven: Yale University Press.

Trost, Caroline T. 1991. "'Belle-Belle ou le Chevalier Fortuné': A Liberated Woman in a Tale by Mme. D'Aulnoy." *Merveilles & Contes* 5(1): 57–66.

Tubach, Frederic C. 1969. *Index Exemplorum: A Handbook of Medieval Religious Tales.* Helsinki: Academia Scientiarum Fennica.

Tuleja, Tad. 1987. "The Turkey." In *American Wildlife in Symbol and Story*, edited by Angus K. Gillespie and Jay Mechling, 15–40. Knoxville: University of Tennessee Press.

Turner, Kay. 1999. *Beautiful Necessity: The Art and Meaning of Women's Altars.* New York: Thames and Hudson.

Turner, Kay, and Pauline Greenhill, eds. 2012. *Transgressive Tales: Queering the Grimms.* Detroit: Wayne State University Press.

Turner, Kay, and Suzanne Seriff. 1993. "'Giving an Altar to St. Joseph': A Feminist Perspective on a Patronal Feast." In *Feminist Theory and the Study of Folklore*, edited by Susan Tower Hollis, Linda Pershing, and M. Jane Young, 89–117. Urbana: University of Illinois Press.

Tye, Diane. 1993. "'A Very Lone Worker': Woman-Centered Thoughts on Helen Creighton's Career as a Folklorist." *Canadian Folklore canadien* 15 (2): 107–117.

Tye, Diane. 2002. "Tales of Whose Village? Legend as Female Countermemory." *Contemporary Legend*, n.s., 5:1–23.

Tye, Diane. 2010. *Baking as Biography: A Life Story in Recipes.* Montreal: McGill-Queen's University Press.

UNICEF. 2011a. "Child Protection from Violence, Exploitation, and Abuse." Accessed May 25, 2011. http://www.unicef.org/protection/index_orphans.html.

UNICEF. 2011b. "United Nations Convention on the Rights of the Child." Accessed May 20, 2011. http://www.unicef.org/crc/.

United Nations Development Program. 2010. "Gender Inequality Index (Table 4)." *Human Development Report 2010—20th Anniversary Edition: The Real Wealth of Nations—Pathways to Human Development*, 156. New York: Palgrave/United Nations

288	*Bibliography*

Development Programme. Accessed March 30, 2011. http://hdr.undp.org/en /mediacentre/.

United States Department of Agriculture. 2008. *Kentucky Agricultural Statistics and Annual Report, 2007–2008*. Washington, DC: National Agriculture Statistics Service.

U.S. Congress Joint Economic Committee. 2010. "Understanding the Economy: Working Mothers in the Great Recession." http://www.jec.senate.gov/public/?a=Files. Serve&File_id=82216270-c7f0-46bf-a54f-6ab221ac586f.

Uther, Hans-Jörg. 2004. *The Types of International Folktales: A Classification and Bibliography*. 3 vols. Helsinki: Academia Scientiarum Fennica.

Velay-Vallantin, Catherine. 1992. *La fille en Garçon*. Carcassonne: Garae/Hediode.

"Veterans 'Lose Faith' in Poppy Charity Chief." 2010. *Scotsman.com*. Accessed November 10, 2010. http://www.scotsman.com/news/veterans-lose-faith-in-poppy-charity -chief-1-832811.

Visser, Margaret. 1991. *The Rituals of Dinner: The Origins, Evolution, Eccentricities, and Meaning of Table Manners*. New York: Penguin.

Visser, Margaret. 1992. "One Strange Bird." *New York Times* November 26, A27.

Voth, Norma Jost. 1994. *Mennonite Foods and Folkways from South Russia*. Vol. 2. Beaverton, OR: Good Books.

Walker, Margaret Urban. 1998. *Moral Understandings: A Feminist Study in Ethics*. New York: Oxford University Press.

Wallendorf, Melanie, and Eric J. Arnould. 1991. "'We Gather Together': Consumption Rituals of Thanksgiving Day." *Journal of Consumer Research* 18(1): 13–31. http:// dx.doi.org/10.1086/209237.

Ward, Jennifer. 2002. *Women in Medieval Europe, 1200–1500*. New York: Longman Pearson.

Ward, Margaret E. 2011. *Missing Mila, Finding Family: An International Adoption in the Shadow of the Salvadoran Civil War*. Austin: University of Texas Press.

Ware, Carolyn E. 2007. *Cajun Women and Mardi Gras: Reading the Rules Backward*. Urbana: University of Illinois Press.

Warkentin, John. 2000. *The Mennonite Settlements of Southern Manitoba*. Steinbach, MB: Hanover Steinbach Historical Society.

Warner, Marina. 1994. *From the Beast to the Blonde: On Fairy Tales and Their Tellers*. New York: Farrar, Straus and Giroux.

Watts, Trent, ed. 2008. *White Masculinity in the Recent South*. Baton Rouge: Louisiana State University Press.

Weber, Eugen. 1976. *Peasants into Frenchmen: The Modernization of Rural France, 1870– 1914*. Stanford: Stanford University Press.

Weigle, Marta. 1982. *Spiders and Spinsters: Women and Mythology*. Albuquerque: University of New Mexico Press.

"Weird Experiment #4: The Sexual Turkey." 2008. *New Scientist,* March 3. Accessed May 27, 2009. http://www.hip2b2.com/news/weird-experiment-the-sexual-turkey/61097/. Site discontinued.

Weiser, Ron. 1978. "Interview with Carl." *Rollin' Rock* 16–17:26.

Werhun, Cherie, and Pauline Greenhill. Forthcoming. "Identities and Literatures."

Wetherell, Margaret, and Nigel Edley. 1999. "Negotiating Hegemonic Masculinity: Imaginary Positions and Psycho-Discursive Practices." *Feminism & Psychology* 9(3): 335–356. http://dx.doi.org/10.1177/0959353599009003012.

Whatley, Mariamne H., and Elissa R. Henken. 2000. *Did You Hear about the Girl Who . . .? Contemporary Legends, Folklore, and Human Sexuality*. New York: New York University Press.

Wheelwright, Julie. 1989. *Amazons and Military Maids: Women Who Dressed as Men in Pursuit of Life, Liberty, and Happiness.* London: Pandora.

Whiteley, Sheila, ed. 1997. *Sexing the Groove: Popular Music and Gender.* London: Routledge.

Wiebe, Armin. 1984. *The Salvation of Yasch Siemens.* Winnipeg: Turnstone.

Williams, Brett. 1984. "Why Migrant Women Feed Their Husbands Tamales: Foodways as a Basis for a Revisionist View of Tejano Family Life." In *Ethnic and Regional Foodways in the United States: The Performance of Group Identity*, edited by Linda Keller Brown and Kay Mussell, 113–126. Knoxville: University of Tennessee Press.

Williams, Clover Nolan. 1994. "The Bachelor's Transgression: Identity and Difference in the Bachelor Party." *Journal of American Folklore* 107(423): 106–120. http://dx.doi.org/10.2307/541075.

Williams, Clyde E. 1969. "Janneying in 'Coughlin Cove.'" In *Christmas Mumming in Newfoundland: Essays in Anthropology, Folklore, and History*, edited by Herbert Halpert and G. M. Story, 209–215. Toronto: University of Toronto Press.

Williams-Forson, Psyche. 2006. *Building Houses out of Chicken Legs: Black Women, Food, and Power.* Chapel Hill: University of North Carolina Press.

Williamson, Duncan. 2005. *Tales of the Seal People: Scottish Folk Tales.* New York: Interlink.

Willis, Roy. 1974. *Man and Beast.* London: Hart-Davis, McGibbon.

Wolf Howl Animal Preserve. 2009. "Wild Turkey Mating Season." Accessed December 1, 2010. http://www.everythingwolf.com/gallery/showgalleryimage.aspx?galleryid=156.

Woodhouse, Annie. 1989. *Fantastic Women: Sex, Gender, and Transvestism.* New Brunswick, NJ: Rutgers University Press.

Xinran. 2011. *Message from an Unknown Chinese Mother: Stories of Loss and Love.* New York: Scribner.

Yao, Guangxiao, Jin Xie, Jing Wang, and Ji Zou, eds. [1403–1405] 1986. *Yongle dadian* [The Great Canon or Vast Documents of the Yongle Era]. Beijing: Zhonghua shuju.

Yngvesson, Barbara. 2004. "National Bodies and the Body of the Child: 'Completing' Families through International Adoption." In *Cross-Cultural Approaches to Adoption*, edited by Fiona Bowie, 211–226. New York: Routledge.

Yngvesson, Barbara. 2010. *Belonging in an Adoption World: Race, Identity, and Transnational Adoption.* Chicago: University of Chicago Press. http://dx.doi.org/10.7208/chicago/9780226964485.001.0001.

Yu, Anthony C. 1987. "'Rest, Rest, Perturbed Spirit!' Ghosts in Traditional Chinese Prose Fiction." *Harvard Journal of Asiatic Studies* 47(2): 397–434. http://dx.doi.org/10.2307/2719188.

Yu, Rujie. 1991. *Huanxiang he jituo de guodu: zhiguai chuanqi xinlun* [Realms of Fantasy and Desire: Rereading *Zhiguai* and *Chuanqi*]. Taibei: Shuxin chubanshe.

Yuan, Mei. [1788?] 1986. *Zi bu yu* [What Confucius Didn't Speak Of], edited and annotated by Cui Guoguang. Jinan: Qilu shushe.

Zeitlin, Judith T. 2007. *The Phantom Heroine: Ghosts and Gender in Seventeenth-Century Chinese Literature.* Honolulu: University of Hawai'i Press.

Zelizer, Viviana A. 1994. *Pricing the Priceless Child: The Changing Social Value of Children.* Princeton: Princeton University Press.

Zhao, Xiaohuan. 2005. *Classical Chinese Supernatural Fiction: A Morphological History.* New York: Edwin Mellen.

Zipes, Jack. 2001. *The Great Fairy Tale Tradition: From Straparola to the Brothers Grimm.* New York: W.W. Norton.

Zipes, Jack. 2002. *The Brothers Grimm: From Enchanted Forests to the Modern World.* 2nd ed. New York: Routledge.

Zipes, Jack. 2003. "Once There Were Two Brothers Named Grimm." In *The Complete Fairy Tales of the Brothers Grimm*, 3rd ed., edited and translated by Jack Zipes, xxiii–xxxviii. New York: Bantam Books.

Zipes, Jack. 2011. *The Enchanted Screen: The Unknown History of Fairy-Tale Films*. New York: Routledge.

Zipes, Jack. 2012. *The Irresistible Fairy Tale: The Cultural and Social History of a Genre*. Princeton: Princeton University Press.

Zita, Jacquelyn N. 1994. "Male Lesbians and the Postmodern Body." In *Adventures in Lesbian Philosophy*, edited by Claudia Card, 112–128. Bloomington: Indiana University Press, Hypatia.

Zuerner, Adrienne E. 1997. "Reflections on the Monarchy in d'Aulnoy's 'Belle-Belle ou le chevalier Fortuné.'" In *Out of the Woods: The Origins of the Literary Fairy Tale in Italy and France*, edited by Nancy L. Canepa, 194–217. Detroit: Wayne State University Press.

Filmography

Austin Powers in Goldmember. 2002. Directed by Jay Roach. USA: New Line Cinema.

Austin Powers: The Spy Who Shagged Me. 1999. Directed by Jay Roach. USA: New Line Cinema.

Avalon. 1990. Directed by Barry Levinson. USA: Baltimore Pictures.

Braveheart. 1995. Directed by Mel Gibson. USA: Icon Entertainment International.

Breakfast on Pluto. 2005. Directed by Neil Jordan. UK/Ireland: Sony Pictures.

Brokeback Mountain. 2005. Directed by Ang Lee. USA: Alberta Film Entertainment.

The Brothers Grimm. 2005. Directed by Terry Gilliam. USA: Dimension Home Video.

The Butcher Boy. 1997. Directed by Neil Jordan. USA: Warner Brothers.

By the Light of the Silvery Moon. 1953. Directed by David Butler. USA: Warner Brothers.

The Crying Game. 1992. Directed by Neil Jordan. UK: Palace Pictures.

Ever After. 1998. Directed by Andy Tennant. USA: 20th Century Fox.

Flashdance. 1983. Directed by Adrian Lyne. USA: Paramount Pictures.

Gallina Blanca. 1960. Posted by Mark Frauenfelder, July 30, 2008. Accessed July 25, 2011. http://boingboing.net/2008/07/30/burlesque-chicken-co.html.

Grindhouse. 2007. Directed by Robert Rodriguez and Quentin Tarantino. USA: Dimension Films.

Halloween. 1978. Directed by John Carpenter. USA: Compass International Pictures.

"He's Mine!" Crazy Lady at Turkey Drop. 2009. Posted by Liveleak.com, November 28, 2009. Accessed November 15, 2010. http://www.liveleak.com/view?i=36e_1259453783.

Home for the Holidays. 1995. Directed by Jodie Foster. USA: Paramount Pictures.

I Want to Stuff You! 2007. Posted by Flowgo, October 26. Accessed November 15, 2009. http://www.youtube.com/watch?v=NRAww-EIp20&NR=1.

A Knight's Tale. 2001. Directed by Brian Helgeland. USA: Columbia Pictures.

"Merry Christmas Mr. Bean." 1992. *Mr. Bean.* Created by Rowan Atkinson and Richard Curtis. Britain. Episode 7, aired December 29.

Michael Collins. 1996. Directed by Neil Jordan. UK/Ireland/USA: Warner Brothers.

Miss Turkey Trot / Miss Drumsticks Pageant. 2010. Posted by TLC, March 8. Accessed August 14, 2010. http://www.youtube.com/watch?v=p7aFkpX–0ZI.

Olsen-banden på sporet [The Olsen Gang on the Track]. 1975. Directed by Erik Balling. Denmark: Nordisk Film.

Once upon a Brothers Grimm. 1977. Directed by Norman Campbell. USA: VCI Home Video.

Ondine. 2009. Directed by Neil Jordan. Ireland/USA: Wayfare Entertainment.

"The One With The Thanksgiving Flashbacks." 1998. Created by Kevin Bright. *Friends,* 1994–2004, season 5, episode 8. USA: Warner Bros Television.

"Pangs." 1999. Directed by Joss Whedon. *Buffy the Vampire Slayer,* 1997–2003, season 4, episode 8. USA: Mutant Enemy.

Pour Some Gravy on Me. 2007. Posted by Flowgo, October 26. Accessed October 15, 2009. http://www.youtube.com/watch?v=NdkeYmySOUM.

Rob Roy. 1995. Directed by Michael Caton-Jones. USA/UK: United Artists.

The Secret of Roan Inish. 1994. Directed by John Sayles. USA: Sony Pictures.

So I Married an Axe Murderer. 1994. Directed by Thomas Schlamme. USA: TriStar Pictures.

Thanksgiving. 2007. Directed by Eli Roth. USA: Dimension Films.

Turkey Jive Thanksgiving. 2007. Posted by Flowgo, October 26. Accessed July 5, 2009. http://www.youtube.com/watch?v=xpehjZ20j4M&feature=related.

What's Cooking? 2000. Directed by Gurinder Chadha. USA: Flashpoint.

The Wonderful World of the Brothers Grimm. 1962. Directed by Henry Levin and George Pal. USA: Metro-Goldwyn-Mayer.

About the Authors

EMILIE ANDERSON-GRÉGOIRE is a student at the University of Winnipeg and a fairy-tale aficionada.

MARCIE FEHR is in women's and gender studies at the University of Winnipeg. Her work focuses on racial masquerade, critical race theory, and queer theory, and she is English student representative on the executive of the Folklore Studies Association of Canada / Association canadienne d'ethnologie et de folklore.

ANN K. FERRELL is assistant professor of folk studies, Department of Folk Studies and Anthropology, Western Kentucky University. She holds a Ph.D. from Ohio State University and is the author of *Burley: Kentucky Tobacco in a New Century* (2013). Her research with Kentucky farmers continues.

PAULINE GREENHILL is professor of women's and gender studies at the University of Winnipeg. Her recent books include *Make the Night Hideous: Four English-Canadian Charivaris* (2010), *Fairy Tale Films: Visions of Ambiguity* (Sidney Eve Matrix, coeditor, 2010), and *Transgressive Tales: Queering the Grimms* (Kay Turner, coeditor, 2012).

KENDRA MAGNUS-JOHNSTON is a Ph.D. student at the University of Manitoba and teaching/research assistant at the University of Winnipeg, where she completed her B.A. (rhetoric and communications) and M.A. (cultural studies). She has published in *Journal of Folklore Research*, *Children's Literature Quarterly*, *Marvels & Tales*, and *Young Scholars in Writing*.

KIRSTEN MØLLEGAARD is associate professor of English at the University of Hawai'i at Hilo. She teaches literature, film, folklore, and mythology and has published on contemporary legends, retellings of myth and folklore in literature and film, tourism and contemporary legends in Hawai'i, and haunting and history in contemporary literature of the American West.

PATRICK B. MULLEN is professor emeritus in the English department at Ohio State University. His books include *The Man Who Adores the Negro: Race and American Folklore* (2008) and *Listening to Old Voices: Folklore, Life Stories, and the Elderly* (1991). He is working on a book about the roots of rock 'n' roll from a fan's perspective.

WILLIAM G. POOLEY has just completed a doctorate on the Gascon folklorist Félix Arnaudin (1844–1921) at the University of Oxford. His research focuses on the history of the body and folklore in the French-speaking world.

LuANNE ROTH is assistant teaching professor of folklore and film in the University of Missouri's Department of English. She is currently preparing a book manuscript, "Talking Turkey," which examines representations of the Thanksgiving meal in the media, and is curating a digital archive of food scenes in film and television.

PATRICIA SAWIN, associate professor and coordinator of the Folklore Program, Department of American Studies, University of North Carolina, Chapel Hill, researches narrative performance of gender identity and the politics of recycling others' speech. She has written *Listening for a Life: A Dialogic Ethnography of Bessie Eldreth through Her Songs and Stories* (2004).

DIANE TYE is professor of folklore at Memorial University. She is author of *Baking as Biography: A Life Story in Recipes* (2010), coeditor with Pauline Greenhill of *Undisciplined Women: Tradition and Culture in Canada* (1997), and coeditor with Michael Lange of *Digest*, the online journal of the American Folklore Society's Foodways section.

THERESA A. VAUGHAN is professor and chairperson of the University of Central Oklahoma's Department of Humanities and Philosophy. She earned a Ph.D. in folklore from Indiana University, and was coeditor of the *Encyclopedia of Women's Folklore and Folklife*. She is currently co-convener of the American Folklore Society's Women's section.

ANNE B. WALLEN (Ph.D., University of Minnesota in German and Scandinavian studies) is assistant director for national scholarships and fellowships in the University Honors Program at the University of Kansas, where she also teaches a freshman honors seminar in cultural studies. Her research focuses on German-Scandinavian cultural exchange since the eighteenth century.

WENJUAN XIE is a Ph.D. candidate in comparative literature at the University of Alberta. She has written on oral tradition and professional storytellers in China, Chinese-language films, and gender studies. She is currently working on her thesis, "Trans-formation, Trans-ambiguity, and Trans-performance: Reading Transgender Stories from Ming-Qing China, 14th–19th Century."

Index